COURT OFFICER

THE COMPLETE STUDY GUIDE FOR SCORING HIGH

Court Officer

By

DAVID R. TURNER, M.S. in Ed.

arco 219 Park Avenue South
New York, N.Y. 10003

Fifth Edition (B-1576)
Third Printing, 1978

Published by ARCO PUBLISHING COMPANY, INC.
219 Park Avenue South, New York, N.Y. 10003

Library of Congress Catalog
Card Number 71-99892

Arco Catalog Number 668-00519-X

Printed in the United States of America

CONTENTS

HOW TO USE THIS INDEX
Slightly bend the right-hand edge of the book. This will expose the corresponding Parts which match the index, below.

PART

1 2 3 4 5

...continued on next page

CONTENTS continued

PART

PART THREE
DUTIES AND JOB KNOWLEDGE

1
2
3
4
5

PART FOUR
BACKGROUND AND STUDY MATERIAL FOR THE EXAM

CONTENTS continued

PART

1

2

3

4

5

...continued on next page

CONTENTS continued

PART

1

2

3

4

5

PART FIVE
A MODEL EXAM AND SOME FINAL ADVICE

COURT OFFICER
WHAT THIS BOOK WILL DO FOR YOU

To get the greatest help from this book, please understand that it has been carefully organized. You must, therefore, plan to use it accordingly. Study this concise, readable book earnestly and your way will be clear. You will progress directly to your goal. You will not be led off into blind alleys and useless fields of study.

Arco Publishing Company has followed testing trends and methods ever since the firm was founded in 1937. We have specialized in books that prepare people for tests. Based on this experience it is our modest boast that you probably have in your hands the best book that could be prepared to help *you* score high. Now, if you'll take a little advice on using it properly, we can assure you that you will do well.

To write this book we carefully analyzed every detail surrounding the forthcoming examination . . .

* the job itself
* official and unofficial announcements concerning the examination
* all the available previous examinations
* many related examinations
* technical literature that explains and forecasts the examination.

As a result of all this (which you, happily, have not had to do) we've been able to create the "climate" of your test, and to give you a fairly accurate picture of what's involved. Some of this material, digested and simplified, actually appears in print here, if it was deemed useful and suitable in helping you score high.

But more important than any other benefit derived from this research is our certainty that the study material, the text and the practice questions are right for you.

The practice questions you will study have been judiciously selected from hundreds of thousands of previous test questions on file here at Arco. But they haven't just been thrown at you pell mell. They've been organized into the subjects that you can expect to find on your test. As you answer the questions, these subjects will take on greater meaning for you. At the same time you will be getting valuable practice in answering test questions. You will proceed with a sure step toward a worthwhile goal: high test marks.

Studying in this manner, you will get the feel of the entire examination. You will learn by "insight," by seeing through a problem as a result of experiencing *previous similar situations.* This is true learning according to many psychologists.

In short, what you get from this book will help you operate at top efficiency . . . make you give the best possible account of yourself on the actual examination.

CAN YOU PREPARE YOURSELF FOR YOUR TEST?

We believe, most certainly, that you *can* with the aid of this "self-tutor"!

It's not a "pony". It's not a complete college education. It's not a "crib sheet", and it's no HOW TO SUCCEED ON TESTS WITHOUT REALLY TRYING. There's nothing in it that will give you a higher score than you really deserve.

It's just a top quality course which you can readily review in less than twenty hours . . . a digest of material which you might easily have written yourself after about five thousand hours of laborious digging.

To really prepare for your test you must motivate yourself . . . get into the right frame of mind for learning from your "self-tutor". You'll have to urge *yourself* to learn and that's the only way people ever learn. Your efforts to score high on the test will be greatly aided by the fact that you will have to do this job on your own . . . perhaps without a teacher. Psychologists have demonstrated that studies undertaken for a clear goal . . . which you initiate yourself and actively pursue . . . are the most successful. You, yourself, want to pass this test. That's why you bought this book and embarked on this program. Nobody forced you to do it, and there may be nobody to lead you through the course. Your self-activity is going to be the key to your success in the forthcoming weeks.

Used correctly, your "self-tutor" will show you what to expect and will give you a speedy brush-up on the subjects peculiar to your exam. Some of these are subjects not taught in schools at all. Even if your study time is very limited, you should:

- Become familiar with the type of examination you will meet.
- Improve your general examination taking skill.
- Improve your skill in analyzing and answering questions involving reasoning, judgment, comparison, and evaluation.
- Improve your speed and skill in reading and understanding what you read—an important part of your ability to learn and an important part of most tests.
- Prepare yourself in the particular fields which measure your learning—
  - Vocabulary
  - Problem solving
  - Mathematics
  - Arithmetic

This book will tell you exactly what to study by presenting in full every type of question you will get on the actual test. You'll do better merely by familiarizing yourself with them.

This book will help you find your weaknesses and find them fast. Once you know where you're weak you can get right to work (before the test) and concentrate your efforts on those soft spots. This is the kind of selective study which yields maximum test results for every hour spent.

This book will give you the *feel* of the exam. Almost all our sample and practice questions are taken from actual previous exams. Since previous exams are not always available for inspection by the public, these sample test questions are quite important for you. The day you take your exam you'll see how closely this book follows the format of the real test.

This book will give you confidence *now*, while you are preparing for the test. It will build your self-confidence as you proceed. It will beat those dreaded before-test jitters that have hurt so many other test-takers.

This book stresses the modern, multiple-choice type of question because that's the kind you'll undoubtedly get on your test. In answering these questions you will add to your knowledge by learning the correct answers, naturally. However, you will not be satisfied with merely the correct choice for each question. You will want to find out why the other choices are incorrect. This will jog your memory . . . help you remember much you thought you had forgotten. You'll be preparing and enriching yourself for the exam to come.

Of course, the great advantage in all this lies in narrowing your study to just those fields in which you're most likely to be quizzed. Answer enough questions in those fields and the chances are very good that you'll meet a few of them again on the actual test. After all, the number of questions an examiner can draw upon in these fields is rather limited. Examiners frequently employ the same questions on different tests for this very reason.

Probably the most important element of tests which you can learn is vocabulary. Most testers consider your vocabulary range an important indication of what you have learned in your life, and therefore, an important measuring rod of your learning ability. With some concentration and systematic study, you can increase your vocabulary substantially and thus increase your score on most tests.

After testing yourself, you may find that your reading ability is poor. It may be wise to take the proper remedial measures now.

If you find that your reasoning ability or your ability to handle mathematical problems is weak, there are ways of improving your skill in these fields.

There are other things which you should know and which various sections of this book will help you learn. Most important, not only for this examination but for all the examinations to come in your life, is learning how to take a test and how to prepare for it.

PART ONE

Applying and Studying For Your Job

COURT OFFICER

With This Book You Prepare Yourself
For Examinations Leading To . . .

...Federal, State, and City Court positions as Uniformed Court Officer, Court Attendant, Senior Court Officer, Deputy Sheriff.

...Completely revised with newly developed material, it replaces former Arco Books bearing the above titles.

ARCO
BUILDS
CAREERS

COURT OFFICER

Forewarned is Forearmed

Official Sample Questions That Forecast the Test

If you want a preview of your exam, look these questions over carefully. We did . . . as we compiled them from various official announcements. A good part of this book is based on these prophetic questions.

A look at the following questions is the easiest, quickest, most important help you can get from this book. These predictive questions give you foresight by providing an "overview" with which to direct your study. They are actual samples of the question types you may expect on your test.

Before you're finished with this book you'll get plenty of practice with the best methods of answering each of these question types. However, you're going to do a little work yourself. You're going to plan your study to make sure that each available hour is used most effectively. You're going to concentrate where it will do you the most good. And you'll take it easy where you have no trouble.

In other words, discover what you're going to face on the test and make plans to pace yourself accordingly.

Vocabulary

These words are not limited only to words actually used on the job. Vocabulary questions are a good measure of a competitor's general ability, as well as his aptitude for work requiring skill with words.

There is no printed list of all words whose meanings are tested in civil service examinations. Study of a selected list of words is likely to help in preparing for an examination. The general improvement of your vocabulary will help and you will find that this improvement will make other kinds of questions more understandable also.

Directions: In each of the following questions you are to find which one of five words or phrases offered as choices has most nearly the same meaning as the word or phrase in CAPITAL LETTERS or *italics*. On the answer sheet mark the letter of the suggested answer which you think is the best.

1. If a report is VERIFIED it is
   A) changed
   B) confirmed
   C) replaced
   D) discarded
   E) corrected

Since "confirmed," lettered B, means most nearly the same as "verified," the space under B is marked on the answer sheet for question 1.

2. A clerk who shows FORBEARANCE TOWARD THE OPINION OF OTHERS shows
   A) severity
   B) hypercriticism
   C) tolerance
   D) quietness
   E) thankfulness

3. *A controversy* between two persons is
   A) an agreement
   B) a dispute
   C) a partnership
   D) a plot
   E) an understanding

4. To say that a condition is *generally or extensively existing* means that it is
   A) artificial
   B) prevalent
   C) recurrent
   D) timely
   E) transient

5. *Authentic* means most nearly
   A) detailed
   B) reliable
   C) valuable
   D) technical
   E) practical

6. *The two farms lie close to each other, but are not in actual contact.* This sentence means most nearly that the two farms are
   A) adjoining
   B) abutting
   C) touching
   D) adjacent
   E) united

The space under D is marked for this question because "adjacent" best describes the meaning of the sentence in italics. The other choices all indicate that the farms are in contact in some degree or are touching each other.

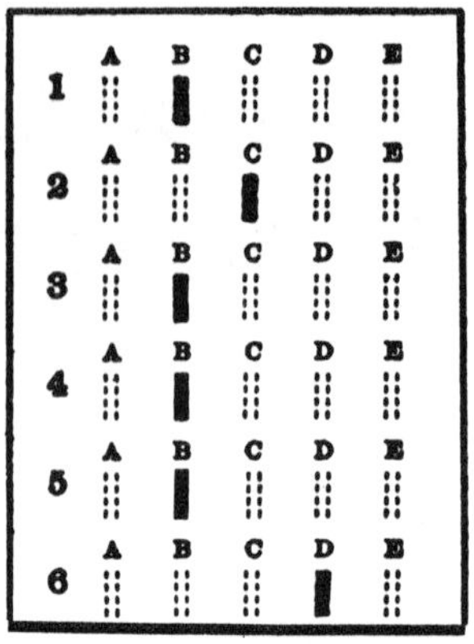

Judgment and Reasoning

These questions are based on a variety of facts, sometimes on facts with which the candidate would be expected to be familiar, sometimes on facts explained in the question itself. The questions are of various degrees of difficulty. In some cases judgment items may pertain to a particular field of subject-matter, knowledge of which is necessary for the job.

1. Hospital beds are usually higher than beds in private homes. Which of the following is the BEST reason for this fact?
   A) Hospital beds are in use all day, instead of at night only.
   B) Many hospital patients are children.
   C) Private homes seldom have space enough for high beds.
   D) The care of patients is less difficult when the beds are high.
   E) The danger of falling out of bed is greater where there are no nurses.

The suggestion lettered D is the answer and is marked on the answer sheet. Of all the suggestions given as possible reasons why hospital beds are higher than other kinds, the one lettered D is clearly the most reasonable and best.

2. Objects are visible because
   A) they are opaque
   B) they are partially in shadow
   C) they absorb light from the sun
   D) light falls on them and is reflected to the eye
   E) light rays penetrate their surfaces

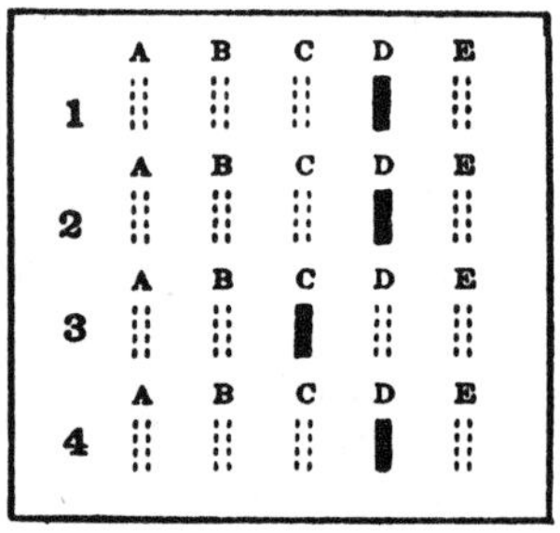

On the section of the answer sheet at the right, the space under D is marked for question 2 because the statement lettered D is the only one that explains why objects are visible. The other statements may be true, but they do not account for the visibility of objects.

3. In starting a load, a horse has to pull harder than he does to keep it moving, because
   A) the load weighs less when it is moving
   B) there is no friction after the load is moving
   C) the horse has to overcome the tendency of the wagon to remain at rest
   D) the wheels stick to the axles
   E) the horse becomes accustomed to pulling the load

4. Which of the following would be the *surest* indication that a druggist may have violated the legal requirement that narcotic drugs be dispensed only on a physician's prescription?
   A) A number of people known to have purchased other drugs from him are believed to possess narcotics, but no prescriptions issued to these persons are in the druggist's file.
   B) He is himself an addict.
   C) His wholesaler refuses to sell him narcotics.
   D) The total of his present narcotics stock and the amount legally accounted for is much less than his purchases.
   E) The supply of narcotics in stock is less than the amount which he recently reported.

The facts related in A do not indicate that these customers have secured their narcotics from this druggist—the narcotics may have been obtained from some other druggist on a proper prescription; B is no indication that prescriptions did not cover all the narcotics he has dispensed, either for his own use or for other people; C might be true for many reasons—for example, his credit may be bad; and E could be explained by legal sales made since his last report. The answer is D, because violation of the requirement mentioned is a likely explanation of the large difference; therefore D is marked on the answer sheet.

VERBAL ABILITIES

Interpretation of Paragraphs

Each question consists of a quotation followed by a series of five statements. Among the five statements there is only one that *must* be true if the quotation is true. Other statements among the five may or may not be true, but they are not necessary conclusions from the quotation. You are to select the *one* statement which is *best supported* by the quotation.

1. (*Reading*) "The application of the steam engine to the sawmill changed the whole lumber industry. Formerly the mills remained near the streams; now they follow the timber. Formerly the logs were floated downstream to their destination; now they are carried by the railroads."

   What besides the method of transportation does the quotation indicate has changed in the lumber industry?
   A) speed of cutting timber
   B) location of market
   C) type of timber sold
   D) route of railroads
   E) source of power

The quotation says nothing about the speed of steam-powered sawmills, location of the market for lumber, the type of timber sold, or the route of railroads. It does, however, mention "the application of the steam engine to the sawmill"—which gave a new source of power for sawmill operations. E is therefore the answer, and the space under E is blackened for question 1.

2. (*Reading*) "More patents have been issued for inventions relating to transportation than for those in any other line of human activity. These inventions have resulted in a great financial saving to the people and have made possible a civilization that could not have existed without them."

   Select the alternative that is best supported by the quotation. Transportation
   A) would be impossible without inventions
   B) is an important factor in our civilization
   C) is still to be much improved
   D) is more important than any other activity
   E) is carried on through the Patent Office

The space on the Answer Sheet under B is marked for question 2 because the statement lettered B is implied in the quotation. A is not strictly true, since manpower without inventions could supply transportation of a sort; C is probably true but is not in the quotation; D is exaggerated; E is not implied in the information given.

3. (*Reading*) "There exists a false but popular idea that a clue is some mysterious fact which most people overlook, but which some very keen investigator easily discovers and recognizes as having, in itself, a remarkable meaning. The clue is most often an ordinary fact which an observant person picks up—something which gains its significance when, after a long series of careful investigations, it is connected with a network of other clues."

   According to the quotation, to be of value, clues must be
   A) discovered by skilled investigators
   B) found under mysterious circumstances
   C) discovered soon after the crime
   D) observed many times
   E) connected with other facts

The quotation does not say that the clue must be (A) discovered by an investigator in order to make it of value; it does not mention (B) the circumstances under which a clue must be found; nothing in the paragraph implies that the value of a clue depends upon the (C) time of its discovery, nor upon the (D) number of times it is observed. E is the answer, because the quotation does say that a clue gains its significance, or value, when *connected with other clues or facts.*

4. (*Reading*) "Just as the procedure of a collection department must be clear-cut and definite, the steps being taken with the sureness of a skilled chess player, so the various paragraphs of a collection letter must show clear organization, giving evidence of a mind that, from the beginning, has had a specific end in view."

   The quotation best supports the statement that a collection letter should always
   A) show a spirit of sportsmanship
   B) be divided into several paragraphs
   C) express confidence in the debtor
   D) be brief, but courteous
   E) be carefully planned

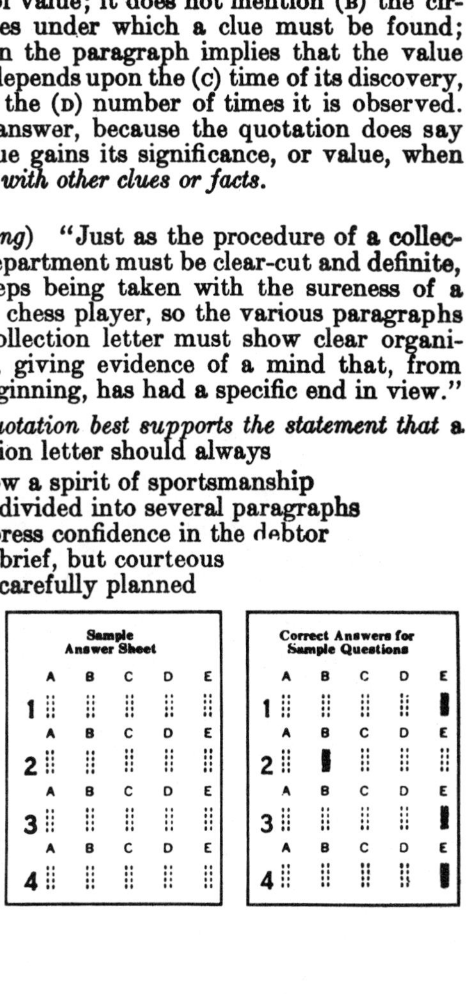

Grammar and English Usage

In each of questions 1 and 2, select the sentence that is preferable with respect to grammar and good usage in a formal letter or report.

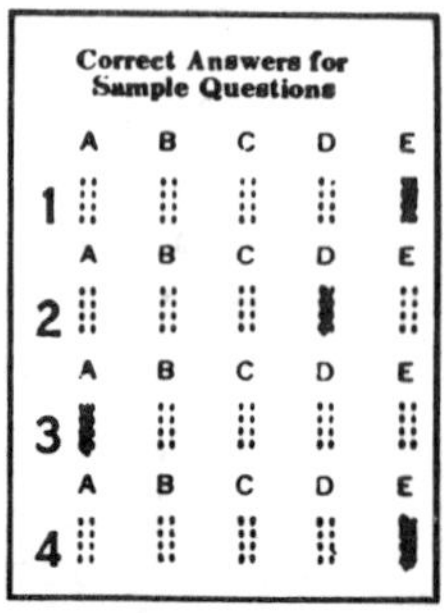

1. A) They do not ordinarily present these kind of reports in detail like this.
   B) Reports like this is not generally given in such great detail.
   C) A report of this kind is not hardly ever given in such detail as this one.
   D) This report is more detailed than what such reports ordinarily are.
   E) A report of this kind is not ordinarily presented in such detail as this one.
2. A) Although that statement is true, I did not leave it influence my decision.
   B) My decision is not effected by that statement, even though it is true.
   C) Although true, I have not let that statement influence my decision.
   D) That statement is true, but it does not affect my decision.
   E) Because that statement is true does not have any effect on my decision.

In questions 3 and 4, four words or phrases have been underlined and lettered A, B, C, and D. If there is an error in usage in one of the underlined words or phrases, mark on the answer sheet the letter of the one in which the error occurs. If there is no error, mark the E space.

3. The gasoline tank bust (A) and escaping (B) gasoline became (C) ignited in an unknown manner (D).
4. The truck was (A) in good mechanical (B) condition when examined (C) ten hours before (D) the accident occurred.

Letter Series

In each of these questions there is a series of letters which follow some definite order, and at the right there are five sets of two letters each. Look at the letters in the series and determine what the order is; then from the suggested answers at the right, select the set that gives the next two letters in the series in their correct order. Mark the space that has the same letter as the set you have chosen.

1. **X C X D X E X** A) **F X** B) **F G** C) **X F** D) **E F** E) **X G**

The series consists of X's alternating with letters in alphabetical order. The next two letters would be F and X; therefore, A is the correct answer.

2. **A B D C E F H** A) **G H** B) **I G** C) **G I** D) **K L** E) **I H**

If you compare this series with the alphabet, you will find that it goes along in pairs, the first pair in their usual order and the next pair in reverse order. The last letter given in the series is the second letter of the pair G—H, which is in reverse order. The first missing letter must, therefore, be G. The next pair of letters would be I—J, in that order; the second of the missing letters is I. The alternative you look for, then, is G I, which is lettered C.

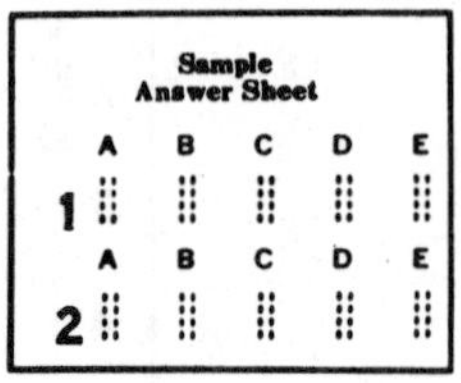

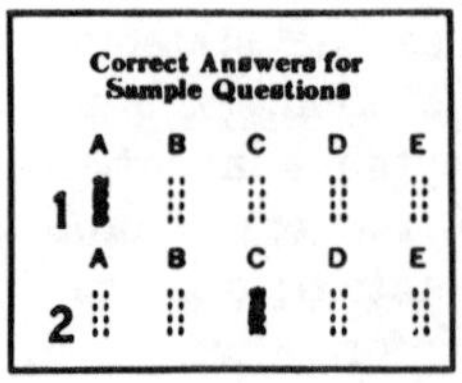

Arithmetic Computations and Problems

Directions: Following each problem below there are several suggested answers. Work each problem in your head or on scratch paper. (There will be space in your test book for you to do scratch work.) Then look at the suggested answers and decide which one is correct.

1. 45.76 written to nearest tenth is
   (A) 45.7 (B) 46.0 (C) 45.8 (D) 45.6

2. A boy picked 31 quarts of huckleberries and sold 24 quarts. How many quarts were left?
   (A) 4 (B) 5 (C) 6 (D) 7

3. A boy leaves his house for school at 7:36 A.M. and arrives at school at 8:02 A.M. How many minutes has it taken him to get to school?
   (A) 26 (B) 30 (C) 38 (D) 40

4. $\begin{array}{r} 3926 \\ \times 82 \\ \hline \end{array}$
   (A) 321,912 (B) 321,932
   (C) 321,962 (D) 321,982

5. 5/8 × 2/3 =
   (A) 1/4 (B) 2/3
   (C) 5/12 (D) 1/2

6. $\begin{array}{r} 8\ 9\ 4\ 2\ 3 \\ -3\ 2\ 8\ 4\ 6 \\ \hline \end{array}$
   (A) 56577 (B) 56587
   (C) 56597 (D) 56607

7. $175\frac{3}{5} + 90\frac{1}{10} =$
   (A) $184\frac{7}{10}$ (B) $265\frac{3}{10}$
   (C) $265\frac{7}{10}$ (D) $265\frac{5}{15}$
   (E) none of these

8. $\frac{3}{8} \times \frac{2}{3} =$
   (A) $\frac{1}{4}$ (B) $\frac{2}{5}$
   (C) $\frac{5}{11}$ (D) $\frac{5}{24}$
   (E) none of these

9. .6) 3618 =
   (A) 6.3 (B) 60.3
   (C) 63 (D) 6030
   (E) none of these

10. If 1 pound = 16 ounces, then
    2) 3 pounds 2 ounces =
    (A) 1 pound $1\frac{1}{4}$ ounces
    (B) 1 pound 2 ounces
    (C) 1 pound 6 ounces
    (D) 1 pound 9 ounces
    (E) none of these

11. Jack earned $2.50 for working 2 hours. At the same rate per hour, how much did he earn in an 8-hour day?
    (A) $5.00 (B) $8.00
    (C) $10.00 (D) $16.00
    (E) $20.00

12. In last week's football game, Bob made kicks of 40, 36, 32, and 36 yards. What was the average length of these kicks, in yards?
    (A) $33\frac{1}{3}$ (B) $33\frac{1}{2}$
    (C) 36 (D) 38
    (E) 72

13. The distance around a circle is about $3\frac{1}{7}$ times the distance across it. Consider two circles—one is 4 feet across and the other is 1 foot across. The distance around the larger circle is about
    (A) $\frac{4}{3}$ times the distance around the smaller
    (B) 2 times the distance around the smaller
    (C) $3\frac{1}{7}$ times the distance around the smaller
    (D) 4 times the distance around the smaller
    (E) $12\frac{4}{7}$ times the distance around the smaller

14. Twenty-two boys and twenty-six girls came to a picnic. If a *quart* of ice cream serves 6 persons, about how many *gallons* of ice cream will be needed?
    (4 quarts = 1 gallon)
    (A) 1 (B) 2
    (C) 4 (D) 6
    (E) 8

Correct Answers for Sample Questions

	A	B	C	D	E
1			■		
2				■	
3	■				
4		■			
5			■		
6	■				
7			■		

Correct Answers for Sample Questions

	A	B	C	D	E
8	■				
9				■	
10				■	
11			■		
12			■		
13				■	
14		■			

APPLYING FOR CIVIL SERVICE POSITIONS

JOB OPENINGS

About seven million people are employed by our state and local departments and agencies—approximately 1,700,000 by the fifty states and over 5,200,000 by the thousands of local government units and school districts. The employment opportunities cover practically every skill and profession in our complex modern social order. Every year thousands of new jobs are created and tens of thousands of replacements are needed on existing jobs.

Most state and municipal units have recruitment procedures for filling civil service positions. They have developed a number of methods to make job opportunities known. Places where such information may be obtained include:

1. The offices of the State Employment Services. There are almost two thousand throughout the country. These offices are administered by the state in which they are located, with the financial assistance of the Federal government. You will find the address of the one nearest you in your telephone book.

2. Your state Civil Service Commission. Address your inquiry to the capital city of your state.

3. Your city Civil Service Commission—if you live in a large city. It is sometimes called by another name, such as the Department of Personnel, but you will be able to identify it in your telephone directory under the listing of city departments.

4. Your municipal building and your local library.

5. Complete listings are carried by such newspaper as the *Civil Service Leader* and *The Chief* (both published in New York City), as well as other city and state-wide publications devoted to civil service employees. Many local newspapers run a section on regional civil service news.

6. State and local agencies looking for competent employees will contact schools, professional societies, veterans organizations, unions, and trade associations.

7. School Boards and Boards of Education, which employ the greatest proportion of all state and local personnel, should be asked directly for information about job openings.

The Job Announcement

WHAT IT CONTAINS

When a position is open and a civil service examination is to be given for it, a job announcement is drawn up. This generally contains just about everything an applicant has to know about the job.

The announcement begins with the job title and salary. A typical announcement then describes the work, the location of the position, the education and experience requirements, the kind of examination to be given, the system of rating. It may also have something to say about veteran preference and the age limit. It tells which application form is to be filled out, where to get the form, and where and when to file it.

Study the job announcement carefully. It will answer many of your questions and help you decide whether you like the position and are qualified for it.

WHERE THE JOB IS LOCATED

There is no point in applying for a position and taking the examination if you do not want to work where it is situated. The announcement gives you the information. The job may be in your community or hundreds of miles away at the other end of the state.

If a state job, be sure you are willing to work in the area indicated. If you are not, study other announcements that will give you an opportunity to work in a place of your choice.

A civil service job close to your home has as an additional advantage the fact that local residents usually receive preference in appointments.

THE DUTIES

The words *Optional Fields*—sometimes just the word *Options*—may appear on the front page of the announcement. You then have a choice to apply for that particular position in which you are especially interested. This is because the duties of various positions are quite different even though they bear the same broad title. A public relations *clerk,* for example, does different work from a payroll *clerk,* although they are considered broadly in the same general area.

Not every announcement has options. But whether or not it has them, the precise duties are described in detail, usually under the heading: *Description of Work.* Make sure that these duties come within the range of your experience and ability.

THE DEADLINE

Most job requirements give a deadline for filing an application. Others bear the words, *No Closing Date,* at the top of the first page; this means that applications will be accepted until the needs of the agency are met. In some cases a public notice is issued when a certain number of applications have been received.

No application mailed past the deadline date will be considered.

EDUCATION AND EXPERIENCE

Every announcement has a detailed section on education and experience requirements for the particular job and for the optional fields. Make sure that in both education and experience you meet the minimum qualifications. If you do not meet the given standards for one job, there may be others open where you stand a better chance of making the grade.

VETERAN PREFERENCE

If the job announcement does not mention veteran preference, it would be wise to inquire if there is such a provision in your state or municipality. There may be none or it may be limited to disabled veterans. In some jurisdictions widows of veteran are given preference. All such information can be obtained through the agency that issues the job announcement.

WHY YOU MAY BE BARRED

Applicants may be denied examinations and eligibles may be denied appointments for any of the following reasons:

—intentional false statements;

—deception or fraud in examination or appointment;

—reasonable doubt concerning loyalty to the United States;

—use of intoxicating beverages to excess;

—criminal, infamous, dishonest, immoral, or notoriously disgraceful conduct.

THE TEST

The announcement describes the kind of test given for the particular position. Please pay special attention to this section. It tells what areas are to be covered in the written test and lists the specific subjects on which questions will be asked. Sometimes sample questions are given.

The test and review material in this Arco book are based on the requirements as given in this section as well as on actual tests.

Usually the announcement states whether the examination is to be assembled or unassembled. In an *assembled* examination applicants *assemble* in the same place at the same time to take a written or performance test. The unassembled examination is one where an applicant does not take a test; instead he is rated on his educaton and experience and whatever records of past achievement he is asked to provide.

There are two main types of tests—competitive and non-competitive.

In a *competitive* examination all applicants for a position compete with each other; the better the mark, the better the chance of being appointed. In a *non-competitive* examination the applicant is tested solely to determine his qualification for a given position; he need only pass to become eligible for appointment.

The method of rating on civil service written tests is on a scale of 100, with 70 as the passing mark.

HOW TO GET AN APPLICATION FORM

Having studied the job announcement and having decided that you want the position and are qualified for it, your next step is to get an application form. The job announcement tells you where to send for it.

The Application Form

On the whole, civil service application forms differ little from state to state and locality to locality. The questions, which have been worked out after years of experimentation, are simple and direct, designed to elicit a maximum of information about you.

Many prospective civil service employees have failed to get a job because of slipshod, erroneous, incomplete, misleading, or untruthful answers. Give the application the serious attention it must have as the first important step toward getting the job you want.

Here, along with some helpful comments, are the questions usually asked on the average application form, although not necessarily in this order.

THE QUESTIONS

Name of examination or kind of position applied for. This information appears in large type on the first page of the job announcement.

Optional job (if mentioned in the announcement). If you wish to apply for an option, simply copy the title from the announcement. If you are not interested in an option, write "None."

Primary place of employment applied for. This would pertain to a state-wide job. The location of the position was probably contained in the announcement. You must consider whether you want to work there. The announcement may list more than one location where the job is open. If you would accept employment in any of the places, list them all; otherwise list the specific place or places where you would be willing to work.

Name and Address. Give in full, including your middle name if you have one, and your maiden name as well if you are a married woman.

Home and Office phones. If none, write "None."

Legal or voting residence. The state in which you vote is the one you list here.

Height wihout shoes, weight, sex. Answer accurately.

Married or single. If you are a widow or widower, you are considered single.

Birthplace. Changes in the borders of European countries make it difficult for many foreign-born American citizens to know which country to list as the land of their birth. One suggestion is to set down the name of the town and the name of the country which now controls it, together with the name of the country to which it belonged at the time of your birth.

Date of birth. Give the exact day, month, and year. Vanity has no place in a civil service application. Sometimes people who have given false ages elsewhere feel they must continue to do so. This would be a mistake.

Lowest grade or pay you will accept. Although the salary is clearly stated in the job announcement, there may be a quicker opening in the same occupation but carrying less responsibility and thus a lower basic entrance salary. You will not be considered for a job paying less than the amount you give in answer to this question.

Will you accept temporary employment if offered you for (a) one month or less, (b) one to four months, (c) four to twelve months? Temporary positions come up frequently and it is important to know whether you are available.

Will you accept less than full-time employment? Part-time work comes up now and then. Consider whether you want to accept such a position while waiting for a full-time appointment.

Were you in active military service in the Armed Forces of the United States? Veterans' preference, if given, is usually limited to active service during the following periods: April 6, 1917, to November 11, 1918; December 7, 1941, to September 2, 1945; June 26, 1950, to July 27, 1953.

Do you claim disabled veterans credit? If you do, you have to show proof of a war-incurred disability. This is done through certification by the Veterans Administration.

Considerable space is allotted on the form for the applicant to tell about all his past employment. Examiners check all such answers closely. DO NOT embroider or falsify your record. If you were ever fired, say so. It is better for you to state this openly than for the examiners to find out the truth from your former employer.

Special qualifications and skills. Even though not directly related to the position for which you are applying, wanted is such information as licenses and certificates obtained for teacher, pilot, registered nurses, and so on. Also experience in the use of machines and equipment, and a list of whatever other skills you have acquired. Also published writings, public speaking experience, membership in professional societies, honors and fellowships received.

Education. List your entire educational history, including all diplomas degrees, special courses taken in any accredited or Armed Forces school. Also give your credits toward a college or a graduate degree.

References. The names of people who can give information about you, with their occupations and business and home address, are often requested.

Your health. Questions are asked concerning your medical record. You are expected to have the physical and psychological capacity to perform the job for which you are applying. Standards vary, of course, depending on the requirements of the position. A physical handicap will not bar an applicant from a job he can perform adequately.

THE EXAMINATIONS

When you have filled out the application as completely as possible, sign it and send it to the address given on the form. If your examination includes a written test, you must wait until it is scheduled. Shortly before it is to be held, you will be notified where and when to report.

YOU ARE TESTED

Sometimes the date of the written test appears on the job announcement. Sometimes it does not and you must simply wait until you receive notification of the time and place.

The period between the filing of the application and the taking of the test can be of immense value to you. If you use it wisely, it will help you score high.

The most important step you can take in preparing for your test is to study questions on previous tests—or questions similar to those asked on previous tests. The purpose of this book is to acquaint you with the kinds of questions that will be asked and to provide you with review material in the subjects that will be covered. A thorough knowledge of the forms of the actual test as well as of the subject matter will give you a great advantage. There are no substitutes for experience and familiarity.

THE DAY OF THE TEST

The importance of knowing beforehand exactly how to reach the test center and how to get there cannot be stressed enough. Lateness will bar you from taking the test. There is nothing more nerve-wracking than to find yourself in a traffic jam and on the wrong bus with little time to spare. If the test is to take place some distance from your house, make the trip a few days earlier to make sure you know how to get there. On the all-important day give yourself more than enough time. In this way you will avoid the risk of an upsetting experience under circumstances that may affect your final score.

THE ELIGIBLE LIST

When all the parts of the examination have been rated (this may include education, experience, and suitability along with the written test), you are notified of your *numerical* rating. If this is high enough to give you a passing mark, you are placed on the eligible list. Appointments are made from this list.

STUDYING AND USING THIS BOOK

Even though this course of study has been carefully planned to help you get in shape by the day your test comes, you'll have to do a little planning on your own to be successful. And you'll also need a few pointers proven effective for many other good students.

SURVEY AND SCHEDULE YOUR WORK

Regular mental workouts are as important as regular physical workouts in achieving maximum personal efficiency. They are absolutely essential in getting top test scores, so you'll want to plan a test-preparing schedule that fits in with your usual program. Use the Schedule on the next page. Make it out for yourself so that it really works with the actual time you have at your disposal.

There are five basic steps in scheduling this book for yourself and in studying each assignment that you schedule:

1. SCAN - the entire job at hand.
2. QUESTION - before reading.
3. READ - to find the answers to the questions you have formulated.
4. RECITE - to see how well you have learned the answers to your questions.
5. REVIEW - to check up on how well you have learned, to learn it again, and to fix it firmly in your mind.

Scan

Make a survey of this whole book before scheduling. Do this by reading our introductory statements and the table of contents. Then leaf through the entire book, paying attention to main headings, sub-headings, summaries, and topic sentences. When you have this bird's eye view of the whole, the parts take on added meaning, and you'll see how they hang together.

Question

As you scan, questions will come to your mind. Write them into the book. Later on you'll be finding the answers. For example, in scanning this book you would naturally change the headline STUDYING AND USING THIS BOOK into *What don't I know about studying? What are my good study habits? How can I improve them? How should I go about reading and using this book?* Practice the habit of formulating and writing such questions into the text.

Read

Now, by reviewing your questions you should be able to work out your schedule easily. Stick to it. And apply these five steps to each assignment you give yourself in the schedule. Your reading of each assignment should be directed to finding answers to the questions you have formulated and will continue to formulate. You'll discover that reading with a purpose will make it easier to *remember* the answers to your questions.

Recite

After you have read your assignment and found the answers to your questions, close the book and recite to yourself. For example, if your question here was "What are the five basic steps in attacking an assignment?" then your answer to yourself would be scan, question, read, recite, and review. Thus, you check up on yourself and "fix" the information in your mind. You have now seen it, read it, said it, and heard it. The more senses you use, the more you learn.

Review

Even if you recall your answers well, review them in order to "overlearn". "Overlearning" gives you a big advantage by reducing the chances of forgetting. Definitely provide time in your schedule for review. It's the clincher in getting ahead of the crowd. You'll find that "overlearning" won't take much time with this book because the text portions have been written as concisely and briefly as possible. You may be tempted to stop work when you have once gone over the work before you. This is wrong because of the ease with which memory impressions are bound to fade. Decide for yourself what is important and plan to review and overlearn those portions. Overlearning rather than last minute cramming is the best way to study.

Your Time is Limited—Schedule Your Study

Plan your program. When you start your Course, look first at the table of contents to give yourself a preliminary idea of the material in the book. If you know the date of your examination, figure out how many half-hour sessions you can set aside for test-preparation, and once you have made up a schedule, stick to it.

STUDY TIMETABLE

Mon.									
Tues.									
Wed.									
Thur.									
Fri.									
Sat.									
Sun.									

HOW TO USE THE STUDY TIMETABLE

At right is a sample timetable filled in for a whole week to show you how a typical schedule might be arranged. The letters *A, B, C,* etc., are keyed to your study subjects so that, for example, *A* might stand for Vocabulary, *B* for Numerical Relations, and so forth. You will note that each day is divided into nine possible study hours and each hour, in turn, is divided into four 15-minute periods.

	7 AM	12 PM		7PM	8 PM	9PM			
Mon.	BB	AA	B	BCC	CCEE	E GG			
		12 PM		7PM	8PM	9PM			
Tues.		FF	A	AABB	DDD	D GG			
	7AM	12PM		7PM					
Wed.	CC	BB	BB	BB					
		12PM		7PM	8PM	9PM	10PM		
Thur.		A	A	A	BBEE	E FF	HH		
	7AM		7PM	8PM					
Fri.	AA	FF	FEE	CC					
	10AM	11AM	12PM	3PM	4PM				
Sat.	DDD	AAA	A	BBB	FF				
	1 PM	2PM	3PM	4PM	8PM				
Sun.	DDD	CCC	CAA	HHH	BB				

Plan to study difficult subjects when you can give them your greatest energy. Some people find that they can do their best work in the early morning hours. On the other hand, it has been found that forgetting is less when study is followed by sleep or recreation. Plan other study periods for those free times which might otherwise be wasted . . . for example lunch or when traveling to and from work.

Plan your schedule so that not more than 1½ or 2 hours are spent in the study of any subject at one sitting. Allow at least a half-hour for each session with your book. It takes a few minutes before you settle down to work.

You will find that there is enough time for your study and other activities if you follow a well-planned schedule. You will not only be able to find enough time for your other activities, but you will also accomplish more in the way of study and learning. A definite plan for study increases concentration. If you establish the habit of studying a subject at the same time each day, you will find that less effort is required in focusing your attention on it.

Where To Study

SELECT A ROOM THAT WILL BE AVAILABLE EACH DAY AT THE SAME TIME. THIS WILL HELP YOU CONCENTRATE.

USE A DESK OR TABLE WHICH WILL NOT BE SHARED SO THAT YOU CAN "LEAVE THINGS OUT". IT SHOULD BE BIG ENOUGH TO ACCOMMODATE ALL YOUR EQUIPMENT WITHOUT CRAMPING YOU. ELIMINATE ORNAMENTS AND OTHER DISTRACTIONS.

SELECT A ROOM WHICH HAS NO DISTRACTIONS. KEEP IT THAT WAY.

PROVIDE FOR GOOD AIR CIRCULATION IN YOUR STUDY ROOM.

KEEP THE TEMPERATURE AROUND 68°.

PROVIDE ADEQUATE LIGHTING . . . USE A DESK LAMP IN ADDITION TO OVERHEAD LIGHTS.

NOISE DISTRACTS SO KEEP RADIO AND TV TURNED OFF.

ARRANGE TO HAVE A PERMANENT KIT OF NECESSARY STUDY EQUIPMENT . . . PEN, PENCIL, RULER, SHEARS, ERASER, NOTEBOOK, CLIPS, DICTIONARY, ETC.

Study On Your Own

As a general rule you will find it more beneficial to study with this book in your room, alone. There are times, however, when two or more individuals can profit from team study. For example, if you can't figure something out for yourself, you might get help from a friend who is also studying for this test. Review situations sometimes lend themselves to team study if everyone concerned has already been over the ground by himself. Sometimes you can gain greater understanding of underlying principles as you volley ideas back and forth with other people. Watch out, though, that you don't come to lean on the others so much that you can't work things out for yourself.

PROVEN STUDY SUGGESTIONS

1. Do some work every day in preparation for the exam.
2. Budget your time—set aside a definite study period for each day during the week.
3. Study with a friend or a group occasionally—the exchange of ideas will help all of you. It's also more pleasant getting together.
4. Answer as many of the questions in this book as you can. Some of the questions that you will get on your actual test will be very much like some of the questions in this book.
5. Be physically fit. Eat the proper food—get enough sleep. You learn better and faster when you are in good health.
6. Take notes.
7. Be an active learner. Participate. Try harder.

TECHNIQUES OF EFFICIENT STUDY

DO NOT ATTEMPT SERIOUS STUDY WHILE IN TOO RELAXED A POSITION.

AVOID SERIOUS STUDY AFTER A HEAVY MEAL.

DO SOMETHING WHILE STUDYING . . . MAKE NOTES, UNDERLINE, FORMULATE QUESTIONS.

BEGIN CONCENTRATING AS SOON AS YOU SIT DOWN TO STUDY. DON'T FOOL AROUND.

MAKE TIME FOR STUDY BY ELIMINATING NEEDLESS ACTIVITIES AND OTHER DRAINS ON YOUR PRECIOUS TIME.

MAKE UP YOUR OWN ILLUSTRATIONS AND EXAMPLES TO CHECK ON YOUR UNDERSTANDING OF A TOPIC.

FIND SOME PRACTICAL APPLICATION OF YOUR NEWLY ACQUIRED KNOWLEDGE.

RELATE NEWLY ACQUIRED KNOWLEDGE TO WHAT YOU KNEW BEFORE.

CONSCIOUSLY TRY TO LEARN, TO CONCENTRATE, TO PAY ATTENTION.

LOOK UP NEW WORDS IN YOUR DICTIONARY.

Concentrating

Most students who complain that they don't know how to concentrate deserve no sympathy. Concentration is merely habit and ought to be as readily acquired as any other habit. The way to begin to study is simply to begin.

Don't wait for inspiration or for the mood to strike you, nor should you permit yourself to indulge in thoughts like, "This chapter is too long" or "I guess I could really let that go until some other time."

Such an attitude throws an extra load on your mental machinery, and by making you work against a handicap, makes it harder for you to begin.

Reading aloud is a good device for those whose minds wander while studying. Articulating "subvocally" for a few moments is another tonic for drifting thoughts. If this doesn't work, write down the point you happen to be dealing with when your mind "goes off track."

Do your studying alone, and you'll find it much easier to concentrate. If you are certain you need help on doubtful or difficult points, check these points and list them; you can go back or ask about them later. In the meantime, proceed to the next point.

A "little tenseness" is a good thing because it helps you keep alert while studying. Do without smoking, or newspapers, or magazines, or novels which may lead you into temptation. Studying in one place all the time also helps.

Boiling it all down, the greatest asset for effective studying is plain, garden variety "common sense" and will power.

Grasshoppers Never Learn

Don't be a "skipper." Jumping around from one part of your course to another may be more interesting, but it won't help you as much as steady progress from page one right through the book.

Studying and learning takes more than just reading. The "text" part of your course can be a valuable tool in test-preparation if you use it correctly. Introductions to the various sections of your book must be "studied." Re-read the paragraph that gives you trouble. Be certain that you understand it before you pass on to the next one. Many persons who have been away from school for a long time, and those people who have a habit of reading rapidly, find that it helps if they hold a piece of white paper under the paragraph they are reading, covering the rest of the page. That helps you concentrate on the facts you are absorbing. Keep a pen or pencil in your hand while reading, and underline important facts. Put a question mark after anything that isn't quite clear to you, so that you can get back to it. Summarize ideas in the margins of your book. You'll be surprised how much easier it is to remember something once you have written it down, and expressed it in your own words.

Taking Notes

Although your "self-tutor" has done a great deal for you in summarizing the information that is essential to success on the test, it's still worth your while to do some notetaking. Your notes, which can be made either in a separate notebook or in the margins of this book, will help you concentrate; are a form of self-recitation; will provide you with concise outlines for review before the test; will help you identify basic and essential materials; will help you retain what you learn, with greater accuracy for a longer period of time; and will help you learn better because they require thinking and active participation on your part.

The following suggestions will help you take the kind of notes that will be of greatest use to you on the test:

RECORD ESSENTIAL FACTS AND AVOID TOO MUCH DETAIL. JOT DOWN CLUES.

ADOPT AN ACTIVE MEANING-SEEKING ATTITUDE. STICK TO BASIC SIGNIFICANCE.

USE YOUR OWN WORDS. BUT BE BRIEF.

DON'T HURRY. WRITE READABLY AND ACCURATELY. YOU'LL BE READING THEM AGAIN.

BE NEAT. WRITE TITLES AND LABELS. DON'T BE SPARING OF PAPER.

USE A SINGLE LOOSELEAF NOTEBOOK SO THAT YOU CAN RE-ORGANIZE AND COMBINE NOTES.

TAKE NOTES IN ALL LEARNING SITUATIONS RELATING TO THIS TEST.

DON'T COPY VERBATIM.

REVIEW YOUR NOTES OF THE PREVIOUS DAY BEFORE STARTING THE CURRENT ASSIGNMENT.

USE QUESTION MARKS IN THE MARGINS OF THE BOOK FOR VAGUE OR DIFFICULT PASSAGES WHICH MAY BE CLARIFIED AS YOU READ ON. YOU MAY WANT TO COME BACK TO THEM TO BE SURE YOU UNDERSTAND THEM.

TRY TO DO SOME FOLLOW UP WORK ON UNDERLINED SECTIONS.

SOME SUGGESTED SYMBOLS FOR MAKING NOTES IN THIS BOOK.

- |, ( ), [ ] A vertical line in the margin, or a bracket, or parenthesis around a sentence or group of sentences is used to indicate an important idea or ideas.
- — Underlining is used to indicate especially important materials, specific points to be consulted during reviews.
- O A circle around a word may be used to indicate that you are not familiar with the word, and that you will come back later to look it up in the dictionary.
- √ E The letter "E" or a check mark (√) in the margin may be used to mark materials that are important and likely to be used in the examination.
- 1, 2, 3, 4 Arabic numerals, circled or uncircled may be placed before a word or at the beginning of a sentence to indicate a series of facts, ideas, important dates, etc.
- D The letter "D" may be used to indicate your disagreement with a passage or a statement.

Keep in mind that effective notetaking is vital to learning. If your notes are effective, your learning is likely to be effective.

Test Yourself Frequently

The major part of your course consists of study questions and answers prepared by experts. Try to answer every question in the book as you reach it. Each study session should end with a self-test.

Develop Careful Reading Habits

While present-day examinations seldom have "trick" questions, the men who make up examinations often frame questions so that careful reading is necessary to understand the question fully and to give the proper answer. Use this book as a personal reading-improver. Rephrase every question in your own words before you answer, to be sure that you really understand what is being asked.

Don't Try to Memorize

It is true that the same questions often reappear on examinations of the same kind, but it would not be worthwhile to try to memorize the hundreds of questions in your book. After all, the *scope* of any examination is fairly limited. Using your book as a self-tester will show you the fields in which you may be weak or strong. The questions and answers will help put you into the important examination-taking frame of mind, and give you an excellent idea of the different types of information about which you will be questioned on your test.

Be Tough With Yourself

One error made by many persons who are preparing for examinations is to give themselves too much of a break. They will peek at the book answer to a question and excuse themselves on the grounds that if they had "really" been taking a test, they would have been more careful and would have given the correct answer. Don't let yourself get away with that!

You have to be a stern teacher to get the most out of any program of self-study. When you test yourself, be as tough as if the test-taker were someone you didn't know. Don't let yourself get away with an "almost right" answer. Today there is keen competition on most tests, and the habits you develop while preparing for your test will show up on the examination in the form of earned or lost percentage points. Mark yourself rigidly. Be honest in appraising your weaknesses, and try to correct them before you sit down to take the real test.

And don't take anything for granted. Even if you find yourself scoring 100% in some area of your test, don't relax too much. When you find that you have answered a question correctly, use that as a lever for self-improvement. Ask yourself *why* your answer was correct. Try to think of other forms in which the same question could have been asked. Try to frame your own questions that are "harder" or more demanding than the ones you can answer easily.

You may find that some sections of this book are difficult, just as some portions of the test will be more difficult than others. Don't worry about it. Don't panic. Remember that the test is a competitive one . . . that your score is relative to the scores of all the oher competitors. What's hard for you will be just as hard (or harder) for them.

When the going gets rough you're on notice to study more carefully. You've discovered one of your weaknesses. You're ahead of the game because you have the opportunity of strengthening yourself. Concentrate on your weak spots and you won't be caught off balance by the test questions.

On the other hand don't permit yourself to be lulled into a false sense of security when you discover material which is very easy for you. Don't quit studying—just give the easy portions less time. Adjust your schedule and use the time you pick up in this way to work where it is most needed.

This technique of devoting as much time and thought as is required by each job (and no more) should be applied to the actual test, with one caution. The easy questions should be answered as rapidly as you can, as you come to them. But if a question appears very difficult and likely to take a lot of time to answer, defer spending too much time on it. Continue on, giving the quick, easy answers. Then go back and use the time remaining to answer the slow, hard ones.

Scissors and Glue for Review

One helpful form of review, as your examination date approaches, is this: Cut out individual questions from your book. Paste them on slips of paper, and mark the correct answers on the back of each question.

Then, whenever you have a few minutes to spare, you can shuffle the questions around and find out whether you have the correct answers in your mind. This is especially helpful in dealing with questions of the "information" type which are basically tests of how well you remember important information and facts.

Another good learning technique is to have someone read the questions and suggested answers to you. "Hearing" will serve as a memory aid after you have read and studied the material.

Analyze Your Weaknesses—And Correct Them

One purpose of this course is to familiarize you with the types of questions you will face and to prepare you for them. Perhaps its more important purpose is to help you find your own weaknesses and to correct them before the examination.

Every time you give the incorrect answer to a practice question you should ask yourself, "Why?" Be honest with yourself and you'll soon discover the subjects in which you're weak. Devote extra time to these subjects and you will have taken giant steps to test success.

We have analyzed test failures and have found time after time that many persons who are perfectly able to pass a test fail it simply because of their weakness in such basic subjects as arithmetic or vocabulary.

If you find that you have such a problem, be brave. Put in the extra effort each day.

COURT OFFICER

HOW TO BE A MASTER TEST TAKER

It's really quite simple. Do things right . . . right from the beginning. Make successful methods a habit by practicing them on all the exercises in this book. Before you're finished you will have invested a good deal of time. Make sure you get the largest dividends from this investment.

SCORING PAPERS BY MACHINE

A typical machine-scored answer sheet is shown below, reduced from the actual size of 8¼ x 11 inches. Since it's the only one that reaches the office where papers are scored, it's important that the blanks at the top be filled in completely and correctly.

The chances are very good that you'll have to mark your answers on one of these sheets. Consequently, we've made it possible for you to practice with them throughout this book.

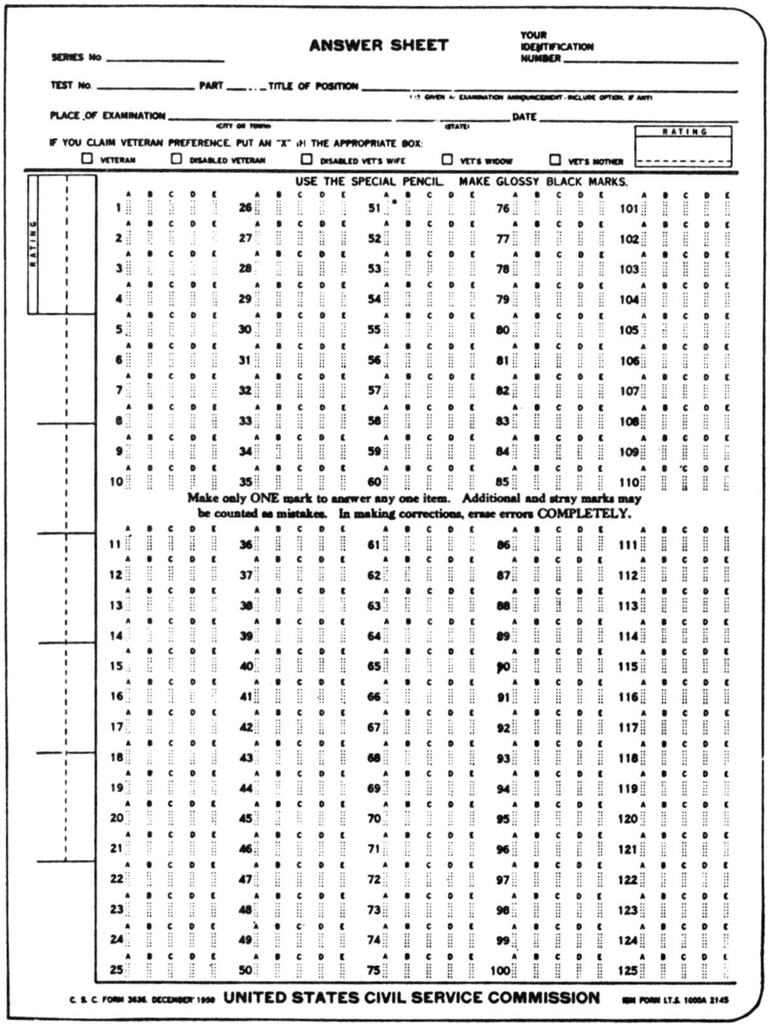
ANSWER SHEET

SERIES No. ________ YOUR IDENTIFICATION NUMBER ________

TEST No. ________ PART ____ TITLE OF POSITION ________

PLACE OF EXAMINATION ________ (CITY OR TOWN) ________ (STATE) DATE ________

RATING

IF YOU CLAIM VETERAN PREFERENCE, PUT AN "X" IN THE APPROPRIATE BOX:

☐ VETERAN ☐ DISABLED VETERAN ☐ DISABLED VET'S WIFE ☐ VET'S WIDOW ☐ VET'S MOTHER

USE THE SPECIAL PENCIL. MAKE GLOSSY BLACK MARKS.

Make only ONE mark to answer any one item. Additional and stray marks may be counted as mistakes. In making corrections, erase errors COMPLETELY.

C. S. C. FORM 3636, DECEMBER 1950 UNITED STATES CIVIL SERVICE COMMISSION

FOLLOW DIRECTIONS CAREFULLY

It's an obvious rule, but more people fail for breaching it than for any other cause. By actual count there are over a hundred types of directions given on tests. You'll familiarize yourself with all of them in the course of this book. And you'll also learn not to let your guard down in reading them, listening to them, and following them. Right now, before you plunge in, we want to be sure that you have nothing to fear from the answer sheet and the way in which you must mark it; from the most important question forms and the ways in which they are to be answered.

HERE'S HOW TO MARK YOUR ANSWERS ON MACHINE-SCORED ANSWER SHEETS:

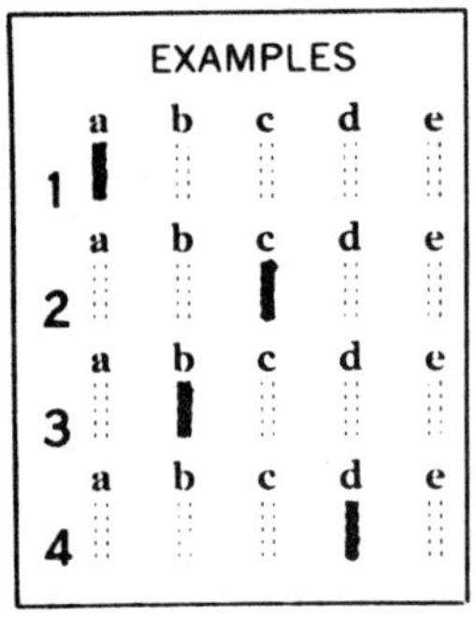

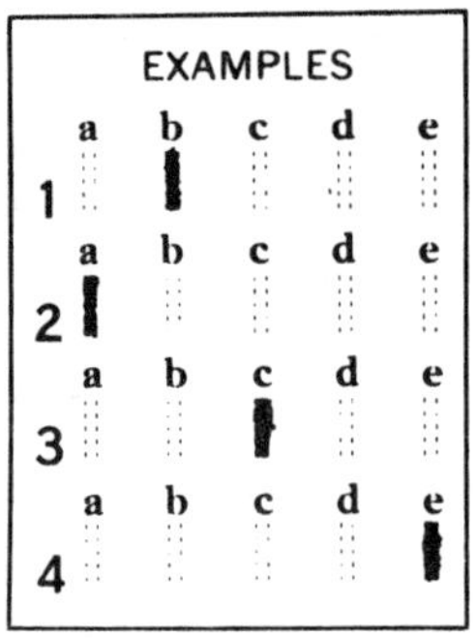

Make only ONE mark for each answer. Additional and stray marks may be counted as mistakes. In making corrections, erase errors COMPLETELY. Make glossy black marks.

(a) Each pencil mark must be heavy and black. Light marks should be retraced with the special pencil.

(b) Each mark must be in the space between the pair of dotted lines and entirely fill this space.

(c) All stray pencil marks on the paper, clearly not intended as answers, must be completely erased.

(d) Each question must have only one answer indicated. If multiple answers occur, all extraneous marks should be thoroughly erased. Otherwise, the machine will give you *no* credit for your correct answer.

MULTIPLE CHOICE METHODS

Multiple choice questions are very popular these days with examiners. The chances are good that you'll get this kind on your test. So we've arranged that you practice with them in the following pages. But first we want to give you a little help by explaining the best methods for handling this question form.

You know, of course, that these questions offer you four or five possible answers, that your job is to select *only* the *best* answer, and that even the incorrect answers are frequently *partly* correct. These partly-true choices are inserted to force you to think . . . and prove that you know the right answer.

USE THESE METHODS TO ANSWER MULTIPLE CHOICE QUESTIONS CORRECTLY:

1. Read the item closely to see what the examiner is after. Re-read it if necessary.
2. Mentally reject answers that are clearly wrong.
3. Suspect as being wrong any of the choices which contain broad statements hinging on "cue" words like

absolute
absolutely
all
always
axiomatic
categorical
completely
doubtless
entirely
extravagantly
forever
immeasurably
inalienable
incontestable
incontrovertible
indefinitely
indisputable
indubitable
inevitable
inexorable
infallible
infinite
inflexible
inordinately
irrefutable
inviolable
never
only
peculiarly
positive
quite
self-evident
sole
totally
unchallenged
unchangeable
undeniable
undoubtedly
unequivocal
unexceptionable
unimpeachable
unqualified
unquestionable
wholly
without exception

If you're unsure of the meanings of any of these words, look them up in your dictionary.

4. A well-constructed multiple choice item will avoid obviously incorrect choices. The good examiner will try to write a cluster of answers, all of which are plausible. Use the clue words to help yourself pick the *most* correct answer.
5. In the case of items where you are doubtful of the answer, you might be able to bring to bear the information you have gained from previous study. This knowledge might be sufficient to indicate that some of the suggested answers are not so plausible. Eliminate such answers from further consideration.
6. Then concentrate on the remaining suggested answers. The more you eliminate in this way, the better your chances of getting the item right.
7. If the item is in the form of an incomplete statement, it sometimes helps to try to complete the statement before you look at the suggested answers. Then see if the way you have completed the statement corresponds with any of the answers provided. If one is found, it is likely to be the correct one.
8. Use your head! Make shrewd inferences. Sometimes with a little thought, and the information that you have, you can reason out the answer. We're suggesting a method of intelligence guessing in which you can become quite expert with a little practice. It's a useful method that may help you with some debatable answers.

NOW, LET'S TRY THESE METHODS OUT ON A SAMPLE MULTIPLE-CHOICE QUESTION.

1. Leather is considered the best material for shoes chiefly because
   (A) it is waterproof
   (B) it is quite durable
   (C) it is easily procurable
   (D) it is flexible and durable
   (E) it can be easily manufactured in various styles.

Here we see that every one of the answer statements is plausible: leather is waterproof if treated properly; it is relatively durable; it is relatively easily procurable; it bends and is shaped easily, and is, again, durable; it constantly appears in various styles of shoes and boots.

However, we must examine the question with an eye toward identifying the key phrase which is: *best* for shoes *chiefly.*

Now we can see that (A) is incorrect because leather is probably not the *best* material for shoes, simply because it is waterproof. There are far better waterproof materials available, such as plastics and rubber. In fact, leather must be treated to make it waterproof. So by analyzing the key phrase of the question we can eliminate (A).

(B) seems plausible. Leather is durable, and durability is a good quality in shoes. But the word *quite* makes it a broad statement. And we become suspicious. The original meaning of *quite* is completely, wholly, entirely. Since such is the case we must reject this choice because leather is *not completely* durable. It does wear out.

(C) Leather is comparatively easy to procure; but would that make it *best* for shoes? And would that be the *chief* reason why it is used for making shoes? Although the statement in itself is quite true, it does not fit the key phrase of the question and we must, reluctantly, eliminate it.

(D) is a double-barreled statement. One part, the durability, has been suggested in (B) above. Leather is also quite flexible, so both parts of the statement would seem to fit the question.

(E) It is true that leather can be manufactured in various styles, but so can many other materials. Again, going back to the key phrase, this could be considered one, but not the *chief* reason why it is *best* for shoes.

So, by carefully analyzing the *key* phrase of the question we have narrowed our choices down to (D). Although we rejected (B) we did recognize that durability is a good quality in shoes, but only one of several. Since flexibility is also a good quality, we have no hesitation in choosing (D) as the correct answer.

The same question, by slightly altering the answer choices, can also call for a *negative* response. Here, even more so, the identification of the key phrase becomes vital in finding the correct answer. Suppose the question and its responses were worded thus:

2. Leather is considered the best material for shoes chiefly because
   (A) it is waterproof
   (B) it is easily colored
   (C) it is easily procurable
   (D) it can easily be manufactured in various styles
   (E) none of these.

We can see that the prior partially correct answer (B) has now been changed, and the doubly-correct answer eliminated. Instead we have a new response possibility (E), "none of these."

We have analyzed three of the choices previously and have seen the reason why none of them are the *chief* reason why leather is considered the *best* material for shoes. The two new elements are (B) "easily colored," and (E) "none of these."

If you think about it, leather *can* be easily colored and often is, but this would not be the chief reason why it is considered *best*. Many other materials are just as easily dyed. So we must come to the conclusion that *none* of the choices are *completely* correct—none fit the key phrase. Therefore, the question calls for a negative response (E).

We have now seen how important it is to identify the key phrase. Equally, or perhaps even more important, is the identifying and analyzing of the key *word*—the qualifying word—in a question. This is usually, though not always, an adjective or adverb. Some of the key words to watch for are: *most, best, least, highest, lowest, always, never, sometimes, most likely, greatest, smallest, tallest, average, easiest, most nearly, maximum, minimum, chiefly, mainly, only, but* and *or*. Identifying these key words is usually half the battle in understanding and, consequently, answering all types of exam questions.

Rephrasing the Question

It is obvious, then, that by carefully analyzing a question, by identifying the key phrase and its key words, you can usually find the correct answer by logical deduction and, often, by elimination. One other way of examining, or "dissecting," a question is to restate or rephrase it with each of the suggested answer choices integrated into the question.

For example, we can take the same question and rephrase it.

(A) The chief reason why leather is considered the best material for shoes is because it is waterproof.

or

(A) Because it is waterproof, leather is considered the best material for shoes.

or

(A) Chiefly because it is waterproof, leather is considered the best material for shoes.

It will be seen from the above three new versions of the original statement and answer that the question has become less obscure because it has been, so to speak, illuminated from different angles. It becomes quite obvious also in this rephrasing that the statement (A) is incorrect, although the *original* phrasing of the question left some doubt.

The rules for understanding and analyzing the key phrase and key words in a question, and the way to identify the *one* correct answer by means of intelligent analysis of the important question-answer elements, are basic to the solution of all the problems you will face on your test.

In fact, perhaps the *main* reason for failing an examination is failure to *understand the question.* In many cases, examinees *do* know the answer to a particular problem, but they cannot answer correctly because they do not understand it.

METHODS FOR MATCHING QUESTIONS

In this question form you are actually faced with multiple questions that require multiple answers. It's a difficult form in which you are asked to pair up one set of facts with another. It can be used with any type of material . . . vocabulary, spatial relations, numbers, facts, etc.

A typical matching question might appear in this form:

Directions: Below is a set of words containing ten words numbered 3 to 12, and twenty other words divided into five groups labeled Group A to Group E. For each of the numbered words select the word in one of the five groups which is most nearly the same in meaning. The letter of that group is the answer for that numbered item.

Although this arrangement is a relatively simple one for a "matching" question, the general principle is the same for all levels of difficulty. Basically, this type of question consists of two columns. The elements of one of the columns must be matched with some or all of the elements of the second column.

3. fiscal
4. deletion
5. equivocal
6. corroboration
7. tortuous
8. predilection
9. sallow
10. virtuosity
11. scion
12. tenuous

Group A
indication ambiguous
excruciating thin

Group B
confirmation financial
phobia erasure

Group C
fiduciary similar
yellowish skill

Group D
theft winding
receive procrastination

Group E
franchise heir
hardy preference

Correct Answers

3. B	6. B	9. C	10. C
4. B	7. D	8. E	11. E
5. A			12. A

There are numerous ways in which these questions may be composed, from the simple one shown above to the most difficult type of arrangement. In many cases the arrangement of the question may be so complicated that more time may be spent upon the comprehension of the instructions than on the actual question. This again, points up the importance of fully and quickly understanding the instructions before attempting to solve any problem or answer any question.

Several general principles apply, however, when solving a matching question. Work with one column at a time and match each item of that column against all the items in the second column, skipping around that second column looking for a proper match. Put a thin pencil line through items that are matched so they won't interfere with your later selections. (This is particularly important in a test that tells you to choose any item only once. The test gets real tricky, however, when you are asked to choose an item more than once.)

Match each item very carefully—don't mark it unless you are certain—because if you have to change any one, it may mean changing three or four or more, and that may get you hopelessly confused. After you have marked all your *certain* choices, go over the unmarked items again and make a *good* guess at the remaining items, if you have time.

USE CONTROLLED ASSOCIATION when you come to an item which you are not able to match. Attempt to recall any and all facts you might have concerning this item. Through the process of association, a fact recalled might provide a clue to the answer.

TRUE-FALSE TACTICS

True-false questions may appear on your test. Because they are easier to answer they are used less frequently than multiple-choice questions. However, because examiners find that they are easier to prepare, here are some suggestions to help you answer them correctly.

1. Suspect the truth of broad statements hinging on those *all or nothing* "cue" words we listed for you in discussing multiple-choice questions.
2. Watch out for "spoilers" . . . the word or phrase which negates an otherwise true statement.

Vegetation is sparse on the Sahara desert where the climate is hot and humid. T F

3. Statements containing such modifiers as *generally, usually, most,* and similar words are usually true.
4. If the scoring formula is "Rights minus Wrongs", don't guess. If you know it's true, mark it T. If you don't know it's true, ask yourself "What have I learned that would make it false?" If you can think of nothing on either side, omit the answer. Of course, if the R-W formula is not being used it is advisable to guess if you're not sure of an answer.
5. Your first hunch is usually best. Unless you have very good reason to do so, don't change your first answer to true-false questions about which you are doubtful.

Single-Statement Question

The basic form of true-false question is the "single-statement" question; i.e., a sentence that contains a single thought, such as:

13. The Statue of Liberty is in New York T F

The same statement becomes slightly more difficult by including a negative element

14. The Statue of Liberty is not in New York T F

or, more subtly:

15. The Statue of Liberty is not in Chicago T F

or, by adding other modifiers:

16. The Statue of Liberty is sometimes in New York T F
17. The Statue of Liberty is always in New York T F

Even from these very simple and basic examples of a "single-statement" true-false question it can be seen that a *complete understanding* of the subject area as well as of the phrasing of the question is essential before you attempt to answer it. Careless or hasty reading of the statment will often make you miss the *key* word, especially if the question appears to be a very simple one.

An important point to remember when answering this type of question is that the statement must be *entirely true* to be answered as "true"; if even just a *part* of it is false, the answer must be marked "false."

Composite-Statement Question

Sometimes a true-false question will be in the form of a "composite statement," a statement that contains more than one thought, such as:

18. The Statue of Liberty is in New York, and Chicago is in Illinois T F

Some basic variations of this type of composite-statemest question are these:

19. The Statue of Liberty is in New York, and Chicago is in Michigan T F
20. The Statue of Liberty is not in New York and Chicago is in Illinois T F
21. The Statue of Liberty is not in New York and Chicago is in Michigan T F

Of the four questions above, only question 18 is true. Each of the other statements (19, 20, 21), is false because each contains at least *one* element that is false.

It can be seen from the above that in a composite statement *both* elements, or "substatements," must be true in order for the answer to be "true." Otherwise, the answer must be "false."

This principle goes for all composite statements that are, or can be, connected by the word "and," even if the various "thoughts" of the statement seem to be entirely unrelated.

We have seen how to handle a composite statement that consists of *unrelated* substatements. Finally, we will examine a composite true-false statement which consists of *related* elements:

22. The Golden Gate Bridge is in San Francisco, which is not the capital of California. T F
23. The Golden Gate Bridge is in San Francisco, the capital of California. T F
24. The Golden Gate Bridge is not in San Francisco, the capital of California. T F
25. The Golden Gate Bridge is not in San Francisco, which is not the capital of California. T F

Again, only the first composite statement (22) is true. All the rest are false because they contain at least one false substatement.

PART TWO

The Previous Exams for Practice

DIRECTIONS FOR ANSWERING QUESTIONS

For each question read all the choices carefully. Then select that answer which you consider correct or most nearly correct. Write the letter preceding your best choice next to the question

Should you want to answer on the kind of answer sheet used on machine-scored examinations, we have provided several such facsimiles. Tear one out if you wish, and mark your answers on it . . . just as you would do on an actual exam.

In machine-scored examinations you should record all your answers on the answer sheet provided. Don't make the mistake of putting answers on the test booklet itself.

On some machine-scored exams you are instructed to "place no marks whatever on the test booklet."

In other examinations you may be instructed to mark your answers in the test booklet. In such cases you should be careful that no other marks interfere with the legibility of your answers.

It is always best NOT to mark your booklet unless you are sure that it is permitted.

It is most important that you learn to mark your answers clearly and in the right place.

To help you understand the procedure, the following sample item is given:

SAMPLE O: The sum of 5 and 3 is

(A) 11 (B) 8 (C) 9 (D) 2 (E) 10.

The sum of 5 and 3 is 8, so that the acceptable answer is shown thus on your answer sheet:

	A	B	C	D	E
SAMPLE O	❘❘	▮	❘❘	❘❘	❘❘

Practice Using Answer Sheets

Alter numbers to match the practice and drill questions in each part of the book.
Make only ONE mark for each answer. Additional and stray marks may be counted as mistakes.
In making corrections, erase errors COMPLETELY. Make glossy black marks.

	A	B	C	D	E		A	B	C	D	E		A	B	C	D	E		A	B	C	D	E		A	B	C	D	E
1	⁞	⁞	⁞	⁞	⁞	1	⁞	⁞	⁞	⁞	⁞	1	⁞	⁞	⁞	⁞	⁞	1	⁞	⁞	⁞	⁞	⁞	1	⁞	⁞	⁞	⁞	⁞
2	⁞	⁞	⁞	⁞	⁞	2	⁞	⁞	⁞	⁞	⁞	2	⁞	⁞	⁞	⁞	⁞	2	⁞	⁞	⁞	⁞	⁞	2	⁞	⁞	⁞	⁞	⁞
3	⁞	⁞	⁞	⁞	⁞	3	⁞	⁞	⁞	⁞	⁞	3	⁞	⁞	⁞	⁞	⁞	3	⁞	⁞	⁞	⁞	⁞	3	⁞	⁞	⁞	⁞	⁞
4	⁞	⁞	⁞	⁞	⁞	4	⁞	⁞	⁞	⁞	⁞	4	⁞	⁞	⁞	⁞	⁞	4	⁞	⁞	⁞	⁞	⁞	4	⁞	⁞	⁞	⁞	⁞
5	⁞	⁞	⁞	⁞	⁞	5	⁞	⁞	⁞	⁞	⁞	5	⁞	⁞	⁞	⁞	⁞	5	⁞	⁞	⁞	⁞	⁞	5	⁞	⁞	⁞	⁞	⁞
6	⁞	⁞	⁞	⁞	⁞	6	⁞	⁞	⁞	⁞	⁞	6	⁞	⁞	⁞	⁞	⁞	6	⁞	⁞	⁞	⁞	⁞	6	⁞	⁞	⁞	⁞	⁞
7	⁞	⁞	⁞	⁞	⁞	7	⁞	⁞	⁞	⁞	⁞	7	⁞	⁞	⁞	⁞	⁞	7	⁞	⁞	⁞	⁞	⁞	7	⁞	⁞	⁞	⁞	⁞
8	⁞	⁞	⁞	⁞	⁞	8	⁞	⁞	⁞	⁞	⁞	8	⁞	⁞	⁞	⁞	⁞	8	⁞	⁞	⁞	⁞	⁞	8	⁞	⁞	⁞	⁞	⁞
9	⁞	⁞	⁞	⁞	⁞	9	⁞	⁞	⁞	⁞	⁞	9	⁞	⁞	⁞	⁞	⁞	9	⁞	⁞	⁞	⁞	⁞	9	⁞	⁞	⁞	⁞	⁞
0	⁞	⁞	⁞	⁞	⁞	0	⁞	⁞	⁞	⁞	⁞	0	⁞	⁞	⁞	⁞	⁞	0	⁞	⁞	⁞	⁞	⁞	0	⁞	⁞	⁞	⁞	⁞

TEAR OUT ALONG THIS LINE AND MARK YOUR ANSWERS AS INSTRUCTED IN THE TEXT

I. THE LATEST PREVIOUS EXAM

"A thousand mile journey begins with a single step." So here's the most recent, available civil service test for your job. It's a reliable indicator of what you're up against, and what you have to study. Get right to work on it. Follow all the instructions carefully, just as though it were the actual test. If you have time, after you've completed the book, you may want to take this test again to compare results and measure your improvement.

DATE OF EXAM: June 25, 1960

The time allowed for the entire examination is 3½ hours. In order to create the climate of the test to come, that's precisely what you should allow yourself . . . no more, no less. Use a watch and keep a record of your time, especially since you may find it convenient to take the test in several sittings.

PREVIOUS TEST QUESTIONS FOR PRACTICE

1. "Physical and mental health are essential to the peace officer". According to this statement, the peace officer must be

   (A) as wise as he is strong (B) smarter than most people (C) sound in mind and body (D) stronger than the average criminal.

2. "Teamwork is the basis of successful law enforcement". The factor stressed by this statement is

   (A) co-operation (B) determination (C) initiative (D) pride.

3. "Legal procedure is a means, not an end. Its function is merely to accomplish the enforcement of legal rights. A litigant has no vested interest in the observance of the rules of procedure as such. All that he should be entitled to demand is that he be given an opportunity for a fair and impartial trial of his case. He should not be permitted to invoke the aid of technical rules merely to embarrass his adversary". According to this paragraph, it is most correct to state that

   (A) observance of the rules of procedure guarantees a fair trial
   (B) embarrassment of an adversary through technical rules does not make for a fair trial (C) a litigant is not interested in the observance of rules of procedure (D) technical rules must not be used in a trial.

4. "One theory states that all criminal behavior is taught by a process of communication within small intimate groups. An individual engages in criminal behavior if the number of criminal patterns which he has acquired exceeds the number of non-criminal patterns". This statement indicates that criminal behavior is

   (A) learned (B) instinctive (C) hereditary (D) reprehensible.

5. "The law enforcement staff of today requires training and mental qualities of a high order. The poorly or partially prepared staff member lowers the standard of work, retards his own earning power, and fails in a career meant to provide a livelihood and social improvement". According to this statement,

(A) an inefficient member of a law enforcement staff will still earn a good livelihood (B) law enforcement officers move in good social circles (C) many people fail in law enforcement careers (D) persons of training and ability are essential to a law enforcement staff.

6. "In New York State, no crime can occur unless there is a written law forbidding the act or the omission in question, and even though an act may not be exactly in harmony with public policy, such act is not a crime unless it is expressly forbidden by legislative enactment." According to the above statement,

(A) a crime is committed with reference to a particular law (B) acts not in harmony with public policy should be forbidden by law (C) non-criminal activity will promote public welfare (D) legislative enactments frequently forbid actions in harmony with public policy.

7. "The unrestricted sale of firearms is one of the main causes of our shameful crime record". According to this statement, one of the causes of our crime record is the

(A) development of firepower (B) ease of securing weapons (C) increased skill in using guns (D) scientific perfection of firearms.

8. "Every person must be informed of the reason for his arrest unless he is arrested in the actual commission of a crime. Sufficient force to effect the arrest may be used, but the courts frown on brutal methods". According to this statement, a person does not have to be informed of the reason for his arrest if

(A) brutal force was not used in effecting it (B) the courts will later turn the defendant loose (C) the person arrested knows force will be used if necessary (D) the reason for it is clearly evident from the circumstances.

9. "An important duty of a court attendant is to keep order in the court." On the basis of this statement it is probably true that

(A) it is more important for a court attendant to be strong than it is for him to be smart (B) people involved in court trials are noisy if not kept in check (C) not every duty of a court attendant is important (D) the maintenance of order is important for the proper conduct of court business.

10. "Ideally, a correctional system should include several types of institutions to provide different degrees of custody." On the basis of this statement, one could most reasonably say that

(A) as the number of institutions in a correctional system increases the efficiency of the system increases (B) the difference in degree of custody for the inmate depends on the types of institutions in a correctional system (C) the greater the variety of institutions, the stricter the degree of custody that can be maintained (D) the same type of correctional institution is not desirable for the custody of all prisoners.

11. "The enforced idleness of a large percentage of adult men and women in our prisons is one of the direct causes of the tensions which burst forth in riot and disorder". On the basis of this statement, a good reason why inmates should perform daily work of some kind is that

(A) better morale and discipline can be maintained when inmates are kept busy (B) daily work is an effective way of punishing inmates for the crimes they have committed (C) law-abiding citizens must work therefore labor should also be required of inmates (D) products of inmates' labor will in part pay the cost of their maintenance.

12. "With industry invading rural areas, the use of the automobile, and the speed of modern communications and transportation, the problems of neglect and delinquency are no longer peculiar to cities but an established feature of everyday life". This statement implies most directly that

(A) delinquents are moving from cities to rural areas (B) delinquency and neglect are found in rural areas (C) delinquency is not as much of a problem in rural areas as in cities (D) rural areas now surpass cities in industry.

13. "Young men from minority groups, if unable to find employment, become discouraged and hopeless because of their economic position and may finally resort to any means of supplying their wants". The most reasonable of the following conclusions that may be drawn from this statement only is that

(A) discouragement sometimes leads to crime (B) in general, young men from minority groups are criminals (C) unemployment turns young men from crime (D) young men from minority groups are seldom employed.

14. "To prevent crime, we must deal with the possible criminal long before he reaches the prison. Our aim should be not merely to reform the law breakers but to strike at the roots of crime: neglectful parents, bad companions, unsatisfactory homes, selfishness, disregard for the rights of others, and bad social conditions." The above statement recommends

(A) abolition of prisons (B) better reformatories (C) compulsory education (D) general social reform.

15. "There is evidence which shows that comic books which glorify the criminal and criminal acts have a distinct influence in producing young criminals". According to this statement,

(A) comic books affect the development of criminal careers (B) comic books specialize in reporting criminal acts (C) young criminals read comic books exclusively (D) young criminals should not be permitted to read comic books.

16. Suppose a study shows that juvenile delinquents are equal in intelligence but three school grades behind juvenile non-delinquents. On the basis of this information only, it is most reasonable to say that

(A) a delinquent usually progresses to the educational limit set by his intelligence (B) educational achievement depends on intelligence only (C) educational achievement is closely associated with delinquency (D) lack of intelligence is closely associated with delinquency.

17. "There is no proof today that the experience of a prison sentence makes a better citizen of an adult. On the contrary, there seems some evidence that the experience is an unwholesome one that frequently confirms the criminality of the inmate". From the above paragraph only, it may be best concluded that

(A) prison sentences tend to punish rather than rehabilitate (B) all criminals should be given prison sentences (C) we should abandon our penal institutions (D) penal institutions are effective in rehabilitating criminals.

18. Some courts are referred to as "criminal" courts while others are known as "civil" courts. This distinction in name is most probably based on the

(A) historical origin of the court (B) link between the court and the police (C) manner in which the judges are chosen (D) type of cases tried there.

19. "Many children who are exposed to contacts and experiences of a delinquent nature become educated and trained in crime in the course of participating in the daily life of the neighborhood". From this statement only, we may reasonably conclude that

(A) delinquency passes from parent to child (B) neighborhood influences are usually bad (C) schools are training grounds for delinquents (D) none of the above conclusions is reasonable.

20. "Old age insurance, for whose benefits a quarter of a million city employees may elect to become eligible, is one feature of the Social Security Act that is wholly administered by the Federal government". On the basis of this paragraph only, it may most reasonably be inferred that

(A) a quarter of a million city employees are drawing old age insurance (B) a quarter of a million city employees have elected to become eligible for old age insurance (C) the city has no part in administering Social Security old age insurance (D) only the Federal government administers the Social Security Act.

21. "A peace officer's revolver is a defensive, and not offensive, weapon". On the basis of this statement only, a peace officer should best draw his revolver to

(A) fire at an unarmed burglar (B) force a suspect to confess (C) frighten a juvenile delinquent (D) protect his own life.

22. "Prevention of crime is of greater value to the community than the punishment of crime". If this statement is accepted as true, greatest emphasis should be placed on

(A) malingering (B) medication (C) imprisonment (D) rehabilitation.

23. "The criminal is rarely or never reformed". Acceptance of this statement as true would mean that greatest emphasis should be placed on

(A) imprisonment (B) parole (C) probation (D) malingering.

24. The most accurate of the following statements about persons convicted of crimes is that

(A) their criminal behavior is almost invariably the result of low intelligence (B) they are almost invariably legally insane (C) they are more likely to come from underprivileged groups than from other groups (D) they have certain facial characteristics which distinguish them from non-criminals.

25. Suppose a study shows that the I.Q. (Intelligence Quotient) of prison inmates is 95 as opposed to an I.Q. of 100 for a numerically equivalent civilian group. A claim, on the basis of this study, that criminals have a lower I.Q. than non-criminals would be

(A) improper; prison inmates are criminals who have been caught (B) proper; the study was numerically well done (C) improper; the sample was inadequate (D) proper; even misdemeanors are sometimes penalized by prison sentences.

Each of questions 26 to 45 consists of a word in capital letters followed by four suggested meanings of the word. In the correspondingly numbered space on your answer sheet, blacken the space between the pair of lines lettered the same as the word which means most nearly the same as the word in capitals.

26.	ABDUCT	(A) lead	(B) kidnap	(C) sudden	(D) worthless
27.	BIAS	(A) ability	(B) envy	(C) prejudice	(D) privilege
28.	COERCE	(A) cancel	(B) force	(C) rescind	(D) rugged
29.	CONDONE	(A) combine	(B) pardon	(C) revive	(D) spice
30.	CONSISTENCY	(A) bravery	(B) readiness	(C) strain	(D) uniformity
31.	CREDENCE	(A) belief	(B) devotion	(C) resemblance	(D) tempo
32.	CURRENT	(A) backward	(B) brave	(C) prevailing	(D) wary
33.	CUSTODY	(A) advisement	(B) belligerence	(C) guardianship	(D) suspicion
34.	DEBILITY	(A) deceitfulness	(B) decency	(C) strength	(D) weakness
35.	DEPLETE	(A) beg	(B) empty	(C) excuse	(D) fold
36.	ENUMERATE	(A) name one by one	(B) disappear	(C) get rid of	(D) pretend

37.	FEIGN	(A) allow	(B) incur	(C) pretend	(D) weaken
38.	INSTIGATE	(A) analyze	(B) co-ordinate	(C) oppose	(D) provoke
39.	LIABLE	(A) careless	(B) growing	(C) mistaken	(D) responsible
40.	PONDER	(A) attack	(B) heavy	(C) meditate	(D) solicit
41.	PUGILIST	(A) farmer	(B) politician	(C) prize fighter	(D) stage actor
42.	QUELL	(A) explode	(B) inform	(C) shake	(D) suppress
43.	RECIPROCAL	(A) mutual	(B) organized	(C) redundant	(D) thoughtful
44.	RUSE	(A) burn	(B) impolite	(C) rot	(D) trick
45.	STEALTHY	(A) crazed	(B) flowing	(C) sly	(D) wicked

Each of the sentences numbered 46 to 50 may be classified under one of the following four categories.

(A) faulty because of incorrect grammar
(B) faulty because of incorrect punctuation
(C) faulty because of incorrect capitalization or incorrect spelling
(D) correct.

Examine each sentence carefully to determine under which of the above four options it is best classified. Then, next to the corresponding number on the answer sheet, blacken the space lettered the same as the capital letter preceding the option which is the best of the four suggested above. Each faulty sentence contains but one type of error. Consider a sentence to be correct if it contains none of the types of errors mentioned, even though there may be other correct ways of expressing the same thought.

46. They told both he and I that the prisoner had escaped.

47. Any superior officer, who,disregards the just complaints of his subordinates, is remiss in the performance of his duty.

48. Only those members of the national organization who resided in the Middle west attended the conference in Chicago.

49. We told him to give the investigation assignment to whoever was available.

50. Please do not disappoint and embarass us by not appearing in court.

51. Suppose a man falls from a two story high scaffold and is unconscious. You should

(A) call for medical assistance and avoid moving the man (B) get someone to help you move him indoors to a bed (C) have someone help you walk him around until he revives (D) hold his head up and pour a stimulant down his throat.

52. For proper first aid treatment, a person who has fainted should be

(A) doused with cold water and then warmly covered (B) given artificial respiration until he is revived (C) laid down with his head lower than the rest of his body (D) slapped on the face until he is revived.

53. If you are called on to give first aid to a person who is suffering from shock, you should

(A) apply cold towels (B) give him a stimulant (C) keep him awake (D) wrap him warmly.

54. Artificial respiration would not be proper first aid for a person suffering from

(A) drowning (B) electric shock (C) external bleeding (D) suffocation.

55. Suppose you are called on to give first aid to several victims of an accident. First attention should be given to the one who is

(A) bleeding severely (B) groaning loudly (C) unconscious (D) vomiting.

56. If a peace officer's weekly salary is increased from $80.00 to $90.00, then the per cent of increase is

(A) 10 per cent (B) 11 1/9 per cent (C) 12 1/2 per cent (D) 20 per cent.

57. Suppose that one half the peace officers in a department have served for more than ten years and one third have served for more than 15 years. Then the fraction of peace officers who have served between ten and fifteen years is

(A) 1/3 (B) 1/5 (C) 1/6 (D) 1/12.

58. In a city prison there are four floors on which prisoners are housed. The top floor houses one quarter of the inmates, the bottom floor houses one sixth of the inmates, one third are housed on the second floor. The rest of the inmates are housed on the third floor. If there are 90 inmates housed on the third floor the total number of inmates housed on all four floors together is

(A) 270 (B) 360 (C) 450 (D) 540.

Suppose that ten per cent of those who commit serious crimes are convicted and that fifteen per cent of those convicted are sentenced for more than 3 years. The percentage of those committing serious crimes who are sentenced for more than 3 years is

(A) 15 per cent (B) 1.5 per cent (C) .15 per cent (D) .015 per cent.

60. Assume that there are 1,100 employees in a city agency. Of these, 15 per cent are peace officers, 80 per cent of whom are attorneys; of the attorneys, two-fifths have been with the agency over five years. Then the number of peace officers who are attorneys and have over five years experience with the agency is most nearly

(A) 45 (B) 53 (C) 132 (D) 165.

61. An employee who has 500 cartons of supplies to pack can pack them at the rate of 50 an hour. After this employee has worked for 1/2 hour, he is joined by another employee who can pack 45 cartons an hour. Assuming that both employees can maintain their respective rates of speed, then the total number of hours required to pack all the cartons is

(A) 4 1/2 (B) 5 (C) 5 1/2 (D) 6 1/2.

62. Thirty-six officers can complete an assignment in 22 days. Assuming that all officers work at the same rate of speed, the number of officers that would be needed to complete this assignment in 12 days is

(A) 42 (B) 54 (C) 66 (D) 72.

The following questions, numbered 63 through 65 inclusive, are to be answered on the basis of the table below. Data for certain categories have been omitted from the table. You are to calculate the missing numbers if needed to answer the questions.

	1958	1959	Numerical Increase
Correction Officers	1,226	1,347	
Court Attendants		529	34
Deputy Sheriffs	38	40	
Supervisors			
	2,180	2,414	

63. The number in the "Supervisors" group in 1958 was most nearly

(A) 500 (B) 475 (C) 450 (D) 425.

64. The largest percentage increase from 1958 to 1959 was in the group of

(A) Correction Officers (B) Court Attendants (C) Deputy Sheriffs
(D) Supervisors.

65. In 1959, the ratio of the number of Correction Officers to the total of the other 3 categories of employees was most nearly

(A) 1:1 (B) 2:1 (C) 3:1 (D) 4:1.

66. "Astronauts" is the name given to

(A) members of a religious sect living in Pennsylvania (B) the first Americans scheduled to be sent into space (C) persons using skin-diving equipment to spear fish underwater (D) the man-made satellites that have been sent into space.

67. The basic document, similar to the Federal constitution, which sets forth the organization and functions of New York City's government is the New York City

(A) Administrative Code (B) Charter (C) Constitution
(D) Home Rule Amendment.

68. The man least likely to be tendered the 1960 Democratic nomination for President is

(A) John Kennedy (B) Nelson Rockefeller (C) Hubert Humphrey
(D) Lyndon Johnson.

69. In municipal government in the United States, the word "referendum", usually refers to the method of

(A) holding elections for political office at stated intervals
(B) nominating persons for political office when political conventions have passed them over (C) obtaining approval from the voters on a specific issue
(D) removing judges or other court officials for cause.

70. Under the provisions for permanent personnel registration, a registered voter in New York to be eligible to vote without the need to register again must vote

(A) at least once every two years (B) at least once every three years
(C) every year in the regular election (D) at least once every four years.

71. The man who has been selected to head the 1964 World's Fair is

(A) Newbold Morris (B) Robert Moses (C) Grover Whalen
(D) Alfred Gruenther.

72. The term "summit conference" has recently been used to refer to a meeting of

(A) military commanders (B) heads of government of the great powers
(C) the President's cabinet and presidential advisers (D) United Nations officials.

73. A person's "real wage" is

(A) his income from stocks and bonds only (B) his total annual income from all sources (C) the purchasing power of his salary (D) the salary from his job only.

74. Of the following, the main purpose of the census is to

(A) determine the economic structure and the spread of wealth in the country
(B) count the population so as to determine representation in Congress
(C) find more equitable bases for taxation than those now existing
(D) prepare a roster of citizens who may be called on for civilian defense.

75. The country whose leader most recently has attacked the United States in his speeches, is

(A) Cuba (B) Puerto Rico (C) Morocco (D) Guatemala.

FOR CORRECTION OFFICER (MEN) CANDIDATES: Continue with questions 76-100.

76. One of the inmates in the institution where you are on duty as correction officer is serving a sentence for having molested a small girl. You should

(A) assume that the man should rightfully be in a mental institution
(B) behave towards this man exactly the same as towards the other inmates
(C) handle this man somewhat more gently because he is not a dangerous criminal
(D) handle this man somewhat roughly because of his contemptible crime.

77. Suppose that one inmate attacks another in a washroom in a correctional institution. From this information only it is safe to infer

(A) that a knife was used in the attack (B) that the attacker was young and strong (C) that the washroom was otherwise empty (D) none of the foregoing.

78. Suppose that an inmate is found badly beaten and unconscious in a corner of the prison laundry where he is employed. Of the following, the question which would be most useful to a correction officer in questioning other inmates to determine the identity of the attacker is

(A) What method of assault was used? (B) When did the assault take place?
(C) Who was the assailant? (D) Why was the inmate assaulted?

79. Of the following circumstances, the one a correction officer should <u>least</u> validly regard with suspicion is

(A) an inmate not being in his cell during the regular check before "lights-out"
(B) an inmate not reporting to his work assignment and who cannot be found
(C) a visitor's attempt to "sneak" an article to an inmate (D) a well-dressed young woman coming to see an inmate during visiting hours.

80. Suppose you are the correction officer in charge of a work group of about 15 inmates in the institutional garage. Of the following, the most practical way to prevent the inmates from concealing tools and carrying them back to their cells is to

(A) assign one or more tools to each inmate and hold him responsible for them
(B) have a definite place for each tool and check to see that it is there at the end of the day (C) require inmates to strip each day before they are taken back to their cells (D) search each man both at the end and the beginning of each day.

81. An inmate stops you and tells you that international bankers are out to "get" him, that already two attempts have been made on his life, and he now fears that the air he breathes is being poisoned. The inmate is an old man who has been in and out of the institution frequently for such minor offenses as vagrancy, alcoholism, loitering, etc. This man is most probably

(A) a victim of amnesia (B) a victim of a persecution complex
(C) covering up an infraction of the rules (D) the object of an international plot.

82. Suppose that while you are off duty and unarmed you recognize on the street an inmate who escaped from your correctional institution a year ago. Apparently he does not see or recognize you. During this escape, the inmate had gotten hold of a gun and seriously wounded a correction officer. The best of the following actions for you to take is to

(A) attack and subdue the man immediately (B) engage the man in conversation to make sure of your identification (C) follow the man until you can summon a patrolman to your aid (D) shout "escaped prisoner" so that passers-by will help you.

83. Suppose a correction officer, feeling that the sentence given an inmate was unfair, permits him to escape. On the basis of this information only, it is safe to assume that the

(A) correction officer used poor judgment (B) correction officer was recently appointed (C) inmate had possession of a large sum of money (D) judge passing sentence was unduly harsh.

84. Suppose that a correctional institution is specially constructed to be escape-proof. Nevertheless, two inmates escape. The most reasonable conclusion on the basis of this information only is that

(A) goals are not always successfully attained (B) not all correction officers are honest (C) the escapers were helped by confederates outside (D) two heads are more resourceful than one.

85. Which one of the following descriptions of an escaped inmate would be most effective in helping to recapture him?

(A) age - 31 years; weight - 168 pounds (B) at time of escape was wearing gray hat, dark overcoat (C) deep scar running from left ear to chin (D) height - 5 feet, 9 inches; complexion - sallow.

86. Allowing inmates to read newspapers in their spare time is

(A) desirable since they should be kept informed of the news (B) undesirable since they will read of crimes they can imitate after release (C) desirable since the advertisements will make them more ambitious (D) undesirable since they will read of prison escapes elsewhere.

87. Suppose an inmate commits an infraction in the mess hall. The main reason why a correction officer might wait until he was back in his cell before reprimanding him would be that

(A) he should be given time to reflect on his error (B) it might interfere with his enjoyment of the meal (C) the correction officer is not busy during meal times (D) there are several hundred other inmates in the mess hall.

88. Of the following, the most important reason why correction officers should see to it that the inmates under their supervision know and understand the rules and regulations of the institution is that

(A) the inmates will become aware of the punishment for each violation (B) the job of the correction officers will be made much easier (C) unintentional violations of the rules will be reduced (D) with full understanding there will be no violations.

89. In considering punishment for an infraction of the rules by an inmate, the disciplinary board in a correction institution is usually guided mainly by the thought that

(A) infractions must be punished whether intentional or unintentional (B) most infractions are deliberate and only few are unintentional (C) the aim of punishment is to achieve better individual adjustment of the inmate (D) the infraction was committed by an individual who is a criminal.

90. "When an inmate commits an infraction of discipline, the disciplinary officer or board shall hold a hearing and recommend disciplinary action". The punishment that should be reserved for the most serious infractions is

(A) a severe reprimand before other inmates (B) denial of athletic privileges (C) loss of time off for good behavior (D) restriction against attending movies.

91. "Parole boards have gradually taken over from the judges the function of specifying terms of imprisonment because they are usually in a better position to perform this task". The main reason for this is most probably that the parole board

(A) can also consider the inmate's prison record (B) has closer contact with the inmate (C) is composed of more than one person (D) usually includes experts in criminology.

92. "In the selection of books for the library of a correctional institution, emphasis should be placed on diversified material". The main reason for this is the

(A) desire of most inmates to prepare themselves for vocations (B) fact that most inmates come from urban areas (C) interest displayed by most inmates in western fiction (D) various age groups and interests of the inmates.

93. "Unscheduled or inconstant patrols by officers will frustrate any planned attempt at irregularity on the part of inmates". According to the preceding quotation, it is most reasonable to assume that

(A) an officer should carefully follow his patrol schedule (B) inmates should be taught regularity in their activities (C) officers should make their patrol intentions known to inmates (D) the element of surprise should be used by officers in their patrols.

94. "Generally the prospect of rehabilitating juvenile delinquents is considerably dimmed by throwing them into the same hopper of criminal procedures and institutions as the adult criminals. Yet it is a fact that some juvenile offenders are more contaminated by contact with some of their peers than by contact with adult offenders." On the basis of the preceding statement, it would be most desirable in the correctional treatment of juvenile offenders to

(A) classify and segregate all prisoners into groups on the sole basis of type of crime they have committed in order to assure that no undesirable contacts will take place (B) recognize no distinction between juvenile and adult offenders and allow them to mingle throughout the custodial and correctional procedures (C) separate only those adult offenders guilty of the most serious crimes from the general prisoner group and allow the others, adult and juveniles, to mingle throughout the correctional and custodial procedures (D) separate the adults from the juveniles but to also further separate the juveniles into groups according to their characteristics.

95. "It is a frequent misconception that correction officers can be recruited from those registers established for the recruitment of city police or firemen. While it is true that many common qualifications are found in all of these, specific standards for correctional institution work are indicated, varying with the size, geographical location and policies of the institution". According to this paragraph only, it may best be inferred that

(A) a successful correction officer must have some qualifications not required of a policeman or fireman (B) qualifications which make a successful patrolman will also make a successful fireman (C) the same qualifications are required of a correction officer regardless of the institution to which he is assigned (D) the successful correction officer is required to be both more intelligent and stronger than a fireman.

96. "A correction officer shall not receive a gift from any inmate or other person on the inmate's behalf". The best explanation for this rule is that

(A) acceptance of a gift has no significance (B) favors may be expected in return (C) inmates cannot usually afford gifts (D) gifts are only an expression of good will.

97. "Correction officers who deal with the inmate who is a habitual offender should have no false impressions about his character. While extending him a square deal, they should always consider him a source of danger." According to this statement only, correction officers should deal with inmates who are habitual offenders

(A) carefully and fairly (B) courageously and with self-reliance
(C) tolerantly and honestly (D) understandingly and with sympathy.

98. Regulations do not permit a correction officer to fire a revolver except when absolutely necessary. On the basis of this information only, it may be most reasonably inferred that

(A) ammunition and bullets are too expensive to be used indiscriminately
(B) many correction officers have been dismissed for unnecessary use of firearms
(C) the cleaning of a firearm after use is a tedious, time-consuming task
(D) the use of a revolver by a correction officer may sometimes be harmful.

99. Suppose that a study of inmates at a correctional institution shows that a comparatively small number of first offenders become second offenders but a very high percentage of second offenders commit further crimes. The most reasonable of the following conclusions from this information only is that

(A) the average age of first offenders is considerably less than that of second offenders (B) it is more difficult to rehabilitate a second offender than a first offender (C) second offenses are likely to be more serious crimes than first offenses (D) the term "offender" as used in the study is scientifically unacceptable.

100. "For the correction officer, the problem of the feeble-minded is one of great importance since this group makes up a large proportion of the offenders in any court or institution". Of the following, the one which is <u>not</u> a cause of this large proportion of feeble-minded inmates is that

(A) a high percentage of dull offenders are caught and convicted (B) many dull delinquents come from poor environment (C) men with low intelligence have natural criminal tendencies (D) the youth of low intelligence is easily led into crime.

101. A defendant comes to trial in the same court in which he had previously been defendant in a similar case. The court attendant should

(A) tell him, "I knew we'd be seeing you again" (B) tell newspaper reporters what he knows of the previous action (C) treat him the same as he would any other defendant (D) warn the judge that the man had previously been a defendant.

102. Suppose in conversation with you, an attorney strongly criticizes a ruling of the judge and you believe the attorney to be correct. You should

(A) assure him you feel the same way (B) tell him the judge knows the law
(C) tell him to ask for an exception (D) refuse to discuss the matter.

103. A court attendant has many contacts with the public. In these contacts, it is most important that he

(A) be brief and complete in his answers (B) be courteous and helpful
(C) go along with what they ask (D) know the law.

104. Suppose a witness becomes engaged in a very heated argument with an attorney who is cross-examining him. The court attendant should

(A) ask the attorney to avoid exciting the witness (B) ask the judge if he wishes any action to be taken (C) await the judge's order before interceding (D) caution the witness to be more respectful.

105. Suppose that you are a court attendant stationed at the door of the courtroom to prevent anyone from entering while the judge is charging the jury. A man whom you recognize as a City Councilman, accompanied by a woman, attempts to enter the courtroom. The best action for you to take is to

(A) apologize and explain why they cannot be permitted to enter (B) permit the man to enter since he is a Councilman but exclude the woman (C) permit them to enter since the judge would surely make an exception for them (D) send a note in to the judge to find if they may be permitted to enter.

106. It is desirable that a court attendant acquire a knowledge of the procedures of the court to which he is assigned mainly because such knowledge will help him

(A) become familiar with anti-social behavior (B) discharge his duties properly (C) gain insight into causes of crime (D) in any personal legal proceeding.

107. "Since he is a city employee, a court attendant who refuses to waive immunity from prosecution when called on to testify in court automatically terminates his employment." From this statement only, it may be best inferred that

(A) a court attendant is a city employee (B) all city employees are court attendants (C) city employees may be fired only for malfeasance (D) court attendants who waive immunity may not be prosecuted.

108. "Referees of the City Court are former judges of this court who have served at least ten years and whose term of office terminated at the age of 55 or over, or any judge who has served in a court of record and has retired." According to this statement, a person can be a referee of the City Court only if he

(A) has been a judge (B) has retired (C) has served at least 10 years in the court (D) meets certain age requirements.

109. Assume that you are assigned to a jury room where you are to guard the jury until 4 P.M., at which time you are to be relieved if the jury has not come to an agreement. At 4 P.M., your relief does not arrive and the jury is still deliberating. Of the following, the best action for you to take is to

(A) ask the foreman of the jury to assume responsibility until your relief arrives (B) find out what the jurors may need, get it, and then lock them in for the night (C) inform your supervisor but remain on duty until you are relieved (D) wait until 5 P.M., your usual closing time, and then leave if the relief has not arrived by then.

110. When, at a trial, a piece of evidence is tagged as "Exhibit A", the chief purpose is to

(A) assure its return to the owner (B) make it possible to examine it for fingerprints without chance of error (C) make it possible to identify and refer to it easily (D) prevent the defendant from denying he had it.

111. "In one case, a mistrial was declared because the indictment used the pronoun 'he' instead of 'she'." The most useful information a court attendant can derive from this statement is that

(A) accuracy is important (B) mistrial is a legal term (C) one must always use good grammar (D) to misrepresent is criminal.

112. omitted

113. Assume that you are the court attendant on duty outside the judge's chambers in the court house. One day, one of the judges informs you that he will be too busy that day to see any visitors and he tells you to refer them to his secretary for new appointments. Later in the day, an important visitor comes in and asks to see the judge about urgent business. Of the following, the best course of action for you to take in this situation is to

(A) ask the visitor to come back another day when the judge may be able to see him (B) call the judge on the phone and tell him that the visitor has urgent business to discuss with him (C) refer the visitor to one of the other judges who may be present in chambers (D) tell the visitor that the judge is not available, but his secretary may be able to help him or make a new appointment.

114. To gain a verdict against X in a trial, it was necessary to show that he could have been at Y Street at 5 P.M. It was proven that he was seen at Z Street at 4:45 P.M. The question that must be answered to show whether the verdict should be against X is:

(A) How long does it take to get from Z Street to Y Street? (B) In what sort of a neighborhood is Y Street located? (C) Was X acting suspiciously on the day in question? (D) Who was with X when he was seen at Z Street at 4:45 P.M.?

115. If, at the instructions of the judge, a court attendant calls the name of a defendant in a lawsuit and the person does not answer, the court attendant should <u>first</u>

(A) ask the judge if he called the person's name correctly (B) call the person's name again (C) look outside the doors of the courtroom for the defendant (D) tell the judge the person doesn't answer.

116. "When X is accused of having cheated Y of a sum of money, and Y is proven to have been deprived of the money, there is an additional requirement for a verdict against X". The additional requirement is to prove that

(A) the money was stolen from Y (B) X had the money after Y had it (C) X had the money before Y had it (D) X cheated Y of the money.

117. Assume that you are on duty in a courtroom and during the judge's absence one of the witnesses for a pending case becomes very angry about the delay. Of the following, the best action for you to take is to

(A) listen to him until he calms down and then explain the reason for the delay (B) tell him your court is no different from any other court (C) walk away from him so that you will not get involved in a dispute (D) warn him that the judge may be back at any minute and will hold him in contempt.

118. Assume that you are assigned to the post outside judge's chambers in the court house. A visitor tells you he has an appointment with Judge Jones who is expected to arrive shortly. He asks for permission to wait in the judge's office which is unoccupied at the present time. For you to permit him to wait there would be

(A) wise; the judge would no doubt wish to speak to the man privately (B) wise; it would keep the anteroom where you are stationed clear, allowing other employees to work without any disturbance (C) unwise; it is rude to allow a visitor to sit alone in an office (D) unwise; there may be confidential material on the judge's desk or bookcases.

119. "A court attendant shall not receive a gift from any defendant or other person on the defendant's behalf". The best explanation for this rule is that

(A) acceptance of a gift has no significance (B) defendants cannot usually afford gifts (C) favors may be expected in return (D) gifts are only an expression of good will.

120. When a jury is selected, the attorney for each side has a right to refuse to accept a certain number of prospective jurors without giving any reason therefor. The reason for this is mainly that

(A) attorneys can exclude persons likely to be biased even though no prejudice is admitted (B) persons who will suffer economically by being summoned for jury duty can be excused forthwith (C) relatives of the litigants can be excused thus insuring a fair trial for each side (D) there will be a greater number of people from which the jury can be selected.

121. "Where the defendant in a criminal case is too poor to afford counsel, the court will assign one and he will be paid by the government". The principle best established by this statement is that

(A) it is improper for the government to provide both prosecuting and defending counsel in a trial (B) laws are usually violated because of poverty and defendants are too poor to employ counsel (C) only wealthy law violators may hope to be represented by competent counsel (D) the government is obligated to shield the innocent as well as punish the guilty.

122. If a visitor to the court asks foolish questions, the best action for the court attendant to take is to

(A) answer in a brusque manner to discourage further foolish questions (B) refer the questioner to his supervisor (C) answer them the same way as he would any other questions (D) ignore them since the person doesn't really expect an answer.

123. "A man plus a uniform makes a good court attendant". This statement is false because

(A) a court attendant is also required to wear a badge (B) a good court attendant is not made merely by putting on a uniform (C) it makes no mention of the fact that the uniform must be neat (D) patrolmen as well as court attendants wear uniforms.

124. "It is a frequent misconception that court attendants can be recruited from those registers established for the recruitment of city police or firemen. While it is true that many common qualifications are found in all of these, specific standards for court work are indicated, varying with the size, geographical location and policies of the court". According to this paragraph only, it may best be inferred that

(A) a successful court attendant must have some qualifications not required of a policeman or fireman (B) qualifications which make a successful patrolman will also make a successful fireman (C) the same qualifications are required of a court attendant regardless of the court to which he is assigned (D) the successful court attendant is required to be both more intelligent and stronger than a fireman.

125. One of the duties of a court attendant is to "assist the public with their problems." A proper exercise of this duty by a court attendant would be for the attendant to

(A) advise members of the public to settle their differences out of court
(B) advise a member of the public how to fill out forms required by the court
(C) lend money to a member of the public to pay the required court fees
(D) recommend a lawyer to a member of the public who does not have one.

FOR COURT ATTENDANT (CITY COURT) CANDIDATES: END OF WRITTEN TEST. Ignore numbers 126 to 150 on your answer sheet.

FOR DEPUTY SHERIFF CANDIDATES: Answer questions 126 to 150. In marking answers, be sure to mark answer to question 126 in space numbered 126 on your answer sheet, answer question 127 in space numbered 127, and so on.

126. Suppose a doorman refuses to admit you to an apartment house in which you are attempting to serve a process on a tenant. Of the following, the best action for you to take is to

(A) bribe the doorman to admit you (B) discard the process since it cannot be served (C) gain entrance by force (D) report the matter to your superior.

127. "False arrest is an offense for which the deputy sheriff may be held liable". Therefore, before making an arrest, the deputy sheriff should

(A) be sure a witness is present (B) be sure it is legal (C) seek assistance from a patrolman (D) deputize a private citizen.

128. "An arrested person should not be transported upon a public conveyance such as a streetcar, subway, or bus, except in an extreme emergency". The reason for this regulation is, most probably, the

(A) danger of escape (B) embarrassment to the prisoner (C) expense involved (D) possible delays.

129. "Except in rare emergencies, a deputy should not attempt to make an arrest without a partner". The best reason for this is that the partner may be needed to

(A) arbitrate the matter (B) lend prestige to the sheriff's office
(C) overcome resistance (D) provide company for the deputy.

130. "At the end of each month, the deputy sheriff must submit to his superior officer an activity report covering the status of his assignments and the extent of his activities in the service of process during the month". It is most important that such report be

(A) accurate (B) brief (C) grammatically correct (D) lengthy.

131. "Deputies are required to hold seized chattels for three days after service of the replevin papers. This means three full 24 hour days, exclusive of the day of service, and the property should not be turned over earlier than 12:01 A.M. on the fourth day. When one day of the period falls on a Sunday or a public holiday, that day is excluded and an additional day must be added to make up the three". According to this statement only, if service of replevin papers is made on Thursday, June 23rd, the property should be turned over on

(A) Sunday, June 26th (B) Monday, June 27th (C) Tuesday, June 28th
(D) Wednesday, June 29th.

132. Certain property is declared by law to be exempt from seizure to satisfy a debt because it is of importance to the comfort of the family although of small money value. On the basis of this law, which of the following would you most expect to be exempt from seizure?

(A) broadloom rug (B) dining table (C) marble statuette (D) modern painting.

133. "As a general rule, a deputy sheriff is justified in refusing to seize an article which differs from the description in the replevin papers, unless the difference is clearly unimportant in the light of other identifying facts". According to this statement, which of the following would a deputy sheriff best be justified in seizing where there is a difference from the description in the papers?

(A) an automobile corresponding in make, year, model and engine number, but differing in color (B) a sofa corresponding in upholstery material, color, width and height, but differing in length (C) a television set corresponding in year, model and size of screen, but differing in number of tubes required (D) a typewriter corresponding in year, model, size of type, and color but differing in name of manufacturer.

134. "The legal aspect of the Sheriff's duties is emphasized by his unique personal liability, not only for his own acts and omissions, but also for those of any deputy or employee in his office". According to the foregoing quotation, it would be most correct to state that the Sheriff

(A) and his employees have unique legal duties to perform (B) is held responsible for actions taken by his subordinates (C) is liable for the acts of his employees only under unique circumstances (D) must personally serve many legal papers.

135. Which one of the following descriptions of a defendant would help most in identifying him?

(A) age - 31 years; weight - 168 pounds (B) at time of escape was wearing gray hat, dark overcoat (C) deep scar running from left ear to chin (D) height - 5 feet, 9 inches; complexion - sallow.

136. Which of the following could a deputy sheriff best accept as proof of a man's identity?

(A) a personal letter (B) automobile driver's license (C) automobile registration certificate (D) social security card.

137. "It was formerly the practice to require someone who knew the defendant by sight to accompany the deputy sheriff. It has been learned through experience that the value of such identification is over-rated". From this paragraph only, it may be best inferred that

(A) circumstantial evidence is not reliable (B) identifications are sometimes inaccurate (C) people are usually for the underdog (D) testimony is often contradictory.

138. "The depositions must set forth the facts tending to establish that an illegal act was committed and that the defendant is guilty". According to this statement only, the one of the following which need <u>not</u> be included in a deposition is evidence that establishes the

(A) fact that an illegal act was committed (B) fact that defendant committed the illegal act (C) guilt of the defendant (D) method of commission of the illegal act.

139. "Each deputy sheriff should understand how his own work helps to accomplish the purpose of the entire agency". This statement means most nearly that the deputy sheriff should understand the

(A) efficiency of a small agency (B) importance of his own job (C) necessity for initiative (D) value of a large organization.

140. "When X is accused of having cheated Y of a sum of money and Y is proven to have been deprived of the money, there is an additional requirement for a verdict against X". The additional requirement is to prove that

(A) the money was stolen from Y (B) X had the money after Y had it (C) X had the money before Y had it (D) X cheated Y of the money.

141. To gain a verdict against X in a trial, it was necessary to show that he could have been at Y Street at 5 P.M. It was proven that he was seen at Z Street at 4:45 P.M. The question that must be answered to show whether X is guilty is:

(A) How long does it take to get from Z Street to Y Street? (B) In what sort of a neighborhood is Z Street located? (C) Was X acting suspiciously on the day in question? (D) Who was with X when he was seen at Z Street at 4:45 P.M.?

142. "The deputy sheriff must give the defendant reasonable time to secure the bail fixed in the process before confining him to jail". The chief purpose of bail is to

(A) permit personnel to act as bondsmen (B) permit the defendant his liberty while assuring his presence at the trial (C) raise additional money for the general fund of the city treasury (D) relieve the city of the necessity of bringing the defendant before a judge.

143. When a jury is selected, the attorney for each side has a right to refuse to accept a certain number of prospective jurors without giving any reason therefor. The reason for this is mainly that

(A) attorneys can exclude persons likely to be biased even though no prejudice is admitted (B) persons who will suffer economically by being summoned for jury duty can be excused forthwith (C) relatives of the litigants can be excused thus insuring a fair trial for each side (D) there will be a greater number of people from which the jury can be selected thus insuring better quality.

144. Suppose a deputy sheriff, feeling that the verdict against a judgment debtor was unfair, permits him to escape. On the basis of this information only, it is safe to assume that

(A) the judge passing sentence was unduly harsh (B) the judgment debtor had possession of a large sum of money (C) the deputy sheriff was recently appointed (D) the deputy sheriff used poor judgment.

145. "A deputy sheriff shall not receive a gift from any defendant or other person on the defendant's behalf". The best explanation for this departmental rule is that

(A) acceptance of a gift has no significance (B) favors may be expected in return (C) gifts are only an expression of good will (D) litigants cannot usually afford gifts.

146. "All concerned are most likely to recognize the deputy sheriff's authority and co-operate with him if he conveys by his manner a complete confidence that they will do so". According to this statement only, a deputy sheriff should display

(A) arrogance (B) agitation (C) assurance (D) excitement.

147. "Since he is a city employee, a deputy sheriff who refuses to waive immunity from prosecution when called on to testify in court automatically terminates his employment." From this statement only, it may be best inferred that

(A) a deputy sheriff is a city employee (B) all city employees are deputy sheriffs (C) city employees may be fired only for malfeasance (D) deputy sheriffs who waive immunity may not be prosecuted.

148. "In one case, a mistrial was declared because the indictment used the pronoun 'he' instead of 'she'." The most useful information a deputy sheriff can derive from this statement is that

(A) accuracy is important (B) mistrial is a legal term (C) one must always use good grammar (D) to misrepresent is felonious.

149. It is desirable that a deputy sheriff acquire a knowledge of the procedures of the division to which he is assigned mainly because such knowledge will help him

(A) become familiar with anti-social behavior (B) discharge his duties properly (C) gain insight into causes of crime (D) in any personal legal proceeding.

150. "It is a frequent misconception that deputy sheriffs can be recruited from those registers established for the recruitment of city police or firemen. While it is true that many common qualifications are found in all of these, specific standards for a sheriff's work are indicated, varying with the size, geographical location and policies of the office". According to this paragraph only, it may best be inferred that

(A) a successful deputy sheriff must have some qualifications not required of a policeman or fireman (B) qualifications which make a successful patrolman will also make a successful fireman (C) the same qualifications are required of a deputy sheriff regardless of the office to which he is assigned (D) the successful deputy sheriff is required to be both more intelligent and stronger than a fireman.

Correct Answers For The Foregoing Questions

(Please try to answer the questions on your own before looking at our answers. You'll do much better on your test if you follow this rule.)

CORRECTION OFFICER

1. C	21. D	41. C	61. C	81. B
2. A	22. D	42. D	62. C	82. C
3. B	23. A	43. A	63. D	83. A
4. A	24. C	44. D	64. D	84. A
5. D	25. A	45. C	65. A	85. C
6. A	26. B	46. A	66. B	86. A
7. B	27. C	47. B	67. B	87. D
8. D	28. B	48. C	68. B	88. C
9. D	29. B	49. D	69. C	89. C
10. D	30. D	50. C	70. A	90. C
11. A	31. A	51. A	71. B	91. A
12. B	32. C	52. C	72. B	92. D
13. A	33. C	53. D	73. C	93. D
14. D	34. D	54. C	74. B	94. D
15. A	35. B	55. A	75. A	95. A
16. C	36. A	56. C	76. B	96. B
17. A	37. C	57. C	77. D	97. A
18. D	38. D	58. B	78. C	98. D
19. D	39. D	59. B	79. D	99. B
20. C	40. C	60. B	80. B	100. C

COURT ATTENDANT

101. C	106. B	111. A	116. D	121. D
102. D	107. A	112.omit	117. A	122. C
103. B	108. A	113. D	118. D	123. B
104. C	109. C	114. A	119. C	124. A
105. A	110. C	115. B	120. A	125. B

DEPUTY SHERIFF

126. D	131. C	136. B	141. A	146. C
127. B	132. B	137. B	142. B	147. A
128. A	133. A	138. D	143. A	148. A
129. C	134. B	139. B	144. D	149. B
130. A	135. C	140. D	145. B	150. A

COURT OFFICER

II. PREVIOUS EXAM FOR PRACTICE

Test yourself now with this civil service exam which was actually given to candidates for your job. Adhere strictly to the test instructions and conditions. You will get a measure of your present knowledge and ability . . . and you will begin real training for the test you must take. You will also discover where your weaknesses lie and can thus concentrate your study in those areas.

DATE OF EXAM: May 7, 1955

The time allowed for the entire examination is 3 hours. In order to create the climate of the test to come, that's precisely what you should allow yourself . . . no more, no less. Use a watch and keep a record of your time, especially since you may find it convenient to take the test in several sittings.

PREVIOUS TEST QUESTIONS FOR PRACTICE

1. A court attendant should regularly read the employee bulletin board in the courthouse to which he has been assigned mainly in order to
(A) learn of changes in the courthouse staff (B) check on how frequently new material is posted (C) show his interest in courthouse activities (D) become familiar with new orders or procedures posted on the bulletin board.

2. A court attendant who has to deal with children should
(A) treat them the same as he treats adults (B) instill in them a fear of the court (C) secure their confidence (D) impress them with the right of the attendant to punish them for wrongdoing.

3. Bail is set by a court chiefly in order to
(A) encourage rehabilitation of criminals pending trial (B) give the prosecuting attorney time to prepare his case against the accused (C) increase the revenues of the courts through forfeitures and interest (D) permit the accused freedom of movement pending the hearing of his case.

4. A court attendant named John Doe is on duty in a courtroom containing a department telephone. This phone is connected to the central switchboard for the court. When he answers the phone, it would be best for the court attendant to say
(A) Hello (B) Attendant Doe (C) Trial Term, Part II, Attendant Doe (D) City Court, Manhattan County.

5. Suppose that an attorney asks you about the amount of the fees received in the different branches of the City Court in the past year. Of the following, the best action for you to take is to
(A) refer him to the Chief Clerk's office (B) find out why he wants the information (C) tell him such information cannot be made public (D) tell him to write in for this information since it isn't issued orally.

6. Of the following, the most important reason for a court attendant to be courteous to persons visiting and using the courts is that
(A) discourtesy will cause fights (B) service to the public should be the court attendant's main purpose (C) people in official uniforms are judged more by their actions than by their words (D) a friendly approach can bring out more honesty in witnesses.

7. A court attendant should familiarize himself with the location of fire boxes in the courthouse. Of the following, the best reason for this action is that

(A) he can spot senders of false alarms (B) he can report defective equipment when he sees it (C) it shows the attendant is alert (D) no time will be lost in looking for a fire box if an emergency arises.

8. If a person in a courtroom asks the court attendant for his name, the attendant should

(A) ask him why he wants this information (B) give him the information asked for (C) inform him that he is not entitled to such information (D) tell him he must get a court order to get the information.

9. It is often observed in a courtroom that two reputable citizens on the stand as witnesses will give contradictory testimony. The most likely reason for this contradiction is that

(A) reputable citizens become nervous when testifying (B) both witnesses favor one side over the other (C) witnesses do not always observe things accurately (D) at least one of the witnesses is lying.

10. A court attendant comes on two citizens fighting in the rear of a courtroom. Several other people have gathered to watch the fight. Of the following actions, the one the attendant should take first is to

(A) summon a patrolman (B) disperse the onlookers and then attend to the fighters (C) try to separate the two fighters without hurting either one (D) ask for assistance from the onlookers and forcibly detain both fighters.

11. You are calling the calendar in your courtroom before the judge appears. One of the attorneys present comments on the way you are performing your task. He makes several suggestions which he claims will speed up the calendar call. The best action for you to take is to

(A) listen to him, thank him, and proceed with the call as you have been doing it (B) stop the call to consult the court clerk about these suggestions (C) order the attorney out of the court, telling him that you know your job (D) tell him to discuss the suggestions with the presiding judge who has the authority to change the procedure.

12. "A court attendant should familiarize himself with first aid methods." Of the following, the best reason for the above statement is that it

(A) is of great advantage that an attendant be prepared to act quickly in an emergency (B) keeps expenses down to have someone available to take care of simple injuries (C) is sometimes better to do nothing than to do the wrong thing (D) may avoid litigation if a simple injury is taken care of promptly.

13. It has been suggested that each court have a roll call of attendants at the beginning of each working day. Of the following, the chief advantage of this procedure would be that

(A) all the men are available in a group for any special job that should be done at once (B) special orders and instructions can be read to all the men (C) the judges are frequently present (D) the same men are always present.

14. Suppose that you are instructed by the presiding judge to mark certain papers as evidence. Of the following, the best reason for these instructions is that

(A) it provides specific identification of evidence in the event the evidence must be referred to again (B) fingerprints found on evidence may often be important (C) you may be required to testify as to the genuineness of the original source of the evidence (D) the judge has the power to determine which evidence may be submitted to the jury.

15. A court attendant should have a good supply of general information mostly because such information

(A) is useful in assisting the public who may consult him (B) sets an example for any youthful offenders with whom he comes in contact (C) helps him in balancing his expenditures (D) will make him popular with other court employees who may need this information.

16. Court attendants have been warned not to accept gratuities from the public. Of the following, the best reason for this rule is that

(A) court attendants should be able to manage on their own salaries (B) accepting a gift may obligate the court attendant (C) gifts are an expression of gratitude by the giver (D) no significance should be attached to a gratuity other than that there was a donor.

17. "The lower courts in the City of New York have rules and regulations which serve a definite and valuable purpose." Of the following, the chief purpose of the rules and regulations of a lower court is to

(A) provide study material for persons who may wish to make this court their career (B) describe the history of this court (C) increase the efficiency of this court (D) explain the operation of this court to laymen.

18. "A court attendant can do his best work when he realizes that his work helps achieve the purpose of the court." This statement means most nearly that

(A) each man should understand the importance of his job (B) a court should be run in a definite way (C) in a complex organization such as a court the overall purpose should be defined (D) each man in an organization should be given an opportunity to direct the entire set-up.

19. "It has often occurred that a criminal proceeding has been dismissed because of the substitution of the pronoun 'he' for the pronoun 'she'." Of the following, the most logical conclusion is that

(A) the law can be a stern taskmaster (B) intentional misrepresentation can nullify a legal process (C) grammatical and literary form are necessary in preparing legal proceedings (D) complete accuracy is often necessary in preparing legal forms.

20. In a jury trial each side is allowed peremptory challenges of members of the panel. Of the following, the best reason for this situation is that it

(A) allows the litigants a greater number of people from which to choose a jury (B) allows each side to try to get persons more favorable to them on the jury (C) enables each side to eliminate jurors who may be biased even though they deny it (D) gives persons who do not wish to serve on the jury a chance to be excused.

"Some creditors have a preference over others." As used in this sentence the word 'preference' means most nearly

(A) lien (B) duty (C) priority (D) security.

22. "The law required compulsory arbitration." As used in this sentence the word 'compulsory' means most nearly

(A) freely given (B) deliberate (C) enforced (D) allowable.

23. "The attorneys signed the stipulation." As used in this sentence the word 'stipulation' means most nearly

(A) affidavit (B) agreement (C) association (D) adjournment.

24. "The judge tried to conciliate the parties." As used in this sentence the word 'conciliate' means most nearly

(A) to cause to agree (B) to enforce calmness (C) to govern (D) to make a decision for.

25. "The law applied to all persons so situated." As used in this sentence the word 'situated' means most nearly

(A) in need (B) convicted (C) sized (D) placed.

26. "The court clerk is the authorized agent of the court." As used in this sentence the word 'authorized' means most nearly

(A) legally empowered (B) substitute (C) assistant (D) protected.

27. "The District Attorney reconstructed the crime before the jury." As used in this sentence the word 'reconstructed' means most nearly

(A) put together again (B) proved (C) established a prima facie case (D) rebutted the defense.

28. "The judge ordered each side to submit a memorandum in two weeks." As used in this sentence the word 'memorandum' means most nearly

(A) a petition addressed to the government (B) a formal request submitted to political superior (C) material to prevent later appeal (D) a brief, written record citing the pertinent law cases.

29. "The defendant allowed the case to go by default." As used in this sentence the word 'default' means most nearly

(A) over his protest (B) without allowing the judge to act (C) without appearing in court (D) after appearing in court.

30. "The judgment was substantial." As used in this sentence the word 'substantial' means most nearly

(A) small (B) considerable (C) imaginary (D) fantastic

31. "It was claimed that the court lacked jurisdiction over this action." As used in this sentence the word 'jurisdiction' means most nearly

(A) authority (B) prestige (C) ascendancy (D) moral force.

32. "A justice presides in each part of the Court." As used in this sentence the word 'presides' means most nearly

(A) protects (B) makes decisions (C) is part of (D) acts as chief officer.

33. "The Board of Justices shall have the duty to establish the procedure for the different parts." As used in this sentence the word 'procedure' means most nearly

(A) results (B) method of operation (C) minutes of (D) setting the proofs.

34. "The foster parents were given custody of the child." As used in this sentence the word 'custody' means most nearly

(A) censorship (B) power to clean (C) safekeeping (D) alternate.

35. "The determination was final." As used in this sentence the word 'determination' means most nearly

(A) decision (B) preparation (C) compound (D) addition.

36. "This court handles cases arising from marital problems." As used in this sentence the word 'marital' means most nearly

(A) emotion (B) marriage (C) imagination (D) war.

37. "The lawyer's stand was inviolable." As used in this sentence the word 'inviolable' means most nearly

(A) not capable of being seen (B) very active (C) not subject to attack (D) very passive.

38. "A court system is a complex organization." As used in this sentence the word 'organization means most nearly

(A) pattern (B) fashion (C) component (D) structure.

39. "Attorneys should be careful to conform all copies of a court order." As used in this sentence the word 'conform' means most nearly

(A) trim evenly (B) bind together (C) make alike (D) complete.

40. "It was obvious that the defendants were acting in collusion." As used in this sentence the word 'collusion' means most nearly

(A) slanderously (B) in a legal way (C) in conspiracy (D) correctly.

41. If you were called to administer first aid to a person whose skin is cold and clammy, whose pulse is weak and irregular and whose breathing is shallow and infrequent, you should treat her for

(A) shock (B) suffocation (C) food poisoning (D) arthritis.

42. A knowledge of "pressure points" is most useful in giving first aid in a case of

(A) shock (B) burns (C) drowning (D) bleeding.

43. Suppose that, while you and a fellow court attendant are resting during a relief period in the employee locker room, he cuts his arm so severely that the blood spurts out. The first action for you to take is to

(A) call a doctor (B) put a bandage on the cut and call a doctor (C) apply a tourniquet (D) go to the nearest telephone, call a doctor and then apply first aid.

44. When blood spurts from a cut, as described in the preceding question, it is a reasonable assumption that the blood comes mostly from

(A) a large vein (B) a lymph duct (C) a mass of capillaries (D) an artery.

45. Of the following, the *least* desirable action to take in the case of a severe shock after an accident on a warm day is to

(A) cover the victim with a blanket (B) splash the victim's face with ice water (C) keep the victim warm with hot water bottles (D) lay the victim flat with head low and feet raised.

46. The Deputy Mayor of the City of New York is

(A) Luther H. Gulick (B) Warren Moscow (C) Henry Epstein (D) Abe Stark.

47. Henry L. McCarthy is commissioner of the Department of

(A) Correction (B) Health (C) Hospitals (D) Welfare.

48. In a city department in which rapid action is essential, the best type of administration is that of a

(A) commission (B) single director (C) manager who submits problems that arise to the Mayor and the City Council (D) panel of judicially minded persons who can determine the merits of problems that arise.

49. The expression "caveat emptor" means most nearly

(A) beware of the dog (B) let the buyer beware (C) let the seller beware (D) beware of cave-ins.

50. A check that is presented to the bank on which it is drawn and marked to show that there are sufficient funds to cover the check is called

(A) certified check (B) indorsed check (C) verified check (D) promissory check.

PART II

51. The Appellate Division is a part of the

(A) Court of Appeals (B) City Court (C) Court of Claims (D) Supreme Court.

52. Children's Court is a division of

(A) Court of Special Sessions (B) City Magistrates' Court (C) Domestic Relations Court (D) Municipal Court.

53. An indictment by a grand jury requires a favorable vote of at least

(A) 21 members (B) 9 members (C) 18 members (D) 12 members.

54. The place where a trial is held is called the

(A) venue (B) jurisprudence (C) jurat (D) examining room.

55. The transportation of prisoners is a responsibility of the

(A) City Marshal (B) City Sheriff (C) Police Department (D) Department of Correction.

56. A writ requiring a person or a corporation to refrain from a particular act is called

(A) an agreement (B) habeas corpus (C) an injunction (D) a warrant.

57. A sworn statement of fact in writing is called

(A) an oath (B) an execution (C) a contract (D) an affidavit.

58. An authority for a person's arrest on a criminal charge with a view to his trial and commitment thereon is called a

(A) subpoena (B) summons (C) warrant (D) complaint.

59. The act of appearing before a competent officer and admitting the execution of a written instrument is called an

(A) acquittance (B) acknowledgment (C) affidavit (D) oath.

60. If a person dies without leaving a will his property is distributed under the supervision of the

(A) Supreme Court (B) City Court (C) Surrogate's Court (D) Court of Claims.

61. An instrument commanding a person to appear in court and to bring with him certain documents and records is called

(A) summons (B) subpoena duces tecum (C) warrant (D) order to show cause.

62. The party who sues in a civil court is called

(A) petitioner (B) complainant (C) plaintiff (D) intervenor.

63. The one of the following which does not have criminal jurisdiction is

(A) Court of Special Sessions (B) Municipal Court (C) Magistrates' Court (D) Court of General Sessions.

64. In a criminal action the party facing the charge is

(A) defendant (B) respondent (C) counsel (D) accomplice.

65. City magistrates are

(A) elected by the voters (B) appointed by the mayor (C) appointed by the chief city magistrate (D) appointed by the governor.

66. An appeal from the Municipal Court is ordinarily taken to the

(A) Appellate Division (B) City Court (C) Court of Appeals (D) Appellate Term.

67. The statement which a judge makes to the members of a jury before they deliberate is called the

(A) challenge (B) direction (C) instruction (D) charge.

68. Evidence which under the law suffices to establish a fact unless rebutted or until overcome by other evidence is known as

(A) prima facie (B) irrelevant (C) cumulative (D) circumstantial.

69. A person who, when examined under oath, deliberately gives false information commits the crime of

(A) barratry (B) forgery (C) perjury (D) slander.

70. A woman comes to you in the court in which you are assigned and asks if she can bring an action to compel a John Brown to acknowledge her child as his. The court to which she should be referred is the

(A) Court of Special Sessions (B) Municipal Court (C) Domestic Relations Court (D) City Magistrates' Court.

71. The one court among the following to which judges are elected by the voters is

(A) Domestic Relations (B) Special Sessions (C) Municipal Court (D) City Magistrates.'

72. If a judge's decision reads "Dismissed without prejudice" it means

(A) the judge has no ill feeling toward the litigants (B) the case has been settled between the parties (C) the case may be brought on again after certain defects are corrected (D) the case may not be brought on again.

73. Of the following, the one court that may try either civil or criminal cases is the

(A) City Court (B) Supreme Court of a county (C) Court of General Sessions (D) Municipal Court.

74. The process of bringing a prisoner before the court to answer the charges against him is called

(A) arrangement (B) recognizance (C) recognition (D) arraignment.

75. An action by a man for $1500 for personal injuries caused by a vehicle operated by another should, if both parties live in the same borough, be brought in the

(A) Supreme Court (B) Municipal Court (C) City Court (D) Court of Claims.

76. The list of cases awaiting trial is called the

(A) lis pendens (B) calendar (C) ledger (D) log.

77. A person imprisoned or restrained in his liberty within the State of New York is entitled to a hearing to inquire into the cause of the imprisonment or restraint. Such hearing is brought on by a writ of

(A) attachment (B) habeas corpus (C) replevin (D) arrest.

78. An objection to a juror for which no reason need be given but upon which the Court must exclude him is called

(A) predatory challenge (B) mandatory chàllenge (C) challenge for cause (D) peremptory challenge.

79. A major function of a grand jury is to

(A) replace the District Attorney in certain criminal cases (B) try cases against public officers (C) make recommendations on the improvement of legal procedures (D) investigate actions in order to determine if a crime exists.

80. In performing his duties, it is most important for a court attendant to recognize that

(A) any law is an abridgement of private freedom (B) undesirable laws should be ignored (C) the law is the last retreat of a clever criminal (D) the law should be obeyed even though it is subject to criticism.

Your answers to questions 81 to 84 are to be based only on the information given in Paragraph A below.

PARAGRAPH A

"A court attendant shall give reasonable aid to a sick or injured person. He shall summon an ambulance, if necessary, by telephoning the Police Department who shall notify the hospital concerned. He shall wait in a place where the arriving ambulance can see him, if possible, so that he can direct the ambulance doctor or attendant to the patient. If the ambulance does not arrive within a half hour, he should call a second time telling the department that this is a second call. However, if the injured person is conscious, the court attendant should ask whether such person is willing to go to a hospital before calling for an ambulance."

81. According to the above paragraph, the court attendant who wishes to summon an ambulance should telephone the

(A) nearest hospital (B) Department of Hospitals (C) Police Department (D) nearest police precinct.

82. According to the above paragraph, if an ambulance doesn't arrive within half an hour, the court attendant should

(A) ask the person injured if he wants to go to the hospital in a cab (B) call the Police Department (C) call the nearest police precinct (D) call the nearest hospital.

83. According to the above paragraph, a court attendant who is called to help a person who has fallen on the courthouse steps and apparently has a broken leg should

(A) put the leg in traction so that the doctor will have no difficulty setting it (B) ask the person, if he is conscious, whether he wishes to go to a hospital (C) attempt to get the story behind the injury to determine if the city is involved (D) put in a call for an ambulance at once.

84. According to the above paragraph, a court attendant who is present when a witness becomes ill while waiting to testify should

(A) wait in front of the room until the ambulance arrives (B) send a bystander to the courtroom to page a doctor (C) ask the witness if he wishes to go to a hospital (D) call the court clerk for instructions.

Your answers to questions 85 to 94 are based only on the information given in the table below:

Summary of Court Business

Court	Arraignments	Fines	Summonses	Warrants
Lower Manhattan	48,175	$74,386	6,388	6,926
Upper Manhattan	20,953	45,183	10,745	5,721
Bay Ridge	6,943	14,238	2,674	1,457
Coney Island	8,481	16,805	2,076	1,476
Flatbush	8,935	15,354	3,301	1,090
Williamsburgh	8,017	13,170	4,454	1,412
Flushing	3,527	8,297	1,971	708
Long Island City	2,261	4,855	1,719	552
Municipal Term, Manhattan	10,521	200,617	2,312	1,324
Municipal Term, Bronx	4,450	78,625	273	683
Municipal Term, Brooklyn	11,242	164,482	1,782	1,342
Municipal Term, Queens	2,680	31,658	576	365
Total		$667,670	38,271	23,056

85. The total of the arraignments for all the courts listed in the table is most nearly
(A) 138,000 (B) 137,000 (C) 136,000 (D) 135,000.

86. The difference between the total collected in fines in Municipal Term, Brooklyn and the total collected in fines in Municipal Term, Bronx is most nearly
(A) $85,860 (B) $85,855 (C) $85,850 (D) $85,845.

87. The number of summonses for Municipal Term, Bronx, when multiplied by 36, is most nearly equal to the number of arraignments for
(A) Lower Manhattan (B) Flatbush (C) Municipal Term, Brooklyn
(D) Municipal Term, Manhattan.

88. The average collected in fines per court for the 12 courts listed is most nearly
(A) $55,640 (B) $55,635 (C) $55,630 (D) $55,625.

89. Of the following, the court with the greatest amount in fines in proportion to the number of arraignments is
(A) Lower Manhattan (B) Upper Manhattan (C) Municipal Term, Queens
(D) Coney Island.

90. Of the following, the court which has most nearly a 4 to 1 ratio of arraignments to summonses is
(A) Flatbush (B) Municipal Term, Brooklyn (C) Municipal Term, Manhattan (D) Flushing.

91. Of the courts with more than 8,000 arraignments, the one which had more than 3 times as many summonses as warrants is
(A) Williamsburgh (B) Coney Island (C) Upper Manhattan (D) Lower Manhattan.

92. Of the Municipal Term Courts,
(A) Manhattan had fewer arraignments but more summonses than Brooklyn (B) Bronx had more summonses but fewer arraignments than Queens (C) Queens had fewer arraignments, fewer summonses and fewer warrants than any other Court (D) Brooklyn had more arraignments, more summonses and more warrants than any other court.

93. The court, with fewer than 3,000 summonses and more than 5,000 arraignments, which had the smallest number of warrants is

(A) Flatbush (B) Municipal Term, Queens (C) Municipal Term, Manhattan (D) Municipal Term, Brooklyn.

94. Of the following, the court which had, most nearly, one-eighth the number of warrants than it had arraignments is

(A) Municipal Term, Queens (B) Coney Island (C) Municipal Term, Bronx (D) Lower Manhattan.

Your answers to questions 95 to 97 are to be based only on the information given in Paragraph B below.

PARAGRAPH B

"The first step in the discharge of our responsibilities is to be certain that the process under which we act is valid in form and fair on its face. Each process must be filed with the county division which has to serve or execute it. Before the entry clerk accepts the process and enters it on the division's records, it must be examined and passed upon by a member of our legal staff. This not only is an insurance against mistakes, but provides an opportunity for professional discussion of any special problems which execution of the process is likely to present. The process then passes through the hands of the under sheriff or other supervisory officer for examination by him and assignment to a deputy sheriff."

95. According to the above paragraph, it may be inferred that the agency referred to is the

(A) County Clerk's Office (B) insurance company (C) Law Department (D) Sheriff's Office.

96. According to the above paragraph, before the entry clerk accepts the process it must be passed upon by

(A) one member of the staff (B) two members of the staff (C) three members of the staff (D) four members of the staff.

97. According to the above paragraph, a process is filed with the

(A) county division (B) legal staff (C) chief clerk (D) under sheriff.

Correct Answers For The Foregoing Questions

(Please try to answer the questions on your own before looking at our answers. You'll do much better on your test if you follow this rule.)

Part I

1. D	8. B	15. A	22. C	29. C	36. B	43. C
2. C	9. C	16. B	23. B	30. B	37. C	44. D
3. D	10. C	17. C	24. A	31. A	38. D	45. B
4. C	11. D	18. A	25. D	32. D	39. C	46. C
5. A	12. A	19. D	26. A	33. B	40. C	47. D
6. B	13. B	20. C	27. A	34. C	41. A	48. B
7. D	14. A	21. C	28. D	35. A	42. D	49. B
						50. A

Part II

51. D	58. C	65. B	72. C	79. D	86. B	93. C
52. C	59. B	66. D	73. B	80. D	87. D	94. A
53. D	60. C	67. D	74. D	81. C	88. A	95. D
54. A	61. B	68. A	75. B	82. B	89. C	96. A
55. D	62. C	69. C	76. B	83. B	90. C	97. A
56. C	63. B	70. A	77. B	84. C	91. A	
57. D	64. A	71. C	78. D	85. C	92. A	

III. PREVIOUS EXAM FOR PRACTICE

Now here's another examination held on another date, but again, quite similar to yours. So you have another opportunity to test and sharpen your skills. The instructions are similar. By this time you should be more familiar with them. But don't relax. Follow them closely. On your actual exam you don't want to waste time puzzling out instructions which you can learn to recognize now without penalty.

DATE OF EXAM: May 10, 1941

The time allowed for the entire examination is 3 hours. In order to create the climate of the test to come, that's precisely what you should allow yourself . . . no more, no less. Use a watch and keep a record of your time, especially since you may find it convenient to take the test in several sittings.

PREVIOUS TEST QUESTIONS FOR PRACTICE

Memorandum

May 10

TO: All Court Attendants.
FROM: Clerk of the Court.
SUBJECT: Assignment of Duties.

Each of you will start on a new assignment on May 13. You will be assigned to either Part 1, Part 2, or Part 4. Definite assignments will be made on Monday.

Those of you who are assigned to Part 4, at which the murder trial of George Jackson is now in progress, are cautioned to be especially alert. Information has been received from the office of the Police Commissioner that the accused may attempt to escape from the courtroom, aided by members of the "Blue Circle" gang with which the accused was connected prior to his arrest.

Known members of this gang include: Patsy "Boots" Brescia, a short, swarthy individual who invariably dresses conservatively. Although this member of the gang has no arrest record, he is known to carry firearms at all times, and is now wanted by authorities in this State.

Fred Fick, alias Frederick Fidens. This individual is 6 feet 4 inches tall, weighs 230 pounds and may be identified by a knife scar on the right cheek. He has been convicted of felonious assault, manslaughter and burglary.

Patrick Ahern. This individual is 6 feet, 2 inches tall and weighs 145 pounds. He is known to be extremely dangerous when under the influence of drugs. Ahern's convictions include those for robbery, breaking and entering, and Sullivan Law violation. He is wanted for kidnapping by the California authorities.

All Court Attendants including those not assigned to the murder trial are, of course, expected to be on the lookout for anyone acting peculiarly. If you observe anyone who answers any of the descriptions given above, or anyone else whose actions are such as to arouse your suspicion, send another Attendant to call the Chief Attendant. Avoid any indication that you are suspicious. Above all, avoid any action which may even remotely jeopardize the safety of spectators. While every precaution will be taken to prevent the admission to the courtroom of anyone carrying arms, do not gamble on the success of these precautions. These men are dangerous, and if convinced that their own safety is in peril, will have no hesitancy in using their weapons should they be able to smuggle them in.

Test One - Memory Test. (Weight 15).

DIRECTIONS: Below are 15 questions numbered 1 through 15, based on the memorandum you have just read. Each question is followed by several suggested answers. Blacken the space on your answer sheet with the same letter of the best ONE of the suggested answers.

1. The memorandum you have just read was issued by the: (A) Clerk of the Court. (B) Presiding Justice. (C) Chief Court Attendant.

2. The number of members in the Blue Circle gang is: (A) 3 to 5. (B) 6 to 9. (C) not definitely stated in the memorandum.

3. According to the memorandum, the man accused of murder is named: (A) Johnson. (B) Jamison. (C) Jackson.

4. Information concerning the possibility of the attempted escape of the accused was received from: (A) the office of the District Attorney. (B) the office of the Police Commissioner. (C) a member of the underworld.

5. The memorandum indicates that, of the members of the Blue Circle gang mentioned: (A) all have been arrested at least once. (B) only one has never been arrested. (C) two have never been arrested.

6. The murder trial mentioned in the memorandum: (A) has already begun. (B) will begin some time next week. (C) will begin on Monday.

7. According to the memorandum, all Attendants: (A) assigned to the murder trial are to personally search all spectators for concealed weapons immediately upon entering the courtroom. (B) will be assigned, at one time or another, to duty at the murder trial. (C) will receive definite new assignments on Monday.

8. Of the members of the gang mentioned in the memorandum: (A) at least one, if apprehended, may be extradited. (B) at least two are said to be wanted by authorities in other states. (C) at least three have been guilty of felonies.

9. The memorandum does not state that Fred Fick has ever been convicted of: (A) manslaughter. (B) robbery. (C) felonious assault.

10. From information given in the memorandum, Patrick Ahern may best be described as: (A) short and stocky. (B) tall and heavy. (C) tall and thin.

11. According to the memorandum, the member of the Blue Circle gang who is known to use drugs is: (A) "Boots" Brescia. (B) Patrick Ahern. (C) Fred Fick.

12. "Boots" Brescia may most readily be identified by: (A) his swarthy complexion. (B) the scar on his right cheek. (C) his flashy clothes.

13. According to instructions contained in the memorandum, if an Attendant observes anyone acting suspiciously he should: (A) report the situation in person to the Chief Attendant. (B) keep the suspect under surveillance until he can turn the job over to another Attendant. (C) send another Attendant to summon the Chief Attendant.

14. On the basis of the information contained in the memorandum, it may be positively stated that: (A) most members of the Blue Circle gang habitually carry firearms. (B) two or more members of the gang are armed at all times. (C) at least one member of the gang is always armed.

15. In dealing with any suspicious characters seen in the courtroom, an Attendant's first concern should be with: (A) maintenance of order. (B) protection of spectators. (C) detention of the suspect.

Test Two

Court Procedure and Legal Terminology (Weight 40).

DIRECTIONS: This test consists of 75 questions numbered 16 through 90. It includes 35 true-false questions numbered 16 through 50, and 40 multiple-choice questions numbered 51 through 90.

In the true-false questions, you are to determine whether each statement is true or false. If a statement is true as a general rule, even though it may have exceptions, write the letter T.
If a statement is false as a general rule, even though it may have exceptions, write the letter F. Examples B and C below have been correctly marked.

EXAMPLES:

B.	Albany is the capital of New York State.	T
C.	Albany is the largest city in New York State.	F

In the multiple-choice questions you are to select the one best answer out of three possible answers that are lettered (A), (B) and (C). You are to blacken the lettered space of the one best answer to each statement.

Examples D and E below have been correctly marked.

EXAMPLES: D. The capital of New York State is: (A) Albany. (B) Syracuse. (C) Elmira. E. The largest city in New York State is: (A) Albany. (B) Rochester. (C) New York City.

NOTE: Unless the context of the statement indicates the contrary, all statements must be answered by applying the general law, rule or procedure (not the exception) in existence in New York State on the date of this examination.

True - False Items.

16. The written authority for one person to act for another in legal matters is called a power-of-attorney.

17. If, during a murder trial, a juror becomes ill and is excused, the trial may proceed with eleven jurors upon consent of the defendant's attorney.

18. The Court of Claims has jurisdiction over claims against the State of New York and any of its civil divisions.

19. A special verdict in a criminal case is one where the jury find the facts only, leaving the judgment to the court.

20. "Supra" appearing in a legal opinion refers to matter following in the same opinion.

21. The Surrogate's Court has jurisdiction over the estates of missing persons who are believed to be dead.

22. If two lawyers sitting at the rear of the courtroom waiting for their cases to be called start talking too loudly, they should immediately be ordered from the courtroom by the Court Attendant.

23. A law dictionary in common use is "Bolivers Law Dictionary."

24. The testimony of a Court Attendant is accepted in court without oath.

25. In an action in the Supreme Court the summons must always state the county which is designated by the plaintiff as the place of trial.

26. There are nine departments of the Appellate Division of the Supreme Court, one for each judicial district in the State.

27. The "Federal Reporter" reports the decisions of the United States Supreme Court.

28. The decisions of the Appellate Division can be found in the Northeastern Reporter.

29. If a Court Attendant sees a juror taking notes on the testimony, for use in the juror's deliberations, he should stop him, because such note taking is not permitted by law.

30. A verdict in a criminal case may be arrived at by the concurrence of five-sixths of the members of the jury.

31. The City Court of the City of New York has no criminal jurisdiction.

32. An "ex parte order" is an order made by the court upon the application of one of the parties to an action, without notice to the other.

33. "Attachment" is a proceeding for the seizure of property after judgment.

34. Hearsay evidence is another term used to describe circumstantial evidence.

35. A row of stars in an opinion, for example (* * *), indicates the omission of matter from a legal quotation.

36. The Supreme Court is limited in its civil jurisdiction to cases involving more than $ 1,000.

37. The provisions of the Children's Court Act of the State of New York apply to all the counties of New York State.

38. A suspended sentence is granted only when there is doubt as to the guilt of the defendant.

39. Where the violation of a right admits of a criminal and also of a civil action, the one is not merged in the other.

40. Under the present law, women cannot constitute more than half the number of persons serving on a jury in the New York State courts.

41. Subordination is the substitution of one person in the place of another with respect to rights or claims.

42. A transcript of a judgment does not include a transcript of the minutes of the trial.

43. Falsely swearing to a material fact before a court is termed contempt of court.

44. The "Code of Criminal Procedure" is contained in McKinney's Consolidated Laws of New York.

45. "Prima facie" evidence is evidence which is conclusive and which cannot be contradicted or rebutted.

46. Coercion exercised upon a person to force him to do some act against his will is legally known as duress.

47. In legal terminology, a citation is a reference to a court docket.

48. The County Court of Kings County has no civil jurisdiction.

49. A "certified" copy of a record is the same as an "exemplified" copy.

50. The giving or offering of anything of value intended to influence a public officer in the discharge of his legal duty is termed extortion.

Official Questions For Court Attendant Multiple-Choice Items.

51. The Court of Appeals consists of: (A) Five judges. (B) Seven judges. (C) Nine judges.

52. Legal proceedings concerning the property of a deceased person are ordinarily held in the: (A) Supreme Court. (B) Surrogate's Court. (C) County Court.

53. A "folio" as used in the measurement of the length of a document in legal or court work consists of: (A) One page. (B) 100 words. (C) Two pages.

54. The best attitude for a Court Attendant to assume toward the public is to: (A) Be always kind and pleasant, ready to assist but never argumentative. (B) Be very friendly and cultivate all the acquaintances possible as they may prove useful in the future. (C) Hold himself apart, and assume a superior haughty manner as the public should be taught to look up to and respect a representative of the law.

55. An affidavit is: (A) An acknowledgment by a notary. (B) The oath administered to a witness before he testifies. (C) A sworn declaration in writing made before a competent authority.

56. A statute is a: (A) Law adopted by initiative and referendum. (B) Legislative appointment. (C) Legislative enactment.

57. The defendant's pleading in a civil action is called the: (A) Reply. (B) Answer. (C) Bill of particulars.

58. Venue in an action refers to: (A) The place of trial. (B) Whether trial is by judge or jury. (C) Whether the pleadings are verified.

59. A criminal action is brought in the name of the: (A) People of the State of New York. (B) Person accused of the crime. (C) District Attorney.

60. The adverse party to an appeal is called: (A) A relator. (B) A respondent. (C) An appellant.

61. To say that directions given by a superior officer are explicit means that they are: (A) Forceful. (B) Exacting. (C) Definite.

62. The one of the following which is a "capital offense" in New York State is: (A) Treason. (B) Rape, first degree. (C) Manslaughter.

63. If a Court Attendant is offered a reward for service rendered in the regular discharge of his duties, he should: (A) Accept the money and turn it over to his superior with a report of the circumstances under which it was received. (B) Keep the money and prefer criminal charges against the person by whom it was paid. (C) Refuse to accept it as a Court Attendant should perform his duties without extra reward.

64. A judge gives you an envelope with important papers to deliver personally at a downtown law office. On the way you are stopped by a stranger who tells you that he was sent by the law office to get the papers. You should: (A) Ask him for his name and give him the papers (B) Have him sign a receipt for the papers and give them to him. (C) Refuse to surrender the papers and proceed on your way.

65. A proceeding to levy on the earnings of income of a judgment debtor is called: (A) Supplementary Proceedings. (B) Summary Judgment. (C) Garnishee Proceedings.

66. The manner of prosecuting and convicting criminals is regulated by the: (A) Civil Practice Act. (B) Penal Law. (C) Code of Criminal Procedure.

67. A group of jurors selected to serve during a term of court is called a: (A) Panel. (B) Jurat. (C) Venire.

68. The request of an attorney to excuse a juror from serving at a particular trial is called: (A) An objection. (B) An exception. (C) A challenge.

69. The legal term used to describe all the means by which the truth regarding any alleged matter of fact is established or disproved in court is: (A) Testimony. (B) Exhibit. (C) Evidence.

70. A suspended sentence is: (A) An indeterminate sentence. (A) A postponed sentence. (C) A decreased sentence.

71. The temperature of a courtroom while the court is in session should be kept at about: (A) 60 degrees Fahrenheit. (B) 80 degrees Fahrenheit. (C) 70 degrees Fahrenheit.

72. A restraining order handed down by a court is called: (A) An injunction. (B) A prohibition. (C) "laissez faire."

73. Admission of attorneys to the practice of law is regulated by the: (A) Court of Appeals. (B) County Court of the county in which the prospective attorney resides. (C) Appellate Division of the Supreme Court.

74. The release of a convicted person, without prison sentence, on condition that, for a stated period he lead an orderly life, is called: (A) Pardon. (B) Probation. (C) Parole.

75. Bringing a defendant to a court to answer a charge is called: (A) Indictment. (B) Attachment. (C) Arraignment.

76. A recidivist is: (A) An incorrigible criminal. (B) A sexual pervert. (C) A first offender.

77. Habeas corpus is the name given to: (A) The body over which an inquest is to be held. (B) The substantial facts showing that a crime has been committed. (C) A writ commanding the bringing of a certain person before a certain court.

78. A subpoena is an order served on: (A) The warden of a jail requiring him to produce a prisoner in court. (B) A person to compel his attendance in court to give testimony as a witness. (C) Any person desired for jury duty.

79. The term "et al" means: (A) And so forth. (B) In reply to. (C) And others.

80. The official terms of justices of the Supreme Court are for: (A) 10 years. (B) 14 years. (C) 4 years.

81. A grand jury consists of: (A) 31 persons. (B) 12 persons. (C) 23 persons.

82. If a spectator in a courtroom faints and falls to the floor, he should be: (A) Placed in a chair in a sitting position. (B) Laid down on a flat surface with his head lower than his body. (C) Picked up and removed to a hospital.

83. The County Clerk of New York County is: (A) Elected for a term of four years. (B) Appointed by the Mayor of New York City. (C) Appointed by the Appellate Division, First Department.

84. Several of the spectators in a courtroom get into a fight and one of them is seriously hurt. As a Court Attendant the first thing you should do is to: (A) Get the facts and make a report. (B) Call an ambulance or a physician. (C) Hold the people who engaged in the fight and have them arrested for creating a public nuisance.

85. If a witness under a severe cross-examination becomes indignant and engages the attorney in a heated argument, a Court Attendant should: (A) Order the witness to be more respectful. (B) Await any action the judge may take. (C) Try to attract the attention of the witness.

86. The Court of General Session has jurisdiction in: (A) All the counties in New York City. (B) The First Judicial Department. (C) Only in New York County.

87. The legal proceeding by which a municipality may take private property for public use is called: (A) Elective franchise. (B) Condemnation. (C) Stare decisus.

88. A bench warrant is a warrant: (A) For the distraint of personal property. (B) Issued by a judge upon the failure of an accused to answer a summons. (C) Authorizing the search of premises in which stolen goods are believed to be stored.

89. A proceeding in the Surrogate's Court is usually commenced by the serving and filing of: (A) A petition. (B) A summons. (C) Letters testamentary.

90. The improper doing of an act which one might lawfully do is known as: (A) Misfeasance. (B) Malfeasance. (C) Non-feasance.

ARITHMETIC (Weight 10.)

DIRECTIONS: Below are 10 arithmetic problems. Each problem is followed by four possible answers lettered (A), (B), (C) or (D). There is ONE CORRECT answer. You are to make the computations necessary in order to obtain the ONE CORRECT answer for each problem.

If you find that none of the four answers given for any problem is correct, indicate that in the space at the right the lettered (E). Note Example H.

EXAMPLE H: The difference between 47 and 19 is: A. 18; B. 32; C. 28; D. 36; E. None of preceding answers.

Since the correct answer is 28, the space lettered C should be blackened.

NOTE: If 28, the correct answer, had not been given in the four suggested answers, the correct method of indicating this fact would have been to blacken the space for E.

1. The sum of the following numbers: 67.05; 89093.9; 1234567.756; 123.653; 654321.08; 4567.101; is: A. 1728940; B. 1892470.540; C. 1987240.540; D. 1982740.540; X. None of the preceding answers.

2. If 49179.2525 is divided by 235.9 the quotient is: A. 208.475; B. 20.8475; C. 207.975; D. 2.08475; X. None of the preceding answers.

3. 41 1/2 + 105 2/9 + 300 3/4 + 241 3/5 + 472 1/4, reduced to lowest terms, equals A. 1159 2/45; B. 1160 418/180; C. 1161 2/9; D. 1160 58/90; X. None of the preceding answers.

4. If 20 attendants can take care of a certain piece of work in 15 days, the correct number which must be added so that the work may be accomplished in 4/5 of the time is: A. 12; B. 5; C. 25; D. 15; D. None of the preceding answers.

5. At a forced sale a bankrupt sold his farm for $ 7500. If this amount was 33 1/3% less than its real value, the value of the farm would be: A. $ 11,250; B. $ 5,000; C. $ 7,500; D. $ 10,000; X. None of the preceding answers.

6. Assume that during the year 1939, the Supreme Court of a certain district handled a total of 16,000 cases, of which 2,400 were of a criminal nature; in 1940 the number of all types of cases increased 25% over 1939, but the percentage of criminal cases remained the same as in 1939. The number of criminal cases handled in 1940 was: A. 3600; B. 3200; C. 2400; D. 5000; X. None of the preceding answers.

7. Assume that you are responsible for the receipt and distribution of pencils and that this duty was delegated to you on Jan. 1, 1940, at which time your inventory showed 1/2 dozen cartons of pencils each carton containing 6 boxes of 12 pencils each; during the first half of the year 2 1/2 gross more pencils were received and 216 pencils used; during the second half of the year 2 more cartons of pencils were received and 42 boxes of pencils used. The number of pencils on hand Jan. 1, 1941, was: A. 432; B. 216; C. None; D. 864; X. None of the preceding answers.

8. From a certain district 4% of the men were drafted for army duty and 5% of the remainder enlisted. The difference between the number who enlisted and those who were drafted was 168. The male population of the district was: A. 210; B. 800; C. 21,000; D. 2,100; X. None of the preceding answers.

9. Assume that a court attendant is allowed 3 1/2 cents a mile for the use of his automobile for the purpose of conducting defendants to and from court sessions. The first month he drove 416 miles; the second month 328; the third 2012; the fourth month 187; the fifth month 713; the sixth month 1608; his expenditures for gasoline averaged 18¢ a gallon and his general average of miles per gallon was 16; he used 32 quarts of oil @ 25¢ quart; and spent $ 70.24 on care and general upkeep of his car for the six months. Without considering the depreciation in value of his car, he would have received above his expenditures: A. $ 46.78; B. $ 59.22; C. $ 8.00; D. $ 52.64; X. None of the preceding answers.

10. Assume that you borrowed $ 2,000 on November 1, 1935, for the use of which you were required to pay simple interest semi-annually at 3 1/2% a year. On May 1, 1941, you would have paid interest amounting to: A. $ 70.00; B. $ 350.00; C. $ 385.00; D. $ 140.00; X. None of the preceding answers.

Correct Answers For The Foregoing Questions

(Please make every effort to answer the questions on your own before looking at these answers. You'll make faster progress by following this rule.)

TEST ONE - MEMORY TEST

1. A	2. C	4. B	6. A	8. A	10. C	12. A	14. C
	3. C	5. B	7. C	9. B	11. B	13. C	15. B

TEST TWO - COURT PROCEDURE AND LEGAL TERMINOLOGY

16. T	21. T	25. T	29. F	33. F	37. T	41. F	46. T
17. F	22. F	26. F	30. F	34. F	38. F	42. T	47. F
18. T	23. F	27. F	31. T	35. T	39. T	43. F	48. T
19. F	24. F	28. F	32. T	36. F	40. F	44. T	49. T
20. F						45. F	50. F

MULTIPLE - CHOICE ITEMS

51. B	56. C	61. C	66. C	71. C	76. A	81. C	86. C
52. B	57. B	62. C	67. A	72. A	77. C	82. B	87. B
53. B	58. A	63. C	68. C	73. C	78. B	83. C	88. B
54. A	59. A	64. C	69. C	74. B	79. C	84. B	89. A
55. C	60. B	65. C	70. B	75. C	80. B	85. B	90. A

ARITHMETIC

1. D	3. X	4. B	5. A	6. X	7. B	8. C	9. A
2. A							10. C

SCORE 1

.... %

NO. CORRECT ÷ NO. OF QUESTIONS ON THIS TEST

SCORE 2

.... %

NO. CORRECT ÷ NO. OF QUESTIONS ON THIS TEST

SCORE 3

.... %

NO. CORRECT ÷ NO. OF QUESTIONS ON THIS TEST

IV. PREDICTIVE PRACTICE EXAMINATION

Based on all the information available before going to press we have constructed this examination to give you a comprehensive and authoritative view of what's in store for you. To avoid any misunderstanding, we must emphasize that this test has never been given before. We devised it specially to provide a final opportunity of employing all you've learned in a situation that closely simulates the real thing.

The time allowed for the entire examination is 8 hours. In order to create the climate of the test to come, that's precisely what you should allow yourself . . . no more, no less. Use a watch and keep a record of your time, especially since you may find it convenient to take the test in several sittings.

A FAIR SAMPLING OF THE QUESTIONS YOU'LL BE ASKED

Part 1

1 The power of the federal government to lay and collect taxes on incomes is provided for in_____.
(A) the body of the Constitution (B) special congressional legislation (C) executive fiat of the President (D) the 16th amendment of the Constitution (E) the 17th amendment of the Constitution

2 The head of the federal Department of Justice is the_____.
(A) Attorney General (B) Secretary of the Interior (C) Solicitor General (D) Chief Justice of the Supreme Court (E) person elected by the members of the United States Supreme Court

3 An example of the government in business for itself is the_____.
(A) automobile industry (B) steel industry (C) oil industry (D) newspaper business (E) postal service

4 A naturalized citizen is one who_____.
(A) is below the age of 21 years (B) has only taken out his first papers (C) has lost the privilege of voting because of a penal offense (D) is a pauper (E) was not born in this country

5 No person shall be a United States Senator who shall not have attained the age of_____.
(A) 35 years (B) 40 years (C) 30 years (D) 45 years (E) 25 years

6 The term of office of a member of the House of Representatives is_____.
(A) one year (B) 3 years (C) 2 years (D) 4 years (E) a variable, depending upon the state from which the representative is elected

7 A fee simple is_____.
(A) a schedule of fees (B) an unrestricted estate of inheritance (C) interest on a fee (D) land held of another in fee (E) reserved rent

8 An impost is a _____.
(A) contract (B) tax (C) penal offense (D) verdict (E) lease

9 One who makes a business of procuring the passage of bills pending before a legislative body is termed a _____.
(A) legislator (B) prosecutor (C) representative (D) lobbyist (E) corporation lawyer

10 It is the primary purpose of a literacy test to determine whether a person____.
(A) can read and write (B) is feebleminded (C) is able to do satisfactory work at a particular job (D) understands the law (E) is guilty of a penal offense

11 The Mayor is primarily the municipal_____.
(A) judicial officer (B) legislative officer (C) financial officer (D) executive officer (E) medium for appeals from the rulings of subordinate officials

12 The most desirable of the following in the administration of a city government is_____.
(A) efficiency (B) speed (C) simplicity (D) complexity (E) rigid formality

13 "The unsatisfactory crime conditions in American cities can be attributed in part to an overcomplicated, technical criminal procedure." This statement can best be interpreted as an argument for_____.
(A) more extensive educational facilities (B) simplicity of judicial organization (C) elimination of the judge from judicial organization (D) honesty in criminal procedure (E) greater formality in criminal procedure

14 "Ballyhoo and showmanship all too often become the determining factors in the selection of municipal judges," is a criticism made most frequently against____.
(A) recommendations by bar associations of persons for appointment as judges (B) popular election of judges (C) appointment of judges by the executive (D) the reorganization of the judicial process (E) the selection of judges by civil service examiners

15 "Merit system" is a term applied particularly to_____.
(A) judicial processes (B) administrative processes (C) municipal liability (D) civil service (E) electoral devices

16 A most serious objection to the initiative is that it_____.
(A) makes for excessively scientific legislation (B) demands little discrimination on the part of the voter (C) lengthens the ballot (D) increases the power of the administrative branch of the government (E) increases the veto power of the principal administrative officer

17 Suppose that party I divides its strength in an election among several candidates while the opposition, party II, agrees on one candidate. It is most likely that_____.

(A) party I will win the election (B) party II will win the election (C) party II will have a distinct advantage in the election (D) after the election party I will cease to exist as a party (E) the election will be very close.

18 One of the most frequent criticisms of the direct primary is that it_____.
(A) increases the cost to the public (B) strengthens party responsibility (C) means everybody can be a candidate for public office (D) reduces the power of the electorate (E) makes for a two party system

19 The one of the following which does not directly result from urbanization is_____.
(A) growth of governmental services (B) assumption by governmental authority of new services (C) massing together of people in cities (D) increase in illiteracy (E) increase in number of municipal employees

20 The primary purpose of the creation of a municipal corporation is to _____.
(A) serve local needs (B) save money (C) enable the municipality to tax its residents (D) facilitate state control (E) reduce size of personnel required for proper administration of the municipality.

21 Inspection by state authorities of the manner in which local services are being performed is a method of_____
(A) administrative control (B) home rule (C) judicial control (D) self determination by municipalities (E) limiting the use of the initiative

22 A grant in aid is a_____.
(A) sum of money usually designed to improve health standards (B) device for setting limits to the municipal indebtedness which may be incurred (C) conditional contributions made by the central government to a unit of the local government to assist in the performance of some function (D) device for the state supervision of local finance (E) method for protecting the credit of local government units

23 "Floater" is a term most generally used to apply to certain_____.
(A) courts (B) governmental councils (C) affidavits (D) types of statutory provisions (E) voters

24 One of the primary purposes of registering voters is to_____.
(A) reduce electoral costs (B) prevent fraudulent voting (C) simplify the voting procedure (D) render party organizations ineffective (E) limit the use of the recall

25 The number of elective municipal offices in this country is_____.
(A) less than 100,000 (B) about 250,000 (C) about 500,000 (D) about 750,000 (E) about 1,000,000

26 "One is not present unless he understands" means most nearly_____.
(A) One is really not present if he does not make his presence known. (B) Absence and fondness are negative correlatives. (C) One should always listen carefully. (D) Court attendants should be alert at all times. (E) Who does not comprehend what is said to him has, in effect, not been addressed.

27 "A wrong is not presumed" means most nearly_____.
(A) The crime rate is a poor index of the amount of immorality in a community. (B) One cannot presume that a man has done wrong just because he committed a crime. (C) Hard cases make bad law. (D) One wrong does not excuse another. (E) A man is innocent until he is found guilty.

28 The sales tax is designed especially to pay for_____.
(A) educational needs (B) general municipal needs (C) improvement of parks (D) emergency relief (E) improved hospital facilities

29 The number of counties in New York City is_____.
(A) 3 (B) 5 (C) 7 (D) 4 (E) 6

30 Of the following, the chief duty of a City Marshal is to_____.
(A) investigate misdemeanor cases (B) examine witnesses in autopsy cases (C) execute the mandates of the Municipal Court (D) hear litigated motions (E) sell municipal property at auction sales

31 The court which hears petitions alleging failure to support wives or children is the_____.
(A) Children's Court (B) Family Court (C) Magistrates' Court (D) Court of Special Sessions (E) Court of General Sessions

32 Appeals from the Surrogates' Courts are taken to the_____.
(A) Court of Appeals (B) Appellate Division (C) Appellate Term (D) Court of Claims (E) Supreme Court

33 The judges comprising the Court of Appeals are usually_____.
(A) appointed by the Governor (B) appointed by the Mayor of New York City (C) selected by the state legislature (D) selected by the municipal assembly (E) elected

34 The City Court has a division in_____.
(A) Brooklyn and Manhattan only (B) Manhattan only (C) each county in New York City (D) Brooklyn only (E) Manhattan and Bronx only

35 The jurisdiction of the Court of General Sessions is_____.
(A) entirely civil (B) criminal and includes cases punishable by life imprisonment or death (C) exclusively of an appellate character (D) both civil and criminal (E) limited to cases not punishable by life imprisonment or death

36 The jurisdiction of the Court of Appeals in New York State is_____.
(A) entirely civil (B) criminal and includes cases punishable by life imprisonment or death (C) exclusively of an appellate character (D) not criminal except in cases involving life imprisonment or death (E) limited to cases not punishable by life imprisonment or death

37 The jurisdiction of the Magistrates' Night Court is confined to_____.
(A) Manhattan, Brooklyn, and The Bronx (B) Manhattan and Brooklyn (C) Manhattan and The Bronx (D) Manhattan (E) Brooklyn

38 The Women's Court does not try women charged with_____.
(A) violations of the multiple dwelling law (B) vagrancy (C) shoplifting (D) keeping a disorderly house (E) larceny of $150

39 A formal record of judicial proceedings is called the_____.
(A) warrant (B) equity (C) devolution (D) probate (E) docket

40 The proofs in a cause which have been offered and admitted are said to be in _____.
(A) interpretation (B) conjunction (C) good consideration (D) malfeasance (E) evidence

41 An order requiring a public officer to do an act demanded by law is called the _____.
(A) mandamus (B) habeas corpus (C) bench warrant (D) writ of covenant (E) writ of execution

42 A writing in which is set down the description of goods sent with a common carrier by land is called the_____.
(A) bill of consignment (B) warehouse receipt (C) receipt (D) way-bill (E) statement

43 A second consideration which the court gives to a cause on a second argument is called_____.
(A) rehearing (B) status quo (C) reinscription (D) rehypothecation (E) rejoinder

44 A tort is a_____.
(A) private or civil wrong or injury (B) kind of toll (C) writ of error (D) form of partnership (E) replevin

45 There is a record of a case in which a conviction for stealing a "pair of boots" was reversed where the evidence showed that the defendant did not steal two mates but that both boots were for the same foot. This case illustrates the _____.
(A) certainty of punishment (B) advantages of using waivers of jury in criminal cases (C) use of ex parte proceedings (D) need for reform in the selection of judges (E) absurd lengths to which appeal for procedural defects may be carried.

46 Legal aid bureaus are designed especially to help persons who_____.
(A)do not have much money (B) may be unjustly convicted because of a prior criminal record (C) have just been released from penal institutions (D)prefer to waive their right of trial by jury (E) prefer to try their cases without the assistance of a lawyer

47 The fundamental basis for allowing people to be free on bail is_____.
(A) the prevention of punishment before trial (B) the centralization of administrative responsibility in criminal cases (C) the detection of violations of the law (D) the simplification of judicial procedures (E) the provision of an orderly means for settling small claims disputes

48 An accusation in the nature of an indictment which is presented by a competent public officer on his oath is known as the _____.
(A) indictment (B) prosecution (C) common law (D) information (E) preliminary hearing

49 The due process clause in the U.S. Constitution occurs in the_____.
(A) preamble (B) body of the Constitution (C) 7th amendment (D) 14th amendment (E) 11th amendment

50 Of the following, the suggestion most generally made for remedying electoral indifference is to_____.
(A) publish the names of non-voters (B) simplify the electoral process (C) raise the minimum age required for eligibility to vote (D) erect high property qualifications for voting (E) promote governmental economy

51 To address with a question is to_____.
(A) interpellate (B) assert (C) codify (D) interpret (E) adjudge

52 The annulling of a law, in whole or in part, by passing a law contrary to it is called _____.
(A) registry (B) surrebutter (C) obrogation (D) conjunctive obligation (E) lien

53 The gift of real property by a last will and testament is called the _____.
(A) remainder (B) marketable title (C) transfer (D) devise (E) quit-claim

54 A certain privilege conferred by grant from government and vested in individuals is called a _____.
(A) franchise (B) contract (C) motion (D) right of action (E) subrogation

55 A proper or legal attestation is called_____.
(A) verification (B) authentication (C) authority (D) declaration (E) signature

56 "Intestate" is a term applied to a person who dies without having _____.
(A) enough money to bury him (B) any living person able to inherit his property (C) made a will (D) provided a burial ground for himself (E) assigned a portion of his estate to his next of kin

57 The release of a person who has been found guilty of an offense, by court order under supervision, instead of sending the individual to an institution is called _____.
(A) parole (B) recidivism (C) incarceration (D) administration and supervision (E) probation

58 The principal purpose of grammatical forms and methods is _____.
(A) assistance in the formulation of spelling rules (B) clear and accurate expression of thought (C) consistency in the uses of tenses and pronouns (D) understanding of the technical meanings of the various parts of speech (E) consistency in punctuation usage

59 The one of the following in which "es" is added to form the plural is _____.
(A) banjo (B) dynamo (C) hero (D) salvo (E) silo

60 "A question rightly asked is a problem half solved" means most nearly_____.
(A) The formulation of a question is important. (B) Half a solution is better than none. (C) Asking many questions is an excellent device for obtaining information. (D) A problem is a kind of question. (E) Courtesy is the most important element in good questioning.

61 The best of the following sentences is _____.
(A) They are alike in this respect. (B) They are both alike in this respect. (C) They are both alike in this respect, especially John. (D) He is alike him in this respect. (E) They are alike to this respect.

62 "Etc." should be preceded by a _____.
(A) semi-colon (B) colon (C) dash (D) comma (E) period

63 The best of the following sentences is_____.
(A) It is they. (B) It is them. (C) It is us. (D) It is me. (E) It be I.

64 The best of the following definitions of style is _____.
(A) consistent use of polysyllabic language (B) use of the right words in the right places (C) use of correct grammatical constructions (D) consistent use of monosyllabic language (E) use of correct spelling and punctuation

65 The best of the following sentences is_____.
(A) Where is he at? (B) At where is he? (C) Whereat is he? (D) Where is he? (E) What place is he at now?

66 The best of the following sentences is _____.
(A) I cannot believe but what he is guilty. (B) I cannot believe but which he is guilty. (C) I cannot believe but where he is guilty. (D) I cannot believe but how he is guilty. (E) I cannot but believe that he is guilty.

67 The best of the following sentences is _____.
(A) This data is correct. (B) Them data is correct. (C) These data are correct. (D) Those data is correct. (E) Them data are correct.

68 The best of the following sentences is_____.
(A) The one is different in the other. (B) The one is different with the other. (C) The one is different to the other. (D) The one is different from the other. (E) The one is different than the other.

69 The best of the following sentences is _____.
(A) The draperies were not hanged well. (B) The draperies were not hanged good. (C) The draperies were not hung well. (D) The draperies were not hung good. (E) The draperies was not hanged well.

70 A verbal message is one which_____.
(A) is given by word of mouth (B) contains a verb (C) is transmitted in a letter only (D) is in words (E) is transmitted through an intermediary only

71 The best of the following sentences is _____.
(A) I will learn him to do it good. (B) I will learn him to do it well. (C) I will teach him to do it good. (D) I will teach him to do it well. (E) I can teach him to do it good.

72 The best of the following sentences is _____.
(A) Opening the door, the chair was seen. (B) Opening the door the chair was seen. (C) Opening the door, the chair was visible. (D) Opening the door, I saw the chair. (E) I opening the door, saw the chair.

73 The best of the following sentences is _____.
(A) He may be here now. (B) He mayhap be here tomorrow. (C) He may have been here now. (D) He might have been here tomorrow. (E) He was here in a few minutes.

74 The best of the following sentences is _____.
(A) Is this the man of who you spoke? (B) Is this the man of whom you spoke? (C) Whom is this man whereof you spoke? (D) Who is this man who you spoke of? (E) Whom is the man to who you spoke?

75 The best of the following sentences is _____.
(A) Each of the attendants was punctual. (B) Each of the attendants were punctual. (C) All of the attendants was punctual. (D) Many of the attendants was punctual . (E) Few of the attendants was punctual.

76 The best of the following sentences is _____.
(A) This is entirely between you and he. (B) That is completely between you and he. (C) This is between you and him. (D) This is between he and you. (E) This is entirely among you and him.

77 The best of the following sentences is _____.
(A) He came almost immediately. (B) He immediately came almost. (C) He immediately almost came. (D) Immediately, he almost came. (E) Almost, he immediately came.

78 The best of the following sentences is _____.
(A) Him, her, and I will do it. (B) He, she, and I will do it. (C) He, she, and I, will do it. (D) He, she, and me will do it. (E) He, her and I will do it.

79 The best of the following sentences is _____.
(A) We proceed from ignorance to knowledge from weakness to strength; and from mortality we hope to immortality. (B) We proceed from ignorance to knowledge; from weakness to strength and from mortality we hope to immortality. (C) We proceed from ignorance to knowledge; from weakness to strength, and from mortality, we hope to immortality. (D) We proceed from ignorance to knowledge; from weakness to strength; and from mortality, we hope, to immortality. (E) We proceed from ignorance to knowledge from weakness to strength and from mortality; we hope to immortality.

80 The _____of voting is denied to few.
(A) priveledge (B) priviledge (C) privilige (D) privelege (E) privilege

81 The _____ of some persons is of little value.
(A) garantee (B) guarantee (C) guarentee (D) garentee (E) guarante

82 His action was entirely_____.
(A) volentary (B) volentery (C) volantary (D) voluntary (E) voluntery

83 This is a _____ of the case.
(A) sumary (B) summery (C) summary (D) sumery (E) sumnary

84 One must _____ his opportunity.
(A) seize (B) seeze (C) sieze (D) ceaze (E) seaze

85 Attendants should always render _____ service.
(A) satisfactery (B) satisffactory (C) sattisfactery (D) satissfactery (E) satisfactory

86 A _____ is one party to a suit.
(A) plaintiff (B) plaintif (C) playntif (D) plainteff (E) plantiff

87 Roosevelt is_____of the United States.
(A) precident (B) president (C) presedent (D) presadent (E) preseidint

88 The _______ of some persons is quite unreadable.
(A) signature (B) signeture (C) signyature (D) signyeture (E) singeture

89 The work is _______ done.
(A) all ready (B) allready (C) already (D) al ready (E) alreddy

90 To divide any number by a fraction, __________.
(A) divide the number by the reciprocal of the fraction (B) change the fraction to a decimal and multiply (C) multiply the number by the fraction (D) multiply the number by the reciprocal of the fraction (E) multiply the number by the reciprocal of the reciprocal of the fraction

91 A house was insured for 80% of its value at 3/8%. The premium paid was $22.50. The value of the house _______.
(A) is $5000 (B) is $1500 (C) is $7500 (D) is more than $10000 (E) cannot be determined from the information given

92 A courtroom contains 72 persons, which is 2/5 of its capacity. The number of persons which the courtroom can hold is _______.
(A) 28 (B) 180 (C) 129 (D) greater than 200 and less than 300 (E) greater than 300 and less than 400

93 The amount of gain in a financial transaction is equal to _______.
(A) cost times rate of gain (B) cost divided by rate of gain (C) cost plus rate of gain (D)cost times selling price divided by rate of gain (E) gain divided by cost

94 7/8% is equal to _______.
(A) 0.0875 (B) 0.00875 (C) 0.0000 7/8 (D) 0.875 (E) 0.000 7/8

95 The total cost of 30 pencils at 18 cents a dozen, 12 paper pads at $27\frac{1}{2}$ cents each, and 8 boxes of paper clips at $5\frac{1}{4}$ cents a box is _______.
(A) more than $10 (B) $1.50 (C) $4.17 (D) $1.52 (E) between $5 and $10

96 $954 is divided among three men in the proportion of 5, 5 and 7 respectively. The amount received by the man who obtains the most money is _______.
(A) about $136 (B) more than $500 (C) between $400 and $500 (D) between $450 and $500 (E) between $350 and $400

97 A house and lot cost $10,000. Taxes, repairs, and other expenses amount to $360. The rent per month which the owner must receive in order to clear 6% on his investment _______.
(A) can not be determined from the information given (B) is $70 (C) is $80 (D) is $40 (E) is $50

98 To multiply a number by 0.13 1/3 _______.
(A) move the decimal place in the number one place to the left and add 1/3 of the obtained result (B) move the decimal place in the number two places to the left and add 1/3 to the obtained result (C) move the decimal in the number one place to the right and add 1/3 of the obtained result (D) move the decimalplace in the number one place to the right and divide the result by 1/3 (E) move the decimal place in the number two places to the left and divide the result by 1/3

Each of the following items contains one word which is not in keeping with the meaning which the sentence is evidently intended to carry. Select the word which does most to spoil the true meaning of the item and write that word in the space provided on the Answer Sheet. If you believe that more than one word may be chosen, write the one of the wrong words which is nearest the beginning of the item.

99 In a number of states there are various high courts of appeal. These have initial jurisdiction in certain types of cases defined by law, and exist chiefly to relieve the pressure upon the highest appellate court of the state.

100 An important aspect of city planning is the problem of courts. This means the districting of the city into special areas or zones which may be used only for certain definite purposes.

101 The care of the indigent is usually shared by public and private agencies, but the ravages of the depression have imposed lesser demands on the public purse.

102 Some reports are left unread and fail to accomplish the purpose for which they were intended because the writer neglected to take into consideration the one who had to file the reports.

103 Budget making is the utilization of future experience in the running of any business enterprise. It estimates as accurately as is possible the income of the business for the following period, and then fixes its expenditures so as to insure a proper relation between the two.

104 Crowding an office force into ample quarters is likely to reduce the output, cause irritation and friction, and lead to unhappiness.

105 The process is a machine designed to reproduce many copies of an original letter or other piece of writing.

106 In the last analysis, the main purpose of a filing system is to enable one to write letters, record cards, bills, documents, catalogues, and other papers into some container in such a logical order that they may be produced, when desired, with the expenditure of a minimum of time and effort.

107 A check is an order directing a person in which one has funds on deposit to pay a specified sum of money to a payee who is named or otherwise indicated in the check.

108 Purposeful reading is similar to, but not exactly the same thing as, study. Purposeful reading is an activity in which one selects books and magazines dealing with a certain subject, or subjects about which one wishes no information.

109 The person who begins to acquire more status regarding words may soon find that he is extending the practice to the acquisition of other types of knowledge.

110 A person who has made a blunder should not attempt to shift the responsibility for his error. He should acknowledge his mistake and attempt to include the error.

111 Speed is of considerable value in handling people. It is desirable, for example, that one be punctual in keeping appointments and avoid keeping people waiting an unreasonable length of time.

112 Should a court attendant wish to know how to write an article which appeared in the newspapers several months ago, it is well to know how it can be found most easily.

Each group of six words below contains two words which are either almost the same or almost the opposite in meaning. Write on the answer sheet the letters of the two words in each group which most nearly have the same or opposite meaning. In writing answers, place the capital letters in alphabetical order.

113 (A) mode (B) habitation (C) patrician (D) vogue (E) permanence (F) constriction

114 (A) pivot (B) axis (C) allusion (D) hitch (E) hollow (F) image

115 (A) proffer (B) acquire (C) serve (D) tender (E) differ (F) obviate

116 (A) complex (B) strict (C) torrid (D) simple (E) meretricious (F) euphuistic

117 (A) calefaction (B) organization (C) reputation (D) convolution (E) requisition (F) refrigeration

118 (A) opposition (B) solution (C) description (D) reduction (E) submission (F) determination

119 (A) coalition (B) jurisdiction (C) union (D) judiciary (E) franchise (F) hindrance

120 (A) resonance (B) reactionary (C) relinquishment (D) relief (E) activity (F) radical

121 (A) puissance (B) fleece (C) postponement (D) posterity (E) confiscation (F) cogency

122 (A) refutation (B) legislature (C) descent (D) correlation (E) substantiation (F) fulmination

123 (A) inconvenience (B) diminish (C) excite (D) express (E) increase (F) prepare

124 (A) circuitous (B) candid (C) chronic (D) inveterate (E) soldierly (F) desirous

125 (A) realize (B) externalize (C) facilitate (D) elucidate (E) extemporize (F) improvise

126 (A) core (B) hard (C) rigor (D) truth (E) nap (F) hub

127 (A) inner (B) indigenous (C) unaffected (D) slender (E) native (F) glorious

128 (A) prolix (B) terse (C) discreet (D) nasal (E) utter (F) idle

129 (A) primary (B) middle (C) initial (D) ostensible (E) systematic (F) conditional

130 (A) regard (B) invent (C) prohibit (D) fabricate (E) depose (F) introduce

131 (A) intellectual (B) fertile (C) legendary (D) illicit (E) uncertain (F) barren

132 (A) contraction (B) expansion (C) expectancy (D) exclusion (E) circulation (F) dejection

133 (A) phlegmatic (B) specified (C) devoted (D) definite (E) tributary (F) deceptive

134 (A) prominent (B) trenchant (C) impossible (D) hasty (E) perverse (F) deliberate

135 (A) cardinal (B) feasible (C) unimportant (D) diffident (E) harried (F) firm

136 (A) celerity (B) liquidity (C) harmony (D) encumbrance (E) ejection (F) dispatch

137 (A) loud (B) tactful (C) consonant (D) meaningful (E) blundering (F) entire

138 (A) portent (B) bias (C) antiquity (D) cleft (E) omen (F) burden

139 (A) violence (B) representation (C) evolution (D) tragedy (E) revolution (F) theory

140 (A) erupt (B) verify (C) substantiate (D) conjugate (E) disconnect (F) disintegrate

141 (A) drop (B) idealize (C) justify (D) dupe (E) trick (F) confer

142 (A) mediocre (B) intermediary (C) obstructive (D) maternal (E) ordinary (F) fundamental

143 (A) absurd (B) brusque (C) injurious (D) acquiescent (E) curt (F) subsidiary

144 (A) preposterous (B) servile (C) painful (D) informative (E) deliberate (F) sensible

145 (A) simultaneous (B) pliable (C) prior (D) ulterior (E) antecedant (F) latent

146 (A) apt (B) arbitrary (C) arboreal (D) aquatic (E) zealous (F) imperious

147 (A) dual (B) edible (C) authoritative (D) austere (E) audacious (F) conclusive

148 (A) facility (B) eviction (C) contraction (D) calamity (E) removal (F) plea

149 (A) imaginary (B) graphic (C) ductile (D) alien (E) extinct (F) actual

150 (A) illegal (B) incompatible (C) congruous (D) succinct (E) enthusiastic (F) capable

Part 2

1. Assume that you are a Court Attendant. Prepare a draft of the principles which should guide you in your relationship with
   (a) the judges
   (b) other court officers and employees.
   (c) attorneys and clients.

2. Assume that you, a Court Attendant, were assigned to deliver a 10 minute talk to a group of high school students visiting your court, on the organization, jurisdiction and work done in your court. Prepare a written draft of your proposed talk.

3. Assume that while the court is in session an air raid alarm has been given. What action should you, as a Court Attendant, take if you were in a crowded court room?

4. (a) Assume that while you are on duty as a Court Attendant, you are approached by a person who attempts to explain to you in broken English what he wants. But other than the fact that he has some kind of court business, you are unable to ascertain what he wants. In addition, you cannot tell what foreign language he is able to understand. What action should you take?

   (b) Assume that while you are on duty as a Court Attendant, you have observed for some time a number of court hangers-on in the halls who are constantly whispering among themselves and who approach and engage in conversation in lowered voices with various litigants and other persons having business in the court. This condition has existed for about a week. What action should you take?

5. It has been proposed that all judges of the five inferior courts be hereafter appointed as a result of competitive examination. Discuss the advantages and disadvantages of this proposal.

6. It has been proposed that all five inferior courts of the city be merged into a single court with jurisdiction over all matters now pertaining to these courts at present. Discuss the advantages and disadvantages of this proposal.

7. Below is a series of 10 words. Each word is divided into its component syllables. With respect to each word, you are to indicate on your answer sheet upon what syllable the primary accent should fall in properly pronouncing the word--
   (a) mu-nic-i-pal
   (b) ab-do-men
   (c) in-tri-cate
   (d) des-pi-ca-ble
   (e) for-mi-da-ble
   (f) pref-er-a-ble
   (g) sol-em-ni ze
   (h) ve-hi-cle
   (i) ve-he-ment
   (j) dis-ci-pline.

8. There has been recently celebrated the Anniversary of the "Bill of Rights". Write an essay explaining what is meant by the "Bill of Rights".

9. Prepare a chart showing the structure of the judicial system of the State of New York.

10. Define or explain the following terms:
   (a) affidavit
   (b) convene
   (c) double jeopardy
   (d) mistrial
   (e) peace officer
   (f) court calendar
   (g) contempt of court
   (h) jurisdiction of a court
   (i) grand jury
   (j) jurat.

The following report is to be written on the accompanying stub sheet only. You may use the second sheets for scratch purposes. Sign your report "J. Doe." If you sign anything else, your report will not be rated. In rating this report, the main consideration will be given to the candidate's organization of the subject matter, including arrangement, punctuation, spelling, grammar, handwriting and neatness. Consideration will also be given to content.

Write a <u>one page</u> report to the Municipal Civil Service Commission on the significance to the administration of criminal justice in this state of placing assistants to the several District Attorneys in the competitive class of the civil service.

NO OFFICIAL ANSWERS WERE RELEASED FOR THIS EXAM

PART THREE

Duties and Job Knowledge

Practice Using Answer Sheets

Alter numbers to match the practice and drill questions in each part of the book.
Make only ONE mark for each answer. Additional and stray marks may be counted as mistakes.
In making corrections, erase errors COMPLETELY. Make glossy black marks.

	A	B	C	D	E		A	B	C	D	E		A	B	C	D	E		A	B	C	D	E		A	B	C	D	E
1						1						1						1						1					
2						2						2						2						2					
3						3						3						3						3					
4						4						4						4						4					
5						5						5						5						5					
6						6						6						6						6					
7						7						7						7						7					
8						8						8						8						8					
9						9						9						9						9					
0						0						0						0						0					

	A	B	C	D	E		A	B	C	D	E		A	B	C	D	E		A	B	C	D	E		A	B	C	D	E
1						1						1						1						1					
2						2						2						2						2					
3						3						3						3						3					
4						4						4						4						4					
5						5						5						5						5					
6						6						6						6						6					
7						7						7						7						7					
8						8						8						8						8					
9						9						9						9						9					
0						0						0						0						0					

	A	B	C	D	E		A	B	C	D	E		A	B	C	D	E		A	B	C	D	E		A	B	C	D	E
1						7						13						19						25					
2						8						14						20						26					
3						9						15						21						27					
4						10						16						22						28					
5						11						17						23						29					
6						12						18						24						30					

TEAR OUT ALONG THIS LINE AND MARK YOUR ANSWERS AS INSTRUCTED IN THE TEXT

COURT OFFICER

Duties of the Court Attendant

Every morning that the court is in session, the Court Attendant should report to the clerk before doing anything else. He should report to the clerk on time dressed in the proper regulation uniform. This uniform should be worn during the entire work day.

The attendant's first duty is to see that the courtroom is in proper condition for the day's business; that it has the correct temperature and atmosphere. Next, he must see that everything is in its proper place so that the opening of court may not be hampered by any minor difficulty. To overlook any detail may later prove costlv.

Throughout the session of the court, he must see that proper order and decorum are maintained in the courtroom. Above everything else, silence must be constantly observed and everything must be eliminated that would delay the most efficient functioning of the court. The attendant must carry out such duties as may be required by the court and clerk. Examples of such duties are directing witnesses to the witness stand and assisting the court clerk and counsel in the handling of exhibits. At times the attendant must act as a messenger in procuring any books from the court library that are required by the attorneys and ordered by the clerk of Court.

The enforcement of the rules of the court require courteous behavior on the part of the court attendant but he must also be firm and strict when the occasion requires such an attitude.

The Court Attendant has important functions in connection with the control of the jury. He must see to it that every juror has his proper place in the box. He must be constantly on the watch to prevent any juror from leaving the jury box while the trial is in progress. Should a juror desire to leave the box while the case is going on, the court attendant must first inform the judge of the juror's desire, to determine whether the judge will grant or refuse the juror's wish. If the judge approves, the trial is stopped and the court attendant is instructed to accompany the juror while he is out of the jury box. In order to prevent any stoppage or possible mistrial, the court attendant must not allow the juror to get out of his sight or hearing. He must always bear in mind that the juror should be returned as quickly as possible; without any unnecessary delay. The juror must not enter into any conversation with anybody or read any matter which he may have or which may be given to him.

The court attendant must be particularly careful when placed in charge of a jury that has retired to deliberate. He must conduct the jury to the jury room and see to it that no juror talks with anyone on the way. If a juror does talk with someone the event may afford grounds for a mistrial.

The jury room must be properly ventilated, heated and lighted and the jurors must be amply supplied with paper, ink, pens, and any other needed stationery. The court attendant immediately locks the door when he leaves the jury rooms and remains at calling or hearing distance for if any jury member requires his services he must respond at a moment's notice. In all cases two attendants are assigned to guard a jury; this is to insure constant guard over the jury. Should one court attendant be dispatched with a message or sent to the court-room for an exhibit, the other would remain on guard. If only one guard were assigned the chances of wrong doing would be heightened.

There arises, at times, a situation in which a jury member desires to communicate with some member of his family while the jury is behind closed doors. The court attendant cannot allow this except with the permission of the judge or the clerk. If the jury member requires the sending of a message to the judge or court he must do so by putting it in writing and requesting that it be delivered by the court attendant.

The jurors may go to dinner only with the permission of the judge. If permission is granted, the court attendant must accompany the jury and make certain that it does not separate. Under no circumstances must the court attendant allow any person to communicate with the jury without official permission or to allow anybody to molest them. The jury must be returned to the jury room as soon as the members have finished eating.

When the jurors agree upon a verdict, one of the court attendants should make it known to the court room and then proceed to announce the court's command, "Return the jury to the court room." After delivering this command the attendants should conduct the jurors back to the jury box and remain near them. The clerk then receives and records the verdict.

A slightly different procedure is followed should the jurors be deliberating on a civil case and be instructed to deliver a sealed verdict. It then becomes necessary for the court attendants to procure an envelope and blank form from the clerk. The jurors are instructed to sign the form, when they have reached a decision, and the foreman is instructed to seal the envelope an keep it in his possession until the following morning or until the opening of the court at the next session. No one is to read the contents of the envelope not even the court attendants.

Another important duty of the court attendants is to see that no witnesses are left standing while others who have no business in the court room have seats. They must also direct witnesses to seats when they present themselves in court to testify. The court attendants must collect all the subpoenas from those who have been summoned and turn them over to the District Attorney--this happens only if a criminal case is being tried.

In order to bring about a smoother conduct of the days business it is best that the court attendant reserve a portion of the court room for the witnesses and thus make it easier to call them to the witness stand. This eliminates much confusion and saves the court much time. When a witness is called to testify the court attendant must direct him to the witness stand. The attendant at the witness stand should direct the witness to face the court while being sworn. He should remain close by to render greater assistance.

TEST QUESTIONS FOR PRACTICE

Directions: In each of the following 35 questions four possible answers are suggested. In the space at the right you are to write the letter A, B, C, or D, preceding the choice which is the best one according to the instructions governing each question. Read all instructions and questions carefully. Work as rapidly and yet as accurately as possible.

1. Which of the following is not a necessary qualification for a court attendant? (a) He should be neat, clean and honest (b) He should be courteous and intelligent (c) He should be alert and willing to obey orders (d) excitable and talkative.

2. When witnesses arrive in the court room it is the duty of the court attendant to (a) see that they are fingerprinted (b) see that they are photographed (c) to relate to them everything that occurred before they entered (d) direct them to seats.

3. In criminal cases, court attendants should take up subpoenas issued by the District Attorney and turn them over to (a) the judge (b) the District Attorney (c) the witnesses (d) the jury.

4. One of the duties of the court attendant is to (a) select the jury (b) find the witnesses (c) assist in the swearing of witnesses and defendants (d) question the defendant.

5. The court attendant asks the witness (a) his religion (b) his political affiliations (c) his name, address and occupation (d) if he was ever arrested.

6. While the witness is testifying, the court attendant is near the stand in order to (a) be on hand if the witness tries to escape (b) guard the witness (c) handle papers, exhibits, etc. (d) record the testimony of the witness.

7. If a witness does not respond after being called by the court, the court attendant should (a) send a telegram to the witness (b) go out himself and locate the witness (c) call out the name loudly in the court rooms and halls and if there is no response after that notify the court (d) call the next witness.

8. If one of the jurors faints during a trial the court attendant should (a) take him home personally (b) take him to the hospital personally (c) take him out of the court room with as little noise as possible and revive him (d) try to revive the juror in the court room.

9. If a fire broke out while a court attendant was in charge of the jury considering a case while the court was still in session, the court attendant should (a) call the fire department (b) call the police department (c) notify the presiding Justice and obey his orders (d) send the jury home.

10. If a man who has been subpoenaed as a witness in an action asks to be excused on the day of the trial because of illness the court attendant should (a) explain to the witness that he must be excused by the attorney who subpoenaed him (b) excuse him and send him home (c) reprimand him for coming to court when he is ill (d) recommend a doctor to him.

11. If a subpoenaed witness whose home is quarantined sends another person to inform the court that he cannot appear, the court attendant should (a) direct that person to the presiding judge (b) direct that person to the district attorney (c) direct that person to the clerk (d) excuse the witness.

12. If during the time that the judge is charging the jury, a woman asks to be admitted because it is vitally important, the court attendant should (a) admit the woman (b) interrupt the judge and notify him (c) refuse admittance to the woman (d) admit the woman explaining however that such procedure is not allowed.

13. After a sealed verdict has been ordered and the Justice has gone for the day, a juror asks permission to telephone his wife that he will be home late. The court attendant should (a) not permit the juror to use the phone (b) permit the juror to use the phone (c) call the juror's wife and let the juror talk to her (d) call the juror's wife and ask her to come down and talk to the husband.

14. If the jurors notify the court attendant that they cannot come to a decision the court attendant should (a) inform the district attorney (b) inform the justice and wait for directions (c) send the jury back until they reach a decision (d) inform the defendant.

15. One of the following which is not a duty of the court attendant is to (a) provide paper, ink, pencils, pens for the jury room (b) maintain proper atmosphere and temperature (c) advise the jurors on their decision (d) lock the door of the jury room and remain near the door.

16. When the jury reaches a verdict, the foreman knocks on the door thus informing the court attendant. The latter should (a) inform the Justice (b) open the door and direct them to their seats in the jury box (c) announce the verdict (d) inform the defendant.

17. If a juror is called and there is no answer, the court attendant should (a) go out and try to find him (b) call up his home (c) announce to the clerk "no answer" (d) select another juror from among the crowd in the court room.

18. When the jury slip is withdrawn from the jury wheel by the clerk, the court attendant should (a) take the jury slip from the clerk (b) announce the name of the juror (c) give the slip to the juror (d) explain to the juror what the case is about.

19. After the jury is complete, it is the duty of the court attendant to (a) direct the jury to the jury box (b) direct the jurors to stand during the administering of the oath by the clerk (c) explain to them the nature of the case (d) explain his opinion of the case to the jurors.

20. When the jury is ready to retire, the two court attendants should (a) direct the jurors to the jury room (b) allow them to communicate with the newspapermen for a few minutes (c) allow them to go to the washrooms (d) outline the case in order to clear up any confusion that may exist in the minds of the jurors.

21. When directing the jurors to the room, the court attendants should (a) not permit anyone to talk or communicate with any one of the jurors at any time (b) allow the jury to make any telephone calls they desire (c) allow the press reporters to interview them (d) take their fingerprints.

22. When a witness is called to testify, it is the duty of the court attendant to (a) question the witness (b) determine his qualifications as a witness (c) admit him and direct the witness to the stand (d) make him feel at ease.

23. Of the following, the one which is not considered the duty of a court attendant is to give information to (a) lawyers (b) jurors (c) press reporters (d) witnesses.

24. The court attendant is not expected to (a) be in correct uniform (b) wash the floors of the court room (c) report on time (d) dress the desk of the judge.

25. The most important duty of the court attendant is to (a) select the jurors (b) determine eligibility of the witnesses (c) maintain order and decorum in the court room (d) approve the decision of the jury.

26. Which of the following statements is most accurate? (a) It is the duty of the court attendant to clean the windows of the court (b) It is the duty of the court attendant to see that subpoenaed witnesses are excused if necessary (c) It is the duty of the court attendant to aid in the care and handling of prisoners in the custody of the court (d) It is the duty of the court attendant to serve the sentence.

27. The court attendant collects fees, handles the papers, and pleading in (a) civil courts (b) city criminal courts (c) state criminal courts (d) federal criminal courts.

28. At close of sessions, the court attendant should (a) sweep up the court room (b) clear the court room putting everything securely in place (c) Lock the court house (d) interview newspaper reporters.

29. The court attendant should act as messenger for (a) the defendant (b) the witnesses (c) the court and clerk (d) the jurors.

30- A court attendant is obligated, when Court is not in session, (a) to carry out all orders directed by the Court which cannot be executed while it is in session (b) to be at constant service of the clerk of the Court (c) to be at constant service of the Justice of the Court (d) to nobody and for no reason whatsoever.

31. If there is disorder in the court room the court attendant should (a) rap for order (b) call the Police (c) restore order immediately (d) explain to the court that improper conduct cannot be tolerated.

32. If persons in a court room continue to act in a disorderly manner, the court attendant should (a) bring them before the court (b) eject them forcibly from the court room (c) arrest them (d) fine them for contempt of court.

33. It is the duty of the court attendant to see that persons who attend court as spectators (a) come in quietly and take seats (b) are informed as to the nature of the cases involved (c) are citizens of the United States (d) are impartial in regard to the cases to be tried.

34. It is necessary for the court attendant who acts in the capacity of a crier to (a) issue all proclamations for the opening and closing of court and adjournments (b) announce the decision of the jury (c) announce his opinion (d) pronounce the sentence.

35. When a court attorney is assigned to a Judge it is not important for him to (a) interview persons desiring to see the judge; inform the Judge of their names and missions (b) know the private life of the judge (c) look after the Judge's minute book, gavel, stationery, etc. (d) secure interpreter when needed.

CORRECT ANSWERS FOR THE FOREGOING QUESTIONS

(Please try to answer the questions on your own before looking at our answers. You'll do much better on your test if you follow this rule.)

1. D	8. C	15. C	22. C	29. C
2. D	9. C	16. B	23. C	30. A
3. B	10. A	17. C	24. B	31. C
4. C	11. C	18. B	25. C	32. A
5. C	12. C	19. B	26. C	33. A
6. C	13. A	20. A	27. A	34. A
7. C	14. B	21. A	28. B	35. B

COURT OFFICER
LAW AND COURTS

The law is the compilation of those customs and traditions, written and unwritten, governing the behavior of men in the state. As the law is a thing continuing and traditional, so it is stable: as the nature of society and the state changes, so law must change to meet new needs.

OLD laws die quietly as the need for them passes away. We no longer have laws concerning heresy or slandering the king: freedom of religion has been greatly extended and we no longer have a king. Old laws are sometimes reborn to fit new needs or the recurrences of old, are modified, and in effect become new laws.

Criminal law and the penal code can (they don't always) vary widely from state to state, city to city, and even between townships in a single county. Under the American system of laws, the policeman only has the most severely limited jurisdiction (and that only by agreement) outside his own community. What might be termed disturbing the peace in one city and subject to a $10 fine might be disorderly conduct in another and merit thirty days in the workhouse.

Lawyers and the court may concern themselves with the law in general, but the police officer must always be aware of changes in particular laws. His question is always, can I make an arrest, and what law gives me the authority to do so? Laws and procedures not only vary from place to place, but they may also undergo changes over the years. A manual of laws can become obsolete—in its definition of law in a particular area—between the day it was compiled and the day it went to press. Even the library of a lawyer specializing in one branch of the law must always be extensive and at least in part out of date.

Law enforcement officers must remain abreast of the law as it affects them in their own jurisdictions. The following questions are based on the criminal law and penal code of one large city, as they have appeared on examinations in recent years. Some of the laws to which they pertain may be obsolete, some of them no longer exist, some of them are not relevant to your community, some of them may have changed over the years, but the form and substance of all of them is still very relevant. The law pertaining to a crime may undergo modification, but the continued existence of law in that area points out society's continuing concern with the crime.

Answer the following questions according to your best judgment and knowledge of the law *in your own jurisdiction.* If you think the law has changed, or if it is different in your jurisdiction, mark an (X) on your answer sheet, and make a point of looking up the law at the nearest opportunity. All of the questions are arranged by subject: make a note of the subjects covered, and in your study of local laws, be sure you have covered all of the subjects.*

GENERAL QUESTIONS

1. A law enforcement officer should regard the law as a kind of
   (A) unreasonable convention
   (B) necessary evil
   (C) rule of action
   (D) inferior substitute for logic.

---

*For a more thorough coverage of this vital subject, see:
Salottolo, Lawrence. CRIMINAL LAW QUIZZER
Arco Publishing Co., Inc., N. Y. 1958

2. The responsibility of policemen in the proper administration of criminal law is to
   (A) attempt to procure the conviction of the person arrested, leaving to the defense attorney the responsibility for obtaining evidence in favor of the accused
   (B) gather all facts concerning the commission of a crime that are favorable to the prosecution, and also indicate to the district attorney any investigative leads which might prove favorable to the defense, but which have not been followed
   (C) gather all the facts pertaining to an incident and to present them all to the proper court
   (D) gather as much information as is necessary to constitute a prima facie case, and not to proceed any further in the investigation.

3. The Fourteenth Amendment to the Federal Constitution provides in part that no state shall "deprive any person of life, liberty, or property, without due process of law." This clause has been construed by the Supreme Court of the United States as prohibiting the use of a coerced confession in a state court. Other authorities for legally excluding involuntary confessions are the
   (A) Administrative Code and the Penal Law
   (B) Civil Practice Act and the Administrative Code
   (C) Code of Criminal Procedure and the State Constitution
   (D) State Constitution and the Penal Law
   (E) Penal Law and the Code of Criminal Procedure.

4. The State Code of Criminal Procedure specifically provides that the only person whose promise of immunity renders a confession inadmissible is
   (A) a desk officer or acting desk officer
   (B) an arresting officer
   (C) any court officer
   (D) a police officer above the rank of sergeant
   (E) the district attorney.

5. Taking by means of force or fear is an element of both
   (A) robbery and extortion
   (B) robbery and burglary
   (C) burglary and extortion
   (D) burglary and larceny.

6. The chief distinction between a felony and a misdemeanor lies in
   (A) the age of the offender
   (B) whether a State or Federal law was violated
   (C) whether the person intended to commit a crime
   (D) the punishment fixed by law.

7. Bail is set chiefly in order to
   (A) permit the accused freedom of movement pending actual hearing of the case
   (B) increase the revenues of the courts through bail bond forfeitures and interest charges
   (C) encourage rehabilitation of criminals pending trial
   (D) give the prosecuting attorneys time to prepare a case against the accused.

8. The chief among the following functions of law is the
   (A) sterilization of the economically incompetent
   (B) maintenance of religion
   (C) guarantee that criminals will not escape from any institution in which they may be incarcerated
   (D) safeguarding of the community against the acts of individuals and groups.

9. To constitute an attempt to commit a crime, there is necessary, beyond mere preparation
   (A) an overt act
   (B) a criminal intent
   (C) a felonious purpose
   (D) a definite motive
   (E) an expression of purpose.

10. In some jurisdictions, persons jointly accused of a crime may request separate trials. The best reason for this procedure is that
    (A) circumstances tending to show guilt sometimes result in disagreement among the jurymen
    (B) known lawbreakers are sometimes able to convince juries of their innocence of a particular crime charged
    (C) no reasonable person would approve of the joint trial of a guilty and an innocent person
    (D) evidence tending to show the guilt of one of the accused may sometimes influence the jury against the other defendant
    (E) persons who are jointly tried for a crime are usually hardened criminals.

11. A person cannot be punished for a crime if he can prove that at the time of its commission he was

(A) suffering from a morbid propensity to commit prohibited acts
(B) in a state of intoxication
(C) a psychopathic inferior person
(D) legally insane.

12. A "dwelling house" as defined in the Penal Law is any building
(A) in which there is at the time a human being
(B) usually occupied by persons lodging therein at night
(C) capable of affording shelter for human beings
(D) a part of which is used as an abode.

Column I lists certain crimes or offenses. In the space to the right of the question next to the number of the crime or offenses in Column I place the letter preceding the statement in Column II which most accurately describes it.

COLUMN I

13. fraud
14. burglary
15. bribery of witness
16. barratry
17. seduction
18. unlawful assembly
19. forgery
20. libel
21. larceny
22. disorderly conduct

COLUMN II

(A) is always a felony
(B) is always a misdemeanor
(C) may be a felony or misdemeanor
(D) is an offense only.

23. The right of one state to demand of another state the return of a fugitive from justice in the demanding state depends upon
(A) comity among the states
(B) treaty between states
(C) provision of the Code of Criminal Procedure
(D) provisions of the Constitution of the United States and federal law.

ADULTERY - PROSTITUTION

24. A person who, after the commission of the offense, harbors, conceals, or aids the offender, with intent that he may avoid or escape from arrest, having knowledge that such offender is liable to arrest, is punishable as a principal when the crime is
(A) statutory rape
(B) seduction
(C) adultery
(D) abduction.

ARREST

25. The one of the following provisions of common law concerning powers of arrest that is most like the State Penal Law is that
(A) any person may arrest any other person whom he suspects on reasonable grounds of having committed a felony if, in fact, a felony has been committed by someone
(B) any person, whether police officer or not, not only may, but must arrest a person committing a felony in his presence
(C) a police officer may arrest any person who is charged by a responsible person with having committed a felony whether, in fact, a felony has been committed or not
(D) a police officer may arrest any person whom he suspects on reasonable grounds of having committed a felony whether, in fact, a felony has been committed or not
(E) no person can be arrested for a misdemeanor without a warrant unless a breach of the peace is taking place and the arrest of the offender is necessary to put a stop to it.

26. The Code of Criminal Procedure of the State is important to the work of a peace officer because it
(A) defines the conditions for legal arrest
(B) describes methods of crime prevention and detection
(C) states the penalty for each crime
(D) contains names and pictures of all known criminals.

ARSON

27. A is charged with setting fire to a building owned by B. Of the following the factor that will be *least* important in determining the degree of arson with which he will be charged is the
(A) time of day or night at which he set fire to the building
(B) value of the building
(C) type of building
(D) occupancy of the building.

ASSAULT

28. A person can be charged with assault in the third degree only, who
    (A) assaults another with intent to prevent the execution of a mandate of a court
    (B) with intent to commit a misdemeanor administers an anesthetic agent to another
    (C) wilfully and wrongfully wounds another but without a weapon
    (D) operates a motor vehicle in a culpably negligent manner, whereby another suffers injury.

BRIBERY

29. A person charged with bribery could be convicted of attempted bribery only if
    (A) the bribe given or received was actually worthless
    (B) the reward offered was not accepted
    (C) no corrupt intent on the part of the officer bribed is shown
    (D) the tendered reward was accepted by the officer after the official act is consummated, without any prior corrupt understanding.

EXTORTION—BLACKMAIL—COERCION

30. A person who, with a view to compel another person to abstain from doing an act which such other person has a legal right to do or to abstain from doing, wrongfully and unlawfully threatens violence or injury upon such other person or his family is guilty of
    (A) blackmail (C) extortion
    (B) coercion (D) fraud.

31. It is *not* an essential element of the crime of blackmail that the
    (A) threat be in writing
    (B) accused had the intent to extort or gain money or property
    (C) contents of the written threat be known to the accused
    (D) threat be calculated to inspire fear or produce terror.

32. A person who wrongfully and unlawfully by means of threat or force attempts the intimidation of another person with a view to compel such person to do an act which such other person has a legal right to do or abstain from doing, is guilty of
    (A) oppression (C) extortion
    (B) coercion (D) entrapment.

33. Extortion is a felony when the threat to injure is
    (A) immediate
    (B) in writing
    (C) accompanied by force
    (D) made by a public officer.

FELONIES

34. A "felony" is defined in the Penal Law as a crime which
    (A) may occasion a forfeiture of civil rights in addition to any other penalty imposed
    (B) is or may be punishable by death or imprisonment in a state prison
    (C) must be prosecuted by indictment rather than by information or complaint
    (D) the state deems injurious to the public at large rather than a particular individual.

35. Regardless of intent, it is a felony merely to possess
    (A) a Browning automatic
    (B) a Thompson sub-machine gun
    (C) a .45 caliber revolver
    (D) any explosive substance.

FORGERY

36. It is essential to constitute the crime of forgery that the
    (A) person in whose name it purports to be made have the legal capacity to make the instrument
    (B) person to whom it is directed be bound to act upon it if genuine, or have a remedy over
    (C) person whose name is forged be an actual living person
    (D) forged instrument would be valid if genuine.

GAMBLING

(Question 40 illustrates the reference to offenses listed in the Penal Code by number. The correct answer to this question, in the jurisdiction from which it was taken, is (B). What would the correct answer be in your jurisdiction?)

37. Where persons are found making bets on a pin-ball machine in a candy store and the proprietor, although present and having full knowledge of the fact, fails to interfere, the proprieter should be charged with violation of section
(A) 722 of the Penal Law
(B) 973 of the Penal Law
(C) 982 of the Penal Law
(D) 899 of the Code of Criminal Procedure.

HOMICIDE

38. If A is accused of having caused the death of B, of the following, the factor which will weigh most heavily in determining whether A should be indicted for murder or manslaughter is
(B) his intent in committing the homicide
(A) his age
(C) the nature of the weapon used
(D) the existence of a corpus delicti.

39. Upon a trial for murder the defendant could be convicted of first degree assault if
(A) premeditation and deliberation were not shown
(B) intent to kill was not proven
(C) the act complained of is not proven to be the cause of death
(D) a deadly weapon was not used.

40. Intent to kill is not a necessary element of
(A) first degree murder
(B) second degree murder
(C) second degree manslaughter
(D) first degree assault.

41. In general, the main difference between murder and manslaughter is that in the latter there is no
(A) premeditation and deliberation
(B) design to kill
(C) use of dangerous weapon
(D) felonious intent.

42. A conviction for 1st degree murder requires proof of
(A) a design to effect death
(B) deliberation and premeditation
(C) malice, express or implied
(D) motive for the killing.

43. To be a homicide the statute requires that the killing result from another's act, a procurement or omission. Under the provisions of Section 2, Penal Law, one whose "procurement" was responsible for a homicide would be punishable as
(A) an accomplice
(B) a conspirator
(C) a principal
(D) an accessory.

44. No person can be convicted of murder or manslaughter unless there is direct proof rather than circumstantial evidence of the
(A) accused's responsibility for the death of the victim
(B) death of the victim
(C) identity of the victim
(D) corpus delecti.

45. A felony murder charge would not be proper in a case where
(A) defendant induced and procured others to rob a certain person but took no part in the commission of the robbery, during which the victim was killed
(B) defendant, imprisoned for a misdemeanor, accidentally killed a fellow prisoner by a misdirected bullet while both were engaged in a conspiracy to escape from prison
(C) defendant, intending to shoot and kill X, fires a revolver and causes the death of B, an innocent bystander
(D) defendant took a human life in the course of an escape from prison where he had been confined on a felony charge.

46. A homicide is manslaughter in the second degree when committed without a design to effect death by
(A) an intoxicated physician's unskillful attendance
(B) advising or encouraging another person to take his own life
(C) inflicting an injury upon the person of a woman which results in the killing of an unborn quick child
(D) administering to a woman any substance intended to procure her miscarriage, which results in her death.

JUVENILE—MINORS

47. A child sixteen years of age who is habitually addicted to the use of drugs or the intemperate use of intoxicating liquors is defined in the Code of Criminal Procedure as a
(A) youthful offender
(B) delinquent child
(C) wayward minor
(D) neglected child.

48. A boy under the age of sixteen may be convicted of the crime of
(A) murder
(B) larceny
(C) rape
(D) arson.

49. A boy 16 years of age who is found of his own free will in a house of prostitution is a

(A) neglected child
(C) youthful offender
(B) delinquent child
(D) wayward minor.

50. The eligibility of a defendant to be adjudged a youthful offender is determined by his age at the time of
(A) commission of the offense
(B) arrest for the offense
(C) indictment for the offense
(D) adjudication as a youthful offender.

51. A woman, believing the girl to be over sixteen years old, induces a girl of fifteen to steal a pair of nylon stockings from a counter in a department store. The most appropriate charge to make against the woman is
(A) juvenile delinquency
(B) impairing the morals of a minor
(C) coercion
(D) criminally receiving stolen goods.

52. A hotel clerk lets a room to a man accompanied by a woman under eighteen years of age. The woman is not the man's wife and the hotel clerk had knowledge of that fact. The hotel clerk could be charged with the crime of
(A) adultery
(B) abduction
(C) seduction
(D) rape.

53. According to the Penal Law the word "neglected" shall include any child under sixteen years of age who
(A) associates with immoral or vicious persons
(B) begs or solicits alms or money in public places under any pretense
(C) frequents any place the existence of which is in violation of law
(D) is found in any place the existence of which is in violation of law
(E) is habitually truant.

54. According to the Penal Law, the possession of a switchblade knife is
(A) permitted when necessary for the purposes of a business or trade
(B) prohibited only when circumstances indicate an intent to use it in an unlawful manner
(C) permitted if used while engaged in certain sporting activities and a currently valid license under the conservation law is being carried
(D) prohibited only when the blade projects from the handle more than six inches.

KIDNAPPING

55. Kidnapping and abduction are similar in that in both crimes
(A) consent is always a defense
(B) the motive is identical
(C) conviction can be had upon the unsupported testimony of the victim
(D) the same acts may constitute the crime.

LARCENY

56. "Consent is no defense." This statement applies *least* accurately to the crime of
(A) blackmail
(B) fraud
(C) larceny
(D) adultery
(E) extortion.

57. No agreement amounts to a conspiracy, unless some overt act besides such agreement be done to effect the object thereof by one or more of the parties to such agreement, if its object is to commit
(A) larceny
(B) arson
(C) burglary
(D) felonious assault.

58. The fact that the defendant was armed with a dangerous weapon does not affect the degree of the crime with which he is charged when he is accused of
(A) larceny
(B) manslaughter
(C) robbery
(D) burglary.

59. A prosecution for petit larceny committed by a fiduciary must be commenced within
(A) two years of the discovery of the facts constituting the crime
(B) two years of the commission of the acts constituting the crime
(C) five years of the discovery of the facts constituting the crime

(D) five years of the commission of the acts constituting the crime.

60. The degree of the crime of larceny is never affected by the
   (A) intent of the taker
   (B) presence of the owner
   (C) place from which the property is taken
   (D) value or amount of property taken.

LIBEL

61. In order to sustain a prosecution for criminal libel
   (A) the person libeled must be living
   (B) there must be evidence of malice on the part of the defendant
   (C) the libelous matter must have been seen by at least one third party
   (D) the matter published must be false.

MALICIOUS MISCHIEF

62. The wilful transmission of a false fire alarm is classified in the Penal Law as
   (A) disorderly conduct
   (B) a public nuisance
   (C) malicious mischief
   (D) a crime involving public safety.

63. According to the Penal Law the one of the following which is *not* malicious mischief is
   (A) defacing an electric light pole in the City without permission of the proper authority
   (B) secretly loitering about a building, with intent to overhear discourse therein, and to repeat the same to injure others
   (C) selling bean-shooters in the City
   (D) breaking or defacing any public urinal in the City
   (E) wilfully giving any false alarm of fire.

MISDEMEANORS

64. A misdemeanor is
   (A) any crime not punishable by death or imprisonment in a state prison
   (B) only such offense as is so defined in the Penal Law
   (C) any violation of a state law or municipal ordinance which does not amount to a crime
   (D) an act for which no penalty is imposed by the Penal Law.

65. According to the Penal Law, the one of the following crimes which is *not* a misdemeanor is for a person
   (A) falsely to represent to the inspectors of election or any of them that he is incapacitated to mark his ballot, for the purpose of obtaining assistance in voting
   (B) having lawfully entered a voting booth with a voter, to reveal to another the name of any candidate voted for by him
   (C) not being lawfully authorized, to make or have in his possession a key to a voting machine which has been adopted and will be used in elections
   (D) to act as an inspector of election without being able to read and write the English language
   (E) to remove any official ballot from a polling place before the closing of the polls.

MOBS

66. A "mob" is defined in the Penal Law as an assemblage of three or more persons
   (A) which shall exercise or attempt to exercise by physical violence and without authority of law any power of correction or punishment over any person
   (B) that disturbs the public peace by using force or violence to any other person or to property or that threatens such disturbance accompanied with the power of immediate execution
   (C) with intent to commit any unlawful act by force or with intent to carry out any unlawful purpose in such manner as to disturb the public peace
   (D) which commits any act of violence on the body of a person in the custody of any peace officer.

NARCOTICS

67. Concerning the sale and possession of hypodermic syringes, the Penal Law provides that
   (A) a written prescription for a hypodermic syringe shall be accessible for inspection

only upon direction of the Board of Health
(B) a written prescription for a hypodermic syringe shall be retained for a period of three years
(C) a written prescription for a hypodermic syringe shall not be used to permit subsequent sales to the person to whom the prescription was issued
(D) every person selling a hypodermic syringe pursuant to a written prescription shall record upon the face of the written prescription, over his signature, the date of the sale of the hypodermic syringe
(E) it shall be unlawful for any person to sell or furnish to any other person a hypodermic syringe except pursuant to a written prescription of a duly licensed physician or veterinarian.

NEGLIGENCE

68. Negligence as used in the Penal Law is best defined as
(A) an act or omission done or left undone in reckless disregard of the life or safety of others
(B) such a gross want of care and regard for the rights of others as to justify the presumption of wilfulness and wantonness
(C) the absence of care according to circumstances
(D) want of such attention to the consequences of one's acts as an ordinarily prudent man would bestow in acting in his own concerns.

PUBLIC NUISANCES

69. A "public nuisance," as defined in the Penal Law, consists in unlawfully doing an act, or omitting to perform a duty, which act or omission
(A) results in the hurt or annoyance of the lands, tenements or hereditaments of another
(B) results in annoyance or injury to the comfort, repose, health or safety of the community as a whole
(C) while not amounting to an assault or battery, annoys or interferes with any person in any place or with the passengers in any public conveyance
(D) results in the wanton and reckless destruction of property or the wilful perpetration of injury to the person.

RAPE—SEDUCTION

70. The previous chaste character of the victim is a material element where the crime is charged is
(A) seduction
(B) first degree rape
(C) statutory rape
(D) abduction.

71. A subsequent marriage between the parties is a complete defense to a prosecution for
(A) first degree rape
(B) abduction
(C) seduction
(D) compulsory prostitution.

72. An act of sexual intercourse perpetrated by a twenty year old boy on a female not his wife, under eighteen years of age, with her consent is punishable as
(A) first degree rape
(B) second degree rape
(C) third degree rape
(D) a misdemeanor.

73. Sexual intercourse is a necessary element of
(A) abduction, seduction and statutory rape
(B) abduction and seduction
(C) seduction and statutory rape
(D) abduction and statutory rape.

74. The corroboration necessary for a first degree rape conviction is supplied by
(A) statements made by the complainant to a policeman within a half hour after the commission of the act
(B) an admission by the defendant that he "fooled" with the defendant
(C) evidence of the birth of a child within one year after the alleged crime
(D) a confession made by the defendant.

RECEIVING STOLEN GOODS

75. An accused could be convicted of the crime of criminally receiving stolen property without proof that he
(A) knew the property was stolen
(B) received the property from the person who stole it
(C) received the property with felonious intent
(D) received, bought, concealed or withheld the property.

ROBBERY

76. Robbery differs from larceny in that to constitute the former
   (A) property must be taken from the person of the victim
   (B) the victim must be the owner of the property taken
   (C) the taking must be accompanied by violence, threats or terror
   (D) there need be no consent to the taking.

THEFT - LARCENY - BURGLARY - ROBBERY

77. In determining whether an arrested suspect should be charged with burglary or unlawful entry, the one of the following factors that will be most decisive is
   (A) the value of property taken from the building
   (B) the kind of building he entered
   (C) the intent with which he entered
   (D) the manner of his entry.

78. The element which distinguishes burglary from larceny is
   (A) break and entry
   (B) appropriation of the property of another
   (C) use of force or fear
   (D) criminal intent
   (E) consent of the victim.

79. The chief distinction between burglary and robbery is that burglary involves
   (A) felonious intent
   (B) the use of an accomplice
   (C) breaking and entering a building
   (D) unlawful taking by means of force.

80. The one of the following elements that is *not* common to both first degree and second degree burglary is
   (A) breaking and entering a dwelling house
   (B) a dwelling house in which there is a human being present
   (C) entry with intent to commit some crime therein
   (D) being armed with a dangerous weapon.

81. If an armed person breaks and enters a dwelling house in the day time, in which there is no human being present at the time, for the purpose of committing a crime therein, the crime is
   (A) burglary, 1st degree
   (B) burglary, 2nd degree
   (C) burglary, 3rd degree
   (D) unlawful entry.

82. A person could not be convicted of burglary if it were shown that the breaking and entering were done with intent to
   (A) open and read a sealed letter belonging to another
   (B) commit vagrancy by loitering in the premises
   (C) commit assault, 3rd degree
   (D) merely intrude upon the property of the owner.

83. Possession by a person of burglar's tools is a felony only if
   (A) found in his possession in the night time
   (B) he is apprehended in the commission of a crime
   (C) he has been previously convicted of possession of burglar's tools
   (D) he has been previously convicted of any crime.

In answering questions 100 to 104 the following definitions of crimes should be applied, bearing in mind that all elements contained in the definition must be present in order to charge a person with that crime:

BURGLARY is the breaking and entering a building with intent to commit some crime therein.

EXTORTION is the obtaining of property from another, with his consent, induced by a wrongful use of force or fear, or under color of official right.

LARCENY is the taking and carrying away of the personal property of another with intent to deprive or defraud the owner of the use and benefit of such property.

ROBBERY is the unlawful taking of the personal property of another from his person or in his presence, by force or violence or by putting him in fear of injury, immediate or future, to his person or property.

84. If A entered B's store during business hours, tied B to a chair and then helped himself to the contents of B's cash register, A upon arrest, should be charged with
   (A) burglary
   (B) extortion
   (C) larceny
   (D) robbery.

85. If A broke the panel of glass in the window of B's store, stepped in and removed some merchandise from the window, he should, upon arrest, be charged with
(A) burglary (C) larceny
(B) extortion (D) robbery.

86. If A, after B had left for the day, found the door of B's store open, walked in, took some merchandise and then left through the same door, he should, upon arrest, be charged with
(A) burglary (C) larceny
(B) extortion (D) robbery.

87. If A, by threatening to report B for failure to pay to the State the full amount of sales tax he had collected from various customers, induced B to give him the contents of his cash register, A should, upon arrest, be charged with
(A) burglary (C) larceny
(B) extortion (D) robbery.

88. If A, on a crowded train, put his hand into B's pocket and removed B's wallet without his knowledge, A should, upon arrest, be charged with
(A) burglary (C) larceny
(B) extortion (D) robbery.

89. The accomplishment of theft or larceny from the person or immediate presence of another in possession thereof by force or intimidation is
(A) swindle (D) burglary
(B) peculation (E) pilfering.
(C) robbery

Correct Answers For The Foregoing Questions

(Please make every effort to answer the questions on your own before looking at these answers. You'll make faster progress by following this rule.)

1. C	12. B	23. D	34. B	45. B	56. C	67. D	78. A
2. C	13. C	24. C	35. B	46. A	57. A	68. D	79. C
3. C	14. A	25. A	36. D	47. C	58. A	69. B	80. D
4. E	15. A	26. A	37. B	48. A	59. A	70. A	81. C
5. A	16. B	27. B	38. B	49. D	60. A	71. C	82. B
6. D	17. A	28. D	39. C	50. A	61. D	72. D	83. D
7. A	18. B	29. D	40. C	51. B	62. C	73. C	84. D
8. D	19. C	30. B	41. B	52. B	63. B	74. D	85. A
9. A	20. B	31. D	42. B	53. D	64. A	75. B	86. C
10. D	21. C	32. B	43. C	54. C	65. A	76. C	87. B
11. D	22. D	33. B	44. B	55. B	66. A	77. D	88. C
							89. C

COURT OFFICER

Previous Exam Questions with Answers Explained

1. A directed verdict is made by a court when
(A) the facts are not disputed (B) the defendant's motion for a directed verdict has been denied (C) there is no question of law involved (D) neither party has moved for a directed verdict

2. Papers on appeal of a case do not include one of the following
(A) summons (B) minutes of trial (C) complaint (D) intermediate motion papers

3. A pleading titled "Smith vs Jones, et al" indicates
(A) two plaintiffs (B) two defendants (C) more than two defendants (D) unknown defendants

4. The basic distinction between the Supreme Court and the County Court of the State of New York is
(A) the Supreme Court may normally try any kind of case (B) the Supreme Court is a court of Record (C) Supreme Court process may be served anywher in the state (D) the County Court has no equity jurisdiction

5. An appeal from the Trial Term of the Supreme Court is taken to
(A) Appellate Division (B) Court of Appeals (C) Appellate Term of Supreme Court (D) the Appellate Term except in capital cases

6. The court in New York County possessing original criminal jurisdiction in felony cases is known as
(A) Court of Special Sessions (B) County Court (C) Court of General Sessions (D) Felony Court

7. A District Attorney makes out a "prima facie" case when
(A) there is proof of guilt beyond a reasonable doubt (B) the evidence is sufficient to convict in the absence of rebutting evidence (C) the prosecution presents more evidence than the defense (D) the defendant fails to take the stand

8. A person is not qualified to act as a trial juror in a criminal action if he or she
(A) has been convicted previously of a misdemeanor (B) is under 21 years of age (C) has scruples against the death penalty (D) does not own property of a value at least $500

9. A court clerk who falsifies a court record commits a (an)
(A) Misdemeanor (B) offense (C) felony (D) no crime but automatically forfeits his tenure

10. Insolent and contemptuous behavior to a judge during a court of record proceeding is punishable as
(A) civil contempt (B) criminal contempt (C) disorderly conduct (D) disorderly person

11. Offering a bribe to a court clerk would <u>not</u> constitute a crime unless
(A) the court clerk accepted the bribe (B) the bribe consisted of money (C) the bribe was given with intent to influence the court clerk in his official functions (D) the court was actually in session

12. When a judge asks the court attendant for a copy of "McKinney's", he wants
(A) Federal Laws (B) Consolidated Laws of N.Y.State (C) Local ordinances
(D) Rules of evidence

13. "37 N.Y.S. (2nd) 49" means
(A) 49th volume (B) 37th page (C) 2nd volume (D) none of the foregoing

14. A writing authorizing one to act for another is known as
(A) verification (B) Power of Attorney (C) a Certification (D) substituted service

15. Statutes which fix the time within which particular actions must be instituted or otherwise be barred, are known as
(A) Statutes of Frauds (B) Exclusionary Acts (C) Statutes of Limitation
(D) Unconsolidated Laws

16. Where a jury has reached a verdict the presence of the defendant is required
(A) in all cases (B) in all criminal cases (C) in civil cases only (D) in felony cases

17. Court Attendants who are members of the Bar
(A) cannot practice law in the county where appointed (B) may have their names listed in the telephone books as attorneys although not permitted to practice law (C) may not appear in any litigation as attorney but may be engaged as Law Consultant (D) may engage in other business activities so long as such activities do not involve the practice of law

18. The basic distinction between an affidavit and a deposition is that
(A) one is sworn (B) the latter is sworn written testimony (C) the former is sworn written testimony (D) the latter is unsigned

19. Arraignment is best defined as
(A) the placing of the accused in custody (B) the opportunity of giving bail (C) the calling of the accused before the court to answer a charge
(D) the justification for an arrest

20. Generally the plaintiff furnishes the court with copies of the summons and pleadings with indications in the margin which allegations are admitted and which are denied. These papers are known as
(A) Supplemental pleadings (B) marked pleadings (C) alternative pleadings
(D) amended pleadings

21. A verdict consisting of answers to specific questions of fact submitted to the jury and the court for the purpose of determining which party as a matter of law is entitled to judgment is called
(A) general verdict (B) sealed verdict (C) special verdict (D) directed verdict

22. Jurisdiction "in rem" requires jurisdiction over
(A) persons (B) property (C) locations (D) chattels

23. The subject matter or property with which the action is concerned is known as the
(A) fee simple (B) freehold (C) res (D) abstract of title

24. The number of Judicial Districts comprising the 2nd Judicial Department is
(A) 1 (B) 2 (C) 3 (D) 4

25. The number of Judicial Departments in the State of New York is
(A) 2 (B) 3 (C) 4 (D) 5

26. Matters which are not triable by a jury in the Supreme Court are heard at
(A) Trial Term (B) Special Term (C) Motion Term (D) Special Proceedings

27. An "ex parte" motion is one which
(A) requires the adversary to appear and be heard (B) is made by the Court in the absence of either party to the litigation (C) is made without notice to an adversary (D) is made by a person not a party to a litigation

28. The best definition of a motion is
(A) an application for an order (B) an application for a dismissal (C) the right to introduce evidence (D) an application to start a suit

29. An attorney may place the case upon the court calendar for trial by filing with the clerk of the court
(A) summons (B) complaint (C) notice of motion (D) note of issue

30. A court order issued now and made effective as of an earlier date is known as
(A) "nunc pro tunc" (B) laches (C) ipso facto (D) interlocutory

31. A reply is served if
(A) there are inconsistencies in the plaintiff's complaint (B) corrections in the plaintiff's complaint are to be made (C) the defendant sets up a counterclaim in his answer (D) the plaintiff intends to set up counterclaims

32. When counsel in a trial takes "exception" to a court ruling, it means that
(A) an adjournment is required before additional evidence is introduced
(B) he formally objects to the court ruling (C) he withdraws his original objection (D) he wishes to give reasons for his original objections

33. Replevin is an action to
(A) recover for personal injuries (B) eject a trespasser (C) recover damages for breach of contract (D) recover personal property

34. Direct appeals from the lower courts are taken to the Court of Appeals where
(A) actions involve constitutional questions (B) the rights of children are involved (C) exceptions to court rulings have been formally recorded
(D) non-residents are involved

35. The term "amicus curiae"
(A) of the same kind (B) friend of the court (C) rebuttal evidence
(D) burden of proof

36. The right of the state to take private property for public use is known as
(A) ejectment (B) easement (C) eminent domain (D) franchise

37. The purpose of the "Affidavit of Service" on the back of a summons is to
(A) verify the personal service of summons upon an individual or a corporation (B) validate the nature of the action (C) make effective the date of the commencement of the action (D) stop the running of the statute of limitations

38. A verification of a pleading is
(A) the same as an "affidavit of service" (B) a verification that the papers have been properly prepared and served (C) an affidavit verifying the facts or contents of a pleading (D) the formal opening of a suit

39. In a civil action, the right to open and close a case is accorded the party who
(A) is not required to offer any evidence (B) defends the action (C) brings the action (D) has the affirmative burden of proof

40. According to the Civil Practice Act, the Court may direct a trial of the issues of fact before a referee where
(A) the plaintiff is an infant (B) there are difficult questions of law involved (C) the trial will require the examination of a long account not involving difficult questions of law (D) the facts are so complicated as to require the application of different laws.

41. If the summons and complaint is served in an action for money only, a notice may be indorsed on the summons setting forth the sum for which judgment will be entered upon default. The purpose of this notice is to
(A) permit the clerk instead of the court to enter judgment in case of default (B) assign the case to the court having proper jurisdiction over the amount stated in the summons (C) permit the court to become aware of the nature of the action (D) expedite the classification of the case

42. If a person dies intestate, his property will be distributed by
(A) an administrator (B) an executor (C) a testator (D) a special guardian

43. Prosecution of all crimes in County Courts must be by
(A) Petition (B) Information (C) Summons (D) Indictment

44. The allegation made to a magistrate that a person has been guilty of a designated crime is known as
(A) Petition (B) Information (C) affidavit (D) Arraignment

45. A jury verdict in a criminal case must be returned by
(A) at least 5/6th of the jurors (B) at least 10 out of twelve jurors (C) the majority of the jurors (D) all the jurors

46. "Polling the jury" means
(A) challenging the jury because of bias (B) requiring each juror to declare what his individual verdict is before it is legally recorded. (C) selecting the jury (D) waiver of trial by jury

47. Of the following laws, the one which does not provide for courts and their jurisdiction, is
(A) Code of Criminal Procedure (B) Penal Law (C) Judiciary Law (D) Civil Practice Act

48. A "challenge to the array" is
(A) challenging a juror "peremptorily" (B) challenging a juror "for cause"
(C) a challenge made "to the favor" (D) a challenge to the entire panel of jurors.

49. Rules of procedure as to selection, drawing, and empanelling of jurors are made by
(A) Appellate Division of 1st and 2nd Departments (B) the County Clerks
(C) the County Jury Board (D) Court on Judiciary

50. The main distinction between riot and unlawful assembly is
(A) disturbance of peace (B) power to make good the threats (C) number of persons (D) threats

51. After cross-examination is completed, the original attorney may ask questions to clarify certain points in the testimony elicited on cross-examination. This examination is called
(A) direct (B) indirect (C) re-direct (D) re-cross - examination

52. Jurors may be excluded from the court room during
(A) testimony regarding the character of the defendant (B) argument of a question concerning the admissibility of evidence (C) motions at the end of the case (D) the examination of expert witnesses

53. A default judgment should not be entered by the clerk of the court if the action is
(A) on a contract for a liquidated amount (B) on a contract to recover a sum of money although not fixed but capable of being ascertained by computation only (C) for the value of property delivered (D) for damages to property due to negligence

54. "A thousand mistakes of every description would be avoided if people did not base their conclusions upon premises furnished by others, take as established fact what is only a possibility and accept as a constantly recurring incident what has been observed only once." Of the following this quotation best supports the statement that a common failing of many persons is
(A) acceptance of unverified assumptions as fact (B) confidence in their own powers of observation (C) failure to mentally record things they have observed (D) prejudice in their observations

55. "In law enforcement work a new man may find himself confronted by the most difficult situations before he has fairly started work. The most perplexing test is as likely to come to the law enforcement officer on his first assignment as it is to the veteran". This quotation implies that the duties which a law enforcement officer is called upon to perform are determined chiefly by
(A) circumstances which cannot be controlled (B) his success on his first assignment (C) the manner with which he masters unpredictable problems
(D) the initiative he displays in overcoming difficult assignments

56. Subject to certain conditions, the one of the following persons who may be permitted to testify in a criminal case without being sworn, is
(A) an adult over 70 years of age (B) a justice of a court of record
(C) a court attendant who witnessed a criminal contempt in court (D) a child under 12 years.

57. The distinction between a criminal contempt and a civil contempt is
(A) one occurs in a court of record (B) one is punishable by jail (C) one is remedial in nature (D) one occurs in a criminal court

58. A witness who has conscientious scruples against taking an oath
(A) shall not be permitted to testify (B) may solemnly affirm to tell the truth instead of taking an oath (C) may testify if the testimony is corroborated by further evidence (D) may testify only in special proceedings

59. If after the service of summons, the plaintiff desires to change his attorney, it shall be necessary to
(A) first compensate the first attorney for his services (B) obtain the permission of the defendant (C) get the attorney's consent (D) either get the attorney's consent or make application to court for the change

60. The one of the following is not a pleading
(A) complaint (B) summons (C) reply (D) answer

61. The personal appearance of the defendant in an appellate court is
(A) not required (B) required only in civil cases (C) required if there is reasonable doubt as to conviction (D) required only in capital cases.

62. In legal parlance, an "information" is
(A) an informer's information to the District Attorney (B) an allegation to a magistrate that a person has committed a designated crime (C) in the nature of a bill of particulars (D) the report of a grand jury after an investigation of crime

63. No jury trials are permitted in matrimonial actions except
(A) in annulment actions where physical incapacity is charged (B) where custody of children are involved (C) where adultery is an issue in divorce proceedings (D)where both parties consent

64. The venue in an action refers to
(A) place of trial (B) the amount of money damages sought (C) the nature of the action (D) probable duration of the trial

65. If a court stenographer insists upon having a witness repeat parts of the testimony
(A) the attorney should dictate the testimony to the stenographer (B) the court attendant should request the witness to repeat the testimony (C) the court should warn the stenographer not to interrupt the questioning (D) the witness should repeat the testimony

66. Under the rules of court procedure, during the summation, counsel may
(A) utilize as much time as is necessary for him to conclude his case
(B) sit during the summation if it is expected to take longer than one hour
(C) refer his remarks to matters outside the record so long as they are not unduly prejudicial (D) not draw inferences from the evidence given

67. A statute is best defined as
(A) a legislative enactment (B) a legal prosecution (C) adjective law
(D) a codification of principles and procedure

68.In the case of a disagreement in a jury
(A) the opinion of the jury foreman shall be the jury's verdict (B) a quotient verdict is obtained (C) court may order a partial retrial if the jury's disagreement was on a separate phase of the litigation (D) the court dismisses the jury and a retrial is ordered without a jury.

69.When the judge enters the court room
(A) every one is directed to rise (B) only the litigants are directed to rise (C) all except court employees are directed to rise (D) all except court employees and women are directed to rise.

70.A statute of limitations places a restriction on
(A) the maximum penalty that may be imposed (B) the time within which an action should be commenced (C) the number of causes of action that may be pleaded at one time (D) the amount and quality of evidence that may be introduced

71.According to the Code of Criminal Procedure, the one of the following who is not a peace officer, is
(A) court attendant (B) criminal investigator attached to District Attorney's office in Westchester County (C) State Parole officer (D) civilian employee of State Prison

72.The maximum age limit for jurors is
(A) 60 years (B) 65 years (C) 70 years (D) 75 years

73.A summons is usually attached to
(A) complaint (B) answer (C) reply (D) counterclaim

74.A case which has been adjourned is
(A) stricken from the calendar (B) postponed for a time (C) dismissed without prejudice (D) tried without a jury

75.In an ex parte proceeding
(A) both sides are heard before the court without a jury (B) each side is heard separately before the court on different days (C) only one side is heard without notice to the other side (D) special relief is sought by both parties in judge's chambers

76.An objection to a juror for which no reason is given is called
(A) an exception (B) peremptory challenge (C) challenge for cause (D) challenge to the favor

77.A trial jury consisting of 12 persons is called a
(A) struck jury (B) special jury (C) grand jury (D) petit jury

78.An answer to a complaint may not contain
(A) denials (B) defenses (C) counterclaims (D) reply

79.A fictitious name used by a person is called
(A) alibi (B) alias (C) facsimile (D) alienist

80.A Youthful Offender is one who is
(A) under 16 years of age (B) under 18 years of age (C) between 16 and 21 years of age (D) between 16 and 18 years of age

81. The official legal publication for the First Judicial Department is the
(A) Journal of Commerce (B) Law Reporter (C) Law Journal (D) City Record

82. The one of the following which is not prohibited on Sunday, is
(A) jury trial (B) court receiving a jury verdict (C) service of summons in a civil action (D) arrest on a misdemeanor warrant without court endorsement

83. A "recidivist" is
(A) mentally incompetent (B) incapable of committing crime (C) a psychopath (D) an habitual offender

84. A "writ of certiorari" is a legal process for the purpose of
(A) reviewing the decision or ruling of an administrative officer (B) reviewing the ruling of a lower court (C) compelling a public officer to perform a duty imposed by law (D) correcting an error or amending the allegations in a pleading

85. A law which increases the punishment for a crime after it has been committed, is called
(A) ipso facto (B) de facto (C) ex post facto (D) ex officio

86. An indictment cannot be found without the concurrence of at least
(A) 12 jurors (B) 14 jurors (C) 16 jurors (D) 23 jurors

87. An examination on the "voir dire" is an examination to
(A) determine the admissibility of documentary evidence (B) determine whether a witness is qualified to testify (C) determine whether the court has proper jurisdiction of the cause of action (D) determine whether the cause of action is outlawed because of the Statute of Limitations

88. The "Statute of Frauds"
(A) defines the several degrees of larceny (B) requires certain contracts to be written (C) requires written instruments to be witnessed and signed (D) makes contracts made by minors voidable

89. The "Code of Criminal Procedure" is
(A) contained in the Civil Practice Act of New York State (B) defines crimes and their punishments (C) a uniform and comprehensive system of criminal procedure (D) a law which regulates criminal procedures uniformly throughout the United States

90. In a civil trial, an exception by counsel is made
(A) after the case is submitted to the jury (B) after an adverse ruling by the court (C) to the introduction of evidence (D) after a contrary jury verdict.

91. The action of a judge in excusing a juror who has been challenged by counsel for the defendant in a criminal case is known as
(A) withdrawal of juror (B) mistrial (C) timely challenge (D) discharge of juror

92. A "mistrial" motion would least likely be granted where
(A) a motion for the withdrawal of a juror is granted (B) a prejudicial remark is made by the court against one of the parties (C) one of the jurors is ill and unable to appear for a continuation of the trial (D) a question is answered by a witness before counsel has had an opportunity to make his objection.

93. "Mayhem" is a form of
(A) arson (B) maiming (C) negligence (D) homicide

94. In the trial of a felony action, the court charges the jury
(A) before People's summation (B) before the defendant's summation (C) after the summation by both parties (D) before the summation of either party.

95. The State Judicial Council
(A) publishes court decisions (B) advises Courts on needed changes in procedures (C) assigns judges to the various courts (D) conducts proceedings as to the qualifications of judges

96. A warrant, order, or process by which a court directs a ministerial officer to take a person to prison or to detain him there is called a
(A) commitment (B) stipulation (C) warrant (D) certificate

97. In legal parlance an "alienist" is one who
(A) has entered this country illegally (B) constantly changes his name
(C) specializes in mental disorders (D) studies the causes of crime

98. The term "obiter dictum" refers to
(A) an answer of a witness which is not responsive to the question asked
(B) the opinion of a court (C) burden of proof (D) a jury's verdict

99. The "polling of a jury" is exercised
(A) before the jury is empannelled (B) after the jurors are sworn (C) after the verdict (D) after the judge's charge

100. A "certificate of reasonable doubt" is an instrument which is intended to
(A) stay execution of judgment because there is reasonable doubt whether the judgment should stand (B) discharge the defendant because of conflicting evidence (C) commute the sentence of a prisoner (D) release a prisoner on a pardon

101. A "ballistics expert" is an expert witness called to testify in connection with
(A) handwriting evidence (B) firearms evidence (C) fingerprints (D) counterfeiting

102. In the trial of a felony action, the jurors must be warned by the court after each adjournment, that
(A) they shall not be separated (B) they shall not converse among themselves
(C) they shall not form any opinion as to the case until the cause is submitted to them (D) they shall not communicate with other persons.

103. Of the following "persons" the one which cannot sue in person, is
(A) a corporation (B) a administrator (C) a poor person (D) executor

104. A person accused of crime may be permitted to testify before a grand jury provided
(A) he has not been arrested (B) it is a capital crime (C) he is a citizen
(D) he files a request to be heard

105. When two defendants are jointly indicted, they can be tried separately provided
(A) they may be convicted of different crimes (B) one has confessed (C) there is a similarity of the offenses charged (D) the court approves

106. If the court deems the evidence insufficient to warrant a conviction of one or more of the crimes in the indictment, it may advise the jury to acquit the defendant thereof. In this connection, the jury
(A) need not follow the recommendation until evidence on both sides has been introduced (B) must follow the advice (C) may disregard the advice if it believes otherwise (D) may accept the advice on condition that a new trial be ordered.

107. In a criminal action, "impeaching a witness" means
(A) compelling a witness to testify (B) rejecting a witness as incompetent (C) attacking the credibility of a witness (D) holding a witness for perjury

108. A prosecution for murder must be commenced within
(A) 5 years (B) 10 years (C) 20 years (D) any period of time after the act

109. The function of the Appellate Term of the Supreme Court is to pass upon appeals from the
(A) Court of Special Sessions (B) Municipal and City Courts of New York City (C) Trial Term of the Supreme Court (D) Special Term of the Supreme Court

110. No guilty plea can be entered by the defendant charged with
(A) murder, 2nd degree (B) treason (C) rape (D) conspiracy

111. To say that testimony is unimpeachable means that it is
(A) is easily refuted (B) not competent (C) irrelevant (D) irrebuttable

112. The number of justices in the highest court of the state is
(A) 5 (B) 6 (C) 7 (D) 9

113. A subpoena duces tecum cannot be issued
(A) to produce original hospital records (B) in a criminal case (C) to produce corporation records (D) unless signed by a judge

114. Barratry is a subject which relates to
(A) guns and bullets (B) inciting groundless law suits (C) disbarment of attorneys (D) contract actions outlawed because of statute of limitations

115. The basic distinction between a tort and a crime is that
(A) crimes are willful or intentional (B) tort is an infringements of man's rights (C) a tort is a private wrong (D) a tort is a wrong against society

116. A party to a felony crime is
(A) either a principal or an accomplice (B) either a principal or an accessory (C) a principal only (D) either an accomplice or an accessory

117. A confession is not admissible as evidence if obtained
(A) while under arrest and without warning (B) by deception (C) by coercion (D) by a private person

118. In legal parlance, an"execution" is
(A) a decree appointing an executor of a decedent's estate (B) a summons (C) a court process directing the satisfaction of a judgment (D) the service of a warrant

119. The least accurate of the following statements, is
(A) a panel is a group of jurors summoned to report for duty at a term of court (B) a criminal action is brought in the name of the People of the State of New York (C) the term "veniremen" means place of trial (D) the term "res" means a thing.

120. The proceedings by which private property is taken for public use upon the payment of just compensation are known as
(A) Supplementary Proceedings (B) Special Proceedings (C) Dispossess Proceedings (D) Condemnation Proceedings

121. The final determination by a judge that a sum of money is owed to one of the parties in a law suit is called
(A) a judgment (B) a decision (C) a verdict (D) a report

122. A defendant on the trial of a felony cannot be convicted on the testimony of an accomplice unless
(A) such testimony is corroborated by other evidence (B) the accomplice is amenable to justice also (C) the accomplice is a relative of the defendant (D) the crime is other than a sex crime

123. The term "jurist" means most nearly
(A) jurat (B) jailer (C) jury (D) judge

124. A witness is incompetent to testify in a civil action
(A) if he has an interest in the litigation (B) if he is an atheist (C) if he has been convicted of a felony (D) in none of the foregoing instances.

125. The person named in a will to carry out its terms is known as the
(A) executor (B) administrator (C) testamentary guardian (D) administrator, c.t.a..

126. A plaintiff is to a complaint as a defendant is to
(A) a rebuttal (B) a reply (C) an answer (D) a demurrage.

127. The one of the following which represents the proper sequence which a court case may follow is
A. (1) Special Term of the Supreme Court; (2) Court of Appeals; (3)Appellate Division of the Supreme Court; (4) Supreme Court of U.S.
B. (1) Trial Term of the Supreme Court; (2) Appellate Division of the Supreme Court; (3) Supreme Court of the United States; (4) Court of Appeals.
C. (1) Special Term of the Supreme Court; (2) Appellate Division of the Supreme Court; (3) Court of Appeals.
D. (1) Appellate Term of the Supreme Court; (2) Appellate Division of the Supreme Court; (3) Supreme Court of the United States.

128. A complaint is to an action as a petition is to
(A) the Congress (B) an indictment (C) a proceeding (D) the Grand Jury.

129. A plaintiff is to a defendant as a petitioner is to
(A) a prosecutor (B) a respondent (C) a reversioner (D) a remainderman.

130. A person whose negligence has caused damage to another is called a (A) tortfeasor (B) decedent (C) testator (D) demurer

131. A "true bill" means most nearly (A) a bailment (B) a bill of particulars (C) a certified statement of taxable costs and disbursements (D) an indictment.

132. A restraining order issued by a court is called (A) a subpoena (B) an injunction (C) a mandamus (D) a rescission.

133. Appeals from convictions for murder in the first degree go in the first instance to the
(A) Appellate Term of the Supreme Court (B) County Court (C) Court of Appeals (D) Appellate Division of the Supreme Court.

134. A person who dies in New York leaving a will disposing of real property in New Jersey is said to have died (A) interstate (B) intestate (C) testate (D) intrastate.

135. The memorandum of a judge explaining the reasons for his decision in a case is called
(A) judgment (B) opinion (C) verdict (D) sentence.

136. A person appointed by a court to represent the interests of a minor litigant is called a
(A) guardian ad litem (B) guardian in socage (C) testamentary guardian (D) temporary guardian.

137. Under New York State Law, a woman
(A) can be required to serve on the Grand Jury but cannot be required to serve on a trial jury (B) cannot serve on a trial jury (C) cannot be required to serve either on a trial jury or on a Grand Jury (D) cannot serve on a Grand Jury.

138. When a case is appealed, the party appealing is called the
(A) plaintiff (B) respondent (C) relator (D) appellant.

139. If a person appears at the Appellate Division before such court has convened, with a notice to serve as a juror, the Court Attendant
(A) should advise him to wait until all the Justices have arrived (B) should refer him to the Central Jury room of such court (C) should advise him that there are no jury trials held in such court (D) should swear him in as a juror.

140. If an attempt is made to free the defendant at a murder trial by the use of automatic firearms, the Court Attendant's primary obligation is
(A) to handcuff himself to the defendant to prevent the latter's escape
(B) to protect the spectators and court officials from possible harm (C) to commit to memory a good description of those assisting in the delivery of the defendant (D) to advise the spectators and court officials not to give way to panic.

141. A misdemeanor
(A) is always a crime (B) may, under certain circumstances, be a crime
(C) is punishable by a fine or by imprisonment, not both (D) is none of the foregoing.

142. Legal proceedings concerning the property of a deceased person are ordinarily held in the
(A) Supreme Court (B) Surrogate's Court (C) County Court (D) Court of Claims

143. A "folio" as used in the measurement of the length of a document in legal or court work consists of
(A) one page (B) 100 words (C) two pages (D) 6 paragraphs

144. The best attitude for a court attendant to assume toward the public is to
(A) be always kind and pleasant, ready to assist but never argumentative
(B) be very friendly and cultivate all the acquaintances possible as they may prove useful in the future .(C) hold himself apart, and assume a superior haughty manner as the public should be taught to look up to and respect a representative of the law. (D) be understanding and sympathetic

145. The legal term used to describe all the means by which the truth regarding any alleged matter of fact is established or disproved in court is
(A) Testimony (B) Exhibit (C) Evidence (D) Proof

146. A suspended sentence is
(A) an indeterminate sentence (B) a postponed sentence (C) a decreased sentence (D) cumulative sentence

147. The improper doing of an act which one might lawfully do is known as
(A) misfeasance (B) malfeasance (C)nonfeasance (D) mala prohibitum

148. A proceeding in the Surrogates' Court is usually commenced by the serving and filing of
(A) a petition (B) a summons (C) letters testamentary (D) letters of administration

149. A bench warrant is a warrant
(A) authorizing the search of premises in which stolen goods are believed to be stored (B) for the seizure of personal property to satisfy a judgment
(C) issued by a judge when a defendant forfeits his bail for non-appearance
(D) issued for the arrest of a person who has disturbed the court proceedings

150. If a witness under a severe cross-examination becomes indignant and engages the attorney in a heated argument, a court attendant should
(A) await any action the judge may take (B) order the witness to be more respectful (C) try to attract the attention of the witness (D) call for assistance

151. If a spectator in a court room faints and falls to the floor, he should be
(A) placed in a chair in a sitting position (B) laid on a flat surface with his head lower than his body (C) picked up and removed to a hospital
(D) placed on his stomach with his head turned to the side.

152. Several of the spectators in a court room get into a fight and one of them is seriously injured. As a court attendant, the first thing you should do is to
(A) get the facts and make a report (B) call an ambulance or a physician
(C) hold the people who engaged in the fight and arrest them for creating a public niusance. (D) evacuate the court room

153. A true legal copy of an official court record is called a
(A) facsimile (B) transcript (C) certificate (D) folio

154. The proof before the surrogate that a will is in fact the last will and testament of a deceased person is legally called
(A) de bonis non (B) citation (C) probate (D) inquest

155. A supplement to a will containing something which the testator added after the original will had been made is called a
(A) codicil (B) appendage (C) novation (D) attestation

156. The legal instrument which evidences the transfer of ownership of real property from one person to another is called a
(A) deed (B) bill of sale (C) stipulation (D) mortgage

157. A summary of the essential points of a court record is called an
(A) abstract (B) amendment (C) abeyance (D) opinion

158. A gift of real property to another by a last will and testament is legally called a
(A) bailment (B) bequest (C) devise (D) legacy

159. Evidence which the law considers to be sufficient to establish the truth of some disputed issue in a legal proceeding unless rebutted or satisfactorily explained by opposite evidence is best defined as evidence which is
(A) res gestae (B) prima facie (C) ex parte (D) conclusive

160. In the citation "People ex rel. Tully v. Fallon, 77 N.Y.S. 292" the abbreviation 'ex rel' means
(A) at the information of (B) in the matter of (C) the respondent
(D) and the following

161. When the doors of a court are closed and only the persons involved in a case are admitted, the proceeding is called
(A) ex parte (B) in camera (C) coram nobis (D) extra judicial

162. To avoid the process of the courts by hiding or leaving the jurisdiction in a clandestine manner is known as
(A) abstention (B) escrow (C) abscond (D) distrain

163. The removal or cessation of a nuisance is known as
(A) abrogation (B) avoidance (C) abridgment (D) abatement

164. That branch of the law which provides procedure for enforcing or maintaining legal rights is called
(A) civil (B) adjective (C) chancery (D) substantive

165. Statement of fact made by a party in a pleading setting forth what he expects to prove is called
(A) assertion (B) affirmation (C) allegation (D) contention

166. Expression which is used to designate a judgment or proceeding dated as of the present but having the effect as of a former date is known as
(A) lis pendens (B) a priori (C) nuncupative (D) nunc pro tunc

167. A book or paper in which is entered a brief resume of all proceedings in a court is called
(A) register (B) docket (C) citation (D) precis

168. Act of going before a competent officer or a court by a person who has executed an instrument and declaring that he has executed such instrument is known as
(A) subornation (B) verification (C) acknowledgment (D) conveyance

169. An obligation of record entered into before a court or officer with condition to do some particular act is known as
(A) undertaking (B) recognizance (C) escrow (D) entrapment

170. Correction of a pleading is done by
(A) amendment (B) amplification (C) novation (D) subrogation

171. A term sometimes used in medical jurisprudence to designate a mercy killing or painless death in the case of an incurable disease is
(A) genocide (B) uxoricide (C) paranoia (D) euthanasia

172. Construing the terms of a written instrument such as a will as near as possible to the intention of the party making such instrument is known as the doctrine of
(A) cy pres (B) res judicata (C) obiter dictum (D) sine qua non.

173. A system of criminal identification based upon the written description of a wanted person is known as
(A) modus operandi (B) portrait parle (C) graphology (D) anthropometry

174. An endorsement signed by the foreman of the grand jury that an indictment has been found on the concurrence of at least twelve grand jurors is known as
(A) a presentment (B) a true bill (C) a commission (D) an ascertainment

175. An allegation made to a magistrate that a person has been guilty of some designated crime is known as
(A) a charge (B) an inquest (C) an incrimination (D) an information

176. A phrase used in criminal cases to indicate the equal guilt of persons involved in the commission of a crime is
(A) pari delicto (B) corpus delicti (C) pari materia (D) crimen falsi

177. A person who, after the commission of a felony, aids the offender to escape arrest, knowing that such offender has committed a felony, is defined in the Penal Law as
(A) a principal (B) an accomplice (C) an accessory (D) a conspirator

178. A term used in law to describe licentious art or literature is
(A) pornography (B) amercement (C) masochism (D) didacticism

179. Law in its regular course of administration is known as
(A) constitutional law (B) adjective law (C) due process of law (D) substantive law

180. The appellation given to a witness in a criminal case whose testimony is necessary is
(A) competent (B) corroborative (C) privileged (D) material

181. An agreement to conceal a crime or to abstain from prosecuting a crime for some consideration is known in the Penal Law as
(A) compounding a crime (B) compromising a crime (C) obstruction of justice (D) misprision of crime

182. The one of the following words which means a wrongdoer is
(A) litigant (B) complainant (C) tortfeasor (D) prosecutor.

183. A paper served on the clerk of the court to have a civil case placed on the calendar for trial
(A) note of issue (B) lis pendens (C) order of trial (D) motion for trial

184. Plaintiff is to a Defendant as an Appellant is to
(A) an Appeller (B) a Petitioner (C) a Relator (D) Respondent

185. Felony is to an Indictment as a Misdemeanor is to
(A) a Presentment (B) a Complaint (C) an Information (D) a Summons

186. A provisional remedy obtainable prior to serving a summons in a civil action is
(A) attachment (B) arbitration (C) sequestration (D) res judicata

187. A proceeding after judgment to levy upon wages, earnings or salary of a judgment debtor
(A) replevin (B) attachment (C) garnishee (D) supros

188. Substitution of one person in the place of another with respect to rights and duties
(A) subrogation (B) subornation (C) rescission (D) novation

189. Verdict in which a jury is instructed to find the facts only, leaving the judgment to the court
(A) general (B) special (C) sealed (D) compromise

190. Defendant is to Counterclaim as Plaintiff is to
(A) Answer (B) Denial (C) Reply (D) Complaint

191. A statement made or an act done which amounts to a prior acknowledgment by one of the parties to an action that one of the facts relevant to the issues is not as he now claims
(A) confession (B) admission (C) tort (D) presumption

192. A Summons is to the Supreme Court as a Citation is to the
(A) Municipal Court (B) Court of Claims (C) City Court (D) Surrogates Court

193. A person who makes application for a writ of habeas corpus is called
(A) appellant (B) complainant (C) relator (D) affiant

194. Action of a court permitting a person convicted of a crime his freedom under supervision without sending him to prison
(A) parole (B) commutation (C) pardon (D) probation

195. An agreement signed by the opposing attorneys during a trial
(A) admission (B) compromise (C) stipulation (D) accordance

196. A judgment entered in consequence of the non-appearance of a party in a civil action is called
(A) interlocutory (B) declaratory (C) non-suit (D) default

197. That which precludes a person from alleging or denying a fact in consequence of his own previous act or allegation of a contrary tenor is called
(A) estoppel (B) escrow (C) abatement (D) escheat

198. The papers which contain the names of the jurors who are being impanelled
(A) exhibits (B) allonges (C) ballots (D) drafts

199. Recognition which a judge officially takes of some fact without requiring evidence in proof thereof
(A) legal presumption (B) judicial notice (C) judicial agreement (D) court ruling

200. Sentences imposed by a court on a defendant convicted of several crimes but with the provision that the sentences shall be served at the same time
(A) consecutive (B) cumulative (C) concurrent (D) intermittent

201. A person appointed by the court to hear and report or to hear and determine facts in dispute
(A) receiver (B) executor (C) referee (D) administrator

202. The voluntary coming into court of a party to a civil action either as the plaintiff or the defendant
(A) arraignment (B) appearance (C) acknowledgment (D) subpoena

203. An inquiry pursuant to a court order into the extent of a judgment debtor's assets
(A) supplementary proceedings (B) contempt proceedings (C) provisional remedy (D) discovery and inspection

204. A legal instrument discharging one party from liability to another party
(A) release (B) judgment (C) liquidation (D) avoidance

205. The science of fingerprint identification
(A) ballistics (B) semantics (C) dactyloscopy (D) anthropometry

206. To pledge personal property without delivering its possession to the pledgee
(A) encumbrance (B) hypothecation (C) filiation (D) bailment

207. A designation given to a crime punishable by imprisonment in a state's prison
(A) malicious (B) lascivious (C) turpitude (D) infamous

208. The inducement which incites or stimulates a person to commit a criminal act
(A) intent (B) deliveration (C) premeditation (D) motive

209. The clause in a statute which reads, "The People of the State of New York, represented in Senate and Assembly, do enact as follows," is called the
(A) proviso clause (B) purview clause (C) preamble clause (D) enacting clause

210. Among the following, a law requiring that a particular instrument be acknowledged is best complied with by a statement at the bottom of such instrument signed by a duly authorized notary public that
(A) "On the first day of July, 1948, the above named person appeared before me and subscribed his name hereto in my presence." (B) "Subscribed and sworn to before me this first day of July, 1948." (C) "I, John Doe, a notary public of the State of New York, do hereby certify and declare that the foregoing instrument was executed and subscribed in my presence on the first day of July, 1948." (D) "On the first day of July, 1948 before me came John Smith to me known to be the individual described in and who executed the foregoing instrument and acknowledged that he executed the same."

211. Among the following, in drafting a statute or rule that is to affect persons who have reached their majority, the most accurate terminology would be: "The provisions hereof shall be applicable to all persons
(A) who have passed their 21st birthday (B) over 21 years of age (C) over twenty years of age (D) twenty-one years of age or over

212. If directed to draft a "saving clause" to be included in a proposed statute, the one of the following that could be most appropriately used as a model is
(A) "The commissioner shall have the power to adopt, promulgate, amend or rescind such rules, regulations or orders as he may deem necessary or proper to effectuate the purpose of this act." (B) "The provisions of this section shall apply to all pending and future proceedings." (C) "If any provisions of this section shall be held invalid, the validity of the remainder of the section shall not be affected thereby." (D) "The provisions of this section shall not be applicable to any federal, state, municipal or other government agency or public authority."

213. Where a New York statute requires five days notice of a hearing to be held at 10 A.M. on June 11, there is sufficient compliance if such notice is served prior to but not later than
(A) the close of business on June 6 (B) 10 A.M. on June 6 (C) midnight on June 5 (D) the close of business on June 5

214. In selecting a jury, the parties to the litigation have a certain number of peremptory challenges. The word "peremptory" means most nearly
(A) arbitrary (B) absolute (C) preliminary (D) inalienable

215. "The testator, at the time of attestation, must tell the witnesses that the document is his will and his signature must be visible to them." The word attestation means most nearly
(A) subscription (B) execution (C) authentication (D) exemplification

216. Originally seizin was the basis upon which real property actions rested. The term seizin means most nearly
(A) inheritance (B) purchase (C) capture (D) possession

217. "The court rendered an interlocutory decree." The term "interlocutory" means
(A) intermediate (B) temporary (C) uniting (D) commingling

218. A "per curiam" opinion is
(A) a memorandum opinion (B) an opinion by the court as a whole (C) a dissenting opinion (D) an unpublished opinion

DIRECTIONS: Each of the terms in Column I #219-224 is generally associated with one of the matters listed in Column II. On the line indicated in Column I, print the letter from Column II with which each item is best associated.

219. ultra vires	A. legal authority
220. stare decisis	B. personal responsibility
221. pari delicto	C. judicial decision
222. obiter dicta	D. statutory construction
223. res adjudicata	
224. injuria sine damno	

225. A fee simple is
(A) a schedule of fees (B) an unrestricted estate of inheritance (C) interest on a fee (D) land held of another in fee (E) reserved rent

226. "A wrong is not presumed" means most nearly
(A) the crime rate is a poor index of the amount of immorality in a community (B) one cannot presume that a man has done wrong just because he has committed a crime (C) hard cases make bad law (D) one wrong does not excuse another (E) a man is innocent until he is found guilty

227. A detailed statement of the plaintiff's cause of action is called a bill of
(A) particulars (B) interpleader (C) review (D) attainder

228. A guardian ad litem is a guardian for
(A) the suit (B) all purposes (C) the purpose of conserving real property (D) the purpose of representing a corporation

229. The fundamental basis for allowing people to be free on bail is
(A) the prevention of overcrowding in prisons (B) the centralization of administrative responsibility in criminal cases (C) the detection of violations of the law (D) the simplification of judicial procedures (E) the prevention of punishment before trial

230. The most important reason among the following for having a jury consist of a number of persons is that
(A) in numbers there is strength (B) no one person is equipped to render valid opinions (C) justice is essentially a matter of majority opinion (D) group opinions are generally less subject to error (E) any person has the right to be tried by a jury of his peers

231. The principal function of a grand jury is to
(A) question witnesses in certain types of criminal cases (B) replace the prosecuting attorney in certain types of cases (C) try important public officials (D) report on methods for the improvement of legal processes (E) review the acts of petit juries

232. An instrument under seal issued by a corporation as security for a loan is called the
(A) debenture (B) stock certificate (C) indenture (D) certificate of debt (E) negotiable instrument

233. The principal object of the Penal Law is to
(A) act as a deterrent to persons who are criminally inclined (B) make people understand that crime does not pay (C) define crimes and prescribe punishment (D) establish police departments in cities of the state (E) provide for the establishment of the criminal courts in New York State

234. The seizure and taking into custody of the Court of the property of a party to a civil action is called
(A) certiorari (B) search warrant (C) attachment (D) mandamus (E) injunction

235. That system of law which does not rest for its authority upon acts passed by the legislature is called
(A) statutory law (B) civil law (C) common law (D) codified law (E) Roman law

236. The statutory proceeding commenced by a landlord to remove a tenant from certain premises is called
(A) ejectment (B) summary judgment (C) supplementary proceedings (D) summary proceedings (E) removal proceedings

237. The opinions of witnesses are usually not admissible in evidence except in the case of experts, because
(A) opinions of ordinary witnesses are quite valuable (B) one of the jury's or court's functions, ordinarily, is to draw inference from the facts testified to (C) opinions of experts are of little value (D) such opinions prolong trials

238. As an attendant assigned to guard the door in a criminal court where an important robbery case is on trial, a man whom you know not to be a police officer, approaches and requests admission. In speaking with him you observe that he has a revolver in his overcoat pocket. You should
(A) refuse to admit him (B) summon another court attendant and search him (C) ask him to identify himself (D) refuse him admittance and call the matter to the attention of the detective who is nearby

239. You are an attendant in charge of a prison pen in which there are a large number of men awaiting trial for felony. One of them falls to the floor and cries out that he has been poisoned. You should
(A) open the door of the pen and, with the assistance of another attendant, remove him (B) summon other attendants to guard the pen while you take him to the doctor's office (C) make him as comfortable as possible pending the arrival of a physician (D) summon a number of other court attendants before opening the pen door

240. As a court attendant in charge of a jury which is deliberating you are approached by one of the attorneys in the case, who asks you to inform him as to how the jury is voting. You should
(A) tell him it is none of his business (B) tell him that the rules prohibit your giving him any information (C) call another attendant and have the attorney arraigned before the court (D) procure his name and report him to the judge immediately

241. If you are in charge of a jury that is deliberating on a case and one of the jurors becomes seriously ill, you should
(A) permit the jurors to continue their discussion of the case (B) stop all discussion and notify the clerk of the court (C) send for an ambulance (D) render first aid and, when the juror recovers, return him to the jury room

242. An attorney in a case on trial in a court in which you are an attendant requests that you refer to him any person who is in need of legal services. You should
(A) tell him that it is against the rules (B) procure his name and address, give it to the judge, and tell him what the attorney has said (C) immediately arraign him before the court and explain what he has said to you (D) warn him that such is a violation of the rules and that if he repeats it, you will report him to the judge

243. You are assigned as an attendant at the door of a criminal court while three desperate criminals are being sentenced for robbery. Your instructions are to admit no one to the court room. The detective who made the arrest and who is late for the proceedings requests that he be admitted, as the judge may want to speak to him. You should
(A) admit him (B) obey the orders given to the letter (C) ask another attendant to find out if the judge wants to see the detective (D) tell the detective to wait until the sentencing is over

244. You are one of three attendants assigned to guard a jury in a hotel where they are confined durin_ the trial of a case. A bell boy tells you that a physician is on the telephone and wants to speak to one of the jurors as his wife has met with a serious accident. You should
(A) convey the message to the juror immediately (B) permit the juror to talk to the physician (C) speak to the juror and tell him that he will have to get in touch with the judge (D) advise the boy to tell the doctor that you will convey the message as soon as you can get the judge's permission to do so

245. You are assigned to the reception desk leading to the Judges' chambers and an emotionally disturbed man insists on being admitted at once to see a particular judge. You should
(A) inform him the judge is ill at home (B) warn those in the judge's chambers that you are admitting the man (C) phone Bellevue Psychiatric Hospital to send an ambulance for the man (D) use as much force as necessary in barring his entrance

246. You are a Court Attendant assigned to a room in which an important trial is being held. A spectator makes a loud outcry while the District Attorney is summing up. You should
(A) assisted by another Court Attendant, take hold of him and rush him to the door (B) take hold of him, wait until the District Attorney gets through, and arraign the spectator before the Judge (C) in a loud tone, order him to desist (D) place him under arrest

247. The maximum term of imprisonment for conviction of a felony for which no penalty is prescribed in the law is
(A) 5 years (B) 7 years (C) 10 years (D) 3 years

248. Under the Penal Law, suicide is
(A) no crime (B) a felony (C) considered the same as manslaughter (D) excusable homicide

249. Evidence of spontaneous acts or utterances proximate to the occurrence of a crime is called
(A) prima facie (B) demonstrative (C) res gestae (D) circumstantial

250. In a criminal trial, the defendant does <u>not</u> have an absolute right to
(A) cross examination (B) aid of legal counsel (C) bail (D) to take the stand

251. A "POLYGRAPH" is a
(A) camera for reproducing copies of the original (B) a lie detector device (C) a burglar alarm device (D) tape recorder

252. A matter which exists by definition of law but which does not have actual existence is called
(A) constructive (B) ex officio (C) demonstrative (D) circumstantial

253. Before taking his confession of a crime, the accused must be warned of his rights by
(A) a magistrate (B) the district attorney (C) an attendant of a County Court (D) peace officer

254. Direct evidence is required in prosecutions of criminal homicides to prove the
(A) identity of the victim (B) death of the victim (C) killing by the accused (D) intent

255. The procuring of another person to commit perjury is known as
(A) compounding a crime (B) subornation (C) accessory (D) perjury

256. The accused has a legal right to a jury trial in New York City if he is charged with
(A) coercion (B) libel (C) conspiracy (D) gambling

257. A search warrant issued for execution in New York City is valid
(A) until executed (B) for 10 days (C) for 5 days (D) for 20 days

258. "Fainting is one of the most common incidents which a court attendant is called upon to treat." The immediate cause of fainting is
(A) an insufficient supply of blood to the brain (B) emotional shock (C) fatigue (D) close confinement

259. A basic distinction between the crime of bigamy and the crime of adultery is that
(A) bigamy requires a validly existing marriage, whereas adultery does not (B) if adultery is committed, both parties to the sexual act are necessarily guilty, whereas bigamy may be committed by one of the two parties to the bigamous act (C) bigamy can be perpetrated only by a male, whereas adultery can be committed by both a male and a female (D) sexual intercourse is essential to bigamy but not to adultery

260. A person who unlawfully threatens to use force or violence upon another with a veiw to compel such other to abstain from doing an act which he has a legal right to do is guilty of
(A) oppression (B) coercion (C) barratry (D) conspiracy

261. A copy of an indictment, to which is attached a certificate in the name of the People of the State of New York attesting to the fact that said copy is a true and exact transcript of the original indictment, is best described as a (n)
(A) exemplified copy (B) certified copy (C) sworn copy (D) examined copy

262. The Parol Evidence Rule provides that evidence of conversations between the parties to a written agreement, either prior to or at the time of its signing, is inadmissible to vary the terms of such agreement. The most probable reason for this rule is that
(A) the parties apparently intended to place themselves beyond the uncertainties of oral proof (B) a written contract always expresses the complete agreement of the parties (C) oral conversations do not express the true agreement between the parties (D) documentary evidence is always superior to testimony

263. The Surrogate's Court does not exercise jurisdiction over
(A) adoption proceedings (B) the estates of deceased persons (C) the appointment of guardians for children (D) the foreclosure of mortgages

264. The crime of bribery differs from the crime of extortion, the misdemeanor in that
(A) only a public officer can be the subject of a bribe (B) this type of extortion requires that compensation be actually received by the public officer (C) the giver as well as the receiver can be guilty of extortion, the misdemeanor (D) bribery requires an intent to influence or to be influenced wrongfully

265. A basic distinction between an indictment and an information is that
(A) an indictment always alleges that a person has committed a felony, whereas an information is used to charge a person with a misdemeanor or minor offense (B) an indictment must be in writing, whereas an information may be oral in form (C) an indictment must be made under oath, whereas an information can consist in an unsworn statement (D) an indictment must state the particular facts constituting the crime with which the defendant is charged, whereas an information need only state the crime alleged to have been committed

266. A Magistrate is
(A) any judicial officer (B) a judicial officer of any court, except those which are not courts of record (C) any officer having power to issue a warrant for the arrest of a person charged with a crime (D) any officer authorized by law to accept bail

267. Evidence that the accused was voluntarily intoxicated at the time of committing the crime for which he is on trial is admissible evidence
(A) as a defense based on excuse or lack of knowledge at time of crime commission (B) whenever a specific intent is a necessary element to constitute a particular degree of the crime charged (C) only when total and not partial intoxication prevented the forming of a specific criminal intent (D) solely for the purpose of mitigating the punishment upon conviction of the crime charged

268. The best evidence rule relates to
(A) all classes of evidence (B) the weight or probative force of hearsay evidence (C) the admissibility of circumstantial evidence (D) evidence of the contents of writings

269. An appeal from which of the following courts is <u>not</u> taken directly to the Appellate Division of the Supreme Court
(A) Surrogate's Court (B) City Court (C) Appellate Term of the Supreme Court
(D) Supreme Court

270. "To control bleeding from a cut artery, pressure may be applied at some point where the main artery to the injured part lies close to a bone. The one of the following which is not a recognized "pressure point" where hand or finger pressure against a bone may stop bleeding is
(A) the body side of the upper arm halfway between the shoulder and elbow
(B) just in front of the ear (C) behind the inner end of the collar bone
(D) about an inch below the kneecap

271. "An ordinary witness may give his opinion on a question at issue whenever the facts involved are such that they cannot be described so as to enable persons, not eye witnesses, to form proper conclusions regarding them." A further requirement for the admissibility of such opinions is that
(A) corroborative evidence must be introduced (B) the witness must be twenty-one years of age or more (C) the case must be one not punishable by death or life imprisonment (D) the subject matter of the opinion must not require a special knowledge or skill

272. The one of the following which is not a recognized principle of first aid is
(A) artificial respiration should be applied first, where an injured person has stopped breathing, even if such person is hemorrhaging seriously (B) water or other liquids should not be given to an unconscious person (C) failure to find a pulse in an injured person is not an indication of death (D) always try to maintain normal body temperature in an injured person

273. "A principal to a crime is not necessarily an accomplice." The correctness of this statement would be indicated by the fact that
(A) a person who knowingly aids a felon to escape from arrest is an accessory to the felony (B) one who actively participates in the commission of a crime is not necessarily a principal to the crime (C) the term "accomplice" has application only in the case where a felony is committed (D) a person who commits acts which would make him an accessory if the crime committed were a felony, is a principal if the crime in question is a misdemeanor.

274. The degree of the crime of larceny is never affected by the
(A) intent of the perpetrator (B) kind of property stolen (C) place from which the property is stolen (D) time when the property is taken

275. When one or more of the facts in issue are communicated to the court and jury by a witness who has actual knowledge of such facts by means of his senses, such evidence would be best described as
(A) circumstantial (B) real (C) direct (D) cumulative

276. "Every injured person is potentially a patient in shock and should be regarded and treated as such." The one of the following which is not a common symptom of shock is
(A) shallow and irregular breathing (B) nausea (C) weak pulse (D) hot, dry skin

277. It would be most incorrect to state that
(A) an "alienist" is a physician or psychiatrist specializing in the mental diseases or conditions of persons (B) a "bill of attainder" is a law which fixes the guilt of a person without the benefit of a trial (C) a "chattel" is an unoccupied house or other building (D) a "defalcation" is an embezzlement

278. There will be a violation of the constitutional privilege against self-incrimination if the defendant is compelled to
(A) stand up and be identified (B) submit to a search (C) reveal bodily marks or scars (D) produce documents or chattels which he claims may tend to indicate criminal responsibility on his part

279. For the purposes of the statute of limitations, criminal prosecution is deemed to have been commenced when
(A) an information is laid before a magistrate (B) the defendant is lawfully arrested (C) an indictment, having been presented by the Grand Jury, is received and filed in court (D) the crime in question becomes or is made known to the police

280. The crime of blackmail differs from the crime of extortion in that blackmail
(A) may result from an oral threat (B) requires that property be actually obtained by the perpetrator (C) is not concerned with the use of threats (D) may be committed without an intent to obtain property

281. Where the Penal Law forbids an act but does not state whether its commission will constitute a felony, misdemeanor or offense, and also fails to indicate the specific penalty therefor, the performance of such act will result in
(A) a felony (B) a misdemeanor (C) an offense (D) an infraction

282. The burden of proof in a criminal prosecution
(A) rests on the People of the State of New York throughout the trial
(B) shifts to the defendant in the course of the trial (C) requires that the guilt of the defendant must be established by a fair preponderance of the evidence (D) rests in the sound discretion of the trial court

283. A search warrant
(A) may always be executed at night (B) may be issued in connection with any property required as evidence (C) may not be issued except when it is incidental to a legal arrest (D) must be executed within 10 days after it has been issued.

284. "There are three kinds of pleas which may be made to an indictment". One of these pleas is
(A) double jeopardy (B) statute of limitations (C) intoxication (D) a demurrer

285. Under the criminal laws of New York State, a child under 16 years of age
(A) may be found guilty of any criminal homicide (B) is not subject to interstate extradition (C) is not allowed to enter a guilty plea to an indictment for murder (D) cannot be found guilty of any attempted crime

286. "The right to recover a debt, or evidence of the debt itself." This statement adequately defines
(A) a "chose in action" (B) laches (C) dictum (D) a remand

287. The term "privileged communications" is used to designate information which one person derives from another by reason of a confidential relationship existing between the parties. A relationship which the law recognizes as privileged is
(A) clergyman and parishioner (B) parent and child (C) reporter and informer (D) dentist and patient

288. The testimony of an accomplice does not warrant a conviction unless it is corroborated by evidence
(A) substantiating all of the essential elements of the crime (B) that the crime charged was in fact committed (C) tending to connect the defendant with the commission of the crime (D) proving that the defendant is guilty beyond a reasonable doubt

289. The least correct of the following statements with respect to the crime of perjury is that
(A) it is no defense that the oath was administered or taken in an irregular manner (B) it is a felony for a witness to give false testimony in a felony prosecution (C) the uncorroborated testimony of only one complaining witness is insufficient to convict (D) a witness who wilfully and knowingly testifies falsely is guilty of perjury even though he admits the truth on cross-examination

290. The phrase "Autoptic Proference" is synonymous with
(A) extra-judicial confession (B) real evidence (C) res gestae (D) legal presumption

291. Evidence which is considered to be sufficient to prove the guilt of the defendant beyond a reasonable doubt, provided it is not rebutted or explained away by the defendant, is best described as
(A) relevant evidence (B) prima facie evidence (C) material evidence (D) conclusive evidence

292. "Never administer a liquid to an unconscious person." The basic reason for this admonition is most probably the fact that
(A) liquids will have a harmful effect on the heart under these circumstances (B) the body of the person may already be overheated (C) the liquids may cause the person to choke (D) alcohol is an excessive stimulant

293. An indictment
(A) must charge but one crime (B) is the first pleading on the part of the People of the State of New York (C) must state the precise time at which the crime was committed (D) shall contain the true name of the defendant

294. The Grand Jury
(A) cannot act officially without a quorum of 23 members (B) may inquire only into those crimes which were actually committed within the county (C) is bound to hear any evidence which a defendant seeks to introduce (D) should find an indictment when the evidence before them is such as in their judgment would, if unexplained or uncontradicted, warrant a conviction by a trial jury

295. It would be incorrect to define an admission as
(A) an express acknowledgment of guilt by the accused (B) an act or declaration of a defendant which is inconsistent with his innocence (C) an act done or a statement made by the accused which amounts to a prior acknowledgment that one of the relevant facts in issue is not as he now claims (D) a declaration by or the conduct of a defendant from which his guilt may be inferred

296. No person can be convicted of murder unless direct evidence is introduced which tends to prove
(A) the death of the person alleged to have been killed (B) the fact that the defendant accomplished the killing in question (C) the identity of the person alleged to have been killed (D) an intent to kill on the part of the accused

297. The term "neglected child" includes any person under 16 years of age who
(A) is habitually truant (B) frequents any place the existence of which is in violation of law (C) associates with immoral persons (D) wanders about without lawful occupation

298. A break in a bone should be classified as a compound fracture if
(A) one or more parts of the bone protrude through the surface of the skin (B) any portion of the bone is splintered (C) the bone is broken in two or more places (D) the break in the bone is vertical rather than horizontal

299. The basic reason for the exlusion of hearsay evidence is
(A) there is no assurance of its reliability (B) the origiral information was not given under oath (C) the human memory cannot be trusted (D) corroboration is impossible

300. The Code of Criminal Procedure provides that
(A) a defendant may be tried in his absence for any crime which has been the subject of an indictment (B) one or two alternate jurors must be selected whenever the crime which is to be tried is punishable by death or life imprisonment (C) when several defendants are tried together, all must join if a valid challenge of a prospective juror is to be made (D) there shall be a mathematical limit on the number of challenges for cause which may be exercised by a defendant

301. The defendant in a criminal action is not entitled to
(A) be confronted by all witnesses against him in the presence of the court
(B) a speedy and public trial (C) appear and defend himself in person
(D) produce as a witness in his own behalf a person who is then detained in a state prison

302. The essential distinction between a felony and a misdemeanor under the criminal laws of New York State depends primarily upon the
(A) seriousness of the injury caused by the criminal act (B) actual penalty imposed upon the perpetrator after conviction (C) inherent evil in the act itself which the community recognizes as socially and morally wrong (D) maximum penalty that the court may legally impose upon the perpetrator after conviction of the crime charged

303. If a witness in a criminal prosecution is solicited by two persons to give false testimony but refuses and is thereupon threatened or intimidated, the solicitors could be charged with all of the following crimes except
(A) coercion (B) conspiracy (C) suppressing evidence (D) subornation of perjury

304. The Code of Criminal Procedure provides that
(A) where a grand jury has investigated a charge of crime and has reported no bill, the defendant concerned is not subject to prosecution thereafter
(B) an indictment voted by the Grand Jury against a defendant who is not as yet in custody shall not be presented in open court (C) a defendant may properly demur to an indictment when it appears upon the face thereof that the facts stated do not consitute a crime (D) a plea of guilty can be put in only by the attorney for the defendant concerned

305. With respect to the proper functioning of a grand jury, it would be most correct to state that
(A) where a grand jury receives any illegal evidence, an indictment voted in connection with such investigation must be dismissed (B) the grand jury may not inquire into the wilful and corrupt misconduct of a public officer within the county (C) the district attorney or his assistants may be present with the grand jury during the expression of their opinions or the giving of their votes on any matter (D) every member of the grand jury is sworn to keep secret the manner in which he or any other grand juror may have voted on a matter before them

306. "With an evil intent to vex, annoy or injure another person". This statement best defines which of the following legal terms?
(A) knowingly (B) corruptly (C) wilfully (D) maliciously

307. A confession will be deemed involuntary and hence incompetent as evidence, if the confession was made by the accused
(A) under a promise of immunity by the police (B) because of deceptive and fraudulent representations (C) in a case in which he was not advised of his constitutional rights (D) under the influence of fear produced by threats

308. A person is not qualified to act as a trial juror in a criminal action if he or she
(A) has been convicted previously of a misdemeanor (B) is under 21 years of age (C) has scruples against the death penalty (D) does not own property which is worth at least five hundred dollars

309. An overt act would be best defined as
(A) a design to effect a certain purpose (B) an act of the mind (C) an act which is witnessed by one or more other persons (D) any physical act

310. Which of the following is not a valid presumption of law? (A) every man is presumed to be sane (B) the defendant in a criminal prosecution is presumed to be innocent (C) the unlawful use of a deadly weapon on another creates a presumption of intent to kill (D) the exclusive possession of the fruits of a recent crime, if unexplained or falsely explained, raises a presumption of guilty possession

311. "An exemption from liability to serve as a trial juror must be claimed at the time the person is examined as to his qualifications for jury duty, except that a woman may claim her right to exemption at any time". The law does not grant such an exemption from jury duty to a practicing (A) embalmer (B) barber (C) pharmacist (D) dentist

312. An unmarried person who enters into a marriage with another, with full knowledge that the other has a husband or wife living and hence is committing bigamy thereby, is best described as a (n) (A) accessory (B) accomplice (C) bigamist (D) consort

313. The Governor may not grant a pardon or commutation of sentence where a defendant has been convicted of (A) murder in the first degree, without a recommendation of mercy by the jury (B) treason (C) kidnapping, and has been sentenced to death (D) criminal anarchy

314. The People of the State of New York may appeal as a matter of right from a determination of the trial court (A) in all cases (B) whenever the People of the State of New York are the aggrieved party (C) where a further prosecution for the same crime would not place the defendant in double jeopardy (D) under no circumstances

315. The most accurate of the following statements is (A) a chattel is a section of real property (B) affinity is a blood relationship between persons descended from a common ancestor (C) adjective law includes those laws which relate to methods of procedure (D) capital punishment includes punishment by death or by life imprisonment

316. "Smith says that Jones broke into a safe in a factory office at 2 A.M. Brown swears that he saw Jones walking out of the factory shortly after that time." The evidence of Brown is said to be (A) hearsay (B) demonstrative (C) corroborative (D) presumptive

317. The principal purpose of cross-examination is to (A) reveal defects in the testimony of the witness (B) show that the witness is committing perjury (C) compel the witness to admit his bias (D) prove that the witness is incompetent to testify

318. Witnesses not actually testifying may be excluded from the court room while another witness is testifying. The most logical basis for such procedure is (A) to avoid the possibility of being prejudiced (B) to permit the testifying witness to testify without fear of reprisal (C) to prevent perjury (D) to keep certain matters in confidence

319. As a general rule, witnesses must testify to facts and not to their opinions and conclusions on the facts in issue. The principal reason to justify the foregoing requirement is that
(A) opinion evidence cannot be tested by oath and cross-examination (B) the function of a witness is to state the facts from which the court or jury draw inferences (C) only the opinions of qualified experts have evidential value (D) opinions of witnesses are invariably derived from hearsay rather than from personal observations

320. The most correct of the following statements is that
(A) the burden of proof in every criminal prosecution is always on the people (B) a person cannot be tried twice for the same crime (C) the right to appeal a conviction is guaranteed to a defendant by the State Constitution (D) the weight of evidence in a criminal case is determined by the number of witnesses testifying to the same fact

321. An attack in court upon a witness' general reputation for truth and veracity is most properly described as
(A) denunciation (B) impeachment (C) neutralization (D) rebuttal

322. The term "criminal conversation" is most closely associated with
(A) illicit sexual intercourse (B) criminal libel (C) actionable slander (D) the hearsay rule

323. When a witness testifies to the date of his birth, such evidence is
(A) incompetent (B) admissible only if corroborated by documentary proof (C) real evidence (D) hearsay

324. Motive would be correctly defined as
(A) the result which a person means to accomplish by the acts which he performs (B) the cause or reason why an act is done (C) the natural and probable results of an act performed (D) a design or purpose to accomplish a certain end

325. The jury which has been chosen for a criminal trial may visit the place in which the crime is alleged to have been committed provided
(A) the crime charged is a felony (B) the court believes that such a visit is proper (C) the jury feels that such a visit might prove helpful (D) the crime charged is murder

326. The law will allow a compulsory disclosure of
(A) the deliberations of a grand jury (B) the deliberations of a trial jury (C) matters which transpired during a criminal trial (D) the deliberations of the court

327. If evidence is illegally seized, its use in the courts of New York State would be
(A) illegal (B) compulsory self-incrimination (C) incompetent (D) legal

328. The expression "caveat emptor" means most nearly
(A) to encourage another to commit crime (B) the right to collect damages for a tort (C) the buyer of property should be alert (D) the right of the government to seize property for the use of the public

329. Upon an appeal by the defendant in a criminal case, the People of the State of New York become known as the
(A) petitioner (B) respondent (C) appellant (D) defendant

330. The main objection to requiring a witness to a crime to answer all questions by "Yes" or "No" is that
(A) too many questions tend to confuse the witness (B) a witness is prevented from telling all that he knows about the subject under investigation
(C) no opportunity is afforded the witness to change his answers in cases of inadvertent errors (D) short answers are easier to falsify than lengthy answers

331. The term "forensic" means most nearly
(A) an idea which has popular approval (B) a subject matter which relates to the use of firearms (C) the psychological reason for doing an act (D)the application of a knowledge or skill in court proceedings

332. Lie detector machines are operated on the principle that
(A) most persons are unable to tell a consistent story (B) emotional stress causes physiological changes in a person (C) many individuals are not afraid to lie (D) a guilty person will unconsciously associate ideas in an indicative manner

333. A single action which is divided into two or more separate actions each of which terminates in a separate judgment is known as
(A) Consolidation (B) severance (C) joinder (D) election of remedies

334. If an attorney is assigned to represent a poor person in a civil action, such attorney
(A) may be allowed a reasonable fee out of any recovery in his favor
(B) will be allowed a reasonable fee irrespective of the success of the action (C) is entitled to costs expended by him in defending the action
(D) must file an undertaking if one is required

335. The term "substituted service" refers to
(A) a change of attorneys (B) a change of pleadings (C) a method of serving summons (D) a change in the parties

336. The purpose of a "supplemental summons" is to
(A) replace a technically defective summons (B) bring in additional parties after the action has begun (C) to bring in additional causes of action
(D) complete the pleadings on appeal

337. An infant may make application for the appointment of a guardian-ad-litem provided he is at least
(A) 12 years of age (B) 14 years of age (C) 15 years of age (D) 16 years of age

338. A "contested motion" is one which
(A) will be argued in opposition by the adversary (B) is defective because of improper service (C) is made by the court (D) requires submission of the facts to a referee

339. A motion is "made" when
(A) the notice of motion is filed (B) the papers are served on the adversary
(C) the hearing is held (D) the order is granted

340. A "request to charge" is made when
(A) there are comples principles of law governing the case (B) an attorney's motion for a directed verdict has been denied (C) there are only questions of law involved (D) counsel believes that certain matters have been insufficiently explained to the jury in the judge's charge

341. The "judgment roll" is
(A) the official record of every action that goes to judgment (B) a lied on all property of the defendant (C) a transcript of the judgment (D) prepared by the clerk of the court for the attorney for the successful party

342. "Laches has always been a bar to a petition for relief". The term "laches" as used in this sentence means
(A) defective papers (B) failure to establish a cause of action (C) unreasonable delay (D) failure to sue by the "real parties in interest"

343. The determination of a controversy in an arbitration proceeding is called
(A) a decree (B) a judgment (C) an award (D) a decision

344. Of the following instances, the one which the Court of Appeals has the power to review the questions of fact, is
(A) contested divorce actions (B) any felony committed by a minor (C) death penalty case (D) personal injury case based on negligence

345. A motion for a "non-suit" is usually made
(A) at the close of the plaintiff's case (B) at the close of the defendant's summation (C) after the judge's charge to the jury (D) by the plaintiff at the beginning of the defendant's case

346. A summons must be subscribed in the name of the
(A) court clerk (B) defendant (C) attorney for the plaintiff (D) judge

347. The abbreviation "et seq." means
(A) and others (B) and the following (C) in the same place (D) above

348 A "covenant" in a deed is
(A) an agreement between two or more parties (B) the attestation at the end of the deed (C) the consideration (D) the description of the property

349. That a court is a court of record means that
(A) its process is valid anywhere in the State (B) the justices are elected rather than appointed (C) it was created by the State Constitution (D) its records are perpetuated

350. Where a complaint is dismissed "without prejudice", it means that
(A) it is final determination on the merits (B) no costs will be charged against the plaintiff (C) the cause of action may be brought again (D) the defendant will hold no prejudice against the plaintiff

* * * * * * * * * *

COURT OFFICER

Answers Explained

1. (A) Where the facts are not disputed, it is a question of law for the court, since the jury has nothing to find. The judge may direct a verdict when he would set aside a contrary verdict as against the weight of evidence.

2. (D) Papers on appeal will consists of those which will enable the appeal court to familiarize itself with the facts necessary to an intelligent understanding of the subject matter of the appeal. If a party feels aggrieved because of a decision on an intermediate motion, an appeal from said decision should be taken. Therefore, any appeal other than one from a decision on an intermediate motion will not include the subject matter of said motion.

3. (C) "et al" means "and others"; since "others" is plural, it indicates two or more defendants in addition to Jones.

4. (A) Supreme Court jurisdiction is unlimited (civil and criminal jurisdiction); Equity jurisdiction as well as law jurisdiction. County Court has limited law jurisdiction as well as equity jurisdiction (outside New York City)

5. (A) Appeals from Municipal Courts and City Courts (NYC) go to Appellate Term of Supreme Court; Appeals from Trial Term of Supreme Court go to Appellate Division of Supreme Court; Appeals from the Appellate Division go to Court of Appeals.

6. (C) General Sessions Court in New York County has jurisdiction over felonies committed in New York County; In other counties in New York City, County Courts have similar jurisdiction over felonies. Special Sessions jurisdiction - misdemeanors; Felony Court is a Special Magistrate's Court in N.Y.C. for the purpose of arraigning defendants in felony cases.

7. (B) It is said to be prima facie when the law regards it as sufficient to establish the fact, unless rebutted.

8. (B) Trial juror qualifications: At least 21 years and not more than 70 years of age; own real or personal property at least $250 in value; no previous conviction for a felony or a misdemeanor (involving moral turpitude. Scruples against the death penalty will <u>not</u> hinder the selection of a juror in a case where the death penalty is not involved.

9. (C) Pen.Law. 1838 Includes every deputy or subordinate of any ministerial officer of the court.

10. (B) Criminal contempt in a court of record: disorderly, contemptuous, or insolent behavior, committed during its sitting, in its immediate view and presence, and directly tending to disrupt its proceedings, or to impair the respect due to its authority. Criminal contempt proceedings are punitive in their nature whereas, civil contempt is remedial and coercive in nature.

11. (C) Offering or giving a bribe to a public officer with intent to influence him in respect to any act, decision, vote, opinion or other proceeding, in the exercise of the powers or functions which he has or may have, is punishable as a felony.

12. (B) McKinney's Consolidated Laws of N.Y. State; Includes all State Laws, Criminal & Civil with annotations from State and Federal Courts.

13. (D) 37 Volume, New York Supplement, 2nd edition, page 49.

14. (B) Power of Attorney must be in writing to be effective. Verification: an affidavit attached to a pleading, wherein the party swears that the contents of the pleading are true or that he believes them to be true. Certification: statement signed by clerk stating that he has compared a copy of a document with the original and has found the copy to be the exact copy of the original. Substituted service: a form of service of summons other than by personal service (affixing to door.)

15. (C) The effect of a statute of limitations is not to extinguish the obligation but merely to bar the particular remedy, so that if any other remedy is still open the creditor may avail himself thereof. (Action on contract must be instituted within 6 years, etc) Statute of Frauds: certain agreements must be in writing in order to be recoverable such as in sale of real property.

16. (D) In civil cases, the presence of litigants is not required; in criminal cases, the presence of the defendant is required if the charge is a felony. In misdemeanor cases, defendant need not be present so long as his counsel is present.

17. (A) Cannot practice law in any county, nor have their names listed in the telephone books as attorneys; cannot engage in any other business or outside activity.

18. (B) Both are sworn statements and signed; a deposition contains testimony of deponent reduced to writing, usually in the form of questions and answers.

19. (C) When the accused is brought before the court, the charge is read to him and he is given an opportunity to answer it. It is incidental to the arraignment that the accused is released on bail.

20. (B) Marked pleadings enable the court to determine the nature of the action, the issues of fact, and the questions of law which will be presented. Supplemental Pleading: pleadings which show additional causes of action and new facts which occurred after the commencement of the action. Amended Pleadings: corrections to the original pleadings. Alternate Pleading: usually not permitted - pleadings should be clear and unequivocal.

21. (C) A special verdict is returned by the jury on framed issues submitted to it, generally in equity actions. General verdict: one which decides in favor of one of the parties and may assess damages. Sealed verdict: usually ordered when the jury continues its deliberations beyond the closing hour of the court. The court instructs the jury to write out its verdict and seal it in an envelope for the clerk to read in open court the next day. Directed verdict: on motion of either party or on Court's own motion, jury may be directed to find a verdict in favor of either party.

22. (B) "In Rem" means jurisdiction over property; "In personam" means jurisdiction over persons. An action in rem is an action against property.

23. (C) To confer jurisdiction "in rem" upon the court, there must be some property or subject matter constituting the "res" with which the action is concerned and relating to which the judgment will be rendered. Fee Simple: full ownership in lands; Freehold: an estate of inheritance or a life estate. Abstract of title: Title companies search title records of property for liens, taxes, judgments etc and present their findings in the form known as "abstract of title".

24. (C) 2nd Dept: 2nd, 9th, and 10th Judicial Districts (Kings, Queens, Richmond, Nassau, Suffolk, Westchester, Putnam, Dutchess, Orange, and Rockland Counties)
1st Dept: 1st judicial District. (Bronx and New York Counties)

25. (C) 4 Judicial Departments throughout the State.
1st Dept: New York County (Location)
2nd Dept: Brooklyn
3rd Dept: Albany
4th Dept: Rochester

26. (B) Special Term: Matters not triable by jury.
Trial Term: Term for jury trials or the trial of law action in which a jury has been demanded.

27. (C) Ex parte: Made by a party without notice to an adversary, thereby giving him no opportunity to oppose. It is made in those cases where the applicant is entitled to relief as a matter of right upon the presentation of certain proof. Motions which require that the adversary be notified so as to rebut the motion are said to be contested motions.

28. (A) During the pendency of an action, numerous applications may be made to the court for various orders, such as an order to set aside service of a summons, or an order to amend the complaint etc. All these applications must be brought to the attention of the court on proper papers commonly called "motion papers".

29. (D) Note of issue: The note of issue states the title of the action, names and addresses of the attorneys, the time when the last pleading was served, whether the action is triable by jury, the term at which the trial is desired, and the specific nature and object of the action. The case is given a calendar number and when it appears for trial the parties must be ready to proceed.

30. (A) "now for then"; A phrase used to express that a thing is done at one time which ought to have been performed at another; dated as if occurring at an earlier date. Laches: negligent delay in enforcing a right. Cases are often dismissed because of "laches" Ipso Facto: (Lat: By the fact itself) Interlocutory: a provisional decree which is not final; thus Interlocutory decree of divorce means a temporary decree not yet final.

31. (C) Reply: Plaintiff's pleading which responds to the Defendant's answer. It consists of denials and defenses; it cannot contain contain any counterclaims; it must not be inconsistent with the allegations in the plaintiff's complaint since both the complaint and the reply are pleadings of the plaintiff. If the answer sets up a counterclaim, a reply thereto must be served, otherwise the defendant may obtain a default judgment on his counterclaim.

32. (B) Exception: a formal objection to the action of the court in denying a request or overruling an objection. Counsel must record his objection by taking exception otherwise the alleged error cannot be raised on appeal.

33. (D) Replevin: Common Law action to recover a chattel. A person who has a present right to possession of a chattel, may maintain the action against any person who has wrongfully taken or detained the property.

34. (A) Appeals are taken to the Court of Appeals from: (1) the Appellate Division, (2) direct appeals from the lower courts where actions involve constitutional questions, and (3) direct appeals from lower courts in capital cases.

35. (B) Amicus Curiae:a friend of the court; advises the court on some legal matter which the court was unaware at the time; one who aids the court by giving information to it. Burden of Proof (onus probandi)

36. (C) The right of sovereignty to seize any private property for public good (Police power of the state) Ejectment: An action which lies to get possession of real property with damages for its unlawful detention. Easement: The right in the owner of one parcel of land, to use the land of another for special purposes, not inconsistent with the general property of the owner (Right to cross another's property in order to get access to his own) Franchise: Privilege of using public property for public use (Bus franchise)

37. (A) After a summons has been served, the server should fill out and sign the form on the back of the summons and have it notarized. The form states that the server was over 18 years of age, that he served the summons on the defendant, that he knew the person served to be the defendant. If the defendant later makes a direct attack against the service, the plaintiff subpoenas the server for the purpose of sustaining the service.

38. (C) Verification: Affidavit attached to the pleading wherein the party swears that the contents of the pleading are true or that he believes them to be true. As a general rule, once a pleading is verified, each subsequent pleading should be verified.

39. (D) Whoever has the affirmative burden of proof, opens and closes the case. Generally, the plaintiff has this right. However, if from the state of the pleadings the plaintiff is not required to offer any evidence because his cause of action is admitted, then the defendant has the right to open and close the case. The party who opens first, sums up last; Party who opens last, sums up first.

40. (C) A compulsory reference may be ordered by the court upon application of either party or upon its own motion without consent where there are issues of fact and the trial will require the examination of a long account on either side and will not require the decision of difficult questions of law. The referee's decision is called a report.

41. (A) Under these circumstances, if there is a default in answering, the clerk can immediately enter the judgment since amount demanded is liquidated or capable of ascertainment.

42. (A) Intestate:Dies without a will; administrator appointed by the court distributes the property. Testator:dies leaving a will, executor appointed by the testator distributes the property. Special Guardian appointed by the court to protect interests of children where an estate is involved.

43. (D) County Courts:Felony jurisdiction, hence prosecution by indictment. Information:basis for prosecution of misdemeanors.

44. (B) C.C.P. Sec. 145. It is distinguished from affidavit, indictment, complaint. Prosecution is commenced when the information is laid before a magistrate that a crime has been committed. It is a written allegation or accusation made by a person without intervention of grand jury and submitted to a magistrate, charging a named person with crime. It is the foundation of a magistrates jurisdiction to take depositions and issue a warrant.

45. (D) Criminal cases: unanimous verdict Civil cases: 5 out of 6 jurors, or 10 out of 12 jurors may agree upon a verdict. If 10 out of 12 jurors cannot agree in a civil case, jury will be discharged and new trial ordered.

46. (B) When a verdict has been reached, the attorney for the losing party will call each juror by name and ask each one whether or not the verdict was his true verdict. This is done to see whether or not jurors have been improperly influenced in reaching their verdict.

47. (B) Penal Law: Defines crimes and their punishment. Code of Crim Proc.: Provides for criminal courts and their jurisdiction. C.P.A.: Civil Courts Judiciary Law: All courts

48. (D) Challenge to the entire panel based upon an irregularity in the selection of the panel itself. Such a challenge is infrequently made. Challenge peremptorily: arbitrarily made and no reason need be given for the objection. Challenge for cause: based upon a charge of bias (related by affinity etc). Challenge to the favor: juror is so prejudiced or biased that he cannot render an impartial verdict. (employed by one of the parties)

49. (A) In 1st & 2nd Departments, Appellate Division makes the rules regulating the procedures as to jurors. Such rules apply to cities having 1 million population. The rules also regulate the duties of the County Clerk and County Jury Board.

50. (B) Riot: 3 or more persons actually disturb the peace by force or violence, or threaten to disturb the peace coupled with the power of immediate execution. (Felony)
Unlawful Assembly: 3 or more assembled with intent to commit unlawful act with force or threaten to commit breach of peace. (Misd)

51. (C) Re-direct follows cross-examination.
Re-cross-examination and re-re-direct examination depends upon the circumstances and the discretion of the judge.

52. (B) During the argument as to the admissibility of evidence the jury would be listening to the evidence in question and if the judge later ruled against its admissibility it would be too late to expel the evidence from the minds of the jurors.

53. (D) Such damages must be proved and cannot be assessed by the clerk of the court. In contract cases for the recovery of money, the alleged amount is the amount sought and if there is a default in answering the clerk may enter the default judgment without application to the court.

54. (A) To form a conclusion upon facts given by others is accepting as true what others say - this is unverified assumption of fact. To say that a thing is a possibility doesn't mean that it has happened.

55. (A) Since difficult situations may occur even before he has started to work, it is apparent then that he has no control over such circumstances.

56. (D) Child under 12 may testify without oath if in the opinion of the court the child does not understand the nature of an oath and is otherwise sufficiently intelligent to justify the reception of the evidence. However such testimony must be corroborated and allowed only in a criminal case.

57. (C) Civil Contempt: Remedial and coercive in nature; involves a neglect or violation of duty, or other misconduct, by which a right or a remedy of a party to a civil action or proceeding, pending in the court may be defeated, impaired or prejudiced.
Criminal Contempt: Punitive in nature; the state and the people are interested in its prosecution. It does not involve any personal right or injury.

58. (B) "No person shall be rendered incompetent to be a witness on account of his opinions on matters of religious belief. "(NY Const) He may be sworn according to his own religious practices.

59. (D) Attorney may be changed: (a) By court, plus consent of party and attorney, or (b) on application of the party. Attorney is allowed reasonable compensation for his services and has a statutory lien on client's interest.

60. (B) There are only 3 pleadings: Complaint: Plaintiff's cause of action; Answer: Defendant's opposition to the complaint; Reply: Plaintiff's answer to the defendant's counterclaim if any.

61. (A) Appellate court reviews the case for possible errors; does not try the defendant since it does not have original jurisdiction.

62. (B) It is the basis of the magistrate's jurisdiction for the issuance of a warrant of arrest. It alleges the facts which constitute the crime; Presentment: Report of a grand jury after an investigation of corruption etc. in the county.

63. (C) Jury trials granted: Divorce actions where the answer puts in issue, the claim of adultery; In annulment actions, (except where physical incapacity is charged); Other cases in the court's discretion on framed issues of fact (jury trial in this case is advisory and not conclusive upon the court).

64. (A) Venue: place of trial; place where the legal cause of action arose; venue selected by the plaintiff. If an improper county is selected and no objection is made by the defendant, the case will proceed in the county selected.

65. (C) The testimony should not be interrupted. At the conclusion, the stenographer requests that certain portions should be repeated after reading the portions which has been taken down.

66. (C) Counsel must stand during summation; shall not exceed an hour unless court permits otherwise. He is given wide latitude in referring to the evidence, commenting thereon, and drawing inferences therefrom. However, if his remarks refer to matters outside of the record and they are unduly prejudicial, a mistrial may be ordered.

67. (A) Statute: legislative enactment. Common Law: law developed in the courts, decisions, customs, traditions, etc. Adjective Law: law governing procedures, such as C.P.A. Substantive Law: law defining rights, obligations, duties, etc ex: Penal Law

68. (C) Disagreement ordinarily means that in a civil action, less than 5/6 of jurors agreed; in criminal case, disagreement occurs when only one juror is in disagreement. If the disagreement is on a separate phase of the litigation, rather than have the entire case retried, the court may order a partial retrial on the phase involved since the jurors were in agreement on the main phase. Quotient Verdict: Striking an average of the jurors (in dollars) and dividing by 12. This is forbidden.

69. (A) Every one is directed to rise, except of course invalids. This is a symbol of respect and dignity which attaches to the court.

70. (B) Stat. Of Limitation: Prescribes the time periods within which various actions should be commenced. Ex: Contract actions should be commenced within 6 years otherwise outlawed; Felonies prosecuted within 5 years etc..

71. (D) Court attendant is peace officer while engaged as such in a court room.

72. (C) Min: 21 years Max: 70 years

73. (A) Summons usually attached to complaint. However, in the Supreme Court, a summons may be served without the complaint. If summons is served with the complaint, then the defendant has to file an answer; if the summons served without the complaint, then the defendant need not answer but must serve a notice of appearance on the attorney for the plaintiff.

74. (B) Adjournment means postponement.

75. (C) Ex-parte: One-sided proceeding without notice to the other side. It is made in those cases where the applicant is entitled to relief as a matter of right upon the presentation of certain proof, or where it is impossible to give notice to an adversary. The police in applying for a wire-tap order, make ex-parte application.

76. (B) Peremptory: No reason given; limited number allowed. For Cause: Reason given,as bias. To the Favor: Reason given, as interested party, such as employee of one of the parties. Exception: Attorney's objection to a court ruling.

77. (D) Petit Jury: trial jury of 12 persons. Struck Jury: a special or Blue Ribbon jury. Grand Jury: 16 to 23 persons, not a trial jury.

78. (D) Reply: Plaintiff's pleading in answer or opposition to defendant's counterclaim or defense. Answer: may contain denials of plaintiff's claims, defense of new matter such as "payment" or counterclaim which is a counter-cause of action to offset Plaintiff's claim.

79. (B) Alias: fictitious name. Alibi: a claim of being at another place at the time in question. Facsimile: an exact copy. Alienist: a psychiatrist; doctor specializing in mental diseases.

80. (C) Youthful Offender: at least 16 but not yet 21 years of age. Youths charged with crimes (except capital crimes and life imprisonment crimes) tried in Youthful Offender Courts.

81. (C) Law Journal: Publishes calendars, motions heard, Court decisions, etc.

82. (B) Court may receive a jury verdict and discharge a jury on Sunday; jury trials are prohibited. Service of summons in a civil action is void. Arrest on a misdemeanor warrant shall not be made unless magistrate endorses the warrant for such service. Felony warrant may be executed on Sunday without endorsement.

83. (D) Recidivist: crime repeater; habitual offender.

84. (A) An order from the Supreme Court to a trial body (not judiciary) to send the minutes of a trial or hearing to it so as to determine the legality of the hearing. Thus, where a public employee has been dismissed from the service, his only relief is "certiorari" to have the Court determine whether or not the dismissal was just and reasonable and not based on the arbitrary or capricious act of the administrator.

85. (C) Ex Post Facto: (after the fact) A law passed after an act was done which retroactively makes such act a crime, or which increases the punishment after the act was committed. Such laws are prohibited by State and Federal Constitutions. Ipso Facto: by the fact itself. De Facto: in fact, actually.DeJure:of right, lawful. Ex Officio:by virtue of the office

86. (A) Grand Jury: 16 to 23 members; quorum consists of at least 16 jurors; an indictment requires concurrence of at least 12 jurors.

87. (B) Voir Dire: a preliminary oath administered to a witness, for the purpose of ascertaining whether he has such an interest in the cause in which he is offered to testify, as would disqualify him.

88. (B) Statute of Frauds: Certain contracts are not enforceable unless evidenced in writing. It protects the individuals concerned. Ex: Contracts for more than a year; real estate conveyance, etc. Attestation: witnessing a written instrument and signing to that effect.

89. (C) Code of Criminal Procedure: Consolidated Law of N.Y.State; Established 1881; established the practice in all criminal cases and the authority for the orders and judgments of the courts. Divided in 6 parts: (1) criminal courts & jurisdiction, (2) Prevention of Crime, (3) Impeachment proceedings etc. (4) Prosecutions by indictments, (5) Special Proceedings & Police Courts, (6) Special Proceedings of a criminal nature.

90. (B) An exception is automatically deemed taken to every adverse ruling, whether before or after the case is submitted to the jury, so long as counsel makes known his position by objection or otherwise.

91. (D) If the challenge is allowed, the court must discharge the juror. Withdrawal of Juror: In civil cases during the course of the trial, the plaintiff discovers that he cannot prove his case because of the absence of a material witness who has been subpoened or for some other reason beyond his immediate control, he may move for the "withdrawal of a juror". If the motion is granted the jury is discharged. The case may thereafter be retried on the same pleadings and other papers; it need not be begun "de novo" (anew).

92. (D) The remedy in this case is for a motion to strike out testimony so that it shall not be considered part of the record and the jury may be asked to disregard it. The other choices (A, B, and C) are grounds for mistrials.

93. (B) Mayhem: form of maiming (to mutilate, cripple etc.) Arson: Wilfull and unlawful burning; Homicide: the killing of one human being by another.

94. (C) Charge to Jury: After both sides have summed up their case. It states to them all matters of law which the court thinks necessary for their information in giving their verdict. And, if requested, informs the jury that they are the exclusive judges of all questions of fact; that they must not consider the punishment since that rests with the judge.

95. (B) State Judicial Council: Continuous survey and study of all the courts of the state; publishes judicial statistics; investigates criticisms, recommends changes in procedures.

96. (A) Commitment : Direct sheriff, peace officer etc. to take or receive person for detention. Stipulation: written agreement between attorneys for both sides on any undisputed matter.

97. (C) Alienist: psychiatrist; specializes in mental disorders. Criminologist: Studies causes of crime and human behavior.

98. (B) Obiter Dictum: Opinion expressed by a court on a matter not essentially involved in a case and hence not a decision. Onus Probandi: Burden of proof.

99. (C) Polling the Jury: After the verdict, counsel may request each juror to declare what his verdict is - whether the verdict as rendered was his verdict.

100. (A) Certificate of Reasonable Doubt: Its purpose is to determine whether there is a reasonably arguable question which ought to be settled by an appellate court; a certification by a judge that there is a reasonable doubt that a conviction should stand. The appellate court may order a new trial if it finds that the verdict was against the weight of evidence.

101. (B) Ballistics: Science of firearms and projectiles.

102. (C) It is their duty not to converse among themselves or others on any subject connected with the trial, or to form or express any opinion thereon, until the cause is finally submitted to them. They may be permitted to separate during trial provided they do not discuss the case with any one.

103. (A) Since a corporation is a legal entity, a fictitious person, it cannot sue "in person" but by a representative. The other choices (B,C, and D) can sue in their own names.

104. (D) Accused may request that he be heard in person before the grand jury; files request with foreman of grand jury and with the District Attorney. However, the grand jury will not hear the accused unless he files a waiver of immunity with the county clerk.

105. (D) Defendants jointly indicted, may be tried separately or jointly, in the discretion of the court.

106. (B) If at any time after evidence on either side is closed, the court deem it insufficient to warrant a conviction of one or more of the crimes in the indictment or information, it may advise the jury to acquit the defendant thereof and they must follow the advice. However, it cannot advise the jury to convict.

107. (C) Impeaching Witness: Attacking credibility of witness by showing his bad reputation as a liar, his character as being vicious and not worthy of belief; that he has made conflicting statements; showing bias, hostility; conviction of a crime, etc.

108. (D) No time limit for the prosecution of murder or kidnapping; 5 years for other felonies (except seduction, 2 years) and 2 years for misdemeanors (except conspiracy to commit a felony, 5 years)

109. (B) In New York City, the Appellate Term of the Supreme Court hears appeals from the Municipal and City Courts only.

110. (B) No guilty plea in Murder 1st degree, Treason, and kidnapping (capital crimes)

111. (D) Irrebuttable, irrefutable, cannot be attacked etc.

112. (C) Court of Appeals: 7 judges; elected for 14 years. The court has appellate jurisdiction only in both civil and criminal cases.

113. (A) Subpoena duces tecum: requires the production of books, records etc; usually the attorney issues and signs it. Court order is necessary to produce original hospital records; however, subpoena duces tecum permissible for the production of a transcript of hospital records. In a criminal action, attorney for defendant may issue subpoenas.

114. (B) Barratry: Misdemeanor; to practice the exciting of groundless judicial proceedings. No conviction can be had unless proof that the person has excited actions or legal proceedings in at least 3 instances, and with a corrupt and malicious intent to vex and annoy.

115. (C) Tort: Violation of an inherent right that a person has as an individual as distinguished from a right arising out of a contract; it may be called a private wrong. A crime also, in most cases, wrongs an individual; but it is more than a private wrong. It is looked upon as a wrong against society. A violation of a man's rights may be either a tort or a crime depending upon the nature of the act.

116. (B) In felony cases, a party to a crime is either a principal or an accessory; in misdemeanor cases, all parties concerned are deemed principals (there are no accessories in misdemeanors) Accomplice: a co-conspirator or co-principal; tried and convicted as a principal.

117. (C) Confession Inadmissible if involuntary, coerced, forced. Admissible even though deception used or made while under arrest; defendant under these circumstances is not entitled to any warning.

118. (C) Execution: Process of the court, signed by the attorney for the person at whose instance it is issued. It generally is directed to the sheriff, describes the judgment, and direct the sheriff to enforce or satisfy the judgment - either to recover the specific property or the payment of money. Letters Testamentary: decree appointing an executor of an estate (In Surrogates Court)

119. (C) Veniremen: means jurors; also called "talesmen"

120. (D) Condemnation Proceedings: Example: State in building highways will condemn private properties in its path and offer reasonable value for such property; if owner refuses amount, condemnation proceedings are instituted whereby owner is compelled to surrender property upon payment of amount reached by arbitrators; This right is the effect of eminent domain.

121. (B) Decision: By court, upon which is entered the judgment. A court or judge does not render a judgment - it renders a decision, and from the decision, judgment is entered. Also, a judgment is entered on the verdict of a jury. Judgment: final determination of the rights of the parties in an action.

122. (A) Accomplice: No conviction can be had upon such testimony unless corroborated by independent evidence tending to prove defendant's connection with the crime and to indicate that the accomplice is not lying.

123. (D) Jurist: Judge; Jurat: The memorandum or clause at the foot of an affidavit showing when and before whom it was sworn; the notary statement.

124. (D) Competency of Witnesses: Witnesses having an interest in the litigation are not disqualified as witnesses. The interest of the witness may still be shown for the purpose of affecting his credibility. Previous conviction does not disqualify; however it may be used to attack his credibility.

125. (A) Executor: carries out the provisions of a will
Administrator: Appointed by the court to distribute the property according to law where there is no will.
Testamentary Guardian: guardian appointed by the last will of a father, for the person, and real and personal estate of his child.
Administrator, c.t.a.: Administration with the will annexed; administration granted in cases where a testator makes a will, without naming any executors, or where executors are incompetent to act, or refuse.

126. (C) Plaintiff files a complaint; Defendant files an answer to complaint. Complaint is plaintiff's pleading; answer is defendant's pleading. Demurrage: a charge for the detention of a vessel by a freighter, beyond the time allowed by the charter party for loading or unloading.

127. (C) Special Term of Supreme Court to Appellate Division to Court of Appeals to (if constitutional question involved) U.S.Supreme Court.

128. (C) Petition: A written instrument containing a prayer (a request) for the redress of some wrong or for some favor. They are frequently presented to the court in order to bring some matter before them as in equity cases. As in Summary Proceedings (dispossess) a petition commences the action. It is similar to a complaint in other actions in that it is a writing, containing an allegation as to the legal grounds for the action. Frequently used in Surrogates Court, Domestics Relations Court etc.

129. (B) Since the defendant answers the plaintiff's complaint, the respondent answers the petitioner's petition. Remainderman: one who is entitled to the remainder of property.

130. (A) Tortfeasor: a wrongdoer; a trespasser. Decedent: deceased person Testator: decedent leaving a will. Demurrer: Legal objection by a defendant to an indictment because of some irregularity etc.

131. (D) "True Bill": When 12 grand jurors concur on an indictment, and signed by the foreman, it is called a "true bill". Bailment: a delivery of goods in trust, upon a contract, that the trust shall be faithfully executed on the part of the bailee. Bill of Particulars: Amplifies the pleading by supplying the details or the particulars of the claim in question; it is intended to prevent surprise at the trial and to limit the scope of the proof to the particulars stated in the Bill.

132. (B) Injunction: Restraining order; to restrain the adverse party in the suit from committing any acts in violation of the plaintiff's rights. Subpoena: request for appearance of witness in court. Mandamus: A Supreme Court order to a public officer commanding him to perform an official duty. Rescission: The annulling of a contract by mutual agreement, or by one of the parties, or by a court.

133. (C) Appeals from murder 1st degree convictions go directly to the court of Appeals. Appeals from other convictions ordinarily go to the Appellate Division of the Supreme Court.

134. (C) Testate: deceased leaving a will
Intestate: deceased leaving no will. Interstate: As between states. Intrastate: within a state.

135. (B) Opinion: Statement or memorandum of a judge usually accompanying his decision. Sentence: The judgment of a court prounounced after the hearing of a cause.

136. (A) Guardian Ad Litem: person designated by a court to represent a child in a lawsuit as plaintiff or defendant.
Guardian in socage: a person who is the custodian of property coming to an infant by descent. Testamentary Guardian: One appointed by the last will of a father. Temporary Guardian: One appointed temporarily to protect the interests of a litigant.

137. (C) Women are qualified for jury service in N.Y.State but are not usually called unless they request it. If otherwise called, they are entitled to exemption merely by requesting same.

138. (D) Appellant: one who appeals a case. Respondent: One who answer an appeal. Relator: A person in whose behalf certain writs are issued, such as attachments for contempt, mandamus etc.
Plaintiff: one who institutes a law suit.

139. (C) The Appellate Division is a court of appellate jurisdiction; it has no original jurisdiction (except in disbarment proceedings) and hence no trials are conducted therein.

140. (B) Since the assailant is armed, the first consideration on the part of the court attendant is the safety of the spectators. He should make every effort to subdue the armed person inorder to prevent any possible injury to others.

141. (A) A crime is either a felony or a misdemeanor. If the crime is punishable in a state prison, it is a felony, otherwise it is a misdemeanor.

142. (B) Surrogates Court: Decedent's estates, probate of wills, etc. Court of Claims: Suits against the State of New York

143. (B) Folio: 100 words

144. (A) Ready to assist, friendly but never argue with parties to litigations.

145. (C) Evidence: the means used to prove or disprove a fact Proof: the result of evidence. Exhibit: Any writing which is exhibited as evidence. Testimony: spoken or written evidence

146. (B) Suspended Sentence: postponed sentence. Cumulative sentence: accumulated sentence, the one sentence to be served after the completion of the first etc. Indeterminate Sentence: Not fixed, but having a minimum and a maximum; the exact time of release not known but dependent upon the behavior of the inmate.

147. (A) Misfeasance: improper performance of a lawful act Malfeasance: the doing of a wrongful act Nonfeasance: neglect of duty Mala prohibitum: prohibited by statute but not inherently evil.

148. (A) Petition: an application to the court in writing Summons: order issued by court requiring person to appear and answer a charge or complaint of plaintiff. Letters Testamentary: authority granted by Surrogates Court to an executor after probate of will, authorizing him to act as executor. Letters of Administration: The authority of an administrator to act in the distribution of the estate of a person dying without will (intestate)

149. (C) Bench Warrant: A warrant of arrest issued after indictment, for the arrest of a person, or failure to appear on the return day of bail. Search Warrant: authorizes peace officer to search named premises for stolen goods. Attachment: Seizure of personal property to satisfy a judgment.

150. (A) The court attendant should do nothing but wait for any instructions from the bench. If the witness becomes unruly and disorderly, the attendant being a peace officer should then try to restrain the witness.

151. (B) Fainting: Loss of blood circulation in his head, becomes pale, and weak. Place body in such a position as to have blood flow back to his head; keep warm.

152. (B) Render first aid as soon as possible; thereafter as a peace officer be guided accordingly as to arrest procedure.

153. (B) Transcript: true copy of original court record Facsimile: a duplicate of anything

154. (C) Probate: The process of proving a will De Bonis Non: a new administrator to replace another Citation: process used in Surrogates Court requiring the attendance of parties on a probate of a will. Inquest: a judicial inquiry or examination.

155. (A) Codicil: an addition to a will
Appendage: a subordinate addition or adjunct: accessory
Novation: a substitution of a new engagement, indebtedness, obligation, creditor or debtor for an existing one.
Attestation:

156. (A) Deed: a written instrument which conveys land to another
Bill of Sale: an agreement in writing by which one person sells his interest in personal property to another.
Stipulation: an agreement or contract
Mortgage: A grant or conveyance of an estate or property to a creditor to secure a debt.

157. (A) Abstract: a compendium; a summary
Abeyance: Where there is no person in existence in whom an inheritance can vest, it is said to be in abeyance.

158. (C) Devise; granting of real property by will
Bequest: giving personal property by will (same as legacy)
Bailment: Delivery of goods to another to be returned when a certain purpose has been accomplished.

159. (B) Prima Facie: evidence which if uncontradicted is sufficient to establish the disputed fact. Rebuttable evidence.
Res Gestae: Hearsay evidence of a spontaneous statement or action occurring at about the time the incident took place.
Ex Parte: One sided; no notice to the adversary

160. (A) "ex rel": from the recital of facts of
in re: in the matter of
et seq: and the following

161. (B) In camera: in chambers
Extra judicial: outside the judicial proceedings
Coram nobis: writ of error on a judgment given by a previous court.

162. (C) Abscond: To flee from a jurisdiction to avoid process.
Abstention: a refraining or abstaining;
Escrow: A bond or deed left with another to be delivered by him to a 3rd person upon the performance of some act.

163. (D) Abatement: To do away with, annul, remit, lessen, mitigate.
Abrogate: cancel, destroy, repeal, abolish
Abridgement: To condense
Avoidance: The evading or escaping from the legal effect of a pleading by alleging new matter in answer to it.

164. (B) Adjective Law: Rules of pleading and procedure (C.P.A. etc)
Substantive Law: Deals with rights and duties (Penal Law etc)
Civil Law: Roman Law
Chancery: Court of equity; equity proceedings

165. (C) Allegation: statement or pleading
Affirmation: an indulgence allowed by law to persons having religious scruples against taking an oath.

166\. (D) Nunc pro tunc: now for then; a term applied to such acts as the entry of judgment made at a later date but to have the effect as of an earlier date.
A priori: from cause to effect
Lis pendens: a pending civil or criminal action. A notice of lis pendens is one of the proceedings in a foreclosure action
Nuncupative: oral (not written) especially in wills.

167\. (B) Docket: An abridged entry of an instrument or proceeding in an action; a list or register of such abridged entries.
Citation: Surrogate's Court process requiring attendance of persons on a probate of a will.
Precis: a brief summary of a book or article.

168\. (C) Acknowledgement: Declaring before a competent officer (notary) that an executed instrument is one's own act or deed.
Subornation: inducing another to commit perjury
Verification: Sworn statement that the contents of an instrument are true.
Conveyance: A written instrument conveying an interest in real property. (deed)

169\. (B) Recognizance: A written statement before the court to do an act specified or suffer a penalty
Undertaking: a written agreement to appear in court when released on bail.
Escrow: Delivering a bond or deed to a third party to be held by him until the performance of a certain act and then te deliver the document to another.
Entrapment: inducing one to commit a crime so as to arrest him

170\. (A) Amendment: Making corrections or entering new allegations.
Novation: substitution of a new obligation for an old one
Subrogation: substitution of one person for another with respect to rights or claims. (insurance companies suing in behalf of assured)

171\. (D) Euthanasia: mercy killing
Genocide: the crime of exterminating certain races, nationalities etc.
Paranoia: persecution complex
Uxoricide: Killing of a wife by husband

172\. (A) Cy Pres Doctrine: construing written instruments as near to the intention of the parties as possible. (usually wills)
Res Judicata: a thing already adjudicated upon
Obiter Dictum: opinion of the court on a matter not involved in the case. (not a decision)

173\. (B) Portrait Parle: spoken picture; photograph with description
Modus Operandi: Criminal's method of operation
Anthropometry: Measurements of body structure and bones.
Graphology: Study of handwriting

174\. (B) True Bill: an indictment on the concurrence of 12 grand jurors and signed by the foreman.
Presentment: report of a grand jury on an investigation conducted by them with respect to conditions in the county.

Commission: An authority granted by a court to a person named to perform certain acts or to exercise certain jurisdiction(attorney to take written deposition of a non-resident)

175. (D) Information: Basis for magistrate's jurisdiction; allegation before a magistrate charging a person with crime. Same as a complaint. In felony cases, an indictment is basis for felony trial.

176. (A) Pari delicto: equally at fault
Corpus delicti: body or substance of the crime
pari materia: equally relevant
Crimen falsi: the crime of falsifying (forgery, perjury etc)

177. (C) Accessory: One knowing that a felony has been committed, aids the felon to avoid arrest, trial, punishment, by harboring and sheltering him. In misdemeanor cases, such a person is not deemed an accessory but a "principal"

178. (A) Pornography: obscene art or literature
Masochism: sexual pleasure in being beaten by another
Amercement: punishment by an exactment, assessment or fine
Didacticism: art of teaching

179. (C) Due Process of Law: Law in its regular course of administration through courts of justice. It imports a judicial trial, and not a mere declaration of legislative will by the passing of a law.
Adjective Law: law regulating pleadings and procedures
Substantive Law: defines rights and obligations of persons.

180. (D) Material Witness: an important key witness
Competent Witness: One not disqualified because of mental capacity, etc

181. (A) Compounding: The crime of taking a reward for forbearing to prosecute a crime or to withhold evidence etc
Compromising: An adjustment of misdemeanors by mutual concession without resort to the law. Compromise is legal if done according to law.
Misprision: failure to reveal crime

182. (C) Tortfeasor: wrongdoer
Litigant: one of the parties to a law suit

183. (A) Note of Issue: After issue joined, either party may place the case on the calendar by filing a note of issue. It contains all the pertinent information: title of the case, names and addresses of the attorneys, time when last pleading was served, whether triable by jury, specific nature of the action.

184. (D) Respondent: answers the appellant's appeal
Appellant: one who appeals

185. (C) Information: basis of jurisdiction over misdemeanors
Indictment: basis of jurisdiction over felonies

186. (A) Provisional Remedy (attachment, Arrest, Injunction, Replevin Receiver) Temporary nature, during pending action and before final adjudication of the rights of the parties. It makes the final judgment more effective.
Attachment: To seize the property of the defendant within the jurisdiction and hold it as security for any judgment subsequently recovered against the defendant.
Arbitration: submitting the matter in conflict before an unofficial person designated by the court for a ruling
Sequestration: Depositing a thing which is in controversy in the hands of a 3rd person to hold for the contending parties.

187. (C) Garnishee: A party in whose hand money or property is attached by the creditor of another, and who is compelled to set aside this property in payment of the creditor's claim.
Replevin: Provisional remedy for the recovery of specific property.

188. (A) Subrogation: Substituting one person for another with respect to certain rights and claims. Ex: An insurance company after paying damage claim of the assured sues the negligent party in the name of the assured - this is subrogation.

189. (B) Special Verdict: When the jury finds the facts only and the court is to determine who is liable under such finding. It is in writing and entered by the clerk in the minutes.
General Verdict: jury pronounces generally in favor of a party and may assess damages.
Sealed Verdict: usually ordered when the jury continues its deliberations beyond the closing hour of the court. The jury writes out its verdict, encloses it in a sealed envelope to be delivered to the clerk who reads the verdict the following day in open court.

190. (D) The counterclaim is in effect the defendant's "complaint" or "counter-complaint" just as the complaint is the Plaintiff's claim.

191. (B) Admission: Statement of fact from which guilt or liability may be inferred.
Confession: a voluntary declaration of guilt made by a person who has committed a crime.
Presumption: an inference as to the existence of some fact not known arising from its connection with facts that are known.

192. (D) Just as a summons requests the attendance of a person in court to answer a complaint, a citation requests the appearance of persons on a probate of a will (in Surrogates Court)

193. (C) Relator: a person in whose behalf certain writs are issued
Appellant: one who institutes an appeal
Complainant: one who brings complaint
Affiant: one who signs an affidavit.

194. (D) Probation: Instead of prison sentence, defendant is released on probation for a definite period of time.
Parole: after part of the sentence is served, prisoner may be released for the duration of the sentence.
Commutation: Governor's privilege in reducing the punishment of a prisoner.
Pardon: Governor's authority to release a prisoner from serving the balance of his sentence.

195. (C) Stipulation: a written agreement, generally between attorneys, agreeing to a certain condition or set of facts, or mutual agreement as to adjournment of the case etc.

196. (D) Default Judgment: Judgment rendered in favor of the party who appeared when the opposing party fails to appear on the trial date. Default judgments may be opened if the court deems the default was excusable.
Interlocutory Judgment: Provisional; not final
Declaratory Judgment: Supreme Court power in any action or proceeding to declare the rights of parties upon request for such declaration. The declaration made has the force and effect as a final judgment. It is advisory but with final effect.
Non-suit: The name of a judgment given against a plaintiff when he is unable to prove his case.

197. (A) Estoppel: That which prevents a person from alleging or denying a fact because of his own previous act or allegation of a contrary nature.
Escheat: reversion of property to the state in default of a person who may inherit it.

198. (C) Ballot: contains the names of the prospective jurors

199. (B) Judicial Notice: The knowledge which a court will officially take of a fact without proof. It dispenses with the necessity of offering evidence as to such fact. Ex: Laws of the state, etc.
Legal Presumption: a legal inference which may or may not be rebutted. Ex: Child under 7 years cannot commit crime (conclusive presumption) whereas, every man is presumed innocent is a legal presumption but rebuttable.

200. (C) Concurrent Sentence: Sentences instead of being served one after other (cumulative) are served at the same time. Thus, a defendant who received 5 years for burglary and 2 years for wiretapping, need serve only the 5 year sentence, since the 2 year sentence is being served at the same time as the 5 year sentence.
Consecutive: same as cumulative; one after the other

201. (C) Referee: a person appointed by the court to hear and determine a matter in dispute. Its finding is called a report (not decision).
Receiver: a person appointed by the court with authority to receive the rents and profits of the lands or other property in dispute, to hold them until the dispute has been settled.

202. (B) Appearance: to appear in court as plaintiff, defendant, etc.
Arraignment: bringing the accused before the court in order to answer a charge placed against him.

203. (A) Supplementary Proceedings: Proceedings instituted after judgment, to inquire of the defendant what properties and possessions he owns so that execution on such possessions may be had in satisfaction of judgment. Frequently, defendants try to conceal from the creditors their assets. Contempt Proceedings: proceedings for the punishment of those charged with contempt of court. Discovery and Inspection: a procedure on notice, authorizing an attorney to prepare his case for trial, to obtain certain information contained in books, papers, documents, photographs which are under the control of the adverse party.

204. (A) Release: a legal instrument which states that for a consideration one party releases the other from all liability.

205. (C) Dactyloscopy: science of fingerprinting
Ballistics: science of projectiles (firearms)
Semantics: study of linguistics which deals with meaning; words.
Anthropometry: measurements of body bones

206. (B) Hypothecate: To pledge a thing without delivering the possession of it to the pledgee.
Encumbrance: a lien or liability attached to real property
Filiation: judicial fixing of paternity of child born out of wedlock.
Bailment: holding of property (persons) according to the purpose of delivery and to be returned when the purpose has been accomplished.

207. (D) Infamous: atrocious, base, notorious.
Turpitude: any act contrary to justice, honesty, and morals.

208. (D) Motive: reason for doing an act
Intent: state of mind to do or omit an act
Deliberation: a weighting in the mind whether to do or not do an act
Premeditation: the thinking of an act before hand

209. (D) Enacting Clause: To put into the form of an act; to give legislative sanction to a bill.
Proviso: A condition inserted in a deed, on the observance whereof the validity of the deed depends.
Preamble: The introduction or commencement of a statute, setting forth by way of recital, the intention of the legislature in framing it, the circumstances which occasioned its passage, etc.
Purview: the providing part of a statute; that which follows the preamble, and contains the direct and express provisions of the law.

210. (D) Acknowledgement: The act by which a party who has executed an instrument, declares it before a competent officer, to be his act and deed.

211. (D) If it is to affect those reaching their majority, then the law should include the 21 year olds as well as those over 21.

212. (C) Saving Clause: Usually inserted at the end of a lengthy statute. Its purpose is to salvage as much of the original statute as possible should any part be declared unconstitutional.

213. (A) The date of the hearing is June 11; hence count back 5 days including June 11, we have June 7; consequently, the day prior to June 7th is the last day of the notice, or June 6th.

214. (B) Peremptory: No reason need be given; absolute; without cause

215. (C) Attestation: Witnessing a written instrument and signing to that effect. It is an act of authentication. Subscription: the signing of a written command directing an officer of the law to enforce a judgment.
Exemplification: A certified transcript under seal of a record

216. (D) Seizin: possession of land; possession of an estate of freehold in lands.

217. (A) Interlocutory: intermediate; something done or determined between the commencement and the termination of an action

218. (B) Per Curiam: by the court

219. (A) Ultra Vires: Acts of a corporation beyond the scope of its authority.

220. (C) Stare Decisis: to stand by decided cases; to uphold the precedents; to maintain former adjudications.

221. (B) Pari Delicto: equal blame

222. (C) Obiter Dicta: An opinion of a judge delivered or expressed by the way , and not upon the point in question before him.

223. (C) Res adjudicata: former adjudication of a thing or action; a former judgment.

224. (B) Injuria Sine Damno: A personal injury without damages; a wrong not resulting in any damages.

225. (B) Fee Simple: absolute ownership of property as distinguished from a lease, mortgage, etc.

226. (E) The basic principle of all criminal prosecutions is the presumption of law that the defendant is presumed innocent until proven guilty.

227. (A) Bill of Particulars: A written statement or specifications of the particulars of the demand for which an action at law is brought.

228. (A) Guardian Ad Litem: A guardian appointed by the court to represent a minor under 21 years in a civil action.

229. (E) Bail: granted under the law in most criminal cases where the release of the defendant is reasonable. The theory behind bail is that a defendant may ultimately be proven innocent and to hold in custody in all cases would be deemed unwarranted punishment.

230. (D) Juries are made up of 12 persons, except in Municipal Courts (6 jurors). There is less likely to be bias and prejudice among the panel of persons selected as jurors.

231. (A) Grand Jury: Inquire into the commission of crimes committed within the county. Such an investigation requires the calling and examining of witnesses.

232. (A) Debenture: a form of promissory note issued by a corporation in return for a loan.

233. (C) Penal Law: defines most of the crimes which can be committed within the state and also prescribes their punishment. The Code of Criminal Procedure outlines the manner in which criminal prosecutions are to be taken.

234. (C) Attachment: seizure of property by legal process inorder to bring it into the custody of the law.
Certiorari: court review of the decision of an administrative officer.
Injunction: Restraining order
Mandamus: Order compelling a public official to perform an official duty.

235. (C) Common Law: Decisions of courts in previous cases based upon the same or similar facts. Unwritten laws.
Statutory Laws: Laws passed by the legislature. Written laws.

236. (D) Summary Proceedings: Special proceeding in which a landlord seeks court authority to evict a tenant. (dispossess proceedings) A petition rather than a summons commences the action.

237. (B) The function of a witness is to present the facts inorder that the court or jury may reach a decision as to liability under the law. Opinion evidence by a witness is allowed if he is qualified as an expert in the particular field with which the matter is concerned.

238. (D) Since the court attendant knows that the man has a revolver on his person, whether he has a pistol permit or not is not known, in any event the circumstance bears further investigation and if a detective is nearby the matter should be brought to his attention.

239. (D) This may be a hoax. In any event, take no chances, but have a sufficient number of attendants on hand when you open the door just in case the inmates attempt to escape. If after this is done, and there is apparent need for medical services, remove him from the pen and have a doctor summoned.

240. (D) This is contempt and as such should be reported to the judge presiding in the case.

241. (B) The deliberation should be stopped and the court clerk notified. If there are alternate jurors, the judge will select an alternate to take the place of the ailing juror.

242. (B) This is a violation of the Code of Ethics - soliciting business. The matter should be reported to the judge who will take action

243. (B) Since your instructions are to admit no one, full compliance is expected. If the detective insists on being admitted, he will have to resort to some other means but not through the court attendant.

244. (D) Only the judge has the power to suspend the deliberation in a matter of this nature.

245. (A) Since the man is apparently emotionally disturbed, appeasement seems to be the best choice under the circumstances. Any forceful eviction or language may only disturb him more and may result in serious harm to those about him.

246. (B) If the outcry was deliberate then it would amount to contempt for which proceedings would have to be instituted against him. In any event, the facts do not indicate whether it was intentional or not and hence only an arraignment before the same judge would bring this matter out.

247. (B) If no penalty is prescribed for the felony, the maximum shall be 7 years, and/or $1000 fine; if misdemeanor, maximum is 1 year and/or $500.

248. (A) Suicide is not a crime. But aiding and abetting another to commit suicide is a felony, and if the attempt is successful, the crime is manslaughter 1st degree.

249. (C) Res Gestae: Spontaneous utterances made at about the time the incident took place. It is hearsay evidence but admissible because of the spontaneity (little likelihood of falsification)
Demonstrative: real evidence (the object itself)
Circumstantial: indirect evidence. Evidence as to the existence of certain facts from which the existence of other facts may be inferred.

250. (C) Once trial starts, bail is a matter within court's discretion

251. (B) Polygraph: Lie detection machine. Records blood pressure, pulse, respiration, etc. as a result of questioning the individual.

252. (A) Constructive: construed as if actually occurred or existed.
Ex: constructive possession, constructive intent.

253. (A) Only judicial officers must warn accused before taking his confession.

254. (B) The only instance in law which requires direct evidence - the death of the victim cannot be established by circumstantial evidence.

255. (B) Subornation: Procuring another to commit perjury. If the perjury is committed, then subornation of perjury is the crime committed by suborner.

256. (B) Libel: malicious publication. The only misdemeanor in the state which requires a jury trial (State Constitution)
Coercion: (Misdemeanor) Compelling a person to do something which he does not legally have to do.
Conspiracy: Combination of two or more persons conspiring to commit a crime. (Misdemeanor)

257. (C) The accused must be in custody or appear before the indictment becomes a public record. Any one making known that a person has been indicted prior to person's custody commits a misdemeanor.

258. (A) When an inadequate supply of blood reaches the brain, the senses become dull and irresponsive. Victim becomes weak and pale. Inorder to get recirculation back into the brain the victim must be placed in a reclining position with head a little lower than the rest of his body.

259. (B) Adultery: Sexual intercourse of two persons, either of whom is married to a third person. Both parties are punishable; knowledge of marriage is immaterial. Bigamy: A person, who having a husband or wife living, marries another person. If both parties are married to others, then both may be charged with bigamy; if only one is married, then he alone is charged with bigamy and the other person (single) may be charged with being Consort to bigamy if such person knew the other party was already married at the time.

260. (B) Coercion (Misd): Compelling another to do an act which he is not required to do or to abstain from doing an act which he has a right to do. Oppression: The unlawful use of authority whereby another is injured in his person, property, or rights.

261. (A) Exemplification: A certified transcript under seal of a court record. Certified Copy: A verification by a clerk of a court that a copy of a document on file in the court has been compared by him with the original and has found the copy to be the exact duplicate of the one on file.

262. (A) The rule is based upon an assumed intention of the parties, evidenced by a written instrument, to place themselves beyond the uncertainties of oral testimony, and the courts are not disposed to defeat this presumed intention of the parties. The instrument itself is the thing to be dealt with. It is a protection against fraud and perjury, infirmity of memory, and the death of the witnesses.

263. (D) Foreclosure of Mortgages: An equity action or proceeding in the Supreme Court. A, B, and C are within the jurisdiction of the Surrogates Court.

264. (D) Bribery: The taking of an undue reward by a public official, juror, judge, athlete etc. to influence his behavior in his office. Extortion: The unlawful taking of property of another with his consent induced by a wrongful use of force or fear, or under color of official right.

265. (B) Indictment: Written accusation rendered by a grand jury. Information: The allegation made to a magistrate, that a person has been guilty of some designated crime. In case of trivial misdemeanors in which the officer brings the culprit before the court for a crime committed in his presence, no written information is necessary.

266. (C) Magistrate: An officer, having the power to issue a warrant for the arrest of a person charged with a crime. Examples: Judges of Supreme Court, County Courts, General Sessions Court, Children's Court, Inferior Courts (Magistrate's Courts); also the Mayor or Recorder of a city.

267. (B) Evidence of Intoxication: Not as a defense to the crime because of such intoxication. However, whenever it is necessary to prove motive or intent as a necessary element of a crime, the jury may take into consideration the fact that the accused was intoxicated at the time, for the purpose of determining the motive or intent with which he committed the act.

268. (D) Best Evidence Rule: To prove the contents of a writing one may do so by producing the writing itself, unless sufficient reason shown for not producing the writing. If the original cannot with due diligence be produced then secondary evidence may be permitted (copy of the original)

269. (B) City Court & Municipal Court Appeals go directly to the Appellate Term of the Supreme Court and from thence to the Appellate Division of the Supreme Court.

270. (D) In this portion of the body the artery is not sufficiently close to the bone for application of the pressure needed to stop the flow of blood.

271. (D) Opinion Evidence: As a general rule witnesses must testify to facts and not to their opinions drawn from the facts. It is the sole province of the jury to draw inferences from the facts. However, an exception is permitted where the opinion of an ordinary witness may be reached because of the necessity of the case, for it often happens that it is quite impossible for a witness to describe in detail all the pertinent facts in such a manner as to enable a jury to form a conclusion without the opinion of the witness. Example: where a stain is paint or blood, a witness may give his opinion that it was blood.

272. (A) In cases of severe bleeding, even though the victim has stopped breathing, it is necessary to stop the bleeding first before applying resuscitation. Otherwise, if resuscitation is started first, with each stroke of the method, more blood will be forced out of the body ultimately resulting in death.

273. (D) Felony Cases: Any one knowing that a felony was committed by a person, harbors, shelters, or aids such criminal to escape apprehension - such person is known as an Accessory and not an accomplice, nor is he a principal. Misdemeanor Cases: Such person who aids the misdemeanant after the commission of the crime, would be called principal and not an accessory as in the case of a felony.

274. (A) Intent of the perpetrator is important for the purpose of determining whether the larceny was committed but is not important for determining whether the larceny is of a particular degree. The other elements are important for determining degrees. Example: Pickpocket at night would be charged with 1st degree whereas the act if committed during the day would constitute 2nd degree larceny (assuming the value in either case is not over $100)

275. (C) Direct Evidence: Positive evidence - when the facts in dispute are sworn to by those who by means of their senses have actual knowledge of them.
Circumstantial Evidence: Relates to facts other than those in issue, which by human experience, have been found to be so associated with the fact in issue that the latter may be reasonably inferred.
Real Evidence: (Demonstrative Evidence) The thing itself.
Cumulative Evidence: Accumulated evidence all on the same point. Example: A number of witnesses all testifying to the same point.

276. (D) Shock Symptoms: Pale, clammy skin, cold, weak pulse etc.

277. (C) Chattel: Every tangible type of property, movable or immovable, not realty.

278. (D) The Constitutional provision against compelling an accused person to testify refers only to an oral examination before or upon trial or to a compulsory production of documents or chattels in response to a subpoena or court order. The other items A, B, and C may be compelled without violating this provision.

279. (C) Action Commenced: (1) information laid before a magistrate and a warrant issued, or (2) Indictment rendered, received and filed in the proper court. The compliance with either of these two cases stops the running of the statute of limitations.

280. (D) Blackmail: Intent to extort or gain money or property or to procure any illegal or wrongful act etc. Must be in writing.
Extortion: requires the obtaining of property of another with his consent induced by wrongful use of force or fear etc.

281. (B) If the violation is not denominated a felony or misdemeanor, it shall be deemed a misdemeanor. This does not make a criminal intent on the part of the one doing the prohibited act an element of the crime.

282. (A) Burden of Proof: the obligation which rests on one of the parties to an action to persuade the trier of the facts (the jury) of the truth of a proposition which he has affirmatively asserted by the pleadings. In a criminal case, it rests with prosecution - it never shifts to the defendant. The burden of going forward with the evidence shifts from the one party to the other but not the burden of proof.

283. (D) Search Warrant: Must be executed within 10 days after it has been issued. It cannot be extended but a new warrant must be obtained at the expiration of the 10 day period. Arrest warrants are unlimited.

284. (A) Pleas: (1) Guilty, (2) Not Guilty, and (3) Former judgment of conviction or acquittal (double jeopardy)
Statute of Limitations: Not a plea but a defense under a not guilty plea. Demurrer: A pleading of the defendant but not a plea. It is a formal objection to an indictment.

285. (D) Child under 16 may be charged with and convicted of a crime which is punishable by death or life imprisonment provided the child is 15 years of age. Such crimes are Murder, Lynching, Treason, and Kidnapping. Such child cannot be found guilty of attempted Murder, etc. since such attempted crime would not be punishable by death or life imprisonment.

286. (A) Chose in Action: A thing in action.
Laches: unreasonable delay in bringing an action
Remand: A re-commitment to custody; to send back into custody
Dictum: court's opinion

287. (D) Privileged Communication: Upon grounds of public policy, the parties to such privileged communications, are under certain circumstances, made incompetent by law, to testify to such communications. There are 4 such relationships which the law recognizes as privileged: (1) Attorney and Client, (2) Husband & Wife, (3) Physician or Dentist and patient, and (4) Clergyman & penitent.

288. (C) Corroborated Evidence: Must tend to connect the defendant with the crime. It must be definite, legal character, independent of testimony of accomplice and must fairly and reasonably connect the defendant with the commission of the crime. It is not required that it substantiate all the elements of the crime or to show that the crime was in fact committed.

289.(B) or (D) Perjury: Felony if the falsehood pertained to a material point in issue, a misdemeanor if otherwise. The degree does not depend on whether the trial is for a felony or a misdemeanor but rather on the materiality of the statement made. It is immaterial that the oath was not administered in the regular way so long as some kind of an oath was given. Conviction cannot be had on the uncorroborated testimony of only one witness against the alleged perjurer. If a witness testified falsely at the beginning and later on cross-examination admits the truth, although it would appear that he committed perjury, yet the courts have held that it was not interested in punishing the witness but in extracting the truth.

290. (B) Autoptic: self-inspection: real evidence

291. (B) Prima Facie Evidence: at first glance; sufficient to contradict if uncontroverted.
Relevant Evidence: evidence which is related to the issue; touches upon the issue; Material Evidence: when it has an effective influence or bearing upon question in issue. Competent Evidence: that which by the very nature of the thing to be proved requires, as the fit and appropriate proof in the particular case.
Conclusive Evidence: that which is irrebuttable and final.

292. (C) If the person is unconscious, the administering of the liquid may cause him to choke.

293. (B) Indictment: First pleading on the part of the people. It may contain several crimes if arising out of the same act or transaction. It shall contain a plain concise statement constituting the crime; defendant may be indicted by a fictitious name if the true name be unknown.

294. (D) Grand Jury: 16 to 23 members; 16 members represent a quorum; 12 needed for an indictment; power to inquire into all crimes committed or triable in the county, and to present them to the court. Bound to hear evidence for the prosecution but not necessarily evidence of the defendant.

295. (A) An express acknowledgment of guilt by an accused is a confession. An admission is an act done or a statement made by an accused from which his guilt, or one or more of the facts in issue, may be inferred.

296. (A) The Penal Law provides that no person can be convicted of murder or manslaughter unless the death of the person alleged to have been killed is shown by direct evidence. The criminal agency of the defendant, the identity of the victim of the homicide, and the intent of the killer may be shown by either direct or circumstantial evidence.

207. (D) A child is deemed "neglected" when it is in a condition of physical, mental, or moral need, which is the fault of parent or guardian. However, where the condition of the child is the result of his own voluntary acts and cannot be charged to parent or guardian (see choices A, B, and C), such child is deemed "delinquent".

298. (A) This is the meaning of a compound fracture. However, if a broken bone does not pierce the outer surface of the skin, the break is termed a simple fracture, no matter how serious it may be for other reasons.

299. (A) In hearsay evidence, information is furnished which is not within the personal knowledge of the witness but was obtained from some other source. Hence, because the source of the information is not subject to cross-examination (this is more important than being under oath), there is no assurance that the hearsay evidence is truthful.

300. (C) Jurors must be challenged jointly where there are two or more defendants. A defendant charged with a felony cannot be tried in his absence. The selection of alternate jurors is always within the discretion of the trial judge. There is no limit on the number of challenges for cause, only on the number of peremptory challenges.

301. (A) It is possible to read into evidence at a trial, in the absence of the witness himself, testimony which was given by such witness on a previous trial or at a preliminary examination before a magistrate, or during a conditional examination before trial. The other choices represent basic rights of a defendant in a criminal prosecution.

302. (D) The fundamental distinction between "felony" and"misdemeanor" rests on the maximum penalty that may be imposed. The character of the crime is not determined by the extent of injuries caused thereby. A felony is a crime punishable by death or imprisonment in a state prison and any other crime is a misdemeanor.

303. (D) Subornation cannot be committed unless the person suborned actually committed the perjury. Hence if the witness refused to testify falsely, no subornation can lie. However,the solicitors could be charged with coercion (compelling a person to do something he is not compelled to do) or Conspiracy (two or more agreeing to commit a crime) or Suppressing Evidence (Misdemeanor)

304. (C) Demurrer: The only pleading for the defendant is either a demurrer or a plea. Demurrer to an indictment is not a plea to it - it is trial upon issues of law. It raises objections which appear on the face of the indictment. If the indictment does not state facts which constitute a crime, it may be attacked by a demurrer. If the indictment shows that the grand jury was without jurisdiction, again the demurrer would lie. When an indictment has been filed, the defendant must be arraigned before the court in which it is found. The defendant personally must plead to a felony indictment whereas in a misdemeanor case, the attorney for the defendant may plead for the defendant.

305. (D) Grand Jurors: sworn to secrecy as to how each has voted in an indictment. It is a misdemeanor to violate this provision. If any part of the evidence is illegal, the indictment may nevertheless stand so long as the illegal evidence was not the basis for the indictment.

306. (D) Maliciously: imports an evil intent or design to vex and annoy or injure another; Corruptly: wrongful desire to acquire some pecuniary or other advantage. Wilfully: deliberately Knowingly: knowledge that the facts exist which constitute the act or crime - it does not mean knowledge of the unlawfulness of the act.

307. (D) Confession: Whether in the course of judicial proceedings or to a private person, can be given in evidence against the defendant, unless made under the influence of fear produced by threats, or unless made upon a stipulation of the district attorney, that he shall be immune from prosecution. It will be admissible despite the fact that it was obtained through deception and fraud.

308. (B) Juror's Qualifications: 21 to 70 years of age; own property (real or personal) worth at least $250; Not convicted of a felony or misdemeanor involving moral turpitude. Scruples against the death penalty will disqualify if the case is one involving the death penalty; otherwise it will not disqualify.

309. (D) Overt Act: any physical outward act or gesture. Ex: Walking, writing, raising hand, etc. The act itself need not be criminal.

310. (C) Presumption of Law: A rule of law which requires that a certain fact must be inferred by the court from the existence of certain other facts. It is a definite conclusion of law which must be drawn as soon as a given set of facts is established, even though it may thereafter be rebutted by evidence offered in opposition to it. Ex: Every man is presumed to be sane; a sane man is presumed to intend the natural consequences of his act; every one knows the law; etc. The unlawful use of a weapon does not create a legal presumption of intent to kill -- there is no such presumption. The jury may presume the intent from these facts when it would be called a presumption of fact (an inference based on circumstantial evidence)

311. (B) Jury Exemptions: Clergyman, Doctor, Dentist, Pharmacist, Optometrist, Embalmer, Lawyer, Armed Forces, Fireman, Policeman, Marine pilot, Marine Engineer or Captain, Woman, Reporter.

312. (D) Consort (To Bigamy) A person who marries another knowing that such other person is already married commits the crime of Consort; the married person commits Bigamy. One is not the accomplice of the other since these are separate crimes.

313. (B) Pardon: The governor has power to grant reprieves, commutations and pardons, after conviction, for all offenses, except Treason & cases of Impeachment. Upon a conviction for Treason, he may suspend the execution of sentence until the case can be reported to the legislature which can pardon, commute the sentence, direct the execution thereof, or grant a further reprieve.

314. (D) Appeals By the People: (1) From a judgment for the defendant on a demurrer to an indictment; (2) From an order of the court arresting judgment; (3) From an order of the court dismissing the indictment; (4) In all cases where an appeal may be taken by the defendant, EXCEPT where verdict or judgment of NOT GUILTY has been rendered. It follows then, that the People cannot appeal a verdict of acquittal.

315. (C) Adjective Law: Laws which relate to procedures, such as Civil Practice Act, Code of Criminal Procedure, etc.
Substantive Law: Laws which relate to rights and duties, such as Penal Law, Insurance Law, General Business Law, etc.
Chattel: Personal Property; Affinity: relationship through marriage; Consanguinity: relationship through blood as decendants from a common ancestor. Capital Punishment: Death penalty only (does not include life imprisonment)

316. (C) Corroborative: Confirms or substantiates Smith's statement that Jones was in the factory at about the time alleged. It only confirms the presence of Jones not that Jones committed the crime.
Demonstrative Evidence: Same as Real Evidence; the thing itself.

317. (A) "Cross-examination is the acid test of the truthfulness of a witness' testimony" In cross-examination, the attorney for the opposing party is given every reasonable opportunity to probe the direct testimony of the witness in an effort to discover and show any defects which will minimize or destroy the effect of such testimony. Perjury, bias and incompetency are just some of the defects which may be indicated as the result of a good cross-examination.

318. (A) A witness who has been excluded from the courtroom will be protected against the possible effect which the testimony of another witness might have on his recollection of the events in question. A witness who has been excluded from the courtroom might be tempted and encouraged to commit perjury much more than a witness who was present in court and heard the testimony of other witnesses.

319. (B) The basic function of a witness is to present the facts so that the jury may, after due consideration, reach its own conclusions. Therefore, a witness is ordinarily barred from expressing his own opinion in connection with the facts. However, there are exceptions to this general rule. Where a subject matter is such that a jury should have specialized assistance, an expert witness will be permitted to express his opinion. In addition, where the facts are such that it is very difficult to describe them as such, even an ordinary witness will be allowed to give opinion evidence.

320. (A) The burden of proof in a criminal action is on the plaintiff and never shifts. A person may be tried twice for the same crime provided the trial did not result in a conviction or acquittal or provided the defendant appealed and the case was sent back for a new trial. The right to appeal is fixed by statutory law and not by the Constitution. The weight of evidence is determined by the jury.

321. (B) Any attack made upon the truthfulness and veracity of a witness is termed "impeaching the credibility" of such witness.

322. (A) The term "criminal conversation" is taken from the common law and relates to an act of sexual intercourse under circumstances which are **criminal** or **illicit**.

323. (D) A person cannot know the date of his birth from his own personal knowledge. Since this information depends upon what the person has been informed an appreciable time after his birth, it is clearly hearsay. However, such evidence has always been admissible and does not require corroboration.

324. (B) Motive is always indicated by the answer to the question: "Why did the defendant do what he did?" Choices "A" and "D" relate to intent.

325. (B) The matter of a jury's visit to the scene of a crime is left to the sound discretion of the court, whether the crime being prosecuted before the jury is a felony or a misdemeanor (C.C.P. 411).

326. (C) Any person who comes within the category of being a party properly interested in a trial or its outcome may compel the disclosure of what occurred during such trial. However, a combination of statutory law and court decisions makes the deliberations of judges, grand jurors and trial jurors privileged.

327. (D) Illegally seized evidence is admissible in New York State Courts; the aggrieved party however may bring ciminal and civil actions against the officer or persons illegally seizing the evidence. Conversely, evidence illegally seized by agents of the federal government or by persons acting at their direction is inadmissible in any federal courts.

328. (C) The term "caveat emptor", literally translated, means "let the buyer beware". It is used to explain the legal principle that, where a seller makes no representations or warranties, the buyer purchases at his own risk on an "as is" basis.

329. (B) Where a defendant appeals in a criminal case, the defendant is termed the appellant and the People of the State of New York become known as the respondent. A petitioner is one who institutes a special type of criminal or civil proceeding, such as delinquent or neglected child cases.

330. (B) By restricting a witness to "Yes" or "No" answers to questions, the witness is prevented from relating his own version of the subject under investigation; moreover, this type of questioning is considered leading or suggestive and therefore is unsuited for eliciting desired information from witnesses, particularly friendly witnesses. (MCI 129) Questions should be asked after the witness finishes his narration to test the completeness and accuracy of his story.

331. (D) The word "forensic" is usually linked with some specific skill or field of knowledge, e.g. forensic ballistics, forensic medicine, and indicates an application of such skill or knowledge to the rules of evidence for use in court trials and other legal proceedings.

332. (B) Emotional stress (fear) is occasioned in a person who is knowingly guilty of lying. This apprehension or stress causes physiological changes in blood pressure, pulse, respiration, and electro-dermal responses. The lie detector technique is based upon recording some or all of these changes.

333. (B) Severance is the converse of consolidation. An action may be severed whenever the court deems it desirable in the interests of justice and it can be done without prejudice to a substantial right. Severance is generally appropriate where some but not all of a number of defendants who are severally liable have been served with the summons.

334. (A) Poor Person: One not worth $300 besides his clothes and household furniture may petition the court to sue or defend as a poor person. The court will assign an attorney for him without compensation, although it may allow a reasonable fee out of any recovery in his favor. He is not required to pay any court fees or costs of the action; he need not file any undertaking where it otherwise might be required.

335. (C) Substituted Service: Practical device for coping with people resorting to many ruses to elude the process server. Serving a person of proper age at defendant's residence, or defendant's place of business, or by affixing the summons to the door and mailing additional copies to the defendant. Substituted Service requires a court order.

336. (B) Supplemental Summons: When the court directs a new party to be brought in as defendant after an action has been begun, a "supplemental summons" must be served on the additional party. It is substantially the same as the original summons except that the additional name is added. The additional party answers the original or amended or supplemental complaint, as the case requires.

337. (B) Guardian-ad-litem: If infant is a plaintiff, a guardian-ad-litem should be appointed before the summons is served. If he is 14 or over, he makes the application himself; if under 14, the application is made by his general or testamentary guardian, or by a relative or friend.

338. (A) Contested Motion: A motion which requires notice to the adverse party thus giving him the opportunity to submit proofs and argue in opposition. Every such motion involves three steps: 1. the notice of motion, 2. the hearing and 3. the order.

339. (B) A motion is made when the papers are served on the adversary.

340. (D) A request to charge is made when counsel wishes the court to charge the jury on a matter not covered or insufficiently explained in the charge delivered by the court. The court may grant the request or deny it. Counsel may take "exception" to the court's refusal to charge as requested.

341. (A) Judgment Roll: Consists of the summons, the pleadings, admissions, the judgment and orders which involve the merits or necessarily affect the judgment. It is prepared and filed by the attorney for the successful party. The clerk thereupon enters the judgment in the judgment docket. This has the effect of making the judgment a lien on real property which the debtor has.

342. (C) Laches: Neglect to make a claim within a reasonable time; slackness, negligence or remissness.

343. (C) Award: By arbitrators in an arbitration proceeding. This proceeding is a special proceeding; informal in nature; no pleadings are used; it does not call for a hearing in any court. After an award, a motion is made to confirm the award and a judgment is obtained thereon which has the same effect as any other judgment obtained.

344. (C) Court of Appeals: The essential function of this court is to review questions of law, except in two cases: (1) death penalty cases and (2) civil cases where the Appellate Division has made new findings of fact and has rendered a final judgment or order.

345. (A) Non-Suit: Defendant moves for a non-suit, i.e., to dismiss the complaint on the theory that the proof adduced by the plaintiff fails to support the cause of action alleged in the complaint. This is done at the close of the plaintiff's case.

346. (C) Subscribed in the name of the attorney for the plaintiff with the post office address. If the plaintiff appears without an attorney, he may subscribe the summons.

347. (B) et seq.:and the following
et al : and others
ibid: in the same place
supra: above; infra: below

348. (A) Covenant: The agreement or consent of two or more by deed in writing, sealed, and delivered, whereby either or one of the parties promises to the other that something is done or shall be done.

349. (D) Court of Record: A court where the acts and judicial proceedings are enrolled in paper for a perpetual memory.

350. (C) Without Prejudice: Not a final determination on the merits; perhaps because of some technicality which can be cured by amendment etc. In any event, plaintiff has not lost his right to reinstitute the action.

* * * * * * * * * * *

KNOW YOUR COURTS

This section will familiarize candidates for civil service examinations with the City, County, and State Courts of New York.

The layman who has had only a minimum of contact with our courts may believe our judicial system to be complex and involved. This section will provide an easy, clear, and concise breakdown of the system. By dividing our court system into proper categories, listing them in their relative standings, and defining the most popular terms used in connection with our courts, this system shall be brought well within the understanding of the civil service candidate.

The courts of the City of New York have been revised effective September 1, 1962. This revision had become necessary because of sociological and economic changes in our society. When our courts were originally set up, inflation had not yet reared its ugly head and different types of crimes were being committed from those taking place today. Thus our courts were actually geared for different times and for different conditions than those existing in our present-day modern society.

To illustrate, the jurisdiction of our State Supreme Court, under the old system, included cases where claims were in excess of $6,000. Before inflation, this sum represented a substantial amount of money; today it does not. This court, therefore, was burdened with a tremendous backlog of cases because in a majority of civil cases for the recovery of damages due to negligence the claims were in excess of this sum. Hence, we can now see that the number of cases to be tried in this court became excessive due to the inflationary process.

Under our old system, due to the existence of many different courts, the administrative process was decentralized. Each court more or less ran itself. The result was duplication of similar processes and dire inflexibility. One court could be flooded while another court was practically idle. Still, a case could not be transferred from one court to another because the jurisdiction of the two courts were different. This, in fact, is the crux of the entire revision. Courts have been combined, resulting in more flexibility and a savings in the administrative and supervisory work.

There are three criteria by which a court may be classified. The first is the power which created the court. The courts of this state are in existence for either one of two reasons. Those that exist because they are provided for in the Constitution of the State of New York may be referred to as Constitutional Courts. The other type of court is provided for by local legislation or by the legislature of the State of New York. These have been created because of necessity and are referred to as Statutory Courts.

The second criterion is type of case tried. Those courts which try cases dealing with civil matters (suits for the recovery of damages or property, etc.) are known as Civil Courts. Other courts exist for the trying of persons accused of violations of laws, the conviction of which would make them criminals. These courts are called Criminal Courts. Both Criminal and Civil Courts may be either Constitutional or Statutory.

The third criterion is whether or not a court's verdict sets precedent for future trials. A court of record is one in which the decisions are recorded and may be referred to as a basis for future decisions involving similar circumstances. The newly established Civil Court is a court of record. Its decisions set precedents for the trying of future cases.

New York State Courts

COURT OF APPEALS

Organization: The Court of Appeals is the highest court in the State. (This fact provides for a question which is very frequently given on civil service examinations and which is a common pitfall for the unprepared candidate. The question requires the naming of the highest court in the state and the candidate, influenced by the very nature of the word "Supreme", invariably chooses the Supreme Court as his answer.)

The court of Appeals is composed of a chief judge and 6 associate judges elected for 14-year terms. The Governor, at the request of the court, may assign not more than four justices of the Supreme Court to act as associate judges of the Court of Appeals when warranted by the court's calendar. No more than seven judges sit on any one case. Five constitutes a quorum and four must concur to arrive at a decision.

Jurisdiction: This court is restricted to reviewing questions of law, except where the judgment is death, or where the Appellate Division makes new findings of fact and enters judgment or orders based on these findings. Appeals are heard as of right direct from the trial court where the question involved tests the validity of a statutory provision of the State or the United States, or in criminal cases where the judgment is death. They are heard from the Appellate Division of the Supreme Court as a matter of right from a judgment or order handed down by the Appellate Division granting a new trial. Also, from a decision of the Appellate Division when a construction of the Constitution of the State or of the United States is involved, or in a case where a Justice of the Appellate Division dissents, or from an order of reversal. Also, from questions of law certified by the Appellate Division, which, in their opinion, ought to be reviewed.

Note: Only one appeal is allowed in a criminal case as a matter of right.

No appeal from a final order of the Appellate Division in civil cases originally commenced in a court other than the Supreme, Surrogates', County Court, Court of Claims or Board of Audit, shall be reviewed, except by permission of the Appellate Division. Appeals from the death penalty go directly to this court.

THE COURT ON THE JUDICIARY

Organization: This court is made up of the chief judge of the Court of Appeals who presides over its hearing, the senior associate judge of the Court of Appeals who presides in the absence of the chief judge, and one justice from each department of the Appellate Division.

Jurisdiction: This court has power to remove or retire a judge among the following: Court of Appeals, justice of the Supreme Court, judge of the Court of Claims, surrogate, special surrogate, judge of the Court of Special Sessions, county court judge, justice of any city court of record.

COURT OF CLAIMS

Organization: The law provides that this court is composed of eight judges appointed by the Governor with the approval of the State Senate. Appointees must be attorneys with at least ten years' experience.

Jurisdiction: The State is sovereign and cannot be sued in the usual manner. However, under the Court Claims Act, the State waives its right to immunity for the acts of its employees and officers and consents to have its liability for acts of officers or employees determined in accordance with the same rules of law as apply to actions in the Supreme Court against an individual or corporation. Jurisdiction conferred on the Court of Claims to hear and determine all claims against the State to recover damages, injuries to property, or personal injury because of misfeasance of negligence of the officers or employees of the State while acting in their official capacity. It also has the power to hear and determine such private claims against the State as may be authorized by the State Legislature. It may also hear and determine any claim on the part of the State against a claimant. Appeals from this court may be taken to the Appellate Division in Albany.

COURT FOR THE TRIAL OF IMPEACHMENTS

Organization: This court is composed of the 51 State Senators, the associate judges of the Court of Appeals and the Chief Judge who presides.

Jursidiction: To try impeachments presented by the State Assembly against the Governor or Lieutenant Governor. The court may remove the accused from office, disqualify him from holding office under the State, or both. There is no provision for an appeal from this court.

SURROGATES' COURT

Organization: Surrogates are chosen by voters of their respective counties. Their term of office is six years except in the New York City counties of New York, Kings, Bronx, and Queens, where the term is 14 years, and New York County has two surrogates.

Jurisdiction: Try Will and Inheritance cases. Probate proceedings whether with or without a jury. Appoints guardians and public administrators. Issues letters of administration. Grants adoptions. Appeals from actions of the Surrogate Court are taken to the Appellate Division of the appropriate department. Note: The distinctive office of Surrogate does not exist in many of the counties outside of the City of New York. In counties where there is no separate office of Surrogate, the County Judge acts in that capacity.

THE SUPREME COURT—ALL COUNTIES

Organization: The State of New York is divided into 10 Judicial Districts and 4 Judicial Departments. A number of Supreme Court Justices are elected by the voters of each judicial district. Each district contains 2 or more counties and each department includes one or more districts. In the New York metropolitan area, the First District includes the counties of New York and the Bronx. The Second District takes in Kings and Richmond (Brooklyn and Staten Island) and seven nearby counties. The Tenth District includes Queens, Nassau and Suffolk. The Appellate Division of each department, in the fall of each year, assigns the various Supreme Court Justices within the department to hold the different special and trial terms of the Supreme Court. If the criminal calendar within a county warrants it, a Justice of the Supreme Court is assigned to sit in the Criminal Branch when felony cases are tried.

Jurisdiction: The court has unlimited civil jurisdiction in both civil and criminal cases, even where the death penalty is involved. In criminal cases, the Justice passes upon questions of law, and a petit jury of 12 determined the facts. However, in civil cases, the Justice may try the case with or without a jury. Appeals from this court are taken to the Appellate Division within the same department; except that in cases where the judgment is death, the appeal goes directly to the Court of Appeals.

APPELLATE TERM OF THE SUPREME COURT

Organization: This branch of the Court exists only in the First and Second Departments. It consists of not less than 3 and not more than 5 Supreme Court Justices, designated for a month at a time by the Appellate Division of the department from among the Supreme Court Justices; three sit to hear an appeal; two must concur for a decision.

Jurisdiction: Reviews cases on appeal from the Civil Court.

APPELLATE DIVISION OF THE SUPREME COURT

Organization: This is the second highest State court, ranking just below the Court of Appeals. Justices are appointed by the Governor for 5-year terms from among the Supreme Court Justices. In the larger districts, there are seven justices, in other districts there are five.

Jurisdiction: Normally, all cases on appeal must be heard by the Appellate Division, except where the judgment has been the death penalty, before going to the Court of Appeals. This division hears appeals from the Appellate Term and Trial and Special Terms of the Supreme Court, from the Criminal Court, Surrogates' Courts, and the Family Court. This court admits attorneys to practice and may, after a hearing, disbar them. It may also, after a hearing, remove from office, magistrates, municipal court justices and justices of the Court of Special Sessions. It has the power to issue writs of habeas corpus, mandamus, prohibition, and certiorari.

JUSTICE OF THE PEACE COURTS

Organization: In a number of counties outside of New York City, elected Justices of the Peace serve in a civil capacity hearing cases involving lesser claims.

Jurisdiction: Generally roughly equivalent to that of the Municipal and Small Claims courts. Cases are tried either with or without a jury.

GRAND JURY - ANY COUNTY

Organization: The Grand Jury is an essential part of the judiciary system of the County. It consists of 23 citizens, usually selected for a term of one month by the clerk of the Division of Jurors. One member is designated by the Court as Foreman, another as Assistant Foreman. A secretary is selected by the body itself. Sixteen jurors constitute a quorum. In order to secure an indictment, also known as a "true bill", twelve must vote for it.

Jurisdiction: To inquire into the crimes of the grade of felony, criminal libel, or other misdemeanors as are presented by the district attorney. The jury may also inquire into the condition and management of public prisons, and into willful and corrupt conduct of public officers in the county. The proceedings of the Grand Jury are called "ex parte" as the only witnesses heard are those for the State although occasionally, upon request, the defendant is heard.

CIVIL COURT

Organization: This is a newly created court effective Sept. 1, 1962. It eliminates, by its existence, the City Court and the Municipal Court. The judges elected to preside over this court are elected for a ten-year term.

Jurisdiction: It will have jurisdiction over civil cases up to $10,000. The civil part of the Supreme Court will sit in judgment over cases involving more than that sum.

Appeals from this court are directed to the Appellate Term of the Supreme Court.

CRIMINAL COURT OF NEW YORK CITY

Organization: This is a newly created court effective Sept. 1, 1962. The judges who preside over this court are Magistrates appointed by the Mayor for a ten-year term.

Jurisdiction: This court will assume the jurisdiction previously assigned to the Court of Special Sessions and the Magistrates' Court. Briefly, it will try offenses, misdemeanors, and in general, lesser crimes. The Criminal part of the Supreme Court will be empowered to try felonies in New York City as it previously has been empowered to handle crimes of this nature in other parts of the state. This will eliminate the Court of General Sessions in New York County and the County Courts which existed in other counties located within the city.

This court will have jurisdiction over:

1. Arraignment of persons arrested for all crimes

2. Narcotic proceedings

3. Trials of persons charged with an offense or misdemeanor

4. Arraignments, pleadings, examinations, trials and sentences of persons at least sixteen years of age but who have not yet reached their nineteenth birthday

5. Weekend and holiday arraignments and pleadings of persons arrested and charged with certain misdemeanors and offenses

6. Arraignments, pleadings, examinations, trials, and sentences of persons charged with violation of:

   a. Administrative Code of the City of New York

   b. Local laws of the City of New York

   c. Rules and regulations of a department of the City of New York

   d. Statutes of the State of New York

7. It may issue warrants of arrest and court summonses

8. Arraignments, pleadings, examinations, trials and sentences of persons charged with a violation of the gambling laws.

9. Arraignments, pleadings, trials and sentences of females charged with prostitution

10. Arraignments, pleadings, trials and sentences of males charged with being drunk and disorderly

11. Arraignments and pleadings of persons who are arrested after the day's courts are closed. They may try and sentence these people who are charged with offenses and misdemeanors.

Appeals from this court are directed to the Appellate Term of the Supreme Court.

THE FAMILY COURT

This court, established September 1, 1962, replaces the Children's Court of the State, the Domestic Relations Court of the City of New York, and the Girls' Term Court of the City of New York.

"The Family Court of the State of New York" is to be followed by the name of the county in which it is located.

Organization: This court is presided over by justices who are appointed by the Mayor for a ten-year term.

Jurisdiction: This court has jurisdiction over:

1. Neglect of children proceedings

2. Support of children proceedings

3. Paternity proceedings

4. Custody proceedings of children by reason of neglect

5. Adoption proceedings

6. Proceedings concerning juvenile delinquency and the determination of whether or not delinquents are in need of supervision

7. Proceedings involving acts which would constitute disorderly conduct or an assault between spouses or between parent and child or between members of the same family or household.

Appeals from this court are directed to the Appellate Division of the Supreme Court.

A NYC Court in Operation

CIVIL COURT

The purpose of this section is to present the forms and procedures employed in prosecuting a case in the Civil Court of the City of New York. This is a court of civil jurisdiction handling actions to $10,000.

Venue. In order to bring suit against a person in the Civil Court the plaintiff must first determine the appropriate district in which to institute the action. A suit may be started in any district of the borough where either of the parties resides or has his place of business. In accordance with his rule attorneys usually bring their actions in the district most convenient to them. "Venue" is the term applied to the district in which an action is brought.

The Summons and Complaint. Any number of plaintiffs may sue any number of defendants in the same action, but all the names must appear on the summons. The caption of the summons includes the name of the Court and the parties to the action. The same action must be used on all papers subsequently used in court in the same action. Captions are extremely important since they specify by whom and against whom a case is brought.

One side of a summons orders the defendant to appear before the Clerk of the Court 5 days after the service of the summons in order to answer the Complaint.

In Civil actions, every attorney is an officer of the Court and possesses the power to issue a summons asking the defendant to appear in court and answer the complaint against him. The party summoned does not have to appear to defend himself. But if he doesn't he thereby admits the truth of the complaint and judgment is obtained against him by default.

The Complaint. On the reverse side of the summons, usually in the lower part are the words "the nature and substance of the plaintiff's cause of action is as follows:" Under this, the attorney for the plaintiff writes the complaint which might take the following form: "Action to replevy personal property rightfully belonging to plaintiff." Though written, this is called an oral complaint because it is not sworn to.

Service of the Summons. Any person over 18 who is not a party to the action may serve the summons at any time, except on Sunday. The defendant must be found and the summons personally handed to him. It may be left on a table, or anywhere in his presence, should he refuse to accept it. However, he must first be informed by the person leaving it that he is being served with a summons. The server should never take a summons back. After a copy of the summons has been served on the defendant, the server must make an affidavit of service, which must be in writing and sworn to. The printed form of summons usually has a form of affidavit on the outside with blank space to be filled in.

Form: Affidavit of Service:

STATE OF NEW YORK) ss:
COUNTY OF KINGS)

John Doe being duly sworn, deposes and says: that on the 10th day of May, 1963 at No. 480 Marcy Avenue, in the Borough of Brooklyn, City of New New York, he served the within summons and complaint on Richard Roe, the defendant therein named by delivering to and leaving a true copy thereof with said defendant personally; deponent knew the said person so served as aforesaid to be the same person mentioned and described in said summons, and complaint as the defendant therein, deponent is over the age of 18 years and not a party to the action.

JOHN DOE

Sworn to before me this 11th day of May 1963

ALTON BING
Notary Public, Kings County

Substituted Service. When there is good reason to believe that the defendant is expecting to be served and is deliberately evading service by any of a number of ruses, the process server may make an affidavit in which he details his attempts to serve the summons or subpoena and the attempts at evasion on the part of the defendant. If the facts are in good form, and it appears that diligent efforts have been made to serve the evading defendant, then an order is issued for substituted service in which the judge permits the process in question, together with a copy of the order, to be left with a "person of proper age and discretion" at the defendant's residence. This must be done within five days, otherwise, the order lapses and a new one must be obtained.

Service by Publication. When a defendant leaves the State in order to evade service, and under certain other conditions, service may be consummated by publication after a diligent effort to locate the defendant has been made and it appears certain that he has left. As in substituted service, an affidavit must be submitted before the judge issues an order permitting service by publication. Usually, he specifies the newspapers in which the service is to be publicized and the number of times the statement must appear. This procedure does not apply in the Civil Court except where a warrant of attachment has been granted.

Traverse. When a defendant has not been properly served, his attorney may claim that a traverse has occurred and he may make a motion to vacate the service of the summons and dismiss the complaint on those grounds. Although cases are not usually closed on the grounds of traverse, the process server should avoid falling into such an error because it may be costly in that the defendant can utilize it to delay the trial.

Filing the Summons. Seven days after the copy of the summons is served the original with the affidavit of service must be filed with the Clerk of the Court named in the Summons. At this time, the case receives an index number that must be used on all subsequent papers filed in the case.

The Answer. The answer to the summons and complaint must be given within five days. The answer may be made orally to the clerk or on a regular printed form of answer. It usually contains a general denial, to which defenses may be added and even "counterclaims."

Counterclaims. Counterclaims are included in the answer when the defendant, instead of admitting that he has done any wrong, claims that he has been wronged and recites the details in very much the same manner as the complaint.

Bill of Particulars. The plaintiff and the defendant have the right to ask for a "bill of particulars" and in such a case a detailed statement of charges must be furnished by the party making the charges.

Notice of Trial. After receiving an answer the plaintiff, or his attorney, must serve a notice of trial on the defendant, not less than three nor more than eight days before the time set for trial. The notice, of course, indicates when and where the trial is to be held.

The Trial Calendar. Except in a court of arraignment, a calendar of cases to be tried during the day is posted by the clerk of every court. This calendar is called at the opening of court to determine which cases are to be adjourned and which are to be tried. Both sides must be represented at the calendar call and when their case is reached both must indicate what disposition of the case they desire for the day. If both sides are ready, the case will be called for the day. If there is a request for adjournment, it must be accompanied by an affidavit giving the reasons for such a request.

Inquests. Should the plaintiff be ready and the defendant fail to answer an inquest may be held before the judge or clerk depending upon the nature of the case. A judgment may be rendered in an inquest with only the plaintiff reciting the details, but judgments by inquest are subject to rehearing on motion by the defendant.

Stipulations and Adjournments. However, if one side is not ready for trial on a certain date, the attorneys may arrange, with court approval, to postpone it to some more convenient time. When such an arrangement is made a few days before the date set, then both attorneys sign a "stipulation" or agreement. A copy of this agreement is mailed to the clerk of the court who takes note of the postponement, altering the court calendar in accordance.

Subpoenas. If there is doubt that a witness will appear in court, he must be served with a subpoena, which is a command for him to come and testify. The courts have given all attorneys the power to issue subpoenas. Like a summons a subpoena must be served personally upon the witness. In fact, exactly the same procedure applies in the service of subpoenas with this addition: the person serving a subpoena must give the witness $2.00 as a fee in the Civil Court, and a mileage allowance if his home is outside the confines of the court. An affidavit of service must be obtained because if the witness does not show, the affidavit is essential to the institution of proceedings for contempt of court. A subpoena duces tecum is a special form of subpoena which not only orders the witness to appear but also commands him to produce books, or papers, or other testimony in court.

Motions. Motions are formal requests made by an attorney to a judge asking that the judge order an adversary to do something he is required to do so as to facilitate justice. Sometimes a motion requests a favor or even leave to be relieved of the consequence of one's own mistake. There is an almost unlimited number of different motions that may be made. Thus a defendant to whose store a Marshal comes to collect a judgment may make a motion to "vacate" the judgment which was entered by "default" on the grounds that through an error he was not notified that he had to appear to defend himself on the preceding day.

On the proper day, the attorneys for both sides appear before the judge who listens to the arguments and decides whether or not to grant the motion.

Order to Show Cause. This is practically the same as notice of motion except that it must be signed by the judge and prevents the other party from taking any action until the motion is decided. Thus with an "Order to Show Cause" the Marshal would be restrained from levying until the motion to reopen the case has been heard.

Motion for Summary Judgment. This type of motion is very frequently made and is consequently worthy of note. When a suit is based on a written instrument or is for goods sold and delivered, and an answer has been filed, the plaintiff has the right to make a motion for a summary judgment. In this it is claimed that there is no merit in the defense and a request is made that the answer be stricken out.

The effect of a motion for a summary judgment is to force the defendant to submit an affidavit in which the grounds for his answer must be specified. The judge then examines the affidavits of both parties and from this decides whether or not there is a real issue involved in the case. If he concludes that the arguments of the defense are not pertinent to the case, then he may hand down judgment without a regular trial, in other words a summary judgment.

Judgment by Confession. It sometimes happens that when the plaintiff has a just claim which the defendant recognizes the case may be concluded before the 5 days which ordinarily intervene between the summons and the judgment. This happens when the defendant signs a confession of judgment which enables the clerk of the court to enter judgment immediately.

Judgment by Default. If no answer to the summons has been made in ten or thirty days after its receipt, the plaintiff makes out a "deposition of judgment" in which he attests to exactly what his damages and claims are. This affidavit enables the clerk to enter judgment.

Costs. After a trial has been held, the "loser" shall bear the court costs. These costs are determined from a schedule which is based on the amount of money being sued for. In the event the defendant is successful and the case is dismissed, not only must the plaintiff assume the court costs but he must also assume the cost of the disbursements which include the fees paid for filing and service of process.

Supplementary Proceedings. If a defendant neither is in business nor is a working man, but is suspected of having property of some kind that he is concealing, then, instead of getting out a garnishee order, supplementary proceedings are started by which is meant proceedings following execution. The idea of these proceedings is that the plaintiff, or any one familiar with the facts, swears that an execution after judgment has been returned unsatisfied by the Marshal and that the judgment debtor must be examined under oath to discover whether or not he has property upon which the judgment can be collected. If the judge desires to grant the request he signs an order requiring the defendant to appear for examination. The judgment debtor is examined under oath by the attorney for the plaintiff. No judge is present in the room, but if the debtor refuses to answer a question he may be brought before a judge who, if the question is reasonable, will order him to answer or be held in contempt of court.

QUESTIONS AND ANSWERS

1. The first paper served in a civil action in the Supreme Court is
(A) complaint (B) summons
(C) injunction (D) subpoena.

2. The one of the following which includes the plaintiff's statement of his claims is
(A) reports
(B) writ of attachment
(C) notice to produce
(D) the complaint.

3. The paper containing the defendant's statement of his defense is
(A) the answer
(B) reports
(C) bill of particulars
(D) opening proclamation.

4. Should the defendant allege a claim against the plaintiff, it would be known as
(A) the execution (B) the charge
(C) the counterclaim (D) challenge.

5. When the defendant's claim is denied by the plaintiff, the paper is known as
(A) the deposition (B) the motion
(C) the reply (D) the lien.

6. To bring a witness into court with his books and papers, he must be served with
(A) injunction
(B) subpoena duces tecum
(C) affidavit
(D) summons.

7. A paper having the written testimony of a witness taken outside of the State is the
(A) framed issues
(B) partition proceedings
(C) discontinuance
(D) deposition.

8. A list of cases ready to be tried is the
(A) calendar (B) panel
(C) board (D) proceedings.

9. When referring to the "venue" in an action one means
(A) the place of trial
(B) opening proclamation
(C) the scene of the crime
(D) residence of the witness.

10. A paper that has been properly entered and calls for the collection of a judgment for money is
    (A) special term, ex parte
    (B) presumptive evidence
    (C) bill of particulars
    (D) the execution.

11. The provisions regulating practice in the Supreme Court of New York are in the book known as the
    (A) Charter of New York State
    (B) Civil Practice Act in Civil Courts, Code of Criminal Procedure, Criminal Courts
    (C) New York Law Journal
    (D) Long's Civil Cases.

12. The paper containing the official notice and memoranda on the courts and published daily in New York is the
    (A) Lawyer's Reports
    (B) Code of Criminal Procedure
    (C) New York Law Journal
    (D) Court of Record.

13. The book containing the decisions of the New York Courts is known as the
    (A) Framed Issues (B) References
    (C) Citations (D) Reports.

14. The rules governing the practice in the Supreme Court of New York are formulated by the
    (A) Appellate Division in Supreme, Board of County Judges in County Courts
    (B) Governor of New York State
    (C) the Bar Association of N.Y.S.
    (D) the Senate of N.Y.S.

15. To prove the service of a paper, one signs what is known as an
    (A) answer (B) acknowledgement
    (C) affidavit (D) affirmation.

16. To obtain more complete details of the plaintiff's claim, the defendant must obtain a
    (A) bill of exceptions
    (B) bill of particulars.
    (C) secondary evidence
    (D) writ of inquiry.

17. For the cessation of harmful acts, one applies in Supreme Court for
    (A) discontinuance
    (B) duress
    (C) injunction
    (D) bill of exceptions.

18. In order for a creditor to seize certain property belonging to a nonresident, he must apply in the Supreme Court for a
    (A) writ of attachment
    (B) deposition
    (C) mandatory injunction
    (D) prohibition.

19. The proceedings that are taken in order to punish a person who causes a disturbance in court are known as
    (A) condemnation proceeding
    (B) exhibit
    (C) measure of damages
    (D) contempt proceedings.

20. Papers filed in the Supreme Court are in the custody of the
    (A) presiding judge
    (B) County Clerk
    (C) Board of County Judges
    (D) Attorney General.

21. The term applied to a person appointed to represent an infant in an action in the Supreme Court is the
    (A) administrator
    (B) referee
    (C) guardian-ad-litem
    (D) talesman.

22. The announcement made at the opening of court is the
    (a) summons
    (B) opening proclamation
    (C) cause of action
    (D) judgment roll.

23. Justices in the Supreme Court obtain their positions for full terms through
    (A) election by voters of the various Judicial Districts in States
    (B) appointment by Governor
    (C) appointment by Bar Association of New York State
    (D) civil service appointment.

24. A Supreme Court Justice's full term is
(A) 10 years (B) 7 years
(C) lifetime appointment with good behavior
(D) 14 years.

25. The provisions of a will left by a deceased may be challenged in the
(A) Supreme Court
(B) Civil Court
(C) Court of Claims
(D) Surrogate Court

26. Before testifying and after being called to the stand what does the court do to the witness providing he is of sufficient age and intellect?
(A) Swears in the court attendant first.
(B) Asks him to state his political affiliation.
(C) Swears in the witness or affirms him.
(D) Immediately begins to question him.

27. A group of jurymen selected to serve during a term of court is known as a
(A) panel (B) board
(C) jury (D) judicial group.

28. The papers containing the trial jurymen's names are known as the
(A) document (B) ballots or slips
(C) reference (D) calendar.

29. Should a juryman be objectionable to an attorney, he
(A) challenges the juror: if sustained, the juror is excused
(B) asks clerk to dismiss him
(C) refuses to continue the case
(D) asks the judge to drop the charge.

30. The result of a jury's agreement is known as the
(A) verdict (B) judgment
(C) plea (D) opinion.

31. The statement made by the judge to the jury is known as the
(A) accusation (B) warrant
(C) order (D) charge.

32. One knows the agreement signed by attorneys during a trial as
(A) agreement (B) bargain
(C) stipulation (D) motion.

33. In a trial by jury, questions of fact are decided by the
(A) clerk (B) jury
(C) judge
(D) two opposing attorneys

34. In a trial by jury, questions of law are decided by the
(A) judge (B) clerk
(C) court attendant (D) jury.

35. In order to prevent a witness from answering a question, the attorney may
(A) write his disapproval on paper
(B) do nothing about it
(C) protest to the clerk
(D) object.

36. Should an attorney be dissatisfied with a ruling of a judge he may
(A) rule the judge in contempt of court
(B) protest to the clerk
(C) take an exception
(D) ask for a new trial.

37. The clerk's records kept during a trial of action are known as the
(A) proceedings (B) minutes
(C) records (D) details.

38. In a contested action, what would an attorney do to obtain an order of the court?
(A) Object
(B) Ask for a recess
(C) Resort to a compromise
(D) Bring on a motion.

39. The title of the person to whom a case is sent if the judge decides to try the case out of court is
(A) clerk (B) court attendant
(C) referee (D) district attorney.

40. By whom are the parts in which the Supreme Court justices sit determined?

(A) Appellate division
(B) Governor
(C) Lt. -Governor
(D) Attorney General.

41. The number of justices in the Appellate Term is
(A) 7 to 9 (B) 5 to 7
(C) 6 to 8 (D) 3 to 5.

42. The justices are given their seats in the Appellate Term by
(A) the governor (B) Appellate Division
(C) the Senate (D) the people.

43. The Appellate Term receives appeals from which of the following courts?
(A) Court of Appeals
(B) Criminal Court
(C) Civil Court
(D) Court of Claims.

44. Of the following, the one who designates justices to sit in the Appellate Division is
(A) the governor
(B) the people
(C) the Supreme Court
(D) the Attorney General.

45. The number of justices sitting in the Appellate Division 1st Dept. at one time is
(A) 4 (B) 7
(C) 3 (D) 5.

46. The number of justices in the Appellate Division 1st Dept. is
(A) 8 (B) 7
(C) 4 (D) 3.

47. Of the following groups, the one which contains courts from which appeals are taken to the Appellate Division. Choose one.
(A) Supreme Court and Court of Appeals
(B) Surrogates Court and Court of Impeachment
(C) Court of Impeachment and Court of Appeals
(D) Family Court and Criminal Court

48. The number of Appellate Divisions in New York State is
(A) 5 (B) 4
(C) 7 (D) 8.

49. From the Appellate Division, appeals are taken to the
(A) Court of Appeals
(B) Supreme Court of U.S.
(C) City Court
(D) County Court.

50. Suits for the recovery of small sums in an informal manner may be instituted in the Small Claims Court. This court is part of the
(A) Supreme Court
(B) Court of Claims
(C) Court of the Judiciary
(D) Civil Court.

51. Verdicts which involve the death penalty are appealed directly to the
(A) Court of the Judiciary
(B) Appellate Division
(C) Court of Appeals
(D) Supreme Court.

52. A court whose jurisdiction includes the hearing of divorce actions and marriage separations is the
(A) Family Court
(B) Supreme Court
(C) Civil Court
(D) Justice of the Peace Court.

53. A part of a city court which is in existence to promote the welfare of children is connected to the
(A) Civil Court
(B) Family Court
(C) Supreme Court
(D) Surrogates' Court.

54. A court whose judges are appointed rather than elected to office is the
(A) Family Court
(B) Surrogate Court
(C) Civil Court
(D) Supreme Court.

55. The conduct of attorneys who practice in New York State is governed by rules and procedures formulated by the
(A) Court of Appeals
(B) Court of the Judiciary
(C) Appellate Division of the Supreme Court
(D) Court of Claims.

Correct Answers For The Foregoing Questions

(Please make every effort to answer the questions on your own before looking at these answers. You'll make faster progress by following this rule.)

1. B	8. A	15. C	22. B	29. A	36. C	43. C	50. D
2. D	9. A	16. B	23. A	30. A	37. B	44. A	51. C
3. A	10. D	17. C	24. D	31. D	38. D	45. D	52. B
4. C	11. B	18. A	25. D	32. C	39. C	46. B	53. B
5. C	12. C	19. D	26. C	33. B	40. A	47. D	54. A
6. B	13. D	20. B	27. A	34. A	41. D	48. B	55. C
7. D	14. A	21. C	28. B	35. D	42. B	49. A	

SCORE

.... %

NO. CORRECT ÷

NO. OF QUESTIONS

PART FOUR

Background and Study Material for the Exam

Practice Using Answer Sheets

DIRECTIONS: Read each question and its lettered answers. When you have decided which answer is correct, blacken the corresponding space on this sheet with a No. 2 pencil. Make your mark as long as the pair of lines, and completely fill the area between the pair of lines. If you change your mind, erase your first mark COMPLETELY. Make no stray marks; they may count against you.

SAMPLE

1. CHICAGO is
1-A a country
1-B a mountain
1-C an island
1-D a city
1-E a state

1 A B C D E

SCORES

1 ____ 5 ____
2 ____ 6 ____
3 ____ 7 ____
4 ____ 8 ____

1 A B C D E	2 A B C D E	3 A B C D E	4 A B C D E
5 A B C D E	6 A B C D E	7 A B C D E	8 A B C D E
9 A B C D E	10 A B C D E	11 A B C D E	12 A B C D E
13 A B C D E	14 A B C D E	15 A B C D E	16 A B C D E
17 A B C D E	18 A B C D E	19 A B C D E	20 A B C D E
21 A B C D E	22 A B C D E	23 A B C D E	24 A B C D E
25 A B C D E	26 A B C D E	27 A B C D E	28 A B C D E
29 A B C D E	30 A B C D E	31 A B C D E	32 A B C D E
33 A B C D E	34 A B C D E	35 A B C D E	36 A B C D E
37 A B C D E	38 A B C D E	39 A B C D E	40 A B C D E
41 A B C D E	42 A B C D E	43 A B C D E	44 A B C D E
45 A B C D E	46 A B C D E	47 A B C D E	48 A B C D E
49 A B C D E	50 A B C D E	51 A B C D E	52 A B C D E
53 A B C D E	54 A B C D E	55 A B C D E	56 A B C D E
57 A B C D E	58 A B C D E	59 A B C D E	60 A B C D E
61 A B C D E	62 A B C D E	63 A B C D E	64 A B C D E
65 A B C D E	66 A B C D E	67 A B C D E	68 A B C D E
69 A B C D E	70 A B C D E	71 A B C D E	72 A B C D E
73 A B C D E	74 A B C D E	75 A B C D E	76 A B C D E
77 A B C D E	78 A B C D E	79 A B C D E	80 A B C D E
81 A B C D E	82 A B C D E	83 A B C D E	84 A B C D E
85 A B C D E	86 A B C D E	87 A B C D E	88 A B C D E
89 A B C D E	90 A B C D E	91 A B C D E	92 A B C D E
93 A B C D E	94 A B C D E	95 A B C D E	96 A B C D E
97 A B C D E	98 A B C D E	99 A B C D E	100 A B C D E
101 A B C D E	102 A B C D E	103 A B C D E	104 A B C D E
105 A B C D E	106 A B C D E	107 A B C D E	108 A B C D E
109 A B C D E	110 A B C D E	111 A B C D E	112 A B C D E
113 A B C D E	114 A B C D E	115 A B C D E	116 A B C D E
117 A B C D E	118 A B C D E	119 A B C D E	120 A B C D E
121 A B C D E	122 A B C D E	123 A B C D E	124 A B C D E
125 A B C D E	126 A B C D E	127 A B C D E	128 A B C D E
129 A B C D E	130 A B C D E	131 A B C D E	132 A B C D E
133 A B C D E	134 A B C D E	135 A B C D E	136 A B C D E
137 A B C D E	138 A B C D E	139 A B C D E	140 A B C D E
141 A B C D E	142 A B C D E	143 A B C D E	144 A B C D E
145 A B C D E	146 A B C D E	147 A B C D E	148 A B C D E
149 A B C D E	150 A B C D E		

TEAR OUT ALONG THIS LINE AND MARK YOUR ANSWERS AS INSTRUCTED IN THE TEXT

TECHNIQUES OF READING INTERPRETATION

The reading comprehension question is the pitfall of many a test-taker. He may do well in every other part of the examination, but "messes up" the comprehension part. If you don't want this to happen to you, you should make every effort to improve your ability to interpret a reading passage.

You can markedly upgrade your reading ability —but you must have a plan—a procedure—a method. First, let us understand that there are two aspects of success in reading interpretation:

1. **reading speed**

   and

2. **reading understanding**

There are many individuals who read with excellent comprehension, but who read too slowly. Remember, there is a time limit on your test. On the other hand, there are those who read rapidly but, for reasons that we shall cite later, do not thoroughly understand what they are reading. These exam-takers will answer few of the comprehension test questions correctly.

We must disagree with those who hold the mistaken belief that there is a causal relationship between speed of reading and comprehension of the material read. Each is important during an exam—speed and comprehension—but improvement in reading skill requires two different treatments: improvement in reading speed and improvement in reading comprehension. Let us, then, divide our discussion into two parts:

1. **increasing reading speed**

   and

2. **improving reading comprehension**

A great many people read very slowly and with little comprehension, yet are completely unaware of just how badly they do read. Some people pronounce the words to themselves as they read, saying each word almost as distinctly as though reading aloud; or they think each one separately.

You were probably taught to read letter by letter; gradually, as you matured, you learned to read word by word. As an adult, however, you should be able to read a complete phrase as quickly as you once read just one letter. If you cannot do this, or if you have trouble in understanding what you read, you should practice reading intensively.

There is no need to be discouraged if this is the case, however. Most students, with a little effort, can increase the speed of their reading significantly. Do not be afraid of not understanding what you read quickly. The old idea that slow readers make up for their slowness by better comprehension of what they read has been proven untrue. Your ability to comprehend what you read will keep pace with your increase in speed. You will absorb as many ideas per page as before, and get many more ideas per unit of reading time.

It has been demonstrated that those who read best also read quickly. This is probably due to the fact that heavier concentration is required for rapid reading; and concentration is what enables a reader to grasp important ideas contained in the reading material.

A good paragraph generally has one central thought—that is, a topic sentence. Your main task is to locate and absorb that thought while reading the paragraph. The correct interpretation of the paragraph is based upon that thought, and not upon personal opinions, prejudices or preferences. If a selection consists of two or more paragraphs, the correct interpretation is based on the central idea of the entire passage. The ability to grasp the central idea of a passage can be acquired by practice—practice that will also increase the speed with which you read.

An important rule to follow in seeking to improve your reading ability is to force yourself to increase your speed. Just as you once stopped reading letter by letter, now learn to stop reading word by word. Force yourself to read by whole phrases and sentences. Move your eyes rapidly across the line of type, skimming it. Don't permit your eyes to stop for individual words, but try to reconstruct the whole idea even if a word has been missed. Proceed quickly through the paragraph in this skimming fashion, without rereading or backtracking to a missed word.

If you find yourself failing to comprehend what you read, read it over several times rapidly, until you do understand. Do not slow down on rereading. At first, you may find yourself missing some of the ideas. Persistent practice, however, will result in stepping up both your reading speed and your ability to comprehend what you read.

If you are one of those who mouth over the words you read, or think each one separately in a similar process, your first step is to learn to overcome this handicap to rapid reading. Learn not to move your lips and not to pronounce the words you read. The habit will be almost automatically overcome if you learn to leap from phrase to phrase. Synchronize your eye movements with your mind. Your mind is a great deal nimbler than your lips. Consequently, your lips and vocal cords must not be permitted to intervene in the instantaneous interchange of ideas between eyes and mind.

Certain physical factors affect your reading. You should always read sitting in a comfortable position, erect, with head slightly inclined. The light should be excellent, with both an indirect and a direct source available; direct light should come from behind you and slightly above your shoulder, in such a way that the type is evenly illumined. Hold the reading matter at your own best reading distance and at a convenient height, so you don't stoop or squint. It goes without saying that, if you need glasses, you should certainly use them when reading.

To prepare for a test in reading comprehension, then, you should keep the above ideas firmly in mind. Practice reading, for practice will improve your skill. Never retreat to your older, easier method of reading, once you have grasped the way we have indicated here. In a very short time, you will find the new method of reading easier than the old. You will read faster. You will understand more of what you read. You will enjoy reading more. You will accomplish more reading in less time. It will no longer be a chore, but a pleasant and profitable relaxation.

INCREASING READING SPEED: CAUSES & CURES OF SLOW READING

Cause #1: *Word-by-Word Reading.* Our earliest reading, since it was done aloud, was of necessity word-by-word reading. Unfortunately, for many, this habit has become so firmly implanted that it often persists.
Cure: Use the *eye-span method.* Look at that first part of a sentence—the part which consists of a thought unit. Then look for the next thought unit, if there is one in the same sentence—then, look for still another thought unit. For example, consider this sentence:

> Reading maketh a full man, conference a ready man, and writing an exact man.

How many ideas are there in the sentence? You are right—three. Now, let us employ the eye-span method in reading this sentence:

Reading maketh a full man,
EYE-SPAN 1

conference a ready man,
EYE-SPAN 2

and writing an exact man.
EYE-SPAN 3

Cause #2: *Vocalizing.* Some readers move their lips or whisper while they read "silently." This practice slows down silent-reading time considerably.
Cure: You must consciously refrain from moving your lips or whispering during silent reading. Have someone watch you while you read. Are you vocalizing?
Cause #3: *One-Speed Reading.* One should vary his reading speed according to what he is reading.
Cure: The pace of your reading should change not only from book to book, but even within a reading selection. Flexibility should be employed so that the reader will change his speed from paragraph to paragraph, even from sentence to sentence.

IMPROVING YOUR READING COMPREHENSION: CAUSES AND CURES OF POOR COMPREHENSION

Cause #1: *Vocabulary Weakness.* You must know the meaning of every word in a passage in order to understand the passage thoroughly. The sentence context will sometimes help you to arrive at the meaning of a word, but the context method is not to be depended upon.
Cure: Increase your vocabulary systematically by taking these simple steps:
1. Learn Latin. Don't get scared. We are referring to Latin roots, prefixes, and suffixes. Remember that approximately 70 per cent of our English words are derived from Latin and Greek.
2. Take Word Tests. We recommend the best-selling "2300 Steps to Word Power" ($1.45—Arco) which tests your knowledge of words through programmed instruction, the revolutionary fast-learning method.
3. Read—not only novels. Non-fiction is good, too

—and don't forget to read newspapers and magazines (the more literate type).
4. LISTEN—to people who speak well. Tune in to worthwhile TV programs, also.
5. PLAY WORD GAMES—like Anagrams, Scrabble, and do Crossword Puzzles.
6. USE THE DICTIONARY—frequently and extensively.

Cause #2: *Hint Neglect.* Examination points may be unnecessarily lost by ignoring the author's hints as to what *he* thinks is most important.

Cure: Be on the lookout for such phrases as "Note that . . ." "Of importance is . . ." These give clues to what the writer is stressing. So do topic sentences. Beware of negatives and all-inclusive statements. Watch particularly words like always, never, all, only, every, absolutely, completely, none, entirely.

Cause #3: *Background Lack.* Since most reading comprehension passages deal with science, literature, or social studies, a weakness in background may create much difficulty in interpretation.

Cure: Read widely. Acquaint yourself with various aspects of science, literature, and social studies.

TEN SUCCESS STEPS

Here are proven techniques for getting the right answer to *any* Reading Interpretation question.
1. Read the selection through quickly to get the general sense.
2. Reread the selection, concentrating on the central idea.
3. Can you now pick out the *topic sentence* in each paragraph?
4. If the selection consists of more than one paragraph, determine the *central idea* of the entire selection.
5. Examine the five choices carefully, yet rapidly. Eliminate immediately those choices which are *far-fetched, ridiculous, irrelevant, false,* or *impossible.*
6. Eliminate those choices which may be true, but which have nothing to do with the sense of the selection.
7. Check those few choices which now remain as possibilities.
8. Refer back to the original selection and determine which one of these remaining possibilities is best in view of

a) specific information in the selection
or
b) implied information in the selection

9. Be sure to consider only the facts *given* or *definitely understood* some place in the selection.
10. Be especially careful of trick expressions or "catch-words" which sometimes destroy the validity of a seemingly acceptable answer. These include the expressions: "under all circumstances," "at all times," "never," "always," "under no conditions," "absolutely," "completely," and "entirely."

AVOID THE TRAPS

Trap #1—Sometimes the question cannot be answered on the basis of the stated facts. You may be required to make a deduction from the facts given.
Trap #2—Eliminate your personal opinions.
Trap #3—Search out significant details that are nestled in the paragraph. Reread the paragraph as many times as necessary (with an eye on your watch).

GET PLENTY OF PRACTICE

Read:

(a) Editorial pages of various newspapers.
(b) Book reviews (also drama and movie reviews).
(c) Magazine articles.

For each selection that you read, do the following:

(a) Jot down the main idea of the article.
(b) Look up the meanings of words that you don't know or that you aren't sure of.

A SAMPLE QUESTION ANALYZED

Here is a sample question followed by an analysis. Try to understand the process of arriving at the correct answer.

(Reading) "Too often, indeed, have scurrilous and offensive allegations by underworld creatures been sufficient to blast the career of irreproachable and incorruptible executives who, because of their efforts to serve the people honestly and faithfully, incurred the enmity of powerful political forces and lost their positions."

Judging from the contents of the preceding paragraph, you might best conclude that

(A) the larger majority of executives are irreproachable and incorruptible

(B) criminals often swear in court that honest officials are corrupt in order to save themselves

(C) political forces are always clashing with government executive

(D) underworld creatures make scurrilous and offensive allegations against incorruptible executives

(E) false statements by criminals sometimes cause honest officials the loss of their positions or the ruin of their careers.

Interpretation

(A) can generally be said to be a true statement, but it cannot be derived from the paragraph. Nothing is said in the paragraph about "the larger majority" of executives.

(B) may also be a true statement and can to a certain extent be derived from the paragraph. However, the phrase "in order to save themselves" is not relevant to the sense of the paragraph, and even if it were, this choice does not sum up its central thought.

(C) cannot be derived from the paragraph. The catch-word "always" makes this choice entirely invalid.

(D) This choice is true as derived from the sense of the paragraph. It is open, however, to two exceptions. First, this choice is in the form of a general statement whereas the paragraph starts with the restrictive phrase "too often," thereby precluding a generality. Secondly, this choice does not summarize the central idea of the paragraph which may be better expressed in the remaining choice.

(E) is the *best* conclusion that could be drawn from the contents of the paragraph in the light of the five choices given. It is open to no exceptions and adequately sums up the central thought of the paragraph.

USING THE "SUCCESS STEPS" WITH A PRACTICE PASSAGE

Let us, now, demonstrate with an actual exam-type reading interpretation selection how to apply the ten "success steps":

Vacations were once the prerogative of the privileged few, even as late as the 19th century. Now they are considered the right of all, except for such unfortunate masses as, for example, the bulk of China's and India's population, for whom life, save for sleep and brief periods of rest, is uninterrupted toil.

They are more necessary now than once because the average life is less well-rounded and has become increasingly departmentalized. I suppose the idea of vacations, as we conceive it, must be incomprehensible to primitive peoples. Rest of some kind has of course always been a part of the rhythm of human life, but earlier ages did not find it necessary to organize it in the way that modern man has done. Holidays, feast days, were sufficient.

With modern man's increasing tensions, with the stultifying quality of so much of his work, this break in the year's routine became steadily more necessary. Vacations became mandatory for the purpose of renewal and repair. And so it came about that in the United States, the most self-indulgent of nations, the tensest, and the most departmentalized, vacations have come to take a predominant place in domestic conversation.

1. The title below that best expresses the ideas of this passage is:
   - a. Vacation Preferences
   - b. Vacations: the Topic of Conversation
   - c. Vacations in Perspective
   - d. The Well-Organized Vacation
   - e. Renewal, Refreshment and Repair

2. We need vacations now more than ever before because we have
   A. a more carefree nature
   B. much more free time
   C. little diversity in our work
   D. less emotional stability
   E. a higher standard of living

3. It is implied in the passage that the lives of Americans are very
   A. habitual
   B. ennobling
   C. patriotic
   D. varied
   E. independent

4. As used in the passage, the word "prerogative" (line 1) most nearly means
   A. habit
   B. distinction
   C. request
   D. demand
   E. hope

STEP 1—We read the selection through quickly to get the general sense.
STEP 2—We reread the selection concentrating on the central idea.
STEP 3—We discover that the topic sentence of each paragraph of this selection is the first sentence of each paragraph. This order is almost always the case: the topic sentence is the first sentence of a paragraph.
STEP 4—The central idea of the selection consists of various aspects of vacations.
STEP 5—Question 1. . . . We eliminate Choice D immediately because it is irrelevant. The selection refers in no way to organization of a vacation.
STEP 6—Eliminate Choice B. Vacations are often a topic of conversation—not so in this selection, however.
STEP 7—Since Choices A, C, and E remain as possible correct choices, we check them.
STEP 8—Choice C is an all-inclusive title. Choices A and E are not all-inclusive. Therefore, C is the correct choice as the best title for the passage.
STEP 9—In arriving at the correct answer, we have considered only the facts given or definitely understood.
STEP 10—We were on the alert for trick expressions and "catch-words." There were none in Question 1.

. . . .

Proceed in the same "10-Step" manner in answering the other questions 2, 3 and 4 of the sample selection.

. . . .

PRACTICE PASSAGE ANSWERS

1. C 2. C 3. A 4. B

Practice Using Answer Sheets

Alter numbers to match the practice and drill questions in each part of the book.
Make only ONE mark for each answer. Additional and stray marks may be counted as mistakes.
In making corrections, erase errors COMPLETELY. Make glossy black marks.

	A	B	C	D	E		A	B	C	D	E		A	B	C	D	E		A	B	C	D	E		A	B	C	D	E
1						1						1						1						1					
2						2						2						2						2					
3						3						3						3						3					
4						4						4						4						4					
5						5						5						5						5					
6						6						6						6						6					
7						7						7						7						7					
8						8						8						8						8					
9						9						9						9						9					
0						0						0						0						0					

	A	B	C	D	E		A	B	C	D	E		A	B	C	D	E		A	B	C	D	E		A	B	C	D	E
1						1						1						1						1					
2						2						2						2						2					
3						3						3						3						3					
4						4						4						4						4					
5						5						5						5						5					
6						6						6						6						6					
7						7						7						7						7					
8						8						8						8						8					
9						9						9						9						9					
0						0						0						0						0					

	A	B	C	D	E		A	B	C	D	E		A	B	C	D	E		A	B	C	D	E		A	B	C	D	E
1						7						13						19						25					
2						8						14						20						26					
3						9						15						21						27					
4						10						16						22						28					
5						11						17						23						29					
6						12						18						24						30					

TEAR OUT ALONG THIS LINE AND MARK YOUR ANSWERS AS INSTRUCTED IN THE TEXT

COURT OFFICER

Reading Interpretation Questions.

Laws, Rules and Regulations.

Ouestions 1 and 2 pertain to the following section of the Penal Code:

"Section 1942. A person who, after having been three times convicted within this state, of felonies or attempts to commit felonies, or under the law of any other state, government or country, of crimes which if committed within this state would be felonious, commits a felony, other than murder, first or second degree, or treason, within this state, shall be sentenced upon conviction of such fourth, or subsequent, offense to imprisonment in a state prison for an indeterminate term the minimum of which shall be not less than the maximum term provided for first offenders for the crime for which the individual has been convicted, but, in any event, the minimum term upon conviction for a felony as the fourth or subsequent, offense, shall be not less than fifteen years, and the maximum thereof shall be his natural life."

1. Under the terms of the above quoted portion of Section 1942 of the Penal Law, a person must receive the increased punishment therein provided, if
   (A) He is convicted of a felony and has been three times previously convicted of felonies
   (B) He has been three times previously convicted of felonies, regardless of the nature of his present conviction
   (C) His fourth conviction is for murder, first or second degree, or treason
   (D) He has previously been convicted three times of murder, first or second degree, or treason.

2. Under the terms of the above quoted portion of Section 1942 of the Penal Law, a person convicted of a felony for which the penalty is imprisonment for a term not to exceed ten years, and who has been three times previously convicted of felonies in this state, shall be sentenced to a term the minimum of which shall be
   (A) Ten years
   (B) Fifteen years
   (C) Indeterminate
   (D) His natural life.

Answer questions 3 to 6 on the basis of the following statement:

"Disorderly conduct, in the abstract, does not constitute any crime known to law; it is only when it tends to a breach of the peace under the circumstances detailed in section 1458 of the Consolidation Act, that it constitutes a minor offense cognizable by the police magistrate of the City of New York, and when it in fact threatens to disturb the peace it is a misdemeanor as well under section 675 of the Penal Code as at common law, and not within the jurisdiction of the police magistrate, but of the Court of Special Sessions."

3. Of the following, the most accurate statement on the basis of the above paragraph is that
   (A) An act which merely threatens to disturb the peace is not a crime
   (B) Disorderly conduct, by itself, is not a crime
   (C) Some types of disorderly conduct are indictable
   (D) A minor offense may or may not be cognizable by the police
   (E) Some facts threaten to disturb the peace.

4. Of the following, the least accurate statement on the basis of the above paragraph is that
   (A) Disorderly conduct which threatens to disturb the peace is within the jurisdiction of a police magistrate
   (B) Disorderly conduct which "tends to a breach of the peace" may constitute a minor offense
   (C) Section 1458 of the Consolidated Act discusses a "breach of the peace"
   (D) Disorderly conduct which "tends to a breach of the peace" is not the same as that which threatens to disturb the peace

(E) The Court of Special Sessions considers some cases resulting from disorderly conduct.

5. The above quotation distinguishes least sharply between
 (A) Jurisdiction of a police magistrate and jurisdiction of the Court of Special Sessions
 (B) Disorderly conduct as a crime and disorderly conduct as no crime
 (C) What "tends to a breach of the peace" and what threatens to disturb the peace
 (D) A minor offense and a misdemeanor
 (E) The Penal Code and the Common Law.

6. Of the following generalizations, the one which is best illustrated by the above paragraph is that
 (A) Acts which in themselves are not criminal may become criminal as a result of their effect
 (B) Abstract conduct may, in and of itself, be criminal
 (C) Criminal acts are determined by results rather than by intent
 (D) An act which is criminal to begin with may not be criminal if it fails to have the desired effect
 (E) All law consists of a detailing of circumstances under which a crime is committed.

Answer questions 7 and 8 solely on the basis of the following paragraph:

"If a motor vehicle fails to pass inspection, the owner will be given a rejection notice by the inspection station. Repairs must be made within ten days after this notice is issued. It is not necessary to have the required adjustment or repairs made at the station where the inspection occurred. The vehicle may be taken to any other garage. Re-inspection after repairs may be made at any official inspection station, not necessarily the same station which made the initial inspection. The registration of any motor vehicle for which an inspection sticker has not been obtained as required, or which is not repaired and inspected within ten days after inspection indicates defects, is subject to suspension. A vehicle cannot be used on public highways while its registration is under suspension."

7. According to the above paragraph, the owner of a car which does not pass inspection must
 (A) have repairs made at the same station which rejected his car.
 (B) take the car to another station and have it re-inspected
 (C) have repairs made anywhere and then have the car re-inspected
 (D) not use the car on a public highway until the necessary repairs have been made.

8. According to the above paragraph, the one of the following which may be cause for suspension of the registration of a vehicle is that
 (A) an inspection sticker was issued before the rejection notice had been in force for ten days
 (B) it was not re-inspected by the station that rejected it originally
 (C) it was not re-inspected either by the station that rejected it originally or by the garage which made the repairs
 (D) it has not had defective parts repaired within ten days after inspection.

9. A statute states: "A person who steals an article worth less than $100 where no aggravating circumstances accompany the act, is guilty of petit larceny. If the article is worth $100 or more it may be larceny second degree." If all you know is that Edward Smith stole an article worth $100, it may reasonably be said that
 (A) Smith is guilty of petit larceny
 (B) Smith is guilty of larceny second degree
 (C) Smith is guilty of neither petit larceny nor larceny second degree
 (D) precisely what charge will be placed against Smith is uncertain.

10. An ordinance reads: "All vehicles, such as motorcycles, passenger automobiles, automobile trucks, horsedriven wagons, or any other type of conveyance, are prohibited from using any street designated as a play street, except as the requirements of the residents of the property abutting such play street may call for." John White, who had only recently arrived in the city from Montreal, Canada, where he had lived all his life, was given a summons by Patrolman Kelly for violating this ordinance. At the time he received the summons he was delivering groceries to a resident on the play street for the Smith Grocery Company, for whom he had started to work the day before. There were no children playing on the street at the time and he did not know that it was a play street. Patrolman Kelly should be told that the summons should not have been issued because
 (A) there were no children on the street at the time
 (B) he was delivering groceries to a resident on the street
 (C) not being a citizen of the United States, he is not completely subject to our jurisdiction

(D) he did not know that it was a play street
(E) he did not know that traffic was prohibited on play streets.

Answer Questions 11 to 13 on the basis of the following paragraph:

"The City Police Department will accept for investigation no report of a person missing from his residence, if such residence is located outside of the city. The person reporting same will be advised to report such fact to the police department of the locality where the missing person lives, which will, if necessary, communicate officially with the City Police Department. However, a report will be accepted of a person who is missing from a temporary residence in the city, but the person making the report will be instructed to make a report also to the police department of the locality where the missing person lives."

11. According to the above paragraph, a report to the City Police Department of a missing person whose permanent residence is outside of the city will
(A) always be investigated provided that a report is also made to his local police authorities
(B) never be investigated unless requested officially by his local police authorities
(C) be investigated in cases of temporary residence in the city, but a report should always be made to his local police authorities
(D) be investigated if the person making the report is a city resident
(E) always be investigated and a report will be made to the local police authorities by the City Police Department.

12. Of the following, the most likely reason for the procedure described in the above paragraph is that
(A) non-residents are not entitled to free police service from the city
(B) local police authorities would resent interference in their jurisdiction
(C) local police authorities sometimes try to unload their problems on the City Police
(D) local police authorities may be better able to conduct an investigation
(E) few persons are erroneously reported as missing.

13. Mr. Smith of Oldtown and Mr. Jones of Newtown had an appointment in the city, but Mr. Jones doesn't appear. Mr. Smith, after trying repeatedly to phone Mr. Jones the next day, believes that something has happened to him. According to the above paragraph, Mr. Smith should apply to the police of
(A) Oldtown
(B) Newtown
(C) Newtown and the city
(D) Oldtown and the city
(E) Newtown, Oldtown and the city.

14. Police Department Rule 5 reads as follows: "A Deputy Commissioner acting as Police Commissioner shall carry out the orders of the Police Commissioner, previously given, and such orders shall not, except in cases of extreme emergency, be countermanded." This means most nearly that, except in case of extreme emergency,
(A) the orders given by a Deputy Commissioner acting as Police Commissioner may not be revoked
(B) a Deputy Commissioner acting as Police Commissioner should not revoke orders previously given by the Police Commissioner
(C) a Deputy Commissioner acting as Police Commissioner is vested with the same authority to issue orders as the Police Commissioner himself
(D) only a Deputy Commissioner acting as Police Commissioner may issue orders in the absence of the Police Commissioner himself.

15. "A 'crime' is an act committed or omitted in violation of a public law either forbidding or commanding it." This statement implies most nearly that
(A) crimes can be omitted
(B) a forbidding act if omitted is a crime
(C) an act of omission may be criminal
(D) to commit an act not commanded is criminal
(E) some acts are acts of commission.

16. "He who by command, counsel or assistance procures another to commit a crime is, in morals and in law, as culpable as the visible actor himself, for the reason that the criminal act, whichever it may be, is imputable to the person who conceived it and set the forces in motion for its actual accomplishment." Of the following, the most accurate inference from the above sentence is that
(A) a criminal act does not have to be committed for a crime to be committed

(B) acting as counsellor for a criminal is a crime
(C) the mere counseling of a criminal act can never be a crime if no criminal act is committed
(D) only the visible actor himself can be criminal
(E) a person acting only as an adviser may be guilty of committing a criminal act.

17. "A 'felony' is a crime punishable by death or imprisonment in a state prison, and any other crime is a 'misdemeanor.'" According to this quotation the decisive distinction between "felony" and "misdemeanor" is the
(A) degree of criminality
(B) type of crime
(C) place of incarceration
(D) length of imprisonment
(E) judicial jurisdiction.

Answer questions 18 to 21 on the basis of the following statement:

"The question, whether an act, repugnant to the Constitution, can become the law of the land, is a question deeply interesting to the United States; but, happily, not of an intricacy proportioned to its interest. It seems only necessary to recognize certain principles, supposed to have been long and well established, to decide it. That the people have an original right to establish, for their future government, such principles as, in their opinion, shall most conduce to their own happiness, is the basis on which the whole American fabric has been erected. The exercise of this original right is a very great exertion; nor can it, nor ought it, to be frequently repeated. The principles, therefore, so established, are deemed fundamental: and as the authority from which they proceed is supreme, and can seldom act, they are designed to be permanent."

18. The best title for the above paragraph would be
(A) Principles of the Constitution
(B) The Root of Constitutional Change
(C) Only People Can Change the Constitution
(D) Methods of Constitutional Change.

19. According to the above paragraph, original right is
(A) fundamental to the principle that the people may choose their own form of government
(B) established by the Constitution
(C) the result of a very great exertion and should not often be repeated
(D) supreme, can seldom act, and is designed to be permanent.

20. Whether an act not in keeping with Constitutional principles can become law is, according to the above paragraph
(A) an intricate problem requiring great thought and concentration
(B) determined by the proportionate interests of legislators
(C) an intricate problem but not too complicated to be solved
(D) determined by certain long established principles, fundamental to Constitutional law
(E) an intricate problem, but less intricate than it would seem from the interest shown in it.

21. According to the above paragraph, the phrase, "and can seldom act," refers to
(A) the principles early enacted into law by Americans when they chose their future form of government
(B) the original rights of the people as vested in the Constitution
(C) the original framers of the Constitution
(D) the established, fundamental principles of government
(E) the body of laws by which the life and actions of all people are governed.

Answer Questions 22 to 25 solely on the basis of the following paragraph:

A foundling is an abandoned child whose identity is unknown. Desk officers shall direct the delivery, by a policewoman if available, of foundlings actually or apparently under two years of age to the New York Foundling Hospital, or if actually or apparently two years of age or over, to the Children's Center. In all other cases of dependent or neglected children, other than foundlings, requiring shelter, desk officers shall provide for obtaining such shelter as follows: between 9 a.m. and 5 p.m., Monday through Friday, by telephone direct to the Bureau of Child Welfare, in order to ascertain the shelter to which the child shall be sent; at all other times, direct the delivery of a child actually or apparently under two years of age to the New York Foundling Hospital, or if the child is actually or apparently two years of age or over to the Children's Center.

22. According to this paragraph, it would be most correct to state that
(A) a foundling as well as a neglected child may be delivered to the New York Foundling Hospital
(B) a foundling but not a neglected child may be delivered to the Children's Center
(C) a neglected child requiring shelter, regard-

less of age, may be delivered to the Bureau of Child Welfare
(D) the Bureau of Child Welfare may determine the shelter to which a foundling may be delivered.

23. According to this paragraph, the desk officer shall provide for obtaining shelter for a neglected child, apparenly under two years of age, by
(A) directing its delivery to Children's Center if occurrence is on a Monday between 9 a.m. and 5 p.m.
(B) telephoning the Bureau of Child Welfare if occurrence is on a Sunday
(C) directing its delivery to the New York Foundling Hospital if occurrence is on a Wednesday at 4 p.m.
(D) telephoning the Bureau of Child Welfare if occurrence is at 10 a.m. on a Friday.

24. According to this paragraph, the desk officer should direct delivery to the New York Foundling Hospital of any child who is
(A) actually under 2 years of age and requires shelter
(B) apparently under two years of age and is neglected or dependent
(C) actually 2 years of age and is a foundling
(D) apparently under 2 years of age and has been abandoned.

25. A 12-year-old neglected child requiring shelter is brought to a police station on Thursday at 2 p.m. Such a child should be sent to
(A) a shelter selected by the Bureau of Child Welfare
(B) a shelter selected by the desk officer
(C) the Children's Center
(D) the New York Foundling Hospital when a brother or sister, under 2 years of age, also requires shelter.

Answer Questions 26 to 28 solely on the basis of the following paragraph:

"All applicants for an original license to operate a catering establishment shall be fingerprinted. This shall include the officers, employees and stockholders of the company and the members of a partnership. In case of a change, by addition or substitution, occurring during the existence of a license, the person added or substituted shall be fingerprinted. However, in the case of a hotel containing more than 200 rooms, only the officer or manager filing the application is required to be fingerprinted. The police commissioner may also at his discretion exempt the employees and stockholders of any company. The fingerprints shall be taken on one copy of form C.E. 20 and on two copies of C.E. 21. One copy of form C.E. 21 shall accompany the application. Fingerprints are not required with a renewal application."

26. According to this paragraph, an employee added to the payroll of a licensed catering establishment which is not in a hotel
(A) must always be fingerprinted
(B) must be fingerprinted unless he has been previously fingerprinted for another license
(C) must be fingerprinted unless exempted by the police commissioner
(D) must be fingerprinted only if he is the manager or an officer of the company.

27. According to this paragraph, it would be most accurate to state that
(A) form C.E. 20 must accompany a renewal application
(B) form C.E. 21 must accompany all applications
(C) form C.E. 21 must accompany an original application
(D) both forms C.E. 20 and C.E. 21 must accompany all applications.

28. A hotel of 270 rooms has applied for a license to operate a catering establishment on the premises. According to the instructions for fingerprinting given in this paragraph
(A) the officers, employees and stockholders shall be fingerprinted
(B) the officers and the manager shall be fingerprinted
(C) the employees shall be fingerprinted
(D) the officer filing the application shall be fingerprinted.

Questions 29 and 30 are to be answered solely on the basis of the following paragraph.

"If the second or third felony is such that, upon a first conviction, the offender would be punishable by imprisonment for any term less than his natural life, then such person must be sentenced to imprisonment for an indeterminate term, the minimum of which shall be not less than one-half of the longest term prescribed upon a first conviction, and the maximum of which shall be not longer than twice such longest term; provided, however, that the minimum sentence imposed hereunder upon such second or third felony offender shall in no case be less than five years; except that where the maximum punishment for a second or third felony offender hereunder is five years or less, the minimum sentence must be not less than two years."

29. According to this paragraph, a person who has a second felony conviction, shall receive as a sentence for that second felony an indeterminate term
    (A) not less than twice the minimum term prescribed upon a first conviction as a maximum
    (B) not less than one-half the maximum term of his first conviction as a minimum
    (C) not more than twice the minimum term prescribed upon a first conviction as a minimum
    (D) with a maximum of not more than one-half the longest term prescribed upon conviction for his first crime
    (E) with a maximum of not more than twice the longest term prescribed for a first conviction for this crime.

30. According to this paragraph, if the term for this crime for a first offender is up to three years, the possible indeterminate term for this crime as a second or third felony shall have a
    (A) minimum of not less than five years
    (B) maximum of not more than five years
    (C) minimum of not less than one and one-half years
    (D) maximum of not less than six years
    (E) minimum of not more than two years.

Correct Answers

(You'll learn more by writing your own answers before comparing them with these.)

1. A	7. C	13. B	19. A	25. A
2. B	8. D	14. B	20. E	26. C
3. B	9. D	15. C	21. A	27. C
4. A	10. B	16. E	22. A	28. D
5. E	11. C	17. C	23. D	29. E
6. A	12. D	18. B	24. D	30. C

READINGS IN LAW ENFORCEMENT

Each of the following questions is based upon your understanding, as a law enforcement officer, of a sentence or paragraph. How well have you read the passage? Have you assimilated all the details? What conclusions can you draw? What conclusions would be illogical in the context of the reading?

1. "The force reconciling and co-ordinating all the human conflicts and directing the men in the harmonious accomplishment of their work is the supervisor. To deal with people successfully, the first one a supervisor must learn to work with is himself." According to the above paragraph, the most accurate of the following conclusions is
   (A) human conflicts are not the basic lack in harmonious accomplishment
   (B) a supervisor should attempt to reconcile all the different views his subordinates have
   (C) a supervisor who understands himself is in a good position to deal with others successfully
   (D) the reconciling force in human conflicts is the ability to deal with people successfully.

Answer questions 2 to 6 solely on the basis of the following paragraph:

"If we are to study crime in its widest social setting, we will find a variety of conduct which, although criminal in the legal sense, is not offensive to the moral conscience of a considerable number of persons. Traffic violations, for example, do not brand the offender as guilty of moral offense. In fact, the recipient of a traffic ticket is usually simply the subject of some good natured joking by his friends. Although there may be indignation among certain groups of citizens against gambling and liquor law violations, these activities are often tolerated, if not openly supported, by the more numerous residents of the community. Indeed, certain social and service clubs regularly conduct gambling games and lotteries for the purpose of raising funds. Some communities regard violations involving the sale of liquor with little concern in order to profit from increased license fees and taxes paid by dealers. The thousand and one forms of political graft and corruption which infest our urban centers only occasionally arouse public condemnation and official action."

2. According to the above paragraph, all types of illegal conduct are
   (A) condemned by all elements of the community
   (B) considered a moral offense, although some are tolerated by a few citizens
   (C) violations of the law, but some are acceptable to certain elements of the community
   (D) found in a social setting which is not punishable by law.

3. According to the above paragraph, traffic violations are generally considered by society as
   (A) crimes requiring the maximum penalty set by the law
   (B) more serious than violations of the liquor laws
   (C) offenses against the morals of the community
   (D) relatively minor offenses requiring minimum punishment.

4. According to the above paragraph, a lottery conducted for the purpose of raising funds for a church
   (A) is considered a serious violation of law
   (B) may be tolerated by a community which has laws against gambling
   (C) may be conducted under special laws demanded by the more numerous residents of a community
   (D) arouses indignation in most communities.

5. On the basis of the above paragraph, the most likely reaction in the community to a police raid on a gambling casino would be
   (A) more an attitude of indifference than interest in the raid
   (B) general approval of the raid
   (C) condemnation of the raid by most people
   (D) demand for further action, since this raid is not sufficient to end gambling activities.

6. The one of the following which best describes the central thought of this paragraph and would be most suitable as a title for it is

(A) Crime and the Police
(B) Public Condemnation of Graft and Corruption
(C) Gambling Is Not Always a Vicious Business
(D) Public Attitude toward Law Violations.

Answer questions 7 to 9 solely on the basis of the following paragraph:

"The law enforcement agency is one of the most important agencies in the field of juvenile delinquency prevention. This is so, not because of the social work connected with this problem, however, for this is not a police matter, but because the officers are usually the first to come in contact with the delinquent. The manner of arrest and detention makes a deep impression upon him and affects his life-long attitude toward society and the law. The juvenile court is perhaps the most important agency in this work. Contrary to the general opinion, however, it is not primarily concerned with putting children into correctional schools. The main purpose of the juvenile court is to save the child and to develop his emotional make-up, in order that he can grow up to be a decent and well-balanced citizen. The system of probation is the means whereby the court seeks to accomplish these goals."

7. According to this paragraph, police work is an important part of a program to prevent juvenile delinquency because
(A) social work is no longer considered important in juvenile delinquency prevention
(B) police officers are the first to have contact with the delinquent
(C) police officers jail the offender in order to be able to change his attitude toward society and the law
(D) it is the first step in placing the delinquent in jail.

8. According to this paragraph, the chief purpose of the juvenile court is to
(A) punish the child for his offense
(B) select a suitable correctional school for the delinquent
(C) use available means to help the delinquent become a better person
(D) provide psychiatric care for the delinquent.

9. According to this paragraph, the juvenile court directs the development of delinquents under its care chiefly by
(A) placing the child under probation
(B) sending the child to a correctional school
(C) keeping the delinquent in prison
(D) returning the child to his home.

10. "Crimes against the person are apt to be more spectacular than other types of crime and in consequence, space is accorded them in the public press out of proportion to their actual frequency." This means most nearly
(A) there has been a notable increase in crimes against the person
(B) the newspapers pay more attention to robberies than to cases of fraud
(C) the newspapers pay no attention to crimes against property
(D) crimes against property are not so serious as crimes against the person.

11. "Blasphemy is still a crime but you meet it at every corner." The clearest implication in this statement is
(A) some laws are ignored
(B) blasphemy is a serious offense
(C) the principal purpose of any law is to catch a law-breaker
(D) blasphemy is quite uncommon.

12. "Discipline should be education: instead it is little more than an application to adults of the theory of spanking," means most nearly
(A) whipping is a good way to handle a man who beats his wife
(B) a thieving banker should be imprisoned for life
(C) those who commit crimes exhibit a marked lack of self-control
(D) re-education is really a kind of discipline.

13. "Law must be stable and yet it cannot stand still," means most nearly
(A) law is a fixed body of subject matter
(B) law must adapt itself to changing conditions
(C) law is a poor substitute for justice
(D) the true administration of justice is the firmest pillar of good government.

14. "The treatment to be given the offender cannot alter the fact of his offenses; but we can take measures to reduce the chances of similar acts in the future. We should banish the criminal, not in order to exact revenge nor directly to encourage reform, but to deter him and others from further illegal attacks on society." According to the preceding paragraph, prisoners should be punished in order to

(A) alter the nature of their offenses
(B) banish them from society
(C) deter them and others from similar illegal attacks on society
(D) exact revenge
(E) to directly encourage reform.

15. "On the other hand, the treatment of prisoners on a basis of direct reform is foredoomed to failure. Neither honest men nor criminals will tolerate a bald proposition from anyone to alter their characters or habits, least of all if we attempt to gain such a change by a system of coercion." According to this paragraph, criminals are
(A) incorrigible
(B) incapable of being coerced
(C) absolutely different from honest men
(C) possessed of very firm characters
(E) not likely to turn into law-abiding citizens as a result of being forced to reform.

16. "A moment's reflection will show that it is never possible to determine the exact amount of blame to be attached to the criminal himself. How can we ascertain how much is due to inheritance, how much to early environment, how much to other matters over which the offender has had no control whatsoever?" According to this paragraph, criminals
(A) cannot be held to account for their crimes
(B) cannot be blamed for their crimes
(C) are variously motivated in committing crime and it is senseless to assume that we can know how much blame to attach to a particular violator of the law
(D) can blame their misdeeds on early environment
(E) none of the foregoing.

17. "While much thought has been devoted to the question of how to build walls high enough to keep men temporarily in prison, we have devoted very little attention to the treatment necessary to enable them to come out permanently cured, inclined to be friends rather than enemies of their law-abiding fellow citizens." According to this paragraph, much thought has been devoted to the problem of prisons as
(A) vengeful agencies
(B) efficient custodial agencies
(C) efficient sanatoria
(D) institutions capable of enabling prisoners to come out permanently cured
(E) places from which society's friends might issue.

18. "There has been a tragic failure on the part of the home, the school, the church, industry, and every other social agency to adjust the incompetent individual to his proper sphere and to impart to him wholesome principles of right living. The failure is finally shunted on to the prison in one last desperate effort to make him over. Theoretically the church, the school and the college have a clean page in the mind of the pupil upon which to make their impressions, but the prison school faces the tremendous task of obliterating many erroneous and corrupt notions before it can secure a clean page upon which to write." According to this paragraph, the prison has as pupils
(A) those persons with which society's educational institutions have been able to do nothing
(B) those who have failed in business and the arts
(C) those who have scoffed at God
(D) those whose minds are blanks
(E) those who have learned nothing from the outside world.

Questions 19 to 21 must be answered according to the information given in Paragraph A and not according to any other information you may have.

PARAGRAPH A

"A car will go a certain distance from the point where danger is first detected before any driver is able to apply the brakes. This is called 'reaction distance.' The distance traveled after the brakes are applied is called 'braking distance.' A car traveling at 30 miles per hour has a braking distance of 50 feet, a car traveling at 40 miles per hour has a braking distance of 88 feet, and a car traveling at 50 miles per hour has a braking distance of 138 feet. It takes a certain amount of time after an emergency arises for even the most experienced driver to see the danger and send the impulse to stop to the braking mechanism of his car. The time this requires varies with the individual driver and ranges from three-eighths of a second to a second or more."

19. According to Paragraph A
(A) a car traveling at 40 miles per hour will travel 88 feet before the brakes are applied by the driver while a car traveling at 50 miles an hour will travel 138 feet before the brakes are applied by the driver
(B) a collision will result if a driver traveling at 30 miles an hour applies the brakes at the same time as the brakes are applied

by a driver 50 feet directly behind him traveling at 50 miles per hour
(C) a driver will step on the brakes the instant he sees danger ahead
(D) reaction time is the time required to see the danger.

20. According to Paragraph A
(A) a car traveling at 20 miles per hour will have a braking distance of 44 feet
(B) an experienced driver can bring a car to a stop in less than a second while a driver with very little experience will require a second or more to bring the same car to a stop
(C) braking distance is the distance traveled from the point where the danger is detected to the point where the car is stopped minus the distance traveled before the brakes are applied
(D) reaction distance is always greater than braking distance.

21. According to Paragraph A
(A) braking distance varies with the rate of speed at which the car is traveling
(B) braking time ranges from three-eighths of a second to a second or more
(C) reaction distance is the distance the car travels before danger is detected
(D) the faster a car is traveling, the shorter the time that is required to bring it to a stop.

22. "Community organization most often includes persons whose behavior is unconventional in relation to generally accepted social definition, if such persons wield substantial influence with the residents." The inference one can most validly draw from this statement is that
(A) influential persons are often likely to be unconventional
(B) the success of a community organization depends largely on the democratic processes employed by it
(C) a gang leader may sometimes be an acceptable recruit for a community organization
(D) the unconventional behavior of a local barkeeper may often become acceptable to the community.

23. "Essential to prevention and early treatment of delinquency is discovery of potential or incipient cases. Finding them is not as difficult as making assistance available and acceptable to them and their families." On the basis of the above statement, it is most accurate to state that
(A) the families of delinquents are largely responsible for their behavior
(B) "an ounce of prevention is worth more than a pound of cure"
(C) potentiality to criminality is readily discernible
(D) the family of a delinquent may often reject a recommended plan for therapy.

24. "The safeguard of democracy is education. The education of youth during a limited period of more or less compulsory attendance at school does not suffice. The educative process is a life long one." The statement most consistent with this quotation is
(A) the school is not the only institution which can contribute to the education of the population
(B) all democratic peoples are educated
(C) the entire population should be required to go to school throughout life
(D) if compulsory education were not required, the educative process would be more effective.

25. "Another explanation of the persistence of the criminal is found in the existence of criminality or near-criminality in the general society." The statement *least* consistent with this quotation is
(A) not all criminals are apprehended and sentenced for their crimes
(B) advertisements of many commodities are often fraudulent in their claims
(C) the reformation of the offender would be much simpler if society contained more persons of the near-criminal type
(D) many business concerns are willing to purchase stolen goods.

Law Enforcement Reading Interpretation Key Answers

1. C	6. D	11. A	16. D	21. A
2. C	7. B	12. D	17. B	22. C
3. D	8. C	13. B	18. A	23. D
4. B	9. A	14. C	19. B	24. A
5. A	10. B	15. E	20. C	25. C

TOP SCORES ON VOCABULARY TESTS

Although questions on vocabulary may not actually appear on your test, it is advisable to practice with the kind of material you have in this chapter. Words and their meanings are quite important in pushing up your score on tests of reading, comprehension, effective writing and correct usage. By broadening your vocabulary, you will definitely improve your marks in these and similar subjects.

INCREASE YOUR VOCABULARY

How is your vocabulary? Do you know the meanings of just about every word you come upon in your reading—or do you find several words that stump you? You must increase your vocabulary if you want to read with understanding. Following are six steps that you can take in order to build up your word power:

(a) Read as much as you have the time for. Don't confine yourself to one type of reading either. Read all kinds of things—newspaper, magazines, books. Seek variety in what you read—different newspapers, several types of magazines, all types of books (novels, poetry, essays, plays, etc.). If you get into the habit of reading widely, your vocabulary will grow by leaps and bounds. You'll learn the meanings of words *by context.* That means that, very often, even though you may not know the meaning of a certain word in a sentence, the other words that you are familiar with will help you get the meaning of the hard word.

(b) Take vocabulary tests. There are many practice books which have word tests. We suggest one of these: *2300 Steps to Word Power*—$1.45 (Arco Publishing Co.). These tests are fun to take—and they will build up your vocabulary fast.

(c) Listen to lectures, discussions, and talks by people who speak well. There are some worthwhile TV programs that have excellent speakers. Listen to such people—you'll learn a great many words from them simply by listening to them.

(d) Use a dictionary. Whenever you don't know the meaning of a word, make a note of it. Then, when you get to a dictionary, look up the meaning of the word. Keep your own little notebook—call it "New Words." In a month or two, you will have added a great many words to your vocabulary. If you do not have a dictionary at home, you should buy one. It is just as important in your life as pots and pans, furniture, or a television set. A good dictionary is not expensive. Any one of the following is highly recommended—and costs about five or six dollars:

Standard College Dictionary (Funk and Wagnalls)

Seventh New Collegiate Dictionary (Merriam-Webster)

American College Dictionary (Random House)

You'll never regret buying a good dictionary for your home.

(c) Play word games. Have you ever played Anagrams or Scrabble? They're really interesting. Buy one of these at a stationery store. They are quite inexpensive but effective in building up your vocabulary. Crossword puzzles will teach you new words also. Practically every daily newspaper has a crossword puzzle.

(f) Learn stems, prefixes, and suffixes. It is very important that you know these.

BASIC LETTER COMBINATIONS

One of the most efficient ways in which you can build up your vocabulary is by a systematic study of the basic word and letter combinations which make up the greater part of the English language.

Etymology is the science of the formation of words, and this somewhat frightening-sounding science can be of great help to you in learning new words and identifying words which may be unfamiliar to you. You will also find that the progress you make in studying the following pages will help to improve your spelling.

A great many of the words which we use every day have come into our language from the Latin and Greek. In the process of being absorbed into English, they appear as parts of words, many of which are related in meaning to each other.

For your convenience, this material is presented in easy-to-study form. Latin and Greek syllables and letter-combinations have been categorized into three groups:

1. *Prefixes:* letter combinations which appear at the beginning of a word.
2. *Suffixes:* letter combinations which appear at the end of a word.
3. *Roots or stems:* which carry the basic meaning and are combined with each other and with prefixes and suffixes to create other words with related meanings.

With the prefixes and suffixes, which you should study first, we have given examples of word formation with meanings, and additional examples. If you find any unfamiliar words among the samples, consult your dictionary to look up their meanings.

The list of roots or stems is accompanied by words in which the letter combinations appear. Here again, use the dictionary to look up any words which are not clear in your mind.

Remember that this section is not meant for easy reading. It is a guide to a program of study that will prove invaluable if you do your part. Do not try to swallow too much at one time. If you can put in a half-hour every day, your study will yield better results.

After you have done your preliminary work and have gotten a better idea of how words are formed in English, schedule the various vocabulary tests and quizzes we have provided in this chapter. They cover a wide variety of the vocabulary questions commonly encountered on examinations. They are short quizzes, not meant to be taken all at one time. Space them out. Adhere closely to the directions which differ for the different test types. Keep an honest record of your scores. Study your mistakes. Look them up in your dictionary. Concentrate closely on each quiz . . . and watch your scores improve.

ETYMOLOGY - A KEY TO WORD RECOGNITION

PREFIXES

PREFIX	MEANING	EXAMPLE
ab, a	away from	absent, amoral
ad, ac, ag, at	to	advent, accrue, aggressive, attract
an	without	anarchy
ante	before	antedate
anti	against	antipathy
bene	well	beneficent
bi	two	bicameral
circum	around	circumspect
com, con, col	together	commit confound, collate
contra	against	contraband
de	from, down	descend
dis, di	apart	distract, divert
ex, e	out	exit, emit
extra	beyond	extracurricular
in, im, il, ir, un	not	inept, impossible, illicit
inter	between	interpose
intra, intro, in	within	intramural, introspective

PREFIX	MEANING	EXAMPLE
mal	bad	malcontent
mis	wrong	misnomer
non	not	nonentity
ob	against	obstacle
per	through	permeate
peri	around	periscope
poly	many	polytheism
post	after	post-mortem
pre	before	premonition
pro	forward	propose
re	again	review
se	apart	seduce
semi	half	semicircle
sub	under	subvert
super	above	superimpose
sui	self	suicide
trans	across	transpose
vice	instead of	vice-president

SUFFIXES

SUFFIX	MEANING	EXAMPLE
able, ible	capable of being	capable, reversible
age	state of	storage
ance	relating to	reliance
ary	relating to	dictionary
ate	act	confiscate
ation	action	radiation
cy	quality	democracy

SUFFIX	MEANING	EXAMPLE
ence	relating to	confidence
er	one who	adviser
ic	pertaining to	democratic
ious	full of	rebellious
ize	to make like	harmonize
ment	result	filament
ty	condition	sanity

LATIN AND GREEK STEMS

STEM	MEANING	EXAMPLE
ag, ac	do	agenda, action
agr	farm	agriculture
aqua	water	aqueous
cad, cas	fall	cadence, casual
cant	sing	chant
cap, cep	take	captive, accept
capit	head	capital
cede	go	precede
celer	speed	celerity
cide, cis	kill, cut	suicide, incision
clud, clus	close	include, inclusion
cur, curs	run	incur, incursion
dict	say	diction
duct	lead	induce
fact, fect	make	factory, perfect
fer, lat	carry	refer, dilate
fring, fract	break	infringe, fracture
frater	brother	fraternal
fund, fus	pour	refund, confuse
greg	group	gregarious
gress, grad	move forward	progress, degrade
homo	man	homicide
ject	throw	reject
jud	right	judicial
junct	join	conjunction
lect, leg	read, choose	collect, legend
loq, loc	speak	loquacious, interlocutory
manu	hand	manuscript
mand	order	remand
mar	sea	maritime
mater	mother	maternal
med	middle	intermediary
min	lessen	diminution
mis, mit	send	remit, dismiss
mort	death	mortician
mote, mov	move	remote, remove
naut	sailor	astronaut
nom	name	nomenclature
pater	father	paternity
ped, pod	foot	pedal, podiatrist
pend	hang	depend
plic	fold	implicate
port	carry	portable
pos, pon	put	depose, component
reg, rect	rule	regicide, direct
rupt	break	eruption
scrib, scrip	write	inscribe, conscription
anthrop	man	anthropology

STEM	MEANING	EXAMPLE
arch	chief, rule	archbishop
astron	star	astronomy
auto	self	automatic
biblio	book	bibliophile
bio	life	biology
chrome	color	chromosome
chron	time	chronology
cosmo	world	cosmic
crat	rule	autocrat
dent, dont	tooth	dental, indent
eu	well, happy	eugenics
gamos	marriage	monogamous
ge	earth	geology
gen	origin, people	progenitor
graph	write	graphic
gyn	women	gynecologist
homo	same	homogeneous
hydr	water	dehydrate
logy	study of	psychology
meter	measure	thermometer
micro	small	microscope
mono	one	monotony
onomy	science	astronomy
onym	name	synonym
pathos	feeling	pathology
philo	love	philosophy
phobia	fear	hydrophobia
phone	sound	telephone
pseudo	false	pseudonym
psych	mind	psychic
scope	see	telescope
soph	wisdom	sophomore
tele	far off	telepathic
theo	god	theology
thermo	heat	thermostat
sec	cut	dissect
sed	remain	sedentary
sequ	follow	sequential
spect	look	inspect
spir	breathe	conspire
stat	stand	status
tact, tang	touch	tactile, tangible
ten	hold	retentive
term	end	terminal
vent	come	prevent
vict	conquer	evict
vid, vis	see	video, revise
voc	call	convocation
volv	roll	devolve

VOCABULARY TEST QUESTIONS FOR PRACTICE

The following questions have been selected to give you as broad a sampling as possible of words which have appeared on previous tests. The ease or difficulty with which you answer these questions will indicate whether or not your word power is adequate for the test you are about to take.

YOU will find these questions divided into separate sub-tests of ten questions each. This division has been made for two reasons: (1) the average number of vocabulary questions on tests of this grade is ten: (2) by doing each sub-test separately, you are enabled to see your progress as you proceed from one test to the next.

You will note that following each test, space is provided for recording the time you took to do the test, and for recording the number of correct answers. By comparing the second test with the first, the third with the second, etc., you will be able to see whether or not you are improving your word power as you study. Successful study should result in speedier time on each successive test, accompanied by increasing accuracy. If this is not the case when you have completed all the tests, then you had better begin again until the desired results are obtained.

These tests, as you will see, take several forms. In general, they are multiple-choice type asking for a word's definition or its opposite. Some questions ask whether a word is used correctly or not, and require you to answer "True" if it is, and "False" if it isn't. You will find, however, that a majority of questions are of the former type. The number of questions in any one form reflects its frequency on actual exams.

Use a watch or clock to keep an accurate record of the time consumed by each test. Read the instructions which precede each test carefully. You may check your accuracy by referring to the answers at the end of the chapter. Do not refer to these answers until you have completed each test.

Sample Test Question Analyzed

The questions may appear in one of several forms, but one of the most numerous is that of choosing a word which is most nearly the same in meaning as the question word. The example below has been chosen because it will help to illustrate the way in which vocabulary questions are answered.

Blacken the appropriate space for the letter preceding the word which is most nearly the same in meaning as the *italicized* word in the sentence.

Sample Question. One who is *garrulous* in his relations with others is, most nearly:

(A) complaining
(B) careless
(C) overly talkative
(D) defensive (E) dishonest.

Notice that the instructions ask for the selection of the choice which is *most nearly* the same in meaning as the italicized word.

First, examine the italicized word. If you know its meaning, your task is fairly simple. But suppose you do not know what *garrulous* means. Perhaps we can eliminate some of the choices by analyzing them.

(A) Complaining: Does *complaining* have anything to do with *garrulous*? It might. However, a synonym for *complaining* is querulous. In this case, it is best to avoid *complaining* as a possibility, since it is probably there to confuse you.

(B) Careless: Most people know what careless means. Here again is a word which only sounds like the question word. You would not use *garrulous* to describe a neglectful person.

(C) Overly Talkative: There is nothing to indicate that this phrase is not a synonym for *garrulous*. Do not eliminate it as a possibility.

(D) Defensive: You can think of synonyms for this one, like protective, safe-guarding, and maybe even fortress and garrison may come to mind. In general, any word that sounds like the question word should be avoided. You would do well to eliminate *defensive* as a possibility.

(E) Dishonest: There is not much to indicate that this is not a synonym for *garrulous*, and none of the synonyms for *dishonest* sounds like the question word. It cannot be eliminated entirely.

The choice is now between (C) and (E); *overly talkative* and *dishonest*. If you have no idea at all regarding the meaning of *garrulous*, then you must guess. Since three of the choices have already been eliminated, you have a much better chance to guess correctly.

Garrulous: The dictionary defines *garrulous* as: "given to continual and tedious talking," "habitually loquacious," "chattering," "verbose." Therefore, (C) "overly talkative" is the correct answer.

SIX TEST-TYPE QUIZZES FOR PRACTICE

For each question read all the choices carefully. Then select that answer which you consider correct or most nearly correct. Write the letter preceding your best choice next to the question

Should you want to answer on the kind of answer sheet used on machine-scored examinations, we have provided several such facsimiles.

In machine-scored examinations you should record all your answers on the answer sheet provided. Don't make the mistake of putting answers on the test booklet itself.

On some machine-scored exams you are instructed to "place no marks whatever on the test booklet."

In other examinations you may be instructed to mark your answers in the test booklet. In such cases you should be careful that no other marks interfere with the legibility of your answers.

It is always best NOT to mark your booklet unless you are sure that it is permitted.

It is most important that you learn to mark your answers clearly and in the right place.

To help you understand the procedure, the following sample item is given:

SAMPLE O: The sum of 5 and 3 is

(A) 11 (B) 8 (C) 9 (D) 2 (E) 10.

The sum of 5 and 3 is 8, so that the acceptable answer is shown thus on your answer sheet:

	a	b	c	d	e
SAMPLE O	⁞	▌	⁞	⁞	⁞

ANSWER SHEETS AND CORRECT ANSWERS APPEAR AFTER EACH TEST

SYNONYMS TEST ONE

DIRECTIONS: For each of the following questions, select the choice which best answers the question or completes the statement.

Correct key answers to all these test questions will be found at the end of the test.

1. An amendment is a
   (A) civic center (B) charter
   (C) penalty (D) change.
2. A quorum is a
   (A) minority (B) committee
   (C) majority (D) bicameral system.
3. Clearance refers to a
   (A) weight (B) hoistway
   (C) distance (D) cleaning process.
4. Pasteurized milk is milk that has been
   (A) watered (B) condemned
   (C) embargoed (D) purified.
5. Antitoxin is used in cases of
   (A) corrupt governmental officials
   (B) sanitary inspection
   (C) disease
   (D) elevator construction.
6. Libel refers to the
   (A) process of incurring financial liability
   (B) publication of a false statement which injures others
   (C) deportation of aliens
   (D) necessity for compulsory schooling.
7. Naturalization refers to the process of
   (A) becoming a civil service employee
   (B) being summoned to court
   (C) becoming a citizen
   (D) pledging allegiance to the American flag.
8. To comply with a rule means to
   (A) abide by a rule (B) abrogate a rule
   (C) dislike a rule (D) ignore a rule.
9. A budget is a
   (A) financial statement
   (B) method for training operators
   (C) device for insuring courtesy
   (D) means for selecting judges
10. A fulcrum is part of a
    (A) typewriter (B) lever
    (C) radio (D) lamp.

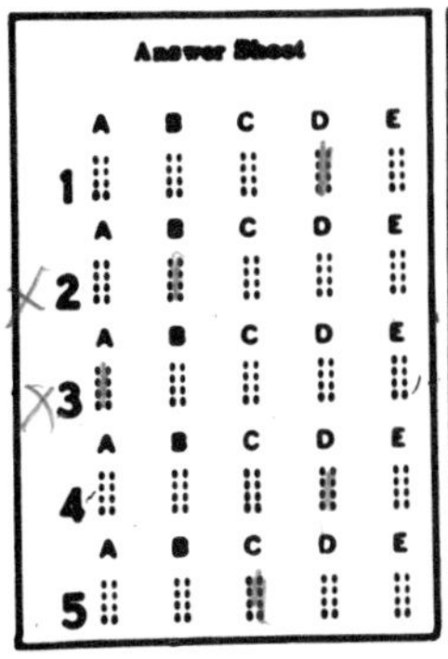

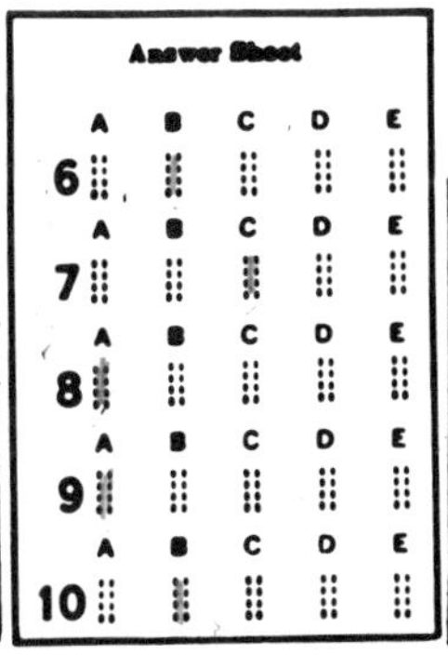

SCORE 80 %

NO. CORRECT ÷ NO. OF QUESTIONS ON THIS TEST

Correct Answers

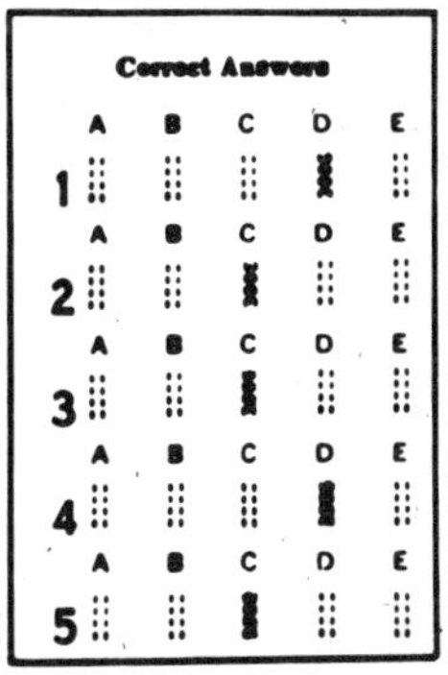

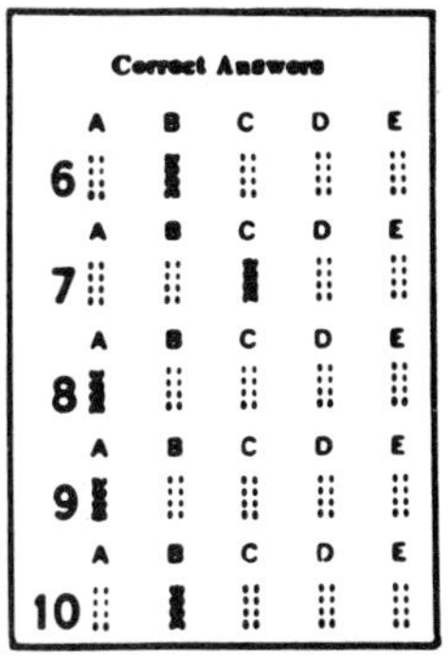

SYNONYMS TEST TWO

DIRECTIONS: Each of the questions in this test is numbered and consists of pairs of words. Each pair of words is preceded by a letter. For each question, select the one pair of words wherein both words are synonymous. Mark the letter, A, B, C, D, or E, preceding that pair on your answer sheet.

Correct key answers to all these test questions will be found at the end of the test.

1. (A) transitory-permanent (B) prohibit-allow (C) beautiful-ugly (D) broken-disunited (E) ferocious-mild.
2. (A) elucidate-clarify (B) recent-ancient (C) enthusiasm-apathy (D) equivocal-indubitable (E) evade-acknowledge.
3. (A) extricate-imprison (B) concur-endorse (C) intimidate-assure (D) lucid-obscure (E) molest-comfort.
4. (A) abandon-hold (B) awkward-skillful (C) consistent-varying (D) constrain-beseech (E) tedious-tiresome.
5. (A) deficient-ample (B) waste-conserve (C) compromise-quarrel (D) sanguine-optimistic (E) desist-persevere.
6. (A) monotony-variety (B) remote-near (C) propitiate-appease (D) many-few (E) veracity-deception.
7. (A) fraud-honesty (B) important-significant (C) mollify-vex (D) abate-maintain (E) authorize-forbid.
8. (A) eradicate-destroy (B) barbarous-humane (C) compulsion-freedom (D) concur-differ (E) incite-quell.
9. (A) morose-cheerful (B) munificent-penurious (C) censorious-fault-finding (D) predominate-subordinate (E) extricate-bind.
10. (A) gratify-displease (B) grudge-good will (C) interpose-withdraw (D) irresponsible-accountable (E) augment-increase.

Correct Answers For The Foregoing Questions

To assist you in scoring yourself we have provided Correct Answers alongside your Answer Sheet. May we therefore suggest that while you are doing the test you cover the Correct Answers with a sheet of white paper.....to avoid temptation and to arrive at an accurate estimate of your ability and progress.

Answer Sheet

	A	B	C	D	E
1					
2					
3					
4					
5					
6					
7					
8					
9					
10					

SCORE

.................%

NO. CORRECT ÷ NO. OF QUESTIONS ON THIS TEST

Correct Answers

	A	B	C	D	E
1				▮	
2	▮				
3		▮			
4					▮
5				▮	
6			▮		
7		▮			
8	▮				
9			▮		
10					▮

SYNONYMS TEST THREE

Although vocabulary questions may not actually appear on your test, it is advisable to try to improve your vocabulary. Words and their meanings are quite important on reading, writing and correct usage tests. By broadening your vocabulary, you will definitely improve your marks in these and similar subjects.

DIRECTIONS: For each of the following statements, mark T if the statement is True, and F if it is False.

1. A *competent* employee is one who is slow and inefficient. T F
2. A person who commits *perjury* does not tell the truth. T F
3. The *prosecutor* in a criminal case is the lawyer who presents evidence against the defendant. T F
4. A *destitute* person has a large amount of money. T F
5. A person with a *florid* complexion has a pale face. T F
6. A noise that is *audible* is capable of being heard. T F
7. Anyone who is *agile* is quick and nimble. T F
8. An employee who gives information in a *curt* manner is sympathetic and courteous. T F
9. A person who is *prudent* is careless in his attention to duty. T F
10. If a person pays an *exorbitant* amount of money for an article, he is paying a fair price. T F

Now, push forward! Test yourself and practice for your test with the carefully constructed quizzes that follow. Each one presents the kind of question you may expect on your test. And each question is at just the level of difficulty that may be expected. Don't try to take all the tests at one time. Rather, schedule yourself so that you take a few at each session, and spend approximately the same time on them at each session. Score yourself honestly, and date each test. You should be able to detect improvement in your performance on successive sessions.

A portion of the standard answer sheet is provided after each test for marking your answers in the way you'll be required to do on the actual exam. At the right of this answer sheet, to make the scoring job simpler (after you have derived your own answers), you'll find our correct answers.

SCORE
%
NO. CORRECT ÷ NO. OF QUESTIONS ON THIS TEST

Correct Answers

(You'll learn more by writing your own answers before comparing them with these.)

1. F	6. T
2. T	7. T
3. T	8. F
4. F	9. F
5. F	10. F

SYNONYMS TEST FOUR

DIRECTIONS: This test contains a list of numbered words, and other words divided into five groups—Group A, Group B, Group C, Group D and Group E. For each of the numbered words, select that word in one of the five groups which is most nearly the same in meaning. The letter of that group is the answer for that item. Your answer sheet and our correct answers follow the last question.

Correct key answers to all these test questions will be found at the end of the test.

Group A

indication ambiguous excruciating thin

Group B

confirmation financial phobia erasure

Group C

fiduciary similar yellowish skill

Group D

theft winding receive procrastination

Group E

franchise heir hardy preference

1. fiscal
2. deletion
3. equivocal
4. corroboration
5. tortuous
6. predilection
7. sallow
8. virtuosity
9. scion
10. tenuous

Correct Answers For The Foregoing Questions

To assist you in scoring yourself we have provided Correct Answers alongside your Answer Sheet. May we therefore suggest that while you are doing the test you cover the Correct Answers with a sheet of white paper.....to avoid temptation and to arrive at an accurate estimate of your ability and progress.

Answer Sheet

	A	B	C	D	E
1					
2					
3					
4					
5					
6					
7					
8					
9					
10					

SCORE

%

NO. CORRECT ÷

NO. OF QUESTIONS ON THIS TEST

Correct Answers

	A	B	C	D	E
1		■			
2		■			
3	■				
4		■			
5				■	
6					■
7			■		
8			■		
9					■
10	■				

SYNONYMS TEST FIVE

DIRECTIONS: This test contains a list of numbered words, and other words divided into five groups—Group A, Group B, Group C, Group D and Group E. For each of the numbered words, select that word in one of the five groups which is most nearly the same in meaning. The letter of that group is the answer for that item. Your answer sheet and our correct answers follow the last question.

Correct key answers to all these test questions will be found at the end of the test.

1. prophylactic
2. palliation
3. redolent
4. indictment
5. misfeasance
6. holograph
7. ancillary
8. hectic
9. obsolescence
10. holocaust

Group A
ruddy retribution mitigation decadence

Group B
dental fragrant accusation symptom

Group C
preventive destruction aggravation testimony

Group D
intimidation subsidiary feverish trespass

Group E
consecration excited corpulence handwritten

Correct Answers For The Foregoing Questions

To assist you in scoring yourself we have provided Correct Answers alongside your Answer Sheet. May we therefore suggest that while you are doing the test you cover the Correct Answers with a sheet of white paper.....to avoid temptation and to arrive at an accurate estimate of your ability and progress.

Answer Sheet

	A	B	C	D	E
1					
2					
3					
4					
5					
6					
7					
8					
9					
10					

SCORE

%

NO. CORRECT ÷
NO. OF QUESTIONS ON THIS TEST

Correct Answers

	A	B	C	D	E
1			■		
2	■				
3		■			
4		■			
5				■	
6					■
7				■	
8				■	
9	■				
10			■		

SYNONYMS TEST SIX

DIRECTIONS: For each question in this test, select the appropriate letter preceding the word which is most nearly the same in meaning as the italicized word in each sentence.

Correct key answers to all these test questions will be found at the end of the test.

1. The person who is *diplomatic* in his relations with others is, most nearly
   (A) well dressed (B) very tactful
   (C) somewhat domineering (D) deceitful and tricky
   (E) verbose.

2. Action at this time would be *inopportune*. The word "inopportune" means most nearly
   (A) untimely (B) premeditated
   (C) sporadic (D) commendable
   (E) fortunate.

3. The word *appraise* means most nearly
   (A) consult (B) attribute
   (C) manage (D) honor
   (E) judge.

4. The word *cognizant* means most nearly
   (A) rare (B) reluctant
   (C) aware (D) haphazard
   (E) correlated.

5. *Probity* is an important requirement of many positions. The word "probity" means most nearly
   (A) analytical ability (B) vision
   (C) tried integrity (D) clear insight
   (E) perseverence.

6. The word *denote* means most nearly
   (A) encumber (B) evade
   (C) furnish (D) indicate
   (E) reduce in rank.

7. The competent employee should know that a method of procedure which is *expedient* is most nearly
   (A) unchangeable (B) based upon a false assumption
   (C) unduly harmful (D) difficult to work out
   (E) suitable to the end in view.

8. An incentive which is *potent* is most nearly
   (A) impossible (B) highly effective
   (C) not immediately practicable (D) a remote possibility
   (E) universally applicable.

9. An employer who is *judicious* is most nearly
   (A) domineering (B) argumentative
   (C) sincere (D) arbitrary
   (E) wise.

10. He presented a *controversial* plan. The word "controversial" means most nearly
    (A) subject to debate (B) unreasonable
    (C) complex (D) comparable
    (E) well formulated.

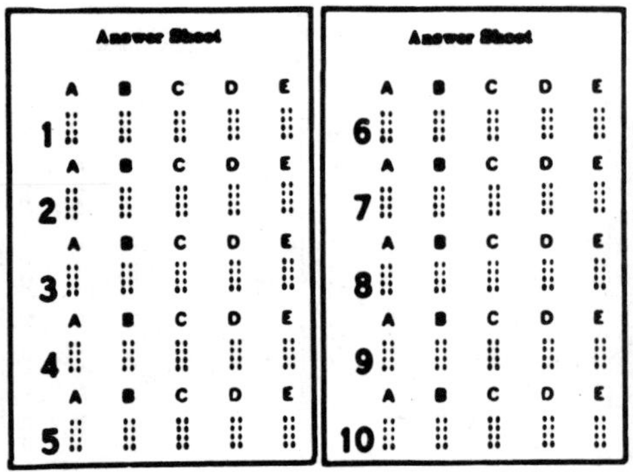

SCORE

%

NO. CORRECT ÷
NO. OF QUESTIONS ON THIS TEST

Correct Answers

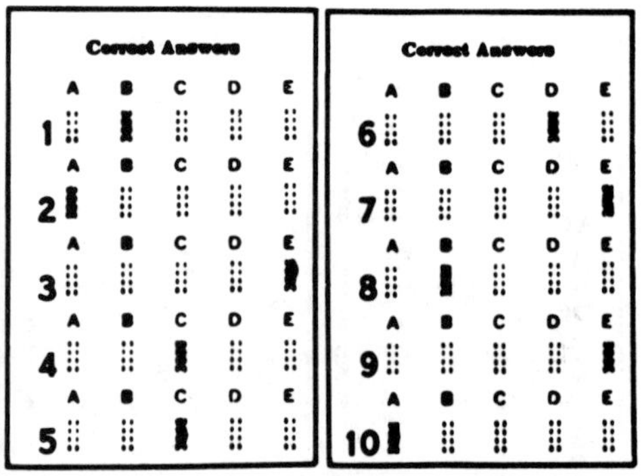

COURT OFFICER

Legal Definitions

You may be asked questions in your examination which require a knowledge of the following definitions. Study them carefully.

Definitions

ABDUCTION: The unlawful act of taking away a virgin, a wife, or a widow against her will.

ABSCOND: To hide from the jurisdiction of a court in order to avoid a legal process.

ACCESSORY BEFORE THE FACT: One who helps another to commit a crime, even though he is absent when the crime is committed.

ACCESSORY AFTER THE FACT: One who harbors, assists, or protects another person although he knows that that other person has committed a crime.

ACCOMMODATION PAPER: A bill or note to which someone has signed his name, without having been paid to do so, for the purpose of benefitting or accommodating some other party who desires to raise money on the paper.

ACKNOWLEDGMENT: The act by which a party goes before a competent officer or court and declares that he has voluntarily performed a certain deed.

ACQUIT: To free a person legally from an accusation of criminal guilt.

ACTION: An ordinary court proceeding wherein one party seeks to uphold his rights under the law.

ACTION TO QUIET TITLE: A proceeding in which the plaintiff declares that the defendant has been claiming some ownership in the plaintiff's land without defining the nature of that ownership. The action calls for definition so that the matter may be settled by decree.

ADJOURNMENT: Postponing a session or a hearing to some other time or place.

ADMINISTRATION OF ESTATES: The management and settlement of the estate of an intestate or a testator who has named no executor. The work is done under the jurisdiction and supervision of the court by a legally appointed administrator.

ADMINISTRATOR, LETTERS OF: Issued by probate court, they empower the administrator to take charge of an intestate's affairs.

ADULT: Any person who is twenty-one years of age or over.

ADULTERY: Voluntary and unlawful sexual intercourse between a man and a woman, at least one of whom is married.

ALIMONY: An allowance paid by a husband for his wife's support when she is living separate from him. Such an allowance is usually made during and after a suit for divorce.

AFFIDAVIT: A written or printed declaration or statement of facts, made voluntarily, and confirmed by the oath or affirmation of the party making it, taken before an officer having authority to administer such oath.

ANCILLARY: Aid, auxiliary; used to describe an action which is dependent upon a principal proceeding.

APPEAL: A case carried to a higher court, in which it is asked that the decision of the lower court, in which the case originated, be altered or over-ruled completely.

ARBITRATION: The settlement of a disagreement out of court by an arbitrator chosen by the parties to the argument. The parties agree that they will adhere to the arbitrator's decision.

ARRAIGN: To cause a person to stand trial for the charge in an indictment.

ARREST: To deprive a person of his liberty by legal authority that he may be held to answer for a crime.

ARREST, ORDER OF: A "provisional remedy" which may be employed in certain civil actions to prevent the object of the action being defeated by the defendant fleeing from the jurisdiction of the court *before judgment*. The order of arrest secures indemnity for the wrong committed, either by holding the defendant personally until the judgment is rendered or by requiring bail for this purpose.

ARSON: Wilfully and maliciously burning property.

ASSAULT: An unlawful attempt to hurt another person physically. Should the person actually be beaten then the act is called "Battery".

ATTACHMENT: This is a proceeding for the seizure of the property of the defendant before judgment and as such it is classified as a "provisional remedy." It cannot exist except as an aid to the action in which it is obtained. The purpose is to obtain possession of property until the recovery of a judgment and thereby prevent the defendant from disposing of it to defeat the object of the action in which the attachment is granted.

ATTAINDER, BILL OF: Is an act passed by the legislature for the special purpose of pronouncing a person guilty of an alleged crime (usually treason) without trial or conviction and passing sentence of death and attainder (deprivation of all civil rights and forfeiture of land) upon him. Bills of attainder are prohibited by the United States Constitution.

ATTESTATION: Witnessing an instrument in writing and recording that act in writing on the instrument.

BAIL: To release a person from jail by guaranteeing that he shall remain within the jurisdiction and call of the court. The bail bond which must be posted is a sum usually proportioned to the seriousness of the crime, and it may be forfeit if the defendant does not appear when called.

BEQUEST: A gift of personal property by will.

BIGAMY: Marriage to two or more persons of the opposite sex.

BILL: A formal declaration of particular things in writing. The word has divers uses in law.

BLACKMAIL: To extort goods or money from another by the threat, in writing, of accusation or exposure.

BRIEF: A summary of the law relating to a case which is prepared by the attorneys for both parties to a case and handed to the judge.

BURGLARY: Breaking into and entering another person's house with the intention of committing a felony therein.

CAPIAS: "That you take". The general name for writs that order the officer to arrest the defendant.

CAPITAL CRIME: Any crime punishable by death.

CAVEAT: A formal notice given to a judge or ministerial officer warning him not to perform contemplated acts within his jurisdiction.

CERTIORARI, WRIT OF: An order issued by a superior court directing an inferior court to send up to the former some or all the record of a case tried in the inferior court for review or trial.

CHAMPERTY: An agreement whereby a stranger to a suit agrees to finance one side in return for a share of the property that is secured through the action.

CHANCERY: see "equity".

CITATION: A writ, issued by a court, ordering a person to appear and perform a certain act.

COMPLAINT: One who sues another in a court of equity. Also one who initiates criminal prosecution.

CONSPIRACY: A secret combination for the purpose of committing a crime.

CONTEMPT OF COURT: Behavior that impugns the authority of a court or obstructs the execution of court orders.

CONVEYANCE: Transfer of ownership in property. Also an instrument in writing which effects this transfer.

CORPUS DELICTI: The actual, visible proof that a crime has been committed. Before murder can be proved in a court the corpus delicti, the murdered person, must be found.

COVENANT: An agreement in writing by which someone pledges to someone else that something has been done or shall be done or that certain facts are true.

DECREE: The judgment of a court of equity or admiralty, answering for most purposes to the judgment of a court of Common Law.

DEED: A written instrument by which one person conveys land to another.

DEFENDANT: The person against whom relief or recovery is sought in an action.

DEMISE: A lease.

DEMUR: To raise an objection in point of law, and rest or pause upon it, referring its decision to the court.

DEMURRER: In court procedure a statement that the opposing party has no sufficient basis in law despite the truth of the facts advanced.

DEPOSITION: The testimony of a witness taken under oath, out of court, and reduced to writing for insertion into the record of the trial.

DEVISE: A gift of real property by will.

DISORDERLY CONDUCT: Minor offenses which tend to endanger public peace, safety or morals.

DISPOSSESS: (summary Proceeding). A legal process instituted by a landlord to regain possession of his own real property. The proceedings are short and simple in comparison with regular court actions.

EMBEZZLEMENT: Fraudulent appropriation by a person acting in fiduciary capacity, of money entrusted by another.

EMBRACERY: The attempt to corruptly influence a juror.

EMINENT DOMAIN: The power of the state to take private property for public use.

EQUITY: A system of jurisprudence and tribunals, separate from the common law courts, the purpose of which is to render the administration of justice more complete by affording relief where the courts of law cannot give it.

ESTOPPEL: A legal prohibition which stops a man from making a particular statement because of something that he has said before.

ET AL.: And others. Used after the names of plaintiffs and defendants to indicate that other persons are involved besides those specifically mentioned.

EX PARTE: Done by or for one side only and without notice to or contestation by any person adversely interested.

EXAMINATION: An investigation of a witness by counsel by means of questions for the purpose of bringing before the court the knowledge possessed by the witness.

EXCEPTION: A formal objection to the action of the court during a trial. The indication is that the excepting party will seek to reverse the court's action at some future proceeding.

EXECUTION AGAINST A PERSON: Such an execution may be obtained after judgment in the same actions in which orders of arrest are obtained. The debtor may be imprisoned for a period not exceeding six months, or until he pays the money. If the defendant serves the six months he may not be imprisoned again in the same action but he is not released of his debt.

EXECUTION AGAINST PROPERTY: After a judgment has been obtained, the attorney for the plaintiff issues an execution against the property. The execution means that the Marshal is ordered to carry out the judgment of the Court. Municipal Court judgments must be executed by the City Marshal. All county and Supreme Court judgments are executed by the Sheriff. Some City Court judgments are executed by the Marshal, others by the Sheriff.

EXECUTION AGAINST WAGES: A "garnishee" execution is issued on any money judgment against "Wages, debts, earnings, salary, income from trust funds or profits which are or will be due the debtor to the amount of $12.00 a week".

EXECUTOR: The person named by a testator to carry out the provisions of his will.

EXTRADITION: Delivery from one state or nation to another of fugitives from justice.

FEE SIMPLE: Complete ownership of property with unconditional power of disposition during life.

FELONY: The term has no very definite or precise meaning, except in most cases where it is defined by statute. Generally speaking, the legislatures of the several states declare whether or not an offense is a felony or not. Aside from this, the term usually connotates an offense or crime of a more serious nature than those designated as misdemeanors.

FIDUCIARY: Having the character of a trustee; invested with rights and powers to be exercised for the benefit of some other person.

GRAND JURY: A jury of inquiry who are summoned and returned by an officer to each session of the criminal courts, and whose duty it is to receive complaints and accusations in criminal cases, hear the evidence adduced on the part of the state, and find bills of indictment in cases where they are satisfied that a trial ought to be held. They are first sworn and instructed by the court. This is called a "grand jury" because it comprises a greater number of jurors than the ordinary trial jury, or "petit jury".

GUARDIAN AD LITEM: A guardian appointed to represent an infant in legal proceedings.

HOMICIDE: Killing of one human being by the act or omission of another human being.

INCHOATE: Imperfect; begun but not completed.

INDICTMENT: A written accusation by a grand jury charging a person with a crime for which he must be tried in court.

INFANT: One who is under twenty-one years of age.

INJUNCTION: An order by a court of equity prohibiting a defendant from committing an act which is injurious to the plaintiff.

INTESTACY PROCEEDINGS: See administration proceedings.

INTESTATE: A person who dies without having made a will.

IPSO FACTO: By the mere effect of an act or a fact.

JEOPARDY: The danger of conviction and punishment which a defendant in a criminal action incurs when a valid indictment has been found. Double jeopardy is prohibited under the constitution, that is, a man may not be tried twice for the same crime.

JUDGMENT: The official decision of a court of justice on the claims of parties to a litigation.

JUSTIFIABLE HOMICIDE: Homicide committed in pursuance of the law as when an executioner kills a criminal sentenced for first degree murder.

LACHES: Failure to assert a right for an unreasonable length of time under circumstances which are harmful to another person.

LARCENY: Unlawfully taking property belonging to another. Grand larceny is established when the property exceeds in value the amount set by statute. Petit larceny is established by stealing anything less than this amount.

LETTERS TESTAMENTARY: The papers which give an executor the power to carry out the provisions of a will.

LEVY: When an execution is given over to a Marshal he must call upon the defendant, announce his position and his business and ask that the debtor pay the money involved. This is known as "making the levy".

LIBEL: Writing calculated to injure the reputation of another by bringing him into ridicule, hatred, or contempt. Slander is of the same nature except that it is verbal not written.

LICENSE: A permission, accorded by competent authority, conferring the right to do some act without which such authorization would be illegal. In no sense can it be construed as a contract between the state and the person licensed.

LIEN ON CHATTEL, FORECLOSURE OF: In cases under municipal court jurisdiction, a lien is held by a seller on the installment plan until the buyer has paid the full purchase price. In an action to foreclose a lien, a warrant is issued commanding the Marshal to seize the chattel and keep it until judgment may be granted by the Court.

MANSLAUGHTER: The killing of another without malice.

MARSHAL: An officer of the courts empowered to carry out court orders. His duties are essentially those of the Sheriff. In New York City the Marshal and Sheriff work for different courts. See "Execution against Property."

MAYHEM: The act of wilfully depriving another of the use of one or more of his limbs so that he is less capable of defending himself.

MISDEMEANOR: An offense punishable by indictment which is not up to the grade of felony. Also offenses for which no punishment is provided.

MORTGAGE: A debt secured by a pledge of land or property.

NEGLIGENCE: That general class of civil suits arising from the defendants' failure to exercise reasonable care.

OBITER DICTUM: A remark made by a judge in his decision which does not bear directly upon the question before him.

ORDINANCE: A law or statute. In a more limited sense, the term is used to designate the enactments of the legislative body of a municipal corporation.

PANEL: A list of names required by competent authority to serve as jurors for the trial of a particular action.

PAROL: Oral or verbal; not expressed in writing.

PAROLE: A conditional release from prison.

PEREMPTORY CHALLENGE: The right of the prisoner and the prosecution in a criminal trial to offer objection to a certain number of proposed jurors without giving any explanation.

PERJURY: The act of wilfully swearing falsely.

PETIT JURY: The ordinary jury of twelve men for the trial of a civil or criminal action.

PLAINTIFF: A person who brings a civil action against another.

PRIMA FACIE: So far as can be judged from the first appearance or at first sight.

PROBATE: The act and process of proving before a proper court, that a document is the valid and legal will of a testator.

PROBATION: The type of penalty whereby a convicted man is put under the jurisdiction of probation officers for a stated time instead of being sent to prison.

QUASI: Best defined as almost. It serves to distinguish between two or more approximately identical things. Thus: — a quasi-contract is "almost" a contract, yet not possessing the full character of a contract.

QUIT CLAIM: A release made out by one man certifying that he has no further cause for action against another man.

REFEREE: A person to whom a court action is referred to take testimony, hear the parties, and report thereon to the court.

RELEASE: The giving up of a right by the person to whom it belongs in favor of the person from whom it might have been demanded.

RELEVANT: Applying to the issue in question and consequently useful in determining the truth or falsity of an alleged fact.

REPLEVIN: Even though chattels rightfully belong to a man, he may not, by himself, take them from another who holds them wrongfully. By recourse to the particular action of replevin, he may cause the court to order a Marshal to retrieve his chattels.

RES: A thing, an object; This word has a very wide use in law taking such forms as Rem, Re, Rerum. Res Judicata means a thing that has been judicially acted upon.

RES GESTAE: Things done; essential circumstances surrounding the subject; the circumstances, facts and declarations which grow out of the main facts and serve to clarify their character.

RESPONDENT: The party against whom a case is brought in a court of equity.

SEARCH WARRANT: A written order issued by the appropriate court for the search of a particular premises.

SUBPOENA: The process by which the attendance of a witness is required is called a subpoena.

SUBPOENA DUCES TECUM: A subpoena not only requiring the witness to testify, but also to compel him to bring all books, documents and papers that may have any bearing on the outcome of the proceedings.

SUBROGATION: Substitution of one person's claims, rights, or securities for those of another person.

SUI JURIS: Being fully able to manage one's own affairs.

SUMMONS: A writ given by legally constituted authority, requiring the authorized person to notify the person named that an action has been commenced against him in a court whence the writ issues, and that he is required to appear, on a day named, and answer the complaint in such an action.

THIRD PARTY PROCEEDINGS: The examination of a third party to find out whether any of the judgment debtor's property is in his possession.

TITLE: The written instrument or other means whereby a person's right to the ownership of property is established.

TITLE, ABSTRACT OF: A condensed history of the ownership of a piece of land, stating all the liens, charges, and liabilities to which it is subject. It is usually prepared for the benefit of a prospective purchaser.

TORT: A legal wrong committed against the person or property, for which reparation may be obtained by a suit at law.

TRUE BILL: An indictment handed down by a grand jury.

VENUE: The neighborhood, place or county in which an injury is declared to have been done, or fact declared to have happened.

VERIFICATION: Confirmation of the correctness or truth of a statement by a sworn statement to that effect.

WARRANT: A writ or precept from a competent authority in pursuance of law, directing the doing of an act, and addressed to an officer or person competent to do the act, and affording him protection from damage if he does it.

WRIT: An instrument in writing ordering a court officer to perform some specified duty.

COURT OFFICER

Legal Terms

PREVIOUS TEST QUESTIONS FOR PRACTICE

1. The word "knowingly," when included in the definition of a crime, means with
   (A) malice aforethought
   (B) deliberation and premeditation
   (C) knowledge that the facts exist which constitute the act or omission
   (D) knowledge of the unlawfulness of the act or omission which constitutes a crime.

2. Jones was charged with the murder of Smith. Brown, Jones' landlord, testified at the trial that Jones had in his home a well-equipped laboratory which contained all the necessary chemicals for producing the poison which an autopsy showed caused Smith's death. Brown's testimony constitutes what is called
   (A) corroborative evidence
   (B) opinion evidence
   (C) hearsay evidence
   (D) circumstantial evidence.

3. A sworn statement of fact is called
   (A) an affidavit
   (B) an oath
   (C) an acknowledgement
   (D) a subpoena.

4. A person who, after the commission of a crime, conceals the offender with the intent that the latter may escape from arrest and trial, is called
   (A) an accessory
   (B) an accomplice
   (C) a confederate
   (D) an associate.

5. The one of the following statements made by a prisoner that is correctly called an *alibi* is
   (A) "He struck me first."
   (B) "I didn't intend to hurt him."
   (C) "I was miles away from there at the time."
   (D) "I don't remember what happened."

6. The procedure, whereby a defendant is brought before a magistrate, is informed of the charge against him and is asked how he pleads thereto, is called
   (A) arraignment (C) presentment
   (B) indictment (D) inquisition.

7. A written accusation of a crime presented by a grand jury is called
   (A) a commitment
   (B) an arraignment
   (C) an indictment
   (D) a demurrer.

8. The delivery of an arrested person to his sureties, upon their giving security for his appearance at the time and place designated to submit to the jurisdiction and judgment of the court, is known as
   (A) bail (C) parole
   (B) habeas corpus (D) probation.

9. A contract that allows individuals or corporations to use public property is known as a
   (A) license (C) patent
   (B) indenture (D) franchise.

10. The term "vagrant" includes persons who
    (A) congregate on public streets and refuse to move when ordered
    (B) jostle against other persons in subways
    (C) follow pedestrians for the purpose of soliciting alms
    (D) appear on public streets with their faces painted or disguised.

11. A child who, through no neglect on the part of his parents, is homeless is called
    (A) a rejected child
    (B) a destitute child
    (C) a delinquent child
    (D) an abandoned child.

12. In the sentence, "The cause of action was barred by laches," the word "laches" means most nearly
    (A) wrongdoing (C) delay
    (B) collusion (D) malice.

13. An instrument in writing, signed by a magistrate, commanding a person to appear at a designated time and place to answer a complaint is called a

(A) subpoena (C) presentment
(B) summons (D) warrant.

14. A writ directed to the person detaining a prisoner, commanding him to produce that prisoner in court at a designated time is called a writ of
(A) prohibition (C) mandamus
(B) habeas corpus (D) extradition.

15. The delivery of an arrested person to his sureties, upon their giving security for his appearance at the time and place designated to submit to the jurisdiction and judgment of the court, is known as
(A) bail (C) parole
(B) habeas corpus (D) probation.

16. A writ or order directed to a person and requiring his attendance at a particular time and place to testify as a witness is properly termed a
(A) summons (C) warrant
(B) subpoena (D) mandamus.

17. Strengthening or confirming evidence given in support of the truth of facts testified to by another witness is most accurately termed
(A) hearsay evidence
(B) corroborative evidence
(C) circumstantial evidence
(D) conclusive evidence.

18. A statute of limitations is a law
(A) limiting the time within which a criminal prosecution or civil action must be commenced
(B) prohibiting a second prosecution for a crime for which a person has once been tried
(C) regulating the descent and distribution of the property of a person dying intestate
(D) limiting the sentence that may be imposed upon conviction for a particular crime.

19. A writ which directs a detaining agent to produce a prisoner at a designated place and time together with the day and cause of his detention is most correctly called a writ of
(A) mandamus (D) surety
(B) execution (E) extradition.
(C) habeas corpus

20. "The purpose and effect of the section are to abolish the distinction which heretofore existed in cases of felony between a *principal* and an *accessory* before the fact." The word "accessory" as used in this sentence means most nearly
(A) appendage
(B) assistant
(C) complement
(D) situation existing
(E) additional.

21. The word "principal" as used in the sentence in the previous question means most nearly
(A) prime mover (D) maximum
(B) probity (E) tenet.
(C) motive

22. Arraignment is most nearly
(A) the statement of pleading on the part of the people of the state regarding an offense in question
(B) directing the arrest of an offender against whom an indictment has been found
(C) preparation of a prisoner to appear before a court for sentence
(D) the assembling of all the charges and evidence supporting the charges
(E) the reading under the jurisdiction of a court of an indictment or information to a defendant and delivering a copy to him.

23. "Any person who by *duress* interferes with the free exercise of the elective franchise by any voter is guilty of a misdeanor." The word "duress" as used in this sentence means most nearly
(A) any illegal means
(B) any fraudulent device
(C) abduction
(D) misdirection
(E) compulsion.

24. "Venue" means most nearly
(A) a list of persons summoned for jury service
(B) intense malice caused by an unbalanced mind
(C) the place within which a jury must be gathered and the case tried
(D) material witnesses for the defense
(E) an illegal sale.

25. "Where the language of an *instrument* has a settled legal meaning, its construction is not open to evidence." The word "instrument" as used in this sentence means most nearly
(A) the formal expression of a legal agreement
(B) a court decision
(C) any legal act
(D) any means of accomplishment
(E) an implement.

26. A "plaintiff" means most nearly a person
(A) who has been confined in a prison
(B) who sues another person
(C) who is suspected of committing a crime
(D) against whom a charge of breaking a law has been made
(E) who requires the services of an attorney.

27. A detailed statement of the plaintiff's cause of action is called a bill of
(A) interpleader (C) particulars
(B) indemnity (D) review.

28. A guardian ad litem is a guardian for
(A) the suit
(B) all purposes
(C) the purpose of conserving real property
(D) the purpose of representing a corporation.

29. Parol means
(A) under seal
(B) hearsay
(C) patent
(D) by word of mouth.

30. The act of going before a competent officer and declaring the execution of an instrument is called
(A) oath
(B) affidavit
(C) acquitance
(D) acknowledgment.

31. If a deceased person left a will and nominated in it someone to manage and distribute his estate, such person, when duly appointed is called
(A) manager (C) administrator
(B) executor (D) guardian.

32. The subscription to a written instrument, signed by the witnesses to its execution, stating that they have witnessed it is called
(A) novation
(B) acknowledgment
(C) consummation
(D) attestation

33. Evidence from which a fact not directly proved is to be inferred as a necessary or probable consequence is called
(A) circumstantial (C) inferential
(B) cumulative (D) collateral.

34. Evidence, such as will prevail, if not rebutted is
(A) corraborative (C) prima facie
(B) cumulative (D) direct.

35. An agreement between two persons, one of whom has a right of action against the other, that the latter should give and the former accept something in satisfaction of such right of action is called
(A) curtilage (C) accord
(B) satisfaction (D) mortgage.

36. The memorandum of the time, place and person before whom an affidavit is sworn is called
(A) subscription (C) jurat
(B) codicil (D) subjunction.

37. A statement of fact made in a legal proceeding is called
(A) affirmation
(B) allegation
(C) affidavit
(D) acknowledgment.

38. An exact copy of a document is called
(A) facsimile (C) execution
(B) exordium (D) habendum.

39. Lis pendens means pending
(A) suit
(B) settlement
(C) medical examination
(D) selection of a jury.

Correct Answers

(You'll learn more by writing your own answers before comparing them with these.)

1. C	9. D	16. B	24. C	32. D
2. D	10. C or D	17. B	25. A	33. A
3. A	11. B	18. A	26. B	34. C
4. A	12. C	19. C	27. C	35. B or C
5. C	13. B	20. B	28. A	36. C
6. A	14. B	21. A	29. D	37. B
7. C	15. A	22. E	30. D	38. A
8. A		23. E	31. B	39. A

Legal Terms and Abbreviations

A

ab ex. - from without
ab init. - from the beginning
abs. re. - defendant being absent
A.D. - in the year of our Lord
ad fin. - to the end
ad init. - at the beginning
ad int. or a.i. - in the meantime
ad lib. - at pleasure
ad loc. - at the place
Admr. - Administrator
Admx. - Administratrix
ad us. - according to custom
ae. or aet. - of age; aged
aff. - affirmative
anon. - anonymous
ans. or A. - answer
ap. - according to
art. - article
Assn. - Association
att. - attached
attn. - attention
Atty. - Attorney
AWOL - absent without leave

B

B/E - bill of exchange
B/L - bill of lading
bbl. - barrel
BTU. - British Thermal Unit
b.v. - book value

C

C - 100; Congress; Centigrade
c. or ca. - about
c.e. - at buyer's risk
cf. or cp. - compare
cit. - citation
c/o - care of
C.O.D. - cash on delivery
C.T.A. - with the will annexed
cy pres. - doctrine that written documents be construed as near as possible to intention of the parties

D

D.B.N. - of the goods not yet distributed; (de bonis non)
dft. - defendant
do. - the same (ditto)
doc. - document
D.Q. - direct question
d.s.p. - died without issue
D.V. - God willing

E

E.D. - Election District
e.g. - for example
et al - and others
etc. - and so forth
et seq.- and the following
et ux - and wife
et vir - and husband
ex - out of; from; without
Exr. - Executor
Exrx. - Executrix
ex parte - from one party
ex rel.- from the recital of facts
exx. - examples

F

ff. - and the following; folios
fec. - he or she made it
f.o.b. - free on board
fwd. - forward
FX - foreign exchange

G

Gov. - Governor
govt. - government
GTC - Good till canceled

H

h.a. - this year
hhd. - hogshead
h.t. - under this title or at this time

I

ib. or ibid. - In the same place
id. - the same
i.e. - that is
ign. - unknown
incog. - in secret
inf. - below or inferior
in lim.- at the outset
in loc.- in the proper place

i.q. - the same as
I.Q. - intelligence quotient
I.R. - Internal Revenue

J

J. - Judge; JJ. is the plural
J.C.D. - Doctor of Civil Law
J.D. - Doctor of Laws
J.S.D. - Doctor of Juristic Science

L

L. - Law
loc. cit. - in the place cited
Leg. - Legislature
ll. - lines
l.l. - in the place quoted
LL.D. - Doctor of Laws
L.S. - place of the seal

M

M - 1000
M.C. - Member of Congress
misc. - miscellaneous
m.m. - necessary changes having been made
ms. - manuscript, plural is mss.
mtg. - mortgage

N

n.b. - note well
nem. con. - unanimously
n.l. - it is not permitted
nol. pros. - to be unwilling to prosecute
non pros. - he does not prosecute
non seq. - it does not follow
N.S.F. - not sufficient funds
n.u. - name unknown

O

ob. - he or she died
ob.s.p. - died without issue
o.p. - out of print
op. cit. - in the work cited

P

p.a. or per an. - by the year
p. ae. - equal parts
pp. - pages
Plf. - Plaintiff
P.P. - by authorization; proxy
P.P.C. - to take leave
p.r.n. - as the occasion arises
pro tem. - for the time being
prox. - of the next month
p.t. - private terms

Q

Q. - Question; plural is QQ.
Q.E.D. - which was to be proved
Q.E.F. - which was to be done
q.v. - which see

R

re - in regard to (sometimes in re)
rev. - revised
R.S. - Revised Statutes
R.I.P. - may he or she rest in peace
R.N. - Registered Nurse
R.S.V.P. - please answer

S

sc., scil., sct., ss., s. - namely or to wit (verifies place of legal action)
s.d. - (sine die) - adjournment without naming a day
seq. - the following
sess. - session
s.f. - near the end
sic - so; thus
s.p. - without issue
s.p.s. - without surviving issue
S.R.O. - standing room only
ss. - namely or to wit
stet - let it stand
sup. - above
supp. - supplement

T

t.a.w. - twice a week
t.f. - till forbidden (advertising)
tx - tax or taxes

U

ut dict. - as directed
u.i. - as below
ult. - of the last month
U.N. - United Nations
u.s. - as above
U.S.C. - United States Code

V

v. or vs. - against
v.i. - see below
vid. - see
v.g. - for example
vi et armis - by force and weapons
viz. - namely
v.v. - vice versa
viva voce - orally

W

WB. - waybill

X

XQ. - cross-question

- A -

A posteriori - from effect to cause.
A priori - from cause to effect.
Ab initio - from the beginning.
Abate - destroy; remove.
Abet - encourage; aid.
Abjure - renounce.
Abridge - reduce; contract.
Abrogate - repeal; annul
Abscond - hide; absent one's self.
Accident - unforeseen event.
Accomplice - principal; helper.
Acknowledgment - act of going before an official authorized to take acknowledgments and acknowledging an act as one's own.
Acquit - release; absolve.
Act - something done voluntarily.
Ad litem - for the suit.
Adduce - offer; present.
Adjacent - near to; close.
Adjective law - rules of procedure.
Adjudicate - to decide finally.
Admiralty - court having jurisdiction over maritime cases.
Adolescent - boys 14 to 21; girls 12 to 21.
Adult - 16 years old or over (in criminal law)
Affiant - one who makes an affidavit.
Affidavit - a sworn, written statement.
Affiliation - order stating one to be the father of a child.
Affinity - relationship between persons through marriage with the kindred of each other; distinguished from consanguinity which is relationship by blood.
Affirm - ratify.
Affirmation - to swear on one's conscience.
Agent - one who represents and acts for another.
Aggressor - one who begins a quarrel.
Aid and comfort - help; encourage.
Alias - a name not one's true name.
Alibi - a claim of not being present at a certain place at a certain time.
Alienist - a doctor specializing in mental diseases - a psychiatrist.
Allegation - the assertion, declaration, or statement of a party to an action, made in a pleading, setting out what he expects to prove.
Ambiguous - not clear, two meanings; equivocal.
Amentia - lack of mind, idiots, imbeciles; mental defectiveness.
Amercement - a pecuniary penalty or a fine imposed as punishment on conviction.
Amicus curiae - a friend of the court or advises on some legal matter.
Animus - mind; intent.
Animus furandi - intent to steal.
Annul - cancel; void.
Annus - a year.
Ante - before.
Ante mortem - before death.
Aphasia - inability to speak although vocal cords are normal.
Appeal - to request a higher court to review a decision of a lower court.
Appearance - to appear in court as defendant, attorney, etc.
Appellant - one who appeals.
Appellee - one who opposes an appellant; a respondent.
Apprehend - arrest
Appurtenant - belonging to.

- A -

Arbiter - one who decides a dispute; a referee.
Arbitrary - an act having no cause or reason; absolute; despotic; peremptory.
Arraign - to call prisoner before the court to answer to a charge.
Artifice - trickery; deception.
Asportation - moving a thing from one place to another as in larceny.
Assert - to state as true.
Asseveration - an affirmation; to swear to the truth.
Asylum - a place of refuge.
At bar - before the court.
At issue - when parties in an action come to a point where one asserts something and the other denies it.
Attach - seize property by court order and sometimes arrest a person.
Attainder - forfeiture of property and corruption of blood of one sentenced to death. (compare with Bill of attainder below).
Attempt - an act done with intent to commit a crime but failing to consummate it.
Attest - to witness a will, etc. attestation.
Authentic - genuine; true.
Authenticate - to give authority to a law, writing, or record.
Axiom - a self-evident truth.

- B -

Bail - to release from custody on written agreement that he appear in court or forfeit property.
Bailee - one to whom personal property is given to improve, care for, etc.,
Bailment - the giving of property to a bailee.
Bailor - the one who gives his property to a bailee.
Barratry - exciting groundless judicial proceedings.
Battery - illegal interfering with another's person.
Bill of attainder - a law pronouncing a person guilty without trial. It is illegal.
Bludgeon - a club heavier at one end than at the other.
Blue laws - rigid Sunday laws.
Blue sky laws - laws regulating investment companies to protect investors from frauds; stop sale of watered stock or fly by night companies selling visionary oil, gold mine stocks.
Bona fide - in good faith.
Bondsman - one who bails another by putting up a bond.
Boycott - a plan to prevent the carrying on of a business by wrongful means.
Breach of the peace - disturbing the public peace by disorder, violence, force, noise, etc.
Bucket shop - a place where people bet on the stock market under pretense of buying and selling stocks.
Bunco game - any trick or cunning calculated to win confidence and to deceive whether by conversation, conduct, or suggestion.

- C -

Cadaver - a dead human body.
Camera - a chamber, room.
Canon - a law, rule.
Capias - an order to arrest.
Carnal - relating to the body.
Carnal abuse - a sex act not amounting to penetration.
Carnal knowledge - sexual intercourse.
Cause of action - matter for which an action may be brought.

- C -

Caveat - let him beware.
Caveat emptor - let the buyer beware.
Certiorari - an order from a high court to a trial body to send the minutes of a trial to it so it may decide their legality.
Challenge - to object to a juror.
Change of venue - to remove place of trial from one county to another.
Character - what a person is; but reputation is what others think or report him to be.
Charge - a complaint, information or indictment.
Chastity - never willingly had unlawful sexual intercourse.
Chattel - personal property.
Chattel mortgage - a mortgage on personal property.
Child - one under 16 years in criminal law.
Cite - to summon; command one's presence.
Civil rights - rights granted to citizens by the Constitution or by statute.
Codicil - an addition to a will.
Coercion- compulsion, duress.
Cognomen - a family name.
Cohabit - living together.
Comity - courtesy, respect; agreement between states to recognize each other's laws.
Commitment - an order to take one to a prison.
Common law - law as it developed in England based on customs, usage, decisions, etc.
Commute - change punishment to one less severe.
Complainant - one who seeks legal redress.
Complaint - a sworn allegation to a magistrate charging one with crime. Also called information.
Compos mentis - sound of mind.
Compromise - an agreement between one charged with certain crimes and the complainant to withdraw charges on payment of money, with court's consent.
Concubinage - cohabiting with one of another sex without marriage.
Concurrent - running together, at the same time.
Condemnation - taking private property for public use on payment therefor.
Confess - to admit the truth of a charge.
Confession - voluntary statement of guilt of crime.
Confidence game - a swindle.
Confrontation - witness testifying in presence of defendant.
Connivance - secret or indirect consent by one to a criminal act by another.
Consanguinity - blood relationship.
Consecutive - successive.
Conspiracy - a plan by two or more to commit crime.
Constitution - the fundamental law of a state or nation.
Constructive intent - if one intends one act and in carrying it out he does another, the intent to do the first is construed to apply to the second.
Contiguous - near by.
Contingency - an event that may or may not happen.
Contra - against.
Contraband - against law; prohibited.
Controvert - to dispute, deny.
Conviction - judgment that one is guilty as charged.
Corporal - bodily.
Corpus delicti - the body of a crime; the crime itself.
Corroborate - to strengthen.
Corrupt - spoiled, tainted, debased.
Corruptly - wrongful desire to acquire an advantage.
Counsellor - a lawyer.

- C -

Counterfeit - to forge, copy, imitate.
Credible - worthy of belief.
Crimen falsi - crimes involving deceit or falsification.
Criminal action - process by which one is accused of crime and brought to trial and punishment.
Criminal conversation - adultery.
Criminal information - same as complaint.
Criminal intent - intent to commit crime, malice.
Criminology - science of crimes and causes and criminals.
Culpable - blamable.
Cumulative - additional, heaping up.
Curtilage - ground and buildings surrounding a dwelling.
Custody - detaining a man's person by legal authority.

- D -

Dangerous weapon - one dangerous to life.
De facto - in fact, actually.
De jure - of right, lawful.
Deadly weapon - one likely to produce death or serious bodily injury.
Debauch - to make lewd, to entice, to seduce.
Decision - a judgment given by a proper court.
Deed - a writing by which one conveys land, etc. to another.
Defalcation - misappropriation of trust funds.
Defamation - injuring one's reputation by false statements.
Defendant - one who defends or denies a charge.
Defraud - to deprive of property by fraud or deceit.
Deliberate - to weigh or ponder before forming a decision.
Delictus - a crime.
Demented - unsound mind.
Deponent - one who gives testimony under oath reduced to writing.
Deposition - sworn written testimony.
Design - plan, scheme, intent.
Dictum - an opinion expressed by a judge, but not a decision.
Dipsomaniac - one who has an irresistible desire for alcohol.
Disfranchise - to deprive of the rights of a citizen.
Dismiss - to discharge a court action.
Disorderly house - a place where people behave so badly as to become a nuisance to the neighborhood.
Document - a written instrument.
Domicile - one's permanent home.
Duress - unlawful constraint on one to force him to do some act.

- E -

Ego - I, myself
Eleemosynary - charitable.
Embezzlement - using money of another entrusted to him for some purpose.
Embracery - unlawful attempt to influence jurors, etc. but not by offering value.
Eminent domain - the right of a state to take private property for public use.
Empirical - based on experience.
Entice - to solicit, persuade, allure by flattery, coaxing, etc.
Entrapment - inducing one to commit a crime so as to arrest him.
Essence - indispensable.
Evidence - all means used to prove or disprove a fact in issue.

ex officio - by virtue of office.
ex parte - on one side only.
ex post facto law - a law passed after an act was done which retroactively makes such act a crime.
examined copy - one compared with the original and sworn to as a correct copy.
exception - a formal objection to the action of the court in denying a request or overruling an objection.
executed - completed.
extradition - surrender of a fugitive from one nation to another.
extrajudicial - outside judicial proceeding.
extremis - near death, beyond hope of recovery.

- F -

facsimile - an exact or accurate copy of an original instrument.
false pretenses - false representations of fact to obtain money.
feasance - to do, doing.
felo de se - one of sound mind who kills himself; suicide.
felonious - criminal, malicious.
fence - one who buys stolen property.
fiduciary - a trustee of property, etc.
filiation, order of - an order declaring one to be the father of an illegitimate child.
finding - the result of the deliberation of a court or jury.
firearm - a weapon that propels bullets by explosion of gunpowder.
forge - to counterfeit or make falsely.
fornication - sexual intercourse between two unmarried persons.
foundling - a deserted child under 2 years of age.
franchise - a privilege granted to one to use public property for private use for the public welfare, elective franchise refers to the voting privilege.
fratricide - killing of one's brother.
freeholder - one who owns real property.
fugitive from justice - one who commits a crime in one state and goes to another.

- G -

gamble - to bet on an event the outcome of which is uncertain.
general verdict - a verdict in which a jury finds defendant guilty or not guilty.
genocide - international crime of exterminating certain races, nationalities or religious groups.
gift enterprise - a scheme for distribution of property by chance among persons who have paid or agreed to pay a consideration; common term for such is lottery.
grand jury - not less 16 not more than 23 citizens of a county sworn to inquire into crimes committed or triable in the county.
grantee - one to whom a grant is made.
grantor - the one who makes the grant.
gravamen - the grievance complained of or the substantial cause of a criminal action.
guardian ad litem - a person designated by a court to represent a child bringing or defending a civil action.

- H -

habeas corpus - an order to produce a person before a court to determine legality of detention.
hearsay - evidence based on repeating the words heard spoken by another and not based on the witness's own personal observation or knowledge of that to which he testifies.
hung jury - one so divided they can't agree on a verdict.
hypothecate - to pledge a thing without delivering it to pledgee.
hypothetical question - question asked of an expert witness assuming facts from which the witness is asked to state his opinion thereon.

- I -

illicit - unlawful.
impeach - to accuse, charge.
inalienable - rights which cannot be lawfully transferred from one person to another.
in loco parentis - in place of parent, a guardian.
incommunicado - denial of the right of a prisoner to communicate with friends or relatives.
indictment - a written accusation of crime presented by a grand jury.
inducement - cause or reason why a thing is done or that which incites the person to do the act or commit a crime; the motive for the criminal act.
infamous crime - a felony.
infant - in civil cases one under 21 years of age.
information - same as complaint, allegation to a magistrate charging a person with a crime.
injunction - legal process requiring a person from doing or from continuing to do a certain action.
intent - state of mind to do or omit an act.
ipso facto - by the fact itself.
issue - in an action what is affirmed by one and denied by another.

- J -

jeopardy - danger, peril.
jostling - interfering with any person by placing one's hand in the vicinity of such person's pocket, pocketbook or handbag.
judicial notice - acceptance by a court or judge of some fact of common knowledge thereby dispensing with the need of offering evidence to prove it; thus, 24 hours in one day.
judiciary - relating to court of justice.
jurat - the part of an affidavit stating where, when and before whom it was signed and sworn.
jurisdiction - power or authority to do something.
jury - a group of citizens sworn to inquire into facts and deliver a verdict. A trial jury tries cases (generally 12). Grand jury indicts (generally 23).

- K -

kleptomanic - irresistible propensity to steal.

- L -

laches - unreasonable delay in bringing an action.
latent - hidden, concealed.
leading question - one so put as to suggest the answer.
lien - a claim a creditor has on property until a debt is paid.
lis pendens - a pending civil or criminal action.
litigant - a party to a lawsuit.
locus delicti - place of the crime.
locus poenitentiae - the abandoning or giving up of one's intention to commit some crime before it is fully completed or abandoning a conspiracy before its purpose is accomplished.
lucri causa - for sake of gain.

- M -

mala in se - bad in themselves; such crimes usually require a specific criminal intent in these cases.
mala prohibita - bad because prohibited by the legislature; not evil in their nature.
malfeasance - to do a wrongful act.
malice-intentional doing of a wrongful act to injure, vex or annoy.
malo animo - evil mind.
mandamus - a court order to a public official to perform an act specified.
maritime - pertaining to the sea or to commerce thereon.

masochism - sexual pleasure in being beaten by another.
mens rea - guilty or criminal intent.
meretricious - unlawful sex acts.
minor - one under 21 years.
miscegenation - marriage or sex intercourse between persons of different races.
misfeasance - improper performance of a lawful act.
mittimus - a warrant of commitment to prison.
moral certainty - evidence which convinces the mind beyond a reasonable doubt; hence the degree of proof required to prove defendant's guilt in a criminal action.
moral turpitude - an act of baseness, vileness, or depravity in the private and social duties which a person owes to his fellow man or to society in general.
motive - reason for doing an act.
mulct - a pecuniary fine imposed as punishment on conviction of a crime; same as amercement.

- N -

natural child - a child born out of lawful wedlock.
night - sunset to sunrise.
nolle prosequi - the prosecutor is unwilling to presecute
nolo contendere - equal to a plea of guilty.
nominal damages - award of a trifling sum where no substantial injury is proved to have been sustained.
nonfeasance - neglect of duty.
noscitur a sociis - meaning of doubtful words in a statute may be ascertained by referring to the meaning of other words associated with it in the definition; also called ejusdem generis.
novation - substitution of a new obligation for an old one.
nunc pro tunc - now for then, dated as if occurring on an earlier date.

- O -

oath - to swear to tell the truth before God.
obiter dictum - opinion expressed by a court on a matter not essentially involved in a case and hence not a decision; also called dicta if plural.
onus probandi - burden of proof.
opinion evidence - inferences or conclusions stated by a witness in testimony as distinguished from facts known to him; generally inadmissible.
overt - open, manifest.

- P -

panel - a group of jurors selected to serve during a term of the court.
pardon - to release an offender from the punishment due his crime.
parens patriae - sovereign power of a state to protect or be a guardian over children and incompetents.
parol - oral, verbal.
parole - to release one in prison before the expiration of his sentence, conditionally.
peculation - stealing.
petit treason - common law crime in which a wife killed her husband, or a servant killed his master or subordinate killed his superior. Abolished as such under N.Y. Statute law since all such killings are classified as criminal homicides - murder or manslaughter.
police power - inherent power of the state or its political subdivisions to enact laws within constitutional limits to promote the general welfare of society or the community.
polling the jury - call the names of persons on a jury and requiring each juror to declare what his verdict is before it is legally recorded.

post mortem - after death.
power of attorney - a writing authorizing one to act for another.
premeditate - to think of an act beforehand.
presentment - a report by a grand jury on something they have investigated on their own knowledge.
presumption - an inference as to the existence of some fact not known arising from its connection with facts which exist or are known to exist.
prima facie - at first sight.
prima facie case - a case where the evidence is very strong against defendant.
primary evidence - term applied to originals of written documents when placed in evidence.
pro and con - for and against.
probation - release of one after conviction, conditionally, without confining him in prison.
probative - tending to prove.

- Q -

quasi crime - violations of law not constituting crimes but punishable as wrongs against the local or general public welfare; thus, minor offenses.
quo warranto - a legal procedure to test an official's right to a public office or the right to hold a franchise, or to hold an office in a domestic corporation.

- R -

reasonable - fit and appropriate.
reasonable doubt - a doubt regarding the guilt of the accused person which entitles him to an acquittal.
rebuttal - evidence to the contrary.
recidivist - habitual criminal.
recognizance - written statement before a court to do an act specified or to suffer a penalty.
recrimination - accusation made by an accused person against his accuser.
rehabilitate - to correct the evil in a criminal, to reform.
remand - to send a prisoner back to jail after a hearing.
removal - a federal procedure by which a fugitive from justice under U.S. laws is returned to the federal district wherein he committed his crime for trial. May also refer to removing trial of a criminal action from one county to another county or to another court.
replevin - an action to recover goods unlawfully taken or withheld.
rescission - annul a contract.
respondeat superior - general rule charging the master or employer with liability for his servant's or employee's negligence in a business causing injury to third persons.
res adjudicata - doctrine that an issue or dispute litigated and determined in a case between the opposing parties is deemed permanently decided between these parties.

- S -

scienter - allegation that the defendant had knowledge or wilfully committed the crime charged against him.
special verdict - verdict by which the jury finds the facts only, leaving the legal judgment to the judge. Must be in writing.
situs delicti - the location of a crime which in most cases is the place where it takes effect. (see locus delicti)
stare decisis - general rule that when an issue has been settled by a court decision, it forms a precedent which is not to be departed from in deciding future similar issues.
struck jury - a special jury or a blue ribbon jury.

suborn - to procure another to commit perjury.
subpoena - a court process requiring one to appear as a witness.
subpoena duces tecum - a subpoena to produce records, books and documents.
subrogation - substitution of one person for another in respect to rights and claims, debts, etc.
sui generis - of the same kind (see noscitur a sociis)
summons - a court order requesting one to appear to answer a charge.
surety - a bondsman.
surname - a family name.
suspend sentence - hold back a sentence pending good behavior of prisoner.

- T -

talesman - person summoned to fill a panel of jurors.
testimony - spoken or written evidence.
tolling the statute - facts which remove the statute of limitations as a bar to a criminal prosecution.
trespass - entry into another's ground, illegally.
true bill - indictment.
trustee - one who lawfully holds property in custody for the benefit of another.
turpitude - anything done contrary to justice, honesty, morals - same as moral turpitude.

- U -

undertaking - a written agreement to appear in court when released on bail.
usury - unlawful interest on a loan.

- V -

veniremen - persons ordered to appear to serve on a jury or composing a panel of jurors.
venue - the place or location where the cause of legal action arose.
verdict - the findings of a jury; decision is the finding by a judge.
vi et armis - phrase used in indictments and informations indicating the crime was committed with force, by violence, weapons, etc.
voir dire - preliminary examination of a witness or a juror to test competency, etc.

- W -

waive - to give up a right.
warrant - a written court order given to a peace officer to arrest one named in it.

- Z -

zoning laws - laws specifying the use to which land in a city may be put; for example, residential, commercial, industrial, etc. May regulate height, width, and size of structures in a certain district. It is justified as a form of police power by the city or state.

* * * * * * * * * * * * * * *

<u>LAW BOOKS</u>

Law Dictionaries - Bouvier; Black; Ballentine
Law of Evidence - Richardson; Wigmore; Wharton; McKelvey
Annual Session Laws of N.Y. - McKinney
Consolidated and Unconsolidated Laws of N.Y. - McKinney
Civil Practice Act; Rules of Civil Procedure; Civil Courts Acts; Rules of Civic Courts - Clevenger Practice Manual
Penal Law and Code of Criminal Procedure - McKinney; Gilbert

* * * * * * * * * * * * * * *

Alienist -A psychiatrist qualified to give expert testimony in court upon the mental conditions of persons.

Ambivalence - Simultaneous contradictory emotions towards the same person; loving and hating a person at the same time.

Amentia - Feeblemindedness; Mental Retardment; Mental defectiveness; usually congenital or from birth. There are three grades: (1) Idiot - does not develop mentally beyond 3 years; I.Q. is 0 to 20. (2) Imbecile; mental development between 3 and 7 years; I.Q. is 20 to 50 (3) Moron - mental development between 7 and 12 years; I.Q. is 50 to 70; persons with I.Q.'s between 70 and 80 are called Borderline cases. Normal intelligence based on I.Q. is between 90 and 110. The I.Q. or Intelligence Quotient is the ratio between a person's mental development and his actual or chronological age. Thus, a 12 year old boy with a mental development of an 8 year old child has an I.Q. of 8/12 x 100 or 66 2/3. This child is classified as a moron.

Amnesia - Loss of memory. Part or total inability to recall past experiences.

Aphasia - Inability to use or understand spoken or written language.

Autoeroticism or Autoerotism - Sexual activity directed toward oneself.

Benign - Of a mild type; opposed to malignant.

Bestiality - Sexual desire for animals - sodomy.

Chorea - St. Vitus Dance.

Compulsion - An irresistible impulse to commit some act such as stealing, setting a fire, etc.

Constitutional Psychopathic Inferiority - Social uneducability in self-control, especially in matters of consideration for others, honesty, or morality.

Cretinism - Mental deficiency and lack of physical and mental development caused by thyroid deficiency.

Degenerate - Person having intense impulses who satisfies them by unnatural acts. Also known as a pervert or a deviate.

Dementia - Loss of sanity or loss of reasoning powers; insanity.

Dipsomania - Abnormal uncontrollable impulse or desire for alcohol.

Electra Complex - An unusual attachment of the daughter for her father.

Erotic - Sexual; anything inciting sexual desires or passions.

Extrovert - A person whose interests are external and objective; seeks action.

Euthanasia - Mercy death to relieve suffering from incurable disease.

Fetichism - Abnormal sexual desire aroused by an object associated with the opposite sex such as shoes, underwear, stockings, etc.

Grand Mal - Epilepsy. Petit Mal is a mild form of epilepsy.

Hermaphroditism - Person with double sex organs.

Heterosexual - Desire for the opposite sex.

Hoboism or Wanderlust - Abnormal desire to wander - nomadic types.

Homosexual - Desire for the same sex; males are called fairies; females are called lesbians.

Hypochondria - Morbid anxiety about one's health by exaggerating every trifling sympton.

Idiot Savant - A feebleminded person who has some outstanding trait or talent.

Insomnia - Inability to sleep.

Introvert - A person whose interests are internal or subjective; not interested in other persons or activities; personal feelings are uppermost.

Kleptomania - Morbid propensity to steal.

Lesbian - A female homo-sexual

Locomotor Ataxia - Muscular incoordination caused by syphilis.

Mesmerism - Hypnotism.

Masochism - Derives sexual pleasure by being put under torture or subject to beating by another.

Mongolism - Mental defectives who have Mongolian features or resemble Mongolians.

Narcissism - Self-centeredness. Individual greatly interested in his own physical satisfactions, his own abilities.

Necrophilia - Sexual desire for dead bodies.
Neurasthenia - Chronic complaints of weakness and fatigue.
Neurosis - Minor mental disorders.
Nymphomania - Abnormal sexual appetite in a female - (white livered)
Obsession - An unreasonable persistent idea.
Oedipus Complex - Unusual attachment of a son for his mother.
Paranoia - Persecution complex.
Pathological Lying - Falsehood not with intent to deceive but more from a habit.
Pederasty - Unnatural sex acts between males or on young boys; buggery, sodomy.
Pedophilia - Desire for sexual relations with children.
Phobia - Fixed, unreasonable fear of some object, person or place.
Psychosis - Any form of severe mental diseases or forms of insanity.
Psychasthenia - Mental cases characterized by fears, compulsions, obsessions.
Psychoneurosis - Minor mental disorder; similar to neurosis.
Psychopath - Great emotional instability not involving a brain disease.
Pyromania - Insane desire to set fires or commit incendiarism.
Sadism - Abnormal sexual satisfaction obtained by torturing another.
Satyriasis - Abnormal sexual appetite in a male.
Schizophrenia - Split personality; extreme disorganization of emotions; hallucinations, fantastic delusions. This term is used now to replace Dementia Praecox.
Somnambulism - Sleep walking.
Sublimation - Expression of some lower urge or instinct in some higher and acceptable form of activity. Thus, repressing sex energy by writing poetry or music.
Transvestism - Abnormal sex satisfaction by wearing clothes of the opposite sex.
Voyeur - A peeping-tom type of sexual deviate.

* * * * * * * * * * * * *

CASE CITATIONS AND REPORTS

The only set of reports covering the entire country is that issued under the NATIONAL REPORTER SYSTEM and published at St. Paul, Minnesota.

U.S. Supreme Court Decisions are published in the "Supreme Court Reporter"
(Fed.) Federal Reporter reports cases of federal courts other than the U.S. Supreme Court.
(N.E.) Northeastern Reporter; Court of Appeals cases only.
(N.Y.S.) New York Supplement (Report cases of Appellate Div. and lower courts.
(N.Y.S. (2nd) Court of Appeals cases and all lower court cases.
(N.Y.) New York Reports: Reports Court of Appeals cases only.
(Misc.) Miscellaneous Reports: Contains reports of cases from New York Courts, but not Appellate Division or Court of Appeals.
(A.D. Reports) or (App. Div.) - Appellate Division Reports; Separate report of cases from this court - but they are now included in the N.Y.S.

CITATIONS ARE READ AS FOLLOWS:

141 N.Y. 65 - Volume 141 of New York Reports (Court of Appeals) Page 65
263 N.Y. 61 - Volume 263, New York Supplement, page 61
18 N.Y.S. 2d 406 - Volume 18, New York Supplement, Second Series, page 406
157 Misc. 69 - Volume 157, Miscellaneous Reports, page 69

* * * * * * * * * * * * *

CORRECTNESS AND EFFECTIVENESS OF EXPRESSION

The questions contained in this section are designed to test your knowledge of grammar, sentence structure, correct usage and punctuation, and to point out some of the main sources of errors that have confounded candidates on past examinations.

SIX TEST-TYPE QUIZZES FOR PRACTICE

Now, push forward! Test yourself and practice for your test with the carefully constructed quizzes that follow. Each one presents the kind of question you may expect on your test. And each question is at just the level of difficulty that may be expected. Don't try to take all the tests at one time. Rather, schedule yourself so that you take a few at each session, and spend approximately the same time on them at each session. Score yourself honestly, and date each test. You should be able to detect improvement in your performance on successive sessions.

A portion of the standard answer sheet is provided after each test for marking your answers in the way you'll be required to do on the actual exam. At the right of this answer sheet, to make the scoring job simpler (after you have derived your own answers), you'll find our correct answers.

ANSWER SHEETS AND CORRECT ANSWERS APPEAR AFTER EACH TEST

CORRECT USAGE TEST ONE

ERRORS IN AGREEMENT OF CASE, TENSE OR NUMBER

DIRECTIONS: In each of the following groups of sentences, select the one sentence that is grammatically INCORRECT. Mark the answer sheet with the letter of that incorrect sentence.

Correct key answers to all these test questions will be found at the end of the test.

1. (A) Everyone at camp must have his medical certificate on file before participating in competitive sports.
(B) A crate of oranges were sent from Florida for all the children in Cabin Six.
(C) John and Danny's room looks as if they were prepared for inspection.
(D) Three miles is too far for a young child to walk.

2. (A) The game over, the spectators rushed out on the field and tore down the goalposts.
(B) The situation was aggravated by disputes over the captaincy of the team.
(C) Yesterday they lay their uniforms aside with the usual end-of-the-season regret.
(D) It is sometimes thought that politics is not for the high-minded.

3. (A) Sandburg's autobiography, as well as his poems, are familiar to many readers.
(B) A series of authentic records of the American Indian tribes is being published.
(C) The Smokies are the home of the descendants of this brave tribe.
(D) Five dollars is really not too much to pay for a book of this type.

4. (A) Being tired, I stretched out on a grassy knoll.
(B) While we were rowing on the lake, a sudden squall almost capsized the boat.
(C) Entering the room, a strange mark on the floor attracted my attention.
(D) Mounting the curb, the empty car crossed the sidewalk and came to rest against a building.
(E) Sitting down, they watched him demonstrate his skill.

5. (A) The text makes the process of developing and sustaining a successful home zoo appear to be a pleasant and profitable one.
(B) The warmth and humor, the clear characterization of the Walmsey family, which includes three children, two dogs and two cats, is such fun to read that this reviewer found herself reading it all over again.
(C) You will be glad, I am sure, to give the book to whoever among your young friends has displayed an interest in animals.
(D) The consensus among critics of children's literature is that the book is well worth the purchase price.

6. (A) Not one in a thousand readers take the matter seriously.
(B) Let it lie there.
(C) You are not so tall as he.
(D) The people began to realize how much she had done.
(E) He was able partially to accomplish his purpose.

7. (A) In the case of members who are absent, a special letter will be sent.
(B) The visitors were all ready to see it.
(C) I like Burns's poem "To a Mountain Daisy."
(D) John told William that he was sure he had seen it.
(E) Both men are Yale alumni.

8. (A) B. Nelson & Co. has a sale of dacron shirts today.
(B) Venetian blinds—called that although they probably did not originate in Ven-

ice—are no longer used as extensively as they were at one time.

(C) He determined to be guided by the opinion of whoever spoke first.

(D) There is often disagreement as to whom is the better Shakespearean actor, Evans or Gielgud.

9. (A) It did not take him long to develop an interest in the great American pastime—baseball.

(B) If you had made your way to the Whipsnade Zoo, you would have had an opportunity of seeing wild animals in more or less natural habitats.

(C) How I should have liked to have spent a few more days in Paris!

(D) Neither baseball pools nor any other form of gambling is allowed in or near the school.

10. (A) If the bill were introduced, it would provoke endless debate.

(B) Since George, with his two dogs is to be with us, it might be better to rent a cabin.

(C) He, not I, is the one to decide.

(D) He is, however, one of those restless people who never seems content in his present environment.

11. (A) Everyone can have a wonderful time in New York if they will just not try to see the entire city in one week.

(B) Being a stranger in town myself, I know how you feel.

(C) New York is a city of man-made wonders awe-inspiring as those found in nature.

(D) He felt deep despair (as who has not?) at the evidence of man's inhumanity to man.

12. (A) A clerk should be careful as well as punctual, even though he or she are otherwise efficient.

(B) Regardless of whether it may be true, some students are not very studious.

(C) Not every writer can say that his opinion is always the best.

(D) We often think of people who assume airs as being affected.

13. (A) We were not entirely dissatisfied with the conditions.

(B) There is a chair and a table in the room.

(C) He was among the few writers who do not experience difficulty with words.

(D) Remember that the man to whom you are speaking is my friend.

Correct Answers For The Foregoing Questions

To assist you in scoring yourself we have provided Correct Answers alongside your Answer Sheet. May we therefore suggest that while you are doing the test you cover the Correct Answers with a sheet of white paper.....to avoid temptation and to arrive at an accurate estimate of your ability and progress.

Answer Sheet

	A	B	C	D	E
1					
2					
3					
4					
5					
6					
7					
8					
9					
10					
11					
12					
13					

SCORE

%

NO. CORRECT ÷

NO. OF QUESTIONS ON THIS TEST

Correct Answers

	A	B	C	D	E
1		▮			
2			▮		
3	▮				
4			▮		
5		▮			
6	▮				
7				▮	
8				▮	
9			▮		
10				▮	
11	▮				
12	▮				
13		▮			

CORRECT USAGE TEST TWO

ERRORS IN AGREEMENT OF CASE, TENSE OR NUMBER

DIRECTIONS: In each of the following groups of sentences, select the one sentence that is grammatically INCORRECT. Mark the answer sheet with the letter of that incorrect sentence.

Correct key answers to all these test questions will be found at the end of the test.

1. (A) This is the woman whom I saw.
   (B) She could solve even this problem.
   (C) She divided the money among the three of us.
   (D) Either she or I are guilty.

2. (A) Consider that the person which is always idle can never be happy.
   (B) Because a man understands a woman does not mean they are necessarily compatible.
   (C) He said that accuracy and speed are both essential.
   (D) Can it be said that the better of the two books is less expensive?

3. (A) Neither the critics nor the author were right about the reaction of the public.
   (B) The senator depended upon whoever was willing to assist him.
   (C) I don't recall any time when Edgar has broken his word.
   (D) Everyone of the campers but John and me is going on the hike.

4. (A) Everyone entered promptly but her.
   (B) Each of the messengers were busily occupied.
   (C) At which exit did you leave him?
   (D) The work was not done well.

5. (A) Never before have I seen anyone who has the skill John has when he repairs engines.
   (B) If anyone can be wholly just in his decisions, it is he.
   (C) Because of his friendliness, the new neighbor was immediately accepted by the community.
   (D) Imagine our embarrassment when us girls saw Miss Maltinge sitting with her beau in the front row.

6. (A) I wondered why it was that the Mayor objected to the Governor's reference to the new tax law.
   (B) I have never read "Les Miserables," but I plan to do so this summer.
   (C) After much talk and haranguing, the workers received an increase in wages.
   (D) The author and myself were the only gay ones at the macabre gathering.

7. (A) The doctor had carelessly left all the instruments on the operating table.
   (B) Was it them whom the professor regarded with such contempt?
   (C) Despite all the power he has, I should still hate to be in his shoes.
   (D) I feel bad because I gave such a poor performance in the play tonight.

8. (A) It seems to me that everyone of the waiters is well able to do his share of the work.
   (B) His parents told him to wait at the station for his uncle and to bring him home in the car.
   (C) Who did you think was going to win the tennis match?
   (D) If he would have answered the detective honestly, he would not have been arrested.

9. (A) The general regarded whomever the colonel honored with disdain.
   (B) Everyone who reads this book will think themselves knights errant on missions of heroism.

(C) The reason why the new leader was so unsuccessful was that he had fewer responsibilities.

(D) All the new mechanical devices we have today have made our daily living a great deal simpler, it is said.

10. (A) The town consists of three distinct sections, of which the western one is by far the larger.

(B) Of London and Paris, the former is the wealthier.

(C) Chicago is larger than any other city in Illinois.

(D) America is the greatest nation, and of all other nations England is the greatest.

11. (A) I can but do my best.

(B) I cannot help comparing him with his predecessor.

(C) I wish that I was in Florida now.

(D) I like this kind of grapes better than any other.

12. (A) Neither Tom nor John was present for the rehearsal.

(B) The happiness or misery of men's lives depends on their early training.

(C) Honor as well as profit are to be gained by these studies.

(D) The egg business is only incidental to the regular business of the general store.

13. (A) It was superior in every way to the book previously used.

(B) His testimony today is different from that of yesterday.

(C) If you would have studied the problem carefully you would have found the solution more quickly.

(D) The flowers smelled so sweet that the whole house was perfumed.

14. (A) When either or both habits become fixed, the student improves.

(B) Neither his words nor his action was justifiable.

(C) A calm almost always comes before a storm.

(D) The gallery with all its pictures were destroyed.

Correct Answers For The Foregoing Questions

To assist you in scoring yourself we have provided Correct Answers alongside your Answer Sheet. May we therefore suggest that while you are doing the test you cover the Correct Answers with a sheet of white paper.....to avoid temptation and to arrive at an accurate estimate of your ability and progress.

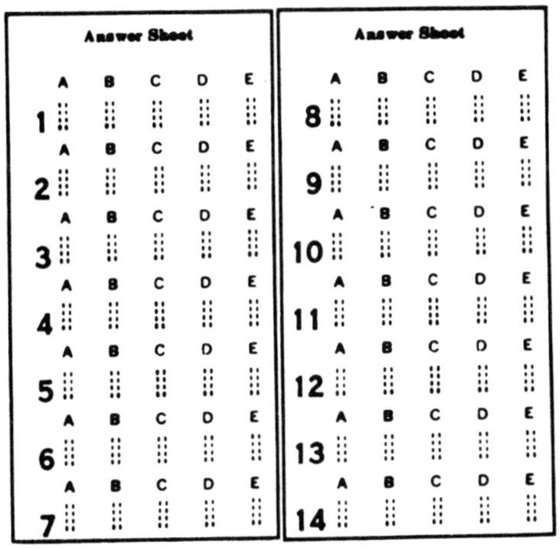

SCORE

%

NO. CORRECT ÷

NO. OF QUESTIONS ON THIS TEST

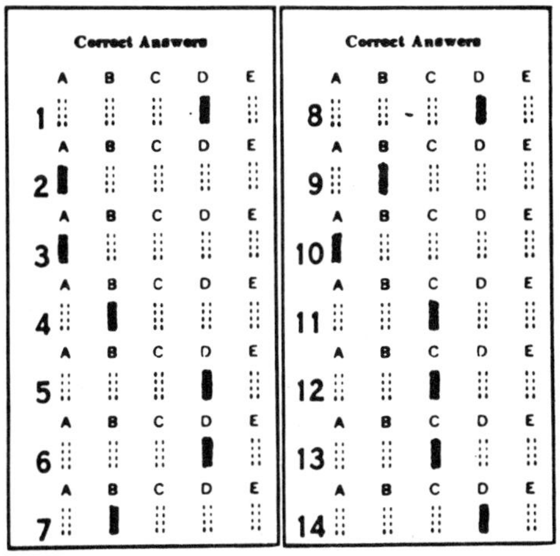

CORRECT USAGE TEST THREE

ERRORS IN AGREEMENT OF CASE, TENSE OR NUMBER

DIRECTIONS: In each of the following groups of sentences, select the one sentence that is grammatically INCORRECT. Mark the answer sheet with the letter of that incorrect sentence.

Correct key answers to all these test questions will be found at the end of the test.

1. (A) Who did they say won?
   (B) The man whom I thought was my friend deceived me.
   (C) Send whoever will do the work.
   (D) The question of who should be leader arose.

2. (A) A box of choice figs was sent him for Christmas.
   (B) Neither Charles nor his brother finished his assignment.
   (C) There goes the last piece of cake and the last spoonful of ice cream.
   (D) Diamonds are more desired than any other precious stones.

3. (A) As long as you are ready, you may as well start promptly.
   (B) My younger brother insists that he is as tall as me.
   (C) We walked as long as there was any light to guide us.
   (D) Realizing I had forgotten my gloves, I returned to the theatre.

4. (A) The supervisor has given you and me difficult assignments.
   (B) This is just between you and I.
   (C) That question is not for you and me to answer.

5. (A) His knowledge of methods and procedures enable him to assist the director in many ways.
   (B) A new set of rules and regulations has been made.
   (C) Reports that the strike has been settled were circulated yesterday.

6. (A) The Credit Bureau rates you as high as him.
   (B) He is no better than you or me.
   (C) You will be notified as soon as I.

7. (A) Neither the stenographer nor the typist has returned from lunch.
   (B) Either the operators or the machines are at fault.
   (C) One or the other of those clerks are responsible for these errors.

8. (A) The Board of Directors has prepared a manual for their own use.
   (B) The company has announced its new policy of advertising.
   (C) The jury were out about thirty minutes when they returned a verdict.

9. (A) Who does he think he is?
   (B) Whom does he consider in making a decision?
   (C) Whom did they say is to be appointed?

10. (A) Who shall I say called?
    (B) The water has frozen the pipes.
    (C) Everyone has left except them.
    (D) Everyone of the salesmen must supply their own car.

11. (A) Two-thirds of the building is finished.
    (B) Where are Mr. Keene and Mr. Herbert?
    (C) Neither the salesladies nor the floorwalker want to work overtime.
    (D) The committee was agreed.

12. (A) Amends have been made for the damage to one of our cars.
    (B) Neither the customer nor the clerk were aware of the fire in the store.
    (C) A box of spare pencils is on the desk.
    (D) There is the total number of missing pens.

13. (A) The company insist on everyone's being prompt.
    (B) Each one of our salesmen takes an aptitude test.
    (C) It is the location that appeals to me.
    (D) Most of the men have left the building.

Correct Answers For The Foregoing Questions

To assist you in scoring yourself we have provided Correct Answers alongside your Answer Sheet. May we therefore suggest that while you are doing the test you cover the Correct Answers with a sheet of white paper.....to avoid temptation and to arrive at an accurate estimate of your ability and progress.

Answer Sheet

	A	B	C	D	E
1					
2					
3					
4					
5					
6					
7					
8					
9					
10					
11					
12					
13					

Correct Answers

	A	B	C	D	E
1		▮			
2			▮		
3		▮			
4		▮			
5	▮				
6		▮			
7			▮		
8	▮				
9			▮		
10				▮	
11			▮		
12		▮			
13	▮				

SCORE

%

NO. CORRECT ÷

NO. OF QUESTIONS ON THIS TEST

CORRECT USAGE TEST FOUR

GOOD AND BAD ENGLISH

DIRECTIONS: In each of the following groups of sentences, select the one sentence that is grammatically INCORRECT. Mark the answer sheet with the letter of that incorrect sentence.

Correct key answers to all these test questions will be found at the end of the test.

1. (A) The students in the dormitories were forbidden, unless they had special passes, from staying out after 11:30 p.m.
   (B) The Student Court rendered a decision satisfactory to both the defendant and the accuser.
   (C) Margarine is being substituted for butter to a considerable extent.
   (D) In this school there are at least fifteen minor accidents a year which are due to this traffic violation.

2. (A) Sailing along New England's craggy coastline, you will relive a bygone era of far-roving whalers and graceful clipper ships.
   (B) The march of history is reenacted in folk festivals, outdoor pageants, and fiestas—local in theme, but national in import.
   (C) Visiting the scenes of the past, our interest in American history is renewed and enlivened.
   (D) What remained was a few unrecognizable fragments.

3. (A) I knew it to be him by the style of his clothes.
   (B) No one saw him doing it.
   (C) Her going away is a loss to the community.
   (D) Mary objected to her being there.
   (E) Illness prevented him graduating in June.

4. (A) No one but her could have recognized him.
   (B) She knew the stranger to be him whom she had given up as lost.
   (C) He looked like he had been in some strange land where age advanced at a double pace.
   (D) It is impossible to include that item; the agenda have already been mimeographed.

5. (A) You have probably heard of the new innovation in the regular morning broadcast.
   (B) During the broadcast you are expected to stand, to salute, and to sing the fourth stanza of "America."
   (C) None of the rocks which form the solid crust of our planet is more than two billion years old.
   (D) "I have finished my assignment," said the pupil. "May I go home now?"

6. (A) The coming of peace effected a change in her way of life.
   (B) Spain is as weak, if not weaker than, she was in 1900.
   (C) In regard to that, I am not certain what my attitude will be.
   (D) That unfortunate family faces the problem of adjusting itself to a new way of life.
   (E) Fred Eastman states in his essay that one of the joys of reading lies in discovering courage.

7. (A) Participation in active sports produces both release from tension as well as physical well-being.
   (B) The problem of taxes is still with them.
   (C) Every boy and every girl in the auditorium was thrilled when the color guard appeared.

(D) At length our club decided to send two representatives to the meeting, you and me.

8. (A) Remains of an ancient civilization were found near Mexico City.
   (B) It is interesting to compare the interior of one of the pyramids in Mexico to the interior of one of the pyramids in Egypt.
   (C) In two days' journey you will be reminded of political upheavals comparable to the volcanic eruptions still visible and audible in parts of Mexico.
   (D) There is little danger of the laws being broken, so drastic is the penalty.

9. (A) Instead of looking disdainfully at London grime, think of it as a mantle of tradition.
   (B) Nobody but the pilot and the co-pilot was permitted to handle the mysterious package.
   (C) Not only is industry anxious to hire all available engineers, but they are being offered commissions by the armed forces.
   (D) For immediate service go direct to the store manager.

10. (A) The delegates alighted and started off in a taxi, their baggage having been taken care of.
    (B) That kind of potatoes is grown in Idaho.
    (C) Besides Alan Stevens, there were eight officers of the organization on the dais.
    (D) As the delegates reached the convention hall late, they blamed their tardiness on the taxi driver.

11. (A) The new system is superior from every point of view to the inefficient system in use until now.
    (B) The reason for the strike, you may recall, was because the union demanded a closed shop.
    (C) Who's to decide whether it is to be installed?
    (D) To suit Mr. Knolls, the new device will have to save time, money, and the dispositions of the employees.

Correct Answers For The Foregoing Questions

To assist you in scoring yourself we have provided Correct Answers alongside your Answer Sheet. May we therefore suggest that while you are doing the test you cover the Correct Answers with a sheet of white paper.....to avoid temptation and to arrive at an accurate estimate of your ability and progress.

Answer Sheet

	A	B	C	D	E
1					
2					
3					
4					
5					
6					
7					
8					
9					
10					
11					

Correct Answers

	A	B	C	D	E
1	■				
2			■		
3					■
4			■		
5	■				
6		■			
7	■				
8		■			
9			■		
10				■	
11		■			

SCORE

%

NO. CORRECT ÷

NO. OF QUESTIONS ON THIS TEST

CORRECT USAGE TEST FIVE

GOOD AND BAD ENGLISH

DIRECTIONS: In each of the following groups of sentences, select the one sentence that is grammatically INCORRECT. Mark the answer sheet with the letter of that incorrect sentence.

Correct key answers to all these test questions will be found at the end of the test.

1. (A) The zinnia has the more vivid color, but the violet is the sweeter-smelling.
   (B) About three-fourths of the review I read was merely a summary of the story; the rest, criticism.
   (C) I shall insist that he not be accepted as a member, since he is very bad-tempered.
   (D) No sooner had he begun to speak when his auditors started to boo and hiss.

2. (A) The children's determination to find their dog almost resulted in tragedy.
   (B) They spent the first night in a house that was unlocked and with no one at home.
   (C) "What he asked me," said the boy, "Was, 'Where can I find your father!' "
   (D) It was the whimpering of the younger child and the comforting words of her brother that a member of the search-party heard about ten feet off the road.

3. (A) This is between you and me.
   (B) These questions are less difficult than those.
   (C) The former is considerably different with the latter.
   (D) We are not unaware of the consequences.

4. (A) This person also wished to state his case.
   (B) He came almost immediately.
   (C) Returning to the room, the book was missing.
   (D) They are both very nearly alike in this respect.

5. (A) What kind of a job have you?
   (B) He did exactly as he was told.
   (C) The red house is differently shaped than the blue.
   (D) We hoped to see you there.

6. (A) He found neither the money or the papers.
   (B) There are no two men in the room.
   (C) Who would file the summons was the question.
   (D) It is possible he may be here now.

7. (A) The choice finally remained between them and us.
   (B) Is this the gardener of whom you spoke?
   (C) The thieves divided the money among themselves.
   (D) Do you know who this package is to be addressed to?

8. (A) I shouldn't have done it.
   (B) After a wearying day, he lay down to rest.
   (C) These problems are difficult as the others.
   (D) She saw neither of us.

9. (A) The incident occurred when he took the book off the desk.
   (B) Helen thinks as clearly as John.
   (C) I cannot believe but what he is guilty.
   (D) He indicated that the two boys were to go.

10. (A) Our child will be successful without any assistance from either you or me.
    (B) Whom do you think we ought to consider for the chairmanship?

(C) Deep in the forest, warmed by the dying embers of our camp-fire, sat the scoutmaster and I.

(D) The part of the story I enjoyed most was where the heroine decided to leave her husband.

11. (A) "Which is the way to Paris?" asked the American soldier glumly.

(B) The physicist muttered in despair, "Will I always be surrounded by fools?"

(C) I never feel badly if after trying hard I fail to win a prize; the effort gives me satisfaction.

(D) Everywhere I go, I find grime and dirt in the air.

12. (A) Parents are the ones who we believe ought to insist upon their children's obeying orders.

(B) The carpenters were lying on the ground and resting when I came in.

(C) I do not understand why mother should object to me playing the piano at the party.

(D) Lie in bed awhile until your aches and pains subside.

13. (A) She avoided my look of surprise, staring at the ceiling steadily.

(B) When I told her I was sorry, I partly meant it.

(C) My father enjoys fresh air, sunshine, and to take long walks.

(D) The greatest pleasure I get is to see my favorite team win a ball game.

14. (A) Students who plan to become physicians are advised to study biology, chemistry, and German.

(B) The critic asked the author which of his plays he considered the best.

(C) I, who am your best friend, should have at least a fair chance of winning the prize.

(D) If you go past the library tomorrow, please bring this book to the librarian who sits at the desk in the children's room.

15. (A) Writers no longer take for granted the mores of the society in which they live.

(B) He is in this country now for five years, but he makes no attempt to speak our language.

(C) The reason the child rebelled was that the order made no sense to him.

(D) His written work has been done in so careless a manner that I refuse to read it.

Correct Answers For The Foregoing Questions

To assist you in scoring yourself we have provided Correct Answers alongside your Answer Sheet. May we therefore suggest that while you are doing the test you cover the Correct Answers with a sheet of white paper.....to avoid temptation and to arrive at an accurate estimate of your ability and progress.

Answer Sheet

	A	B	C	D	E
1	⁞	⁞	⁞	⁞	⁞
2	⁞	⁞	⁞	⁞	⁞
3	⁞	⁞	⁞	⁞	⁞
4	⁞	⁞	⁞	⁞	⁞
5	⁞	⁞	⁞	⁞	⁞
6	⁞	⁞	⁞	⁞	⁞
7	⁞	⁞	⁞	⁞	⁞
8	⁞	⁞	⁞	⁞	⁞
9	⁞	⁞	⁞	⁞	⁞
10	⁞	⁞	⁞	⁞	⁞
11	⁞	⁞	⁞	⁞	⁞
12	⁞	⁞	⁞	⁞	⁞
13	⁞	⁞	⁞	⁞	⁞
14	⁞	⁞	⁞	⁞	⁞
15	⁞	⁞	⁞	⁞	⁞

SCORE

%

NO. CORRECT ÷

NO. OF QUESTIONS ON THIS TEST

Correct Answers

	A	B	C	D	E
1				▮	
2		▮			
3			▮		
4			▮		
5	▮				
6	▮				
7				▮	
8			▮		
9			▮		
10				▮	
11			▮		
12			▮		
13			▮		
14				▮	
15		▮			

CORRECT USAGE TEST SIX

GOOD AND BAD ENGLISH

DIRECTIONS: In each of the following groups of sentences, select the one sentence that is grammatically INCORRECT. Mark the answer sheet with the letter of that incorrect sentence.

Correct key answers to all these test questions will be found at the end of the test.

1. (A) The lines on the map are finely drawn.
   (B) He spoke very slowly.
   (C) The lady looked good in her new suit.
   (D) The cream tasted sour.

2. (A) The day is warm.
   (B) It should be called to his attention.
   (C) The girl was an unusually beautiful child.
   (D) He performed the job easy and quick.

3. (A) The company published its new catalogue last week.
   (B) The man who he introduced was Mr. Carey.
   (C) The Rolls-Royce is the fastest car in England.
   (D) He finished the job satisfactorily.

4. (A) She saw the letter laying here this morning.
   (B) They gave the poor man some food when he knocked on the door.
   (C) The plans were drawn before the fight started.
   (D) He was here when the messenger brought the news.

5. (A) I regret the loss caused by the error.
   (B) The students will have a new teacher.
   (C) It shall rain before the afternoon is over.
   (D) They swore to bring out all the facts.

6. (A) If my trip is a success, I should be back on Thursday.
   (B) We will send a copy of the article to you if you wish it.
   (C) They will have gone before the notice is sent to their office.
   (D) Can I use this information in my speech?

7. (A) He likes these kind of pencils better than those kind.
   (B) That Jackson will be elected is evident.
   (C) He does not approve of my dictating the letter.
   (D) Jack should make some progress in his work each day.

8. (A) The company has moved into its new building.
   (B) They will approve him going to the concert.
   (C) That business is good appears to be true.
   (D) It was he who won the prize.

Correct Answers

Answer Sheet

	A	B	C	D	E
1					
2					
3					
4					
5					
6					
7					
8					

SCORE

%

NO. CORRECT ÷ NO. OF QUESTIONS ON THIS TEST

Correct Answers

	A	B	C	D	E
1			■		
2				■	
3		■			
4	■				
5			■		
6				■	
7	■				
8		■			

COURT OFFICER

JUDGMENT AND REASONING QUESTIONS

In the main, judgment questions relate to general topics. If the candidate is unfamiliar with a particular problem, he should attempt to reason out the various possibilities. By applying a certain amount of common sense, the candidate can, by a process of eliminating those choices which are least correct, deduce the correct or "expected" answer.

JUDGMENT questions are usually multiple-choice questions. Each question consists of a partial statement followed by five choices, *one* and *only one* of which will *best* complete the original statement. In some cases, *several* of the choices will make a true or correct statement. In all cases, however, there is *one* choice which is *more* correct and *less* open to exceptions than any other choice that could be made. In answering sample questions, eliminate immediately from consideration those choices which are least correct, far-fetched, or which otherwise are extraneous to the original statement.

A SAMPLE QUESTION ANALYZED

The following sample test question, which has been analyzed, will help the candidate establish a methodology for answering judgment questions.

Example: The one of the following which is the best source of current business information is the

(A) almanac
(B) dictionary
(C) city directory
(D) telephone directory
(E) newspaper.

First, it is important to analyze the question. Notice the adjectives: *best, current* and *business.* Of the five possible choices, the correct one must have the three qualities. It must be the *best* source of *current business* information.

Ask yourself the following questions regarding the choices: (1) Is it a source of information? (2) Is it a source of *business* information? (3) Is it a source of *current* information? (4) Is it the *best* source of *current business* information?

Let us analyze the five choices:

(A) almanac: (a) The almanac *is* a source of information. (b) The almanac could be called a source of *current* information since an almanac is generally issued annually, and for a time has *current* information. (c) However, an almanac is generally *not* a source of *business* information. An almanac is defined as "a book containing a calendar of days, weeks, and months with the times of the rising and setting of the sun, moon, etc. Therefore, "almanac" is not the proper choice.

(B) dictionary: (a) The dictionary *is* a source of information. (b) The dictionary is a source of *business* information because it gives us the meaning of words, including business terms. (c) Some dictionaries *may* be a source of *current* information right after they come off the press, but any dictionary is not *always* a source of *current* information. Therefore, the dictionary is not the proper answer.

(C) city directory: (a) The city directory *is* a source of information. (b) The city directory is a source of *business* information, because it gives us the names, addresses and business occupations of city inhabitants. (c) The city directory is a source of *current* information because it gives the present or *current* addresses and occupations of people living in the city. So far in our analysis, we see that the city directory *is* a source of *current business* information. (d) Now the question is: Is it the *best* source of current business information? Let us examine the *other* choices before we decide.

(D) telephone directory: (a) The telephone directory *is* a source of information. (b) The telephone directory is a source of *business* information because it gives us the names, addresses, *business* and phone numbers of city inhabitants. (c) The telephone directory is a source of *current* information because like the city directory, it indicates the present or *current* addresses, etc. of city inhabitants, since copies are issued twice a year. (d) Again the question remains: Is it the *best* source of current business information? Let us examine the last choice.

(E) newspaper: (a) The newspaper *is* a source of information. (b) The newspaper is a source of *business* information, since almost all newspapers have a *business section*. (c) The newspaper is a source of *current* information, since it is issued in many cases several times daily.

At this point, it is clear that of the five choices, three of them, the city directory, telephone directory and the newspaper, are all sources of current business information.

We must now decide which is the *best*. Compared to the city directory and the telephone directory, it becomes very apparent that the *newspaper* is the *best* source of *current, business* information. This method should be used in answering the sample test questions which follow.

PREVIOUS TEST QUESTIONS FOR PRACTICE

Read the following questions carefully. From the five suggestions for an answer, select the one choice which best completes the statement. Indicate the letter preceding your choice for the best answer.

1. The average span of life has increased chiefly because
   (A) modern civilization exerts less pressure on the individual
   (B) the individual does not have to work as hard as formerly
   (C) modern inventions conserve the individual's energy
   (D) advances in the field of medicine have made possible control of many formerly fatal diseases
   (E) the human body over a period of centuries has built up greater resistance to disease.

2. Zoning has been introduced for residential districts in order to
   (A) keep the district residential, thereby preventing confusion and unnecessary movement
   (B) maintain real estate values
   (C) fix the growth of the city in definite patterns
   (D) keep unwanted populations out of exclusive districts
   (E) reduce friction between communities.

3. The rate of increase of the farm population in the United States has been greater than that of cultivated farm land. We may conclude from this that
   (A) there will be more farmers than city dwellers in a short time
   (B) the rural population will shortly become too many for the available land
   (C) we may soon expect a movement from the farms to the cities
   (D) there will be more people to cultivate the same land
   (E) too many people are cultivating too little land.

4. An automobile can pick up speed more quickly than a locomotive train chiefly because it
   (A) has a less complicated mechanism than the locomotive
   (B) runs on rubber tires instead of on tracks
   (C) the automobile uses gasoline instead of steam as fuel
   (D) the automobile is lighter in weight than the locomotive
   (E) the automobile is capable of operating at a higher speed than the locomotive.

5. Replacement of obsolete machinery by modern equipment is often a benefit to the manufacturer in that it
   (A) relieves the strain on the workers
   (B) lowers the selling price of his product
   (C) lowers his overhead
   (D) produces a better product at a lower unit cost
   (E) reduces taxes.

6. Which of the following would be the surest indication that a druggist may have violated the legal requirement that narcotic drugs be dispensed only on a physician's prescription?
   (A) a number of people known to have purchased other drugs from him are believed to possess narcotics, but no prescriptions issued to these persons are in the druggist's file
   (B) he is himself an addict
   (C) his wholesaler refuses to sell him narcotics

(D) the total of his present narcotics stock and the amount legally accounted for is much less than his purchases
(E) the supply of narcotics in stock is less than the amount he recently reported.

7. Stars are invisible in the daytime principally because
(A) the distance between the earth and the stars increases during the night
(B) the relative brightness of the sun is greater than that of the stars during the day
(C) the earth's rotation places them on the opposite side of the earth
(D) they do not reflect the light of the sun during the day
(E) they are really still visible as they can be seen from the bottom of a deep well.

8. Sculpture predated painting as an art because
(A) it is more important than painting
(B) it is simpler than painting
(C) it was used as an adjunct in construction
(D) it is more interesting to the primitive mind
(E) it requires primitive strength.

9. Custom regulations concerning the importation of fruit trees exist primarily in order to
(A) prevent the smuggling of fruit trees into the country
(B) aid farmers in maintaining high prices for their fruits
(C) prevent the introduction into the United States of foreign destructive fruit insects
(D) prevent foreign products from flooding the American market
(E) aid in the introduction of new varieties of fruit trees into the United States.

10. In starting a load, a horse has to pull harder than he does to keep it moving because
(A) the load weighs less when it is moving
(B) there is no friction after the load is moving
(C) the horse becomes accustomed to pulling the load
(D) the wheels stick to the axles
(E) the horse has to overcome the tendency of the wagon to remain at rest.

11. The best reason for the rule in criminal cases requiring that the defendant's guilt be established beyond a reasonable doubt is
(A) in a civil case the plaintiff must prove his claim in the same way
(B) a fair preponderance of the credible evidence is necessary in a civil suit
(C) the District Attorney has his own investigators, the Police Department and other official assistance in preparing his case whereas the defendant has to rely mainly on his own lawyer
(D) it is so provided in the State or Federal Constitutions
(E) because it is one of the strongest safeguards under our system of law against unjust convictions.

12. From 1930 to 1940 there was a 7% rise in the population of the United States. During the same period there was a rise of 60% in the numbers of married people. The increase in the number of married people may be attributed to
(A) an increased birth rate
(B) a natural increase in the population of the country
(C) a large number of marriages from 1930 to 1940
(D) unrest in the world
(E) previous population increases.

13. The price of a two-pound can is less than double that of a one-pound can because
(A) packaging costs are not proportional to the quantity of material in a package
(B) a cheaper grade of merchandise is always included in larger packages
(C) the manufacturer would rather sell small packages
(D) more expensive merchandise is usually in smaller packages
(E) large packages are a good advertisement.

14. Men work chiefly because they must
(A) support the state
(B) support themselves
(C) enjoy themselves
(D) utilize leisure time
(E) broaden their viewpoint on life.

15. Mass production results in lower prices chiefly because
(A) the cost of making each unit is lowered
(B) a larger amount of material is used
(C) competition becomes keener
(D) demand for the product increases

(E) the articles produced are of an inferior quality.

16. Your superior directs you to find certain papers. You know the purpose for which the papers are to be used. In the course of your search for the papers, you come across certain material which would be very useful for the purpose to be served by the papers. You should
(A) bring the papers to your superior and ask whether he wishes the other materials
(B) go to your superior immediately and ask whether he wishes both the papers and the materials
(C) bring to your superior the other materials together with the papers
(D) bring only the other materials and point out to your superior how these materials are of greater value than the papers
(E) bring only the papers and say nothing about the other materials.

17. The purpose of new regulations requiring that the use of any excessive flavoring or coloring matter in whiskey be noted on the label is to
(A) keep people from buying such whiskey
(B) make the taste of whiskey less pleasant
(C) let the buyer know the exact quality of his purchases
(D) decrease the number of different blends of whiskey
(E) keep distillers from using any such matters.

18. The fact that ships leaving shore seem to drop below the horizon proves chiefly that
(A) the ocean and the horizon merge at a certain point
(B) the farther from shore, the lower the ship
(C) the earth is round
(D) the distance between the ship and the shore is increased
(E) the ship gradually fades out.

19. The individual distinguishes differences in colors primarily because colors
(A) have different chemical compositions
(B) have different wave-lengths
(C) are all part of the color spectrum
(D) reflect light
(E) are visible except to those who are color blind.

20. The various forms of social insurance are aimed at
(A) eradicating unhappiness
(B) effecting a radical change in our social system
(C) eliminating the causes of dependency
(D) spreading the cost of maintaining those in need over as many people and as wide a period of time as possible
(E) getting the most good to the greatest number.

21. The fact that fossil fish are found on a mountain indicates that
(A) fishes once lived on land
(B) the mountain-top was once below sea-level
(C) fish were one of the first organisms existent upon the earth
(D) the level of the sea and the mountain was once equal
(E) fossil fish are valuable as relics of prehistoric life.

22. The Government does not allow pictures to be made of its paper money because in that way
(A) it preserves the bills
(B) discourages counterfeiting
(C) it stabilizes the currency
(D) it prevents paper money from being used in preference to coins
(E) it conceals the infinite detail in the currency.

23. "All minors everywhere are highly emotional, for they are adolescents." This statement assumes most nearly that
(A) all adolescents who are highly emotional are minors
(B) all adolescents are minors
(C) few minors are not emotional
(D) any person who is an adolescent is highly emotional
(E) some adolescents are not highly emotional.

24. Rare manuscripts are reproduced on photographic film
(A) to reduce the possibility of loss by fire
(B) so that the text may be available without any disturbance to the original manuscript
(C) so that they may be stored in smaller space

(D) to facilitate ready reference
(E) to aid scholars in research.

25. The chief reason why a bank can extend its loans beyond the volume of the cash in its possession is that
(A) it takes a long time for checks drawn upon it to be cashed
(B) checks drawn upon it are likely to be deposited with it instead of being cashed
(C) checks drawn upon it are likely to be deposited in another bank
(D) the bank does not have to supply the required loan immediately
(E) the bank can extend its loan thirty per cent beyond cash at hand by federal law.

26. Water from a spring in the woods should generally be boiled before being used for drinking purposes chiefly because
(A) it may contain dirt
(B) boiling will remove any taste of clay
(C) any sediment contained in the water will settle to the bottom after boiling
(D) it may contain harmful bacteria
(E) the minerals in it will be eliminated by boiling.

27. The air is cool at the bottom of an unused chimney because it is
(A) undisturbed
(B) under pressure
(C) farther from the outside air
(D) heavier and cool air settled there
(E) away from the sun's rays.

28. If the earth were made of lead, objects would
(A) weigh more
(B) weigh less
(C) retain their present weight
(D) tend to decrease in dimension
(E) corrode.

29. The relative position of stars in the sky is continually changing because
(A) of the stellar "drift"
(B) the earth moves eastward around the sun once a year
(C) of the semi-annual increase in the earth's velocity
(D) of changes in the relative distance between the earth and the stars
(E) of phenomena as yet unexplained.

30. Leverage is most useful in
(A) multiplying energy
(B) decreasing work
(C) reducing friction
(D) gaining mechanical advantage
(E) bending heavy bars.

31. Water power is one of the most natural and at the same time most truly economical sources of energy chiefly because
(A) water has a relatively high velocity
(B) water power can be easily harnessed
(C) water is readily available and can be cheaply and easily converted into power
(D) water power readily lends itself to the operation of many machines
(E) water power contains the greatest amount of energy known to man.

32. Winds result from
(A) the effects on the air of the difference in heat of the tropics and the polar regions
(B) the erratic movements of the sea
(C) the movements of the moon
(D) earthquakes
(E) changes in the atmosphere about the equator.

33. It becomes profitable to import a commodity chiefly whenever labor and capital engaged in its domestic productions yield
(A) a profit which is less than the same agents would yield in other fields
(B) a lesser number of products than would be normally expected
(C) a profit similar to that which they would yield in other fields
(D) a very small profit
(E) less profits than a competitive firm.

34. The Government arbitrarily assigns frequencies to radio broadcasting stations
(A) to facilitate licensing procedures
(B) to prevent more than one station broadcasting on the same frequency
(C) to reduce static and interference
(D) to reserve the air for amateur operators
(E) to avoid the necessity of further restrictions.

35. The apparent motion of the sun across the sky is caused by
(A) the earth's speed
(B) the rotation of the earth on its axis
(C) the earth's centrifugal force

(D) the relative variation in so-called "sun-spots"
(E) a spectrum phenomenon.

36. Water tanks are maintained on the top of tall buildings chiefly in order to
(A) maintain a reserve supply of water if the normal water supply should fail
(B) prevent lightning from striking the building by acting as an arrester
(C) have water available in the event of a fire
(D) supply the upper floors with water by a process of first pumping it into the tanks
(E) convert the water into electric power by a turbine process.

37. The fact that the sun seems to rise in the east and set in the west is proof that
(A) only the sun is in motion
(B) only the earth is in motion
(C) either the sun or the earth is in motion
(D) the east and the west are merely abstract concepts
(E) there are 12 hours in the average day.

38. "Because telephone directories contain printed pages, they are called books." This statement assumes most nearly that
(A) some books do not contain printed pages
(B) not all telephone directories are books which contain printed pages
(C) material which contains printed pages is called a book
(D) all books which contain printed pages are called telephone directories
(E) all telephone directories must have printed pages.

39. Leather is considered the best material for shoes chiefly because
(A) it is waterproof
(B) it is durable
(C) it is easily procurable
(D) it is flexible and durable
(E) it can be easily manufactured in various styles.

40. Skyscrapers are a development of city life because
(A) land is limited and expensive
(B) engineers have the knowledge wherewith to build them
(C) people like to live in the upper stories where the air is pure
(D) they are in conformity with zoning regulations
(E) they add to a city's beauty.

41. Automobile accident insurance rates vary from city to city chiefly because
(A) it is difficult for automobile accident insurance companies to arrive at a standard rate applicable to all cities
(B) the accident rate varies from city to city
(C) people in some cities are better educated in safety rules and regulations than in others
(D) safety laws vary from one city to another
(E) the number of automobile drivers varies from city to city.

42. An insulating process is currently being used in modern house construction chiefly because
(A) it makes houses sound-proof
(B) it makes houses less costly to construct
(C) insulation makes a house waterproof
(D) the insulation tends to reduce house fueling costs
(E) it saves time in construction.

43. The ability of elements to produce heat while they are uniting proves chiefly that
(A) all elements unite at extreme heat
(B) heat is a purifying agent
(C) heat is a by-product of every chemical flux
(D) elements contain heat energy
(E) when elements unite a compound is formed.

44. Electricity is used as the chief agent in flashing messages from place to place mainly because
(A) it is less costly in the long run
(B) aerial wiring is eliminated
(C) maximum speed is obtainable
(D) it is applicable to telegrams
(E) the element of space is reduced.

45. The sound which issues from a violin when a bow is drawn across one of the strings is due chiefly to
(A) air waves set in motion by the bow
(B) ether waves set in motion by the bow
(C) a partial vacuum in the vicinity of the sound chamber which is caused by the vibrating motion of the bow

(D) vibration of the string
(E) the tenseness of the string.

46. A clay pitcher of water will crack if the water freezes chiefly because
(A) during the process of freezing the water expands
(B) during the process of freezing the water contracts
(C) the crystallization process of ice formation causes the ice to solidify
(D) the tension strength of clay decreases as the temperature decreases
(E) the rate of expansion of water has the same ratio as that of contraction of the pitcher.

CORRECT ANSWERS FOR THE FOREGOING QUESTIONS

(Please try to answer the questions on your own before looking at our answers. You'll do much better on your test if you follow this rule.)

1. D	7. B	13. A	19. B	25. B	31. C	37. C	43. D
2. A	8. C	14. B	20. D	26. D	32. A	38. C	44. C
3. D	9. C	15. A	21. B	27. D	33. A	39. D	45. D
4. D	10. E	16. A	22. B	28. A	34. B	40. A	46. A
5. D	11. E	17. C	23. D	29. B	35. B	41. B	
6. D	12. C	18. C	24. B	30. D	36. D	42. D	

JUDGMENT FOR LAW ENFORCEMENT OFFICERS

The following questions test your judgment as a law enforcement officer in fundamental problems of police protection and law enforcement. In each question, a certain amount of data is supplied, or it is assumed that you already possess sufficient police knowledge to answer the question. Read each question twice; the first time for overall meaning, the second to be sure you have missed no detail. Beware of trick questions.

1. "One can only see what one observes and one observes only things which are already in the mind." Of the following, the chief implication of this statement is that
   (A) observation, to be most effective, should be directed and conscious
   (B) all aspects of a situation, unless the law enforcement officer exercises caution, are likely to strike him with equal forcefulness
   (C) observation should be essentially indirect if it is to be accurate
   (D) memory is essentially perception one step removed from observation.

2. "The number of arrests made is not always the best indication of a successful policeman." The statement most consistent with the above quotation is that
   (A) a number of factors should be considered in properly evaluating the performance of a policeman
   (B) there is a negative correlation between the number of arrests made and the success of a policeman
   (C) policemen should avoid making arrests whenever possible
   (D) the success of a policeman cannot be precisely and objectively measured.

3. A law enforcement officer is in the habit in his free time of occasionally inventing imaginary law enforcement problems on his post and attempting to provide appropriate solutions to these happenings. This sort of behavior is best characterized as
   (A) undesirable, since it may lead to insanity
   (B) desirable, since it exercises his mind
   (C) useful, because it is conclusive evidence of his competence
   (D) undesirable, in that his attention is less readily given to what is actually happening on his post
   (E) desirable, since he may, as a result, be better prepared for emergencies.

4. "Training produces co-operation and brings about lower unit costs of operation." According to this statement, it is most logical to assume that
   (A) a program of personnel training is a major feature of every large business organization
   (B) training is a factor in improving morale and efficiency
   (C) training is of more value to new workers than to old employees
   (D) unless personnel costs can be lowered, training is of little value.

5. As an intelligent law enforcement officer, you should know that, of the following, the one which is least likely to be followed by an increase in crime is
   (A) war
   (C) poor housing
   (B) depression
   (D) prosperity.

6. In lecturing on the law of arrest an instructor remarked: "To go beyond is as bad as to fall short." The one of the following which most nearly expresses his meaning is
   (A) never undertake the impossible
   (B) extremes are not desirable
   (C) look before you leap
   (D) too much success is dangerous.

7. In addressing a class an instructor remarked: "Carelessness and failure are twins." The one

of the following that most nearly expresses his meaning is
(A) negligence seldom accompanies success
(B) incomplete work is careless work
(C) conscientious work is never attended by failure
(D) a conscientious person never makes mistakes.

8. The cardinal function of a police department is
(A) the prevention of crime
(B) the efficiency and discipline of its members
(C) to preserve property values
(D) to minimize conflicts.

9. Law enforcement officials receive badges with numbers on them so that
(A) their personalities may be submerged
(B) they may be more easily identified
(C) they may be spied upon
(D) their movements may be kept under constant control.

10. If you were asked what you thought of a person you didn't know, what should you say?
(A) I will go and get acquainted
(B) I think he is all right
(C) I don't know him and can't say
(D) I think he is worthless.

11. The best attitude for an officer to take is to
(A) be constantly on the alert
(B) be hostile
(C) vary his watchfulness with the apparent necessity for it
(D) regard tact as his most effective weapon for handling any degree of disorder.

12. An officer who has been assigned to work with you has a receding chin. It is most probable that he will
(A) be much like the other men in your group
(B) lack will power to a marked degree
(C) be a very timid person
(D) constantly carry tales to you about the other officers.

13. The annual number of arrests recorded in City A is 1,000. The annual number of arrests recorded in city B is 1,200. It is safe to infer from this information
(A) that there are more criminals in City A than in city B
(B) that more persons are imprisoned in city A than in City B
(C) there is more disrespect for law in city A than in City B
(D) none of the foregoing.

14. 10 percent of the inmates released from a certain prison are arrested as parole violators. It follows that
(A) 90 percent have reformed
(B) 10 percent have reformed
(C) none has reformed
(D) none of the foregoing is necessarily true.

15. It has been stated that arrests are made in only 44 percent of the crimes committed, while only 40 percent of those arrested are convicted. The most reasonable inference from these data is that
(A) most criminal acts are not immediately followed by the arrest of the criminal
(B) a small number of persons is arrested
(C) most of those persons who are arrested are also convicted
(D) people without influence are most likely to be convicted after arrest.

16. An insane person who has a wife and two children is arrested on a charge of burglary. It follows from these data that
(A) we have here insufficient information from which to draw any conclusions with reference to the relation between crime and insanity
(B) burglary is a crime which attracts lunatics
(C) this proves that not all lunatics are burglars
(D) a burgler is one type of lunatic.

17. A certain committee found that over 90 percent of the murders in the United States are committed by use of pistols. It follows that
(A) almost all murders are caused by the possession of pistols
(B) 90 percent of murders can be eliminated by eliminating the sale and use of pistols
(C) the pistol is a mechanical aid to crime
(D) no information is available with regard to the way murders happen.

18. The causes of crime
(A) are exactly the same today as in the past
(B) have been accurately and completely determined
(C) are an unimportant matter
(D) are an extremely complicated problem.

19. A criminal is typically one who

(A) has a peculiarly shaped head
(B) exhibits a most degenerate kind of behavior
(C) is an intelligent, well educated person
(D) looks like other people.

20. There would be no crime if there were no
(A) weapons
(B) criminals
(C) stupid laws
(D) private property.

21. An officer receives instructions from his supervisor which he does not fully understand. For the officer to ask for a further explanation would be
(A) good; chiefly because his supervisor will be impressed with his interest in his work
(B) poor; chiefly because the time of the supervisor will be needlessly wasted
(C) good; chiefly because proper performance depends on full understanding of the work to be done
(D) poor; chiefly because officers should be able to think for themselves.

22. The FBI reports that the crime rate in New Jersey last year was 10.6 percent higher than in the previous year, while the average increase in crime throughout the United States was 7.6 percent. It may logically be concluded from these facts that
(A) most New Jersey residents have lost their respect for the law
(B) New Jersey police officials are more conscientious than those of other states
(C) New Jersey's laws are more severe than those of other states
(D) New Jersey's increased crime rate may be due to a combination of reasons not listed above.

23. The one of the following statements concerning the behavior of law enforcement officers which is most accurate is
(A) a show of confident assurance on the part of a law enforcement officer will make it possible to cover a shortage of knowledge in any given duty
(B) in ordinary cases, when a newly appointed officer does not know what to do, it is always better to do too much than to do too little
(C) it is not advisable that officers recommend the employment of certain attorneys for individuals taken into custody
(D) a prisoner who is morose and refuses to talk will bear less watching by an officer than one who threatens to kill himself.

24. A law enforcement officer should know that character can be influenced only when and in so far as
(A) the desire for ideals has been aroused
(B) a knowledge of principles of conduct has been acquired
(C) problems of behavior have been clearly defined
(D) plans for meeting specific situations are carried into conduct.

25. In dealing with children a law enforcement officer should always
(A) treat them the same as adults
(B) instill in them a fear of the law
(C) secure their confidence
(D) impress them with the right of the law to punish them for wrong-doing.

26. Of the following, the greatest danger in arming a policeman detailed to guard prisoners in hospitals is that
(A) the gun may accidentally go off, wounding prisoners and others within gunshot
(B) the policeman may use the gun without adequate cause
(C) the prisoners may disarm the policeman
(D) it is hazardous to permit too many people to possess firearms.

27. Charging a fee for fortune-telling is not permitted under the laws of this State. In spite of this, fortune-telling in various forms remains popular. Of the following, the *least* likely reason for this popularity is that many people
(A) fear to make their own decisions in important matters
(B) have such drab lives that they must search for a hope of change
(C) wish to use fortune-tellers for entertainment at their social gatherings
(D) wish to make contacts with loved ones who have died
(E) wish to place blame on some supernatural power for their failures.

28. The one of the following which is the most probable reason for the considerably increasing proportion of serious crimes committed by women is

(A) that the proportion of women in the population is increasing
(B) that greater supervision of women results in a greater number of arrests
(C) the success of women in achieving social equality with men
(D) the increasing number of crime stories in the movies and on television
(E) the increasing number of crime gangs in operation.

29. Of the following types of crimes, increased police vigilance would probably be *least* successful in preventing
(A) murder
(B) burglary
(C) prostitution
(D) automobile thefts
(E) robbery.

30. In most hotels, couples who wish to rent a hotel room are required to carry a suitcase in order to be allowed to register. Of the following, the most valid reason for this regulation is that
(A) the hotel wishes to be protected against possible non-payment of the bill
(B) couples who carry a suitcase are surely married
(C) couples will be discouraged from entering into illicit relations on the impulse of the moment
(D) couples who carry a suitcase are likely to be strangers in town and therefore have a legitimate claim to a hotel room.
(E) the hotel will thus be able to maintain complete respectability.

31. "Undoubtedly the most important influence upon the growing youngster is that wielded by the adults whom he observes day after day." Accordingly, the type of adult behavior that generally would be *least* likely to adversely affect youngsters is
(A) dishonesty by public officials
(B) lack of courtesy in the home
(C) intolerance in the school
(D) racial discrimination in the neighborhood youth club
(E) hypocrisy in religious practices.

32. It frequently happens that a major crime of an unusual nature is followed almost immediately by an "epidemic" of several crimes, in widely scattered locations, which have elements similar to the first one. Of the following, the most likely explanation for this situation is that
(A) the same criminal is likely to commit the same type of a crime
(B) a gang of criminals will operate in several areas simultaneously
(C) newspaper publicity on a major crime is apt to influence other would-be criminals
(D) the same causes which are responsible for the first crime are also responsible for the others
(E) crimes are committed simultaneously to divert the efforts of the police.

33. "In studying juvenile delinquency in an area, it can be noted that the recorded activities of courts dealing with children's cases do not always give a true picture of the extent of juvenile delinquency in the area, especially if the police are so ineffective that many cases of delinquency do not reach the courts." On this basis, it can be stated most accurately that
(A) a population which has many delinquents will necessarily result in high delinquency figures
(B) low delinquency figures are possible only in a population of relatively well-adjusted children
(C) delinquency figures bear no relationship to the number of well-adjusted children in the population
(D) low delinquency figures may mean lax law enforcement or they may mean a population of relatively well-adjusted children
(E) low delinquency figures can result only from lax law enforcement.

34. "Many well meaning people have proposed that officers in uniform not be permitted to arrest juveniles." This proposal is
(A) good; the police are not equipped to handle juvenile offenders
(B) bad; juvenile offenders would lose respect for all law enforcement agencies
(C) good; offending juveniles should be segregated from hardened criminals
(D) bad; frequently it is the uniformed officer who first comes upon the youthful offender
(E) good; contact with the police would prevent any rehabilitative measures from being taken.

35. "A member of the department shall not indulge in intoxicants while in uniform. A member of the department not required to wear a uniform and a uniformed member while out of uniform shall not indulge in intoxicants to an extent unfitting him or her for duty." It follows that a

(A) member off duty, not in uniform, may drink intoxicants to any degree desired
(B) member not on duty, in uniform, may drink intoxicants
(C) member on duty, in uniform, may drink intoxicants
(D) uniformed member, in civilian clothes, may not drink intoxicants
(E) member on duty, not in uniform, may drink intoxicants.

36. The reason police officers have greater authority than private citizens in making arrests is
(A) to protect citizens against needless arrest
(B) to insure a fair trial
(C) that they have greater knowledge of the law
(D) that they are in better physical shape.

37. "The treatment to be given the offender cannot alter the fact of his offense; but we can take measures to reduce the chances of similar acts in the future. We should banish the criminal, not in order to exact revenge nor directly to encourage reform, but to deter him and others from further illegal attacks on society." According to this paragraph the principal reason for punishing criminals is to
(A) prevent the commission of future crimes
(B) remove them safely from society
(C) avenge society
(D) teach them that crime does not pay.

38. "The law enforcement officer's art consists in applying and enforcing a multitude of laws and ordinances in such degree or proportion and in such manner that the greatest degree of social protection will be secured. The degree of enforcement and the method of application will vary with each neighborhood and community." According to the foregoing paragraph
(A) each neighborhood or community must judge for itself to what extent the law is to be enforced
(B) a law enforcement officer should only enforce those laws which are designed to give the greatest degree of social protection
(C) the manner and intensity of law enforcement is not necessarily the same in all
(D) all laws and ordinances must be enforced in a community with the same degree of intensity.

39. It is well known that most criminals in the city
(A) belong to subversive organizations
(B) work at respectable jobs during the day
(C) are professionally trained
(D) come from crowded localities.

40. When arrested, boys under 16 are not brought to the same place of detention as older ones. The reason for this separation is most likely to
(A) keep them with others of their own age
(B) protect them from rough police methods
(C) help them get sound legal aid
(D) keep them from contact with hardened criminals.

41. Many criminals dress well and look like gentlemen, but have no regard for a human life if it stands in their way. A reasonable conclusion from this statement is that
(A) it is almost certain death to combat a criminal
(B) criminals are frequently gentlemen
(C) even some gentlemen have no regard for human lives
(D) a well-dressed man may be a criminal.

Law Enforcement Judgment: Key Answers

1. A	9. B	17. C	25. C	33. D
2. A	10. C	18. D	26. C	34. D
3. E	11. A	19. D	27. C	35. E
4. B	12. A	20. B	28. C	36. A
5. D	13. D	21. C	29. A	37. A
6. B	14. D	22. D	30. C	38. C
7. A	15. A	23. C	31. A	39. D
8. A	16. A	24. A	32. C	40. D
				41. D

COURT OFFICER
FIRST AID

GENERAL CONSIDERATIONS

Definition of First Aid

First aid is the immediate temporary care given by a trained person in case of accident or sudden illness before medical aid is available. It is given in order to prevent death or further injury, to relieve pain and counteract shock. To become *expert* in first aid requires many hours of training and practice.

General Directions

Keep the victim lying down.

Give immediate attention to serious bleeding and asphyxia.

Examine for injuries not clearly seen.

Keep victim warm.

Make injured comfortable.

Keep the crowd away.

See that someone calls a doctor.

Do not give an unconscious person anything to drink.

Do not permit casualty to be moved unless it is necessary and until it is safe.

When a casualty has several injuries, treat the most serious first, especially if it involves severe bleeding.

Remember you are a first aid worker and not a physician.

THE CARE OF WOUNDS

The chief *dangers* of wounds are severe *bleeding,* the introduction of *infection* and the development of *shock.* Bleeding should be controlled at once, for profuse bleeding may be followed by shock or result in lowered resistance to infection. Serious infections frequently develop in neglected wounds. All wounds should, therefore, be treated by a physician.

Make no attempt to clean or wash the wound. Do not apply any antiseptic, disinfectant, or any other material such as ointments, salves, oils, or chemicals. Simply cover the wound with sterile gauze, fix it in place with bandage or adhesive plaster, and take the injured person to the doctor. The gauze used must be large enough to cover the wound and a margin of skin on all sides. It must be sterile, and therefore should be from a freshly opened package. The surface of the gauze to be placed against the wound must not touch anything before it is applied. Do not lift the dressing or slide it about after application.

Casualties with injuries which appear to be minor should be directed to a casualty station. Casualties with serious injuries must be transported by stretcher to a first aid post or sent by a doctor directly to a hospital by ambulance. Because injuries may appear minor on the surface but be severe in the depth, you should not permit an injured person to go home until he has been seen by a doctor.

Watch for fragment wounds, which may be very small, often only a scratch. Such wounds have black edges. They must be considered serious because there will probably be damage to muscle and other tissue below the skin surface, and the fragment may be still embedded. A casualty with a wound in the body, however small, whether made by a bomb fragment or other missile, should be treated as for internal injuries.

Treatment for shock is important, especially if hemorrhage is severe. Lacerated and crushing wounds are often accompanied by severe shock.

If a limb is severely torn or crushed it should be immobilized with a traction splint before the victim is moved. Only moderate traction should be used in these cases.

CARE OF WOUNDS IN SPECIAL LOCATIONS

Head Injuries

Head injuries are common wounds. Severe injury may be caused by a blow on the head from falling timbers or flying debris, or the victim may be thrown against a wall or to the ground by the force of an explosion in such a way as to cause severe injury to his head. The injured person may be unconscious or dazed. Shock is usually present. He often resists efforts to help him. He may tear off bandages or clutch at the first aider as he tries to treat him.

In any case of head injury the brain may be damaged. The skull may be fractured. If this has occurred, blood stained fluid may leak from the ears.

If a casualty is dazed or unconscious and there is no obvious injury, examine the head first.

Look for bruises or bumps. Even persons with slight or doubtful head injuries must be seen by a physician as soon as possible.

Wounds of the scalp are common. Because they bleed profusely they are terrifying to the beginner in first aid.

First aid.—If there is a wound of the scalp apply a sterile compress to the wound and hold it in place with a firmly applied bandage.

If there is bloody or watery discharge from the ears do not plug them with cotton and do not try to clean them. Simply apply a sterile dressing over the ears. Keep the victim warm and quiet. Keep him lying down with his head slightly elevated.

Internal Injury

Serious injury may occur in the abdomen or in the chest as a result of penetration by a missile or crushing. Penetrating wounds about the hip joint or buttocks often cause internal injuries. Internal injury is always accompanied by internal bleeding and shock. The casualty may tear at his clothing in an effort to get more air. He may complain of thirst. If the wound is in the chest he may cough up blood.

First aid.—Treat for shock, which is always present. Keep the victim warm. Never give anything to drink. If the injury is in the abdomen keep the victim lying down, but if it is in his chest prop up the head and shoulders. All cases of internal injury must be transported on stretchers to a hospital as soon as possible. A casualty suffering from chest injuries should be propped up on the stretcher in a semisitting position, leaning toward the injured side. A casualty suffering from an abdominal injury should be transported on his back with legs slightly bent at the knees. No attempt should be made to replace protruding organs. Call a doctor.

Injury to the Face

Probably no injury is so terrifying as an injury to the face. When facial expression is lost the casualty appears to lose his identity as a human being. Bleeding is often profuse. Blood may run into the mouth or nose and strangle the victim. The jaw may be broken, in which case the tongue tends to fall backwards and obstruct the air passages.

In treating victims with facial injuries the first aid worker would do well to remember the miracles accomplished through plastic surgery. Although facial injuries are very gruesome, they are not the most dangerous to life.

First aid.—Determine whether the tongue has fallen into the back of the throat. If it has, grasp it in the fingers and pull it forward. Turn the victim onto his abdomen so that the blood will not run into his nose or mouth. Apply a liberal number of sterile gauze dressings to the wound and bind in place with a triangle bandage as described on page 8 . If the tongue falls backwards pull it forward and apply a bandage to the chin.

HEMORRHAGE

Hemorrhage is a condition which sounds, looks and is serious. Persons with hemorrhage must have priority treatment and transport.

Although the presence of blood requires immediate attention, it is in itself a poor indicator of the severity of the wounds. A little blood goes a long way and may make a minor injury look frightening. On the other hand a severe wound, a torn off limb for example, may bleed very little because of shock.

Many people think the only way to stop bleeding is to apply a tourniquet. They fail to consider its dangers. They would be horrified to know of the number of limbs lost or paralyzed because tourniquets have been left in place without being loosened every 15 minutes.

A pad over the wound and a firm bandage combined with elevation of the limb will stop bleeding in nearly all cases.

Kinds of Bleeding

A. *Bleeding from artery*—blood *spurts* with each beat of heart unless cut artery is deep under tissues, in which case blood will well up.

B. *Bleeding from veins* will be a *steady flow.*

C. Bleeding from injury to very small vessels—*oozing.*

Control of Bleeding

A. *Bleeding from artery.*

1. *Pressure points.*—Pressure points are points where arteries lie close enough to bones to permit sufficient compression by the fingers to control bleeding. Hemorrhage may be controlled by pressure on these points until pressure dressings can be applied to the bleeding wound.

(*a*) *For bleeding from the scalp and forehead,* press with finger or thumb just in front of the opening of the ear on the side nearer the bleeding.

(*b*) *For bleeding from the face below the eyebrows,* press against the side of the lower jaw just in front of the angle of the jawbone on the bleeding side.

(c) *For bleeding from the neck or cut throat,* place finger tips on the neck beside the windpipe on the bleeding side, and with thumb behind the neck, press toward backbone with ball of fingers.

(d) *For bleeding from the shoulder or armpit,* tip the head toward the shoulder on the injured side and press down with thumb at side of neck, just behind the collar bone.

(e) *For bleeding from the arm,* press with fingers on inner side of the arm just below armpit.

(f) *For bleeding from the leg,* put victim on his back and press downward with straight arm pressing the heel of the hand into the middle of the groin.

2. *Tourniquet for arterial bleeding*:

(a) *Materials.*—A cravat bandage or a strip of cloth at least two inches wide folded with enough thicknesses to prevent cutting into skin (*never use wire or any similar materials*), and a stick about 6 inches long.

(b) *Application.*—Wrap folded cloth twice around arm a hand's breadth below the armpit or around leg a hand's breadth below the groin and tie with single knot. Place stick on knot, secure it with square knot and twist. Make certain the tourniquet stops the bleeding. Prevent stick from untwisting by tying ends of stick to the limb with bandage or handkerchief. Record the time the tourniquet was applied by writing the hour and minute on the tourniquet with a pencil.

(c) *Precautions.*—i. *Loosen tourniquet at end of 15 minutes.* If dressing over wound becomes more bloody, tighten tourniquet for another fifteen minutes. If dressing does not show new bleeding, leave tourniquet loose, but in place, ready for use if bleeding starts again. Indicate time of loosening and tightening on tourniquet.

ii. Always mark large letters "*TK*" on victim's forehead with skin pencil to indicate presence of tourniquet, so it may be loosened by those receiving victim.

iii. *Never apply a dressing over a tourniquet.*

B. *Bleeding from veins.*

1. Elevate a bleeding arm or leg unless it is fractured.

2. Apply sterile dressing over the wound and tie firmly in place. *Remember not to touch surface of gauze to be placed over wound.* If no sterile dressing is at hand, use cleanest cloth available, preferably inside surface of freshly laundered handkerchief or towel. If a fracture is present stop the bleeding in this manner and then give first aid for the fracture.

C. *Bleeding from small vessels.*—Treat as a simple wound. Apply a bandage compress so that it presses firmly on the wound.

BURNS

Burns may be extensive and serious. They may be caused by incendiary bombs or shells, by contact with live electric wires or they may occur in burning buildings.

First aid.—The first need is to reduce pain and avoid shock. If a doctor is immediately available, apply a sterile dressing over the wound without removing clothing, wrap the victim in a blanket to keep him warm and call the doctor.

If a doctor is not available, carefully cut the clothing away from the burn. Avoid tearing or pulling. Do not try to remove bits of clothing or dirt which may be stuck to the burned area. Spread tannic acid jelly on a gauze compress, cover the burn, bandage lightly, wrap the victim in blankets and transport immediately to the hospital.

Persons with burns should be treated for shock.

Ointments, salves, or greasy substances should never, under any circumstances be put on a burn. These materials must be removed before proper treatment can be given by the doctor, and because they will not dissolve in water their removal is very difficult.

Chemical burns.—

1. Use large quantities of water to dilute and wash off the chemical, followed by usual first aid for burns.

SHOCK (COLLAPSE)

Shock[1] is present to some extent in all injuries. It is a serious condition which frequently results in death when the injuries would not of themselves prove fatal. It is a depression of the nervous system and the functions of the body. There is a loss of body heat and a decrease in the amount of circulating blood. To compensate for this the heart beats faster. Severe shock may occur in the presence of conspicuous manifestations such as hemorrhage.

The first aid worker must not become so intent on the care of an injury that the victim develops severe shock because simple preventive measures were omitted. The first aid measures for the prevention of shock are so simple and commonplace that the inexperienced might see little harm in omitting them. But, simple as they are, shock treatment is vitally important for *every* case.

[1] The term shock must not be confused with apoplexy or stroke, which is spoken of as "shock" in some sections of the United States.

As the amount of blood in circulation diminishes the brain does not get enough blood. Keep the casualty lying down so that the blood will go to the heart by gravity and may be pumped to the brain. Apply blankets and hot water bottles to prevent loss of body heat. This does not consist merely of piling blankets on top of an injured person—it is important to have as many thicknesses underneath him. Warm drinks (unless the casualty is unconscious) are beneficial. Do not remove more clothes from the victim than necessary to treat his injury. Loosen clothing at the neck, chest and waist.

Shock probably causes more fatalities than any other condition. Do not underestimate its dangers.

Symptoms—Pale (especially about the face and lips),[2] *chilly, clammy sweat,* nausea, mentally confused, *weak rapid pulse,* irregular breathing. May be unconscious.

First aid.

1. Lay flat with *head low* and *feet raised.*
2. Put *blankets* and *wraps under* and *over victim.*
3. *Keep warm with hot water bottles* but do not burn.
4. Give warm and sweetened drinks, but not if the person is unconscious or injured internally.
5. Do *not* give alcoholic drinks.
6. *Get a doctor* without delay.

FRACTURES

Definitions

Fracture—a broken bone.

Simple fracture—bone broken but skin is not.

Compound fracture—bone broken and skin broken.

Splint—an appliance made of wood or metal to keep in place and protect an injured part.

Fixed traction splint—a splint which protects and prevents motion of broken bones by exerting pull from the ends of the bone.

Immobilize—to make broken bone fragments immovable by use of splints.

Displacement—bone fragments out of normal position.

Overriding—overlapping of the ends of a broken bone. This is caused by contraction of muscles and results in shortening of the limb. It may take place shortly after the fracture and may be avoided by early application of a fixed traction splint.

[2] In injured women, do not let make-up confuse you. Remove it.

Recognition of Fractures

1. *Pain* and tenderness.
2. Partial or complete *loss of use.*
3. *Deformity*—may be pronounced or very slight.
4. *Swelling* and discoloration—frequently not present for several hours.
5. Sense of *grating* with motion.
6. In compound fractures, bone may or may not protrude through skin wound.

The Care of Fractures

In making an examination to determine whether or not a fracture has occurred, *be very gentle.* Care must be taken not to move the broken fragments. Sometimes the first touch of an injured limb may give one the feeling of broken edges grating together.

If *fracture* is *suspected, handle* the case as if *a fracture were present.* Large nerves and blood vessels run close to bones. If these should be cut by the sharp edges of the broken bone, paralysis or bleeding will follow. *Pain* and *shock* will be increased *by* the *moving* of bone *fragments.*

It is important to keep persons with fractures *motionless* until the limb has been splinted. Moving a person with a fractured bone without splints may increase shock and result in death. Traction splints most effectively protect the victim from these dangers. Deaths from fractured thighs were halved in the World War after traction splints were applied on the battlefield.

"*Splint them where they lie.*" If you don't know how, get someone who does. If there is a compound fracture. *get a doctor.* If none is immediately available, expose the injury by carefully *cutting* away the clothing without moving the broken bone. Do not pull or tear away clothing. If there is bleeding it must be controlled. Apply sterile dressing, moving the injured part as little as possible while bandaging. The fracture should then be splinted.

Fracture of Spine

Broken backs and *broken necks* are so dangerous that they require special first aid measures. Improper care may result in permanent paralysis or death of a person with these injuries.

Broken neck.—The victim, if conscious, will complain of pain in the neck. Many cases will hold the head and neck stiff and motionless, but some will be completely relaxed and have no control of the head. Injury to the spine may cause paralysis. Can the injured move his hands? Try his grip (both hands).

Keep him lying in the position in which he was

found and prevent motion of the head. Do not give him water as he may move his head to drink. Cover him with blankets or wraps. Get a doctor.

If a victim with a broken neck must be moved get a door, shutter, or wide board and place it beside him with the end at least 4 inches above the top of his head. The board should be at least 15 inches wide and 5 feet or more in length.

One person kneels at the victim's head, holding the head between his two hands and steadies the head so that the head, neck, and shoulders move as a unit with the body without bending. One or more assistants grasp the victim's clothing at the hips and shoulders and carefully slide him sideward onto the board or door so that he remains face upward, arms at his sides, head, trunk, and extremities on the board. The head must not be raised or the neck bent forward or sideways. The arms may then be folded over the chest and held together with safety pins or bandage. Several straps or triangle bandages should then be placed around the victim and the board to hold him in place during transportation. A folded sweater or coat should be placed around his head to hold it in position, or socks filled with sand or earth may be used. The board is then picked up and the victim transported as though he were on a stretcher.

If a victim with a broken neck is found lying on his face a door or wide board should be placed beside him as described above, and the arm at that side brought above the head. The person kneeling at the head grasps it firmly at the sides covering the ear and the back end of the jaw with his hands. Assistants grasp the victim's clothing at the shoulders and hips and gently roll him onto the board, the man at the head steadying the head so that it is kept in line with the rest of the body. Moderate traction should be exerted by the hands holding the head. The head must not be allowed to tilt either forward or backward.

Broken back.—When the backbone is broken below the neck, the only symptom may be pain in the back. If the spinal cord is damaged or under pressure, the victim may be unable to move his feet, but can move his hands.

Any move which doubles the injured man forward may cause death or paralysis for life. He must, therefore, be kept motionless in the position in which he is found. Get a doctor. *Keep him warm. Reassure him. Do not let him move.* If necessary to move a victim found on his back, place a door or wide board beside him as described above. Raise the arm on the side toward the board so that it is straight above the victim's head. Several assistants kneel alongside the board opposite the victim and, grasping his clothing on the far side, they roll him slowly and gently towards them so that he lies face downwards on the board. If a door is used the assistants kneel on the door, leaving enough space for the victim. In making this roll the body must move as a unit. There should be no twisting or jerking. Then bend one forearm so that the head will rest on it.

If a casualty with a broken back is found lying on his belly the door or board should be placed beside him. Assistants grasp his clothing and slide him onto the board, one person guarding his face. He remains in a face-down position. Several straps or bandages should then be placed around the victim and the board to bind him firmly in place during transportation.

Victims with broken backs should, if possible, be moved only on a rigid support. A blanket may safely be used if no rigid support is available. If the victim is on his back he must be rolled onto a blanket. If the victim is found lying on his belly he must be slid onto the blanket. If the victim is found on his side or in a crumpled condition he must be carefully straightened out. With one person at the feet, a second at the head, and one in the middle, the victim is rolled onto his back in the case of a broken neck and onto his belly in the case of a broken back.

If both the neck and back are broken, handle as a broken neck.

In case of doubt, *handle a suspected fracture as if it were actually a fracture.*

ARTIFICIAL RESPIRATION

Common Causes of Arrested Breathing or Asphyxia

1. Electric shock.
2. Carbon monoxide poisoning (illuminating gas, exhaust gas, or coal gas).
3. Drowning.
4. Concussion from explosions, or from blows on the head or abdomen.
5. Suffocation or strangulation due to external obstruction of the air passages.
6. Foreign bodies in the throat or windpipe, which obstruct the air passages.

A person who has stopped breathing from any of these causes must be made to breathe at once or he will die. Do not waste time on unnecessary things but get to work immediately, using the prone pressure or mouth-to-mouth method of artificial respiration. Get the victim into fresh air, clear the mouth or throat of any obstructions, and proceed as follows:

Loosen tight clothing about injured's neck. Place injured on a flat surface in a face down position, one arm extended and the other arm bent; the head resting on the bent arm and turned sidewise. Place yourself astride, in a kneeling position, facing the injured's head.

Place your hands flat over the lower part of the back (i.e., over the lowest ribs of the chest; the little finger should rest directly over the lowest rib), one on each side, and with your arms straight, gradually throw the weight of your body forward on to the injured so as to produce firm pressure. By this means the air (and water if there be any) is forced out of the injured's lungs. Now raise your body slowly so as to remove the pressure, but keep your hands in position. Repeat this forward and backward movement every four or five seconds, i.e., from twelve to fifteen times a minute, without any pause. Every moment counts. Continue, for hours if necessary, until injured is revived or is pronounced dead by the physician. Many persons have been revived after several hours of artificial respiration. If fatigued, have another person replace you without breaking the rhythm. Several persons may alternate in doing this work. If injured must be removed, continue artificial respiration in transit.

Keep injured warm. Do not give anything by mouth until he is fully recovered. When recovered, give stimulants such as hot tea or coffee.

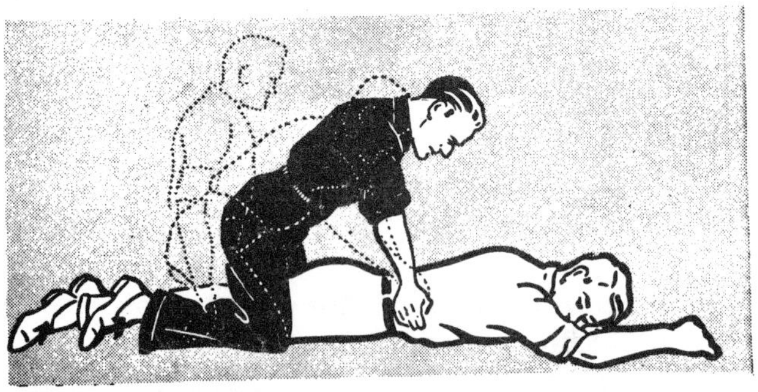

FIGURE 1

Mouth-to-Mouth (Mouth-to-Nose) Method of Artificial Respiration

If there is foreign matter visible in the mouth, wipe it out quickly with your fingers or a cloth wrapped around your fingers.

1. Tilt the head back so the chin in pointing upward (Fig. 2A). Pull or push the jaw into a jutting-out position (Fig. 2B, 2C).

These maneuvers should relieve obstruction of the airway by moving the base of the tongue away from the back of the throat.

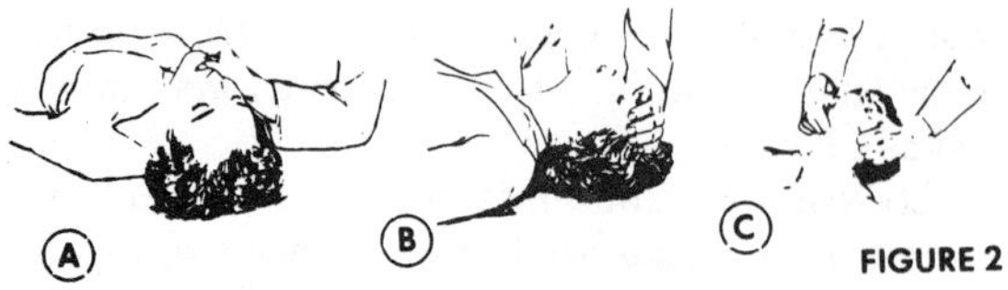

FIGURE 2

2. Open your mouth wide and place it tightly over the victim's mouth. At the same time pinch the victim's nostrils shut or close the nostrils with your cheek. Or close the victim's mouth and place your mouth over the nose. Blow into the victim's mouth or nose. (Air may be blown through the victim's teeth, even though they may be clenched.)

The first blowing efforts should determine whether or not obstruction exists.

3. Remove your mouth, turn your head to the side, and listen for the return rush of air that indicates air exchange. Repeat the blowing effort.

For an adult, blow vigorously at the rate of about 12 breaths per minute. For a child, take realtively shallow breaths appropriate for the child's size, at the rate of about 20 per minute.

4. If you are not getting air exchange, recheck the head and jaw position (Fig. 1 or Fig. 2 and Fig. 3). If you still do not get air exchange, quickly turn the victim on his side and administer several sharp blows between the shoulder blades in the hope of dislodging foreign matter.

Again sweep your fingers through the victim's mouth to remove foreign matter.

Those who do not wish to come in contact with the person may hold a cloth over the victim's mouth or nose and breathe through it. The cloth does not greatly affect the exchange of air.

Prone Pressure Method text and picture reproduced with permission of Johnson & Johnson; Mouth-to-Mouth Method, The American National Red Cross.

MISCELLANEOUS CONDITIONS

Heat Stroke (Sun Stroke)

It is not necessary that the individual be exposed to the sun's rays to develop heat stroke. Clothing which prevents the escape of heat (gasproof clothing or firemen's coats and boots), excessive humidity, fatigue, particularly in the absence of a current of air, increase the danger of heat stroke.

Symptoms.—Headache, dizziness, nausea. The victim may appear flushed or may have a bluish color about the face and lips. He may be unconscious. The body temperature is elevated, the skin is hot and dry.

First aid.—For mild cases wrap the victim in a wet sheet and expose to cold drafts of air, as from a fan. For more severe cases apply ice to the temples and the back of the neck. Place in a cool bath for 20 minutes, at the same time rubbing the limbs and trunk to stimulate circulation.

Heat Exhaustion (Prostration)

Heat exhaustion is a form of shock resulting from exposure to heat. It occurs more frequently when the humidity is high. It is a serious condition requiring prompt first aid treatment.

Symptoms.—The symptoms are those of shock: face pale, cold, clammy sweat, weak and rapid pulse, slow respiration.

Treatment.—The same as the treatment for shock. *Do not confuse this condition with heat or sun stroke.* The treatment is exactly opposite.

Heat Cramps

Persons exposed to intense heat or doing manual labor lose large amounts of salt in their perspiration. As the salt is depleted, muscular cramps may develop.

Symptoms.—Spasmodic cramps of the muscles of the abdomen and limbs.

First aid.—Prevention is more important than treatment. Men at hard work in high temperatures drink large amounts of water to replace the fluid lost in perspiration. The salt lost in the perspiration should be replaced by adding a good-sized pinch of table salt to each glass of water.

After the condition has developed, treatment consists of warm baths, rest, drinks to which salt has been added. If the cramps are severe or persist, a doctor should be called.

Frostbite

Frostbite is more likely to occur in damp and windy weather.

Symptoms.—There is tingling of the skin followed by numbness. As the part becomes numb it takes on a dead whiteness. At this stage the tissues are not actually lifeless, though they may soon become so, even in warm atmosphere. The skin may then appear reddened or purplish and it may crack. Very large blisters are ordinarily formed.

First aid.—Have the victim exercise the part if he can. Do not massage it. Immerse the affected part in cool water or apply warm (not hot) compresses. Allow water temperature to rise slowly. To obtain the best results the thawing process should be drawn out for several hours. Do not break any blisters. Apply a sterile dressing to the part and take the person to a doctor.

Carbon Monoxide Poisoning

The gas is odorless, colorless and tasteless. It may produce death even in low concentrations if breathed for some time. In high concentrations it may produce death in a few minutes. The body stores carbon monoxide. People doing manual labor breathe faster than those at rest and tend to be overcome more rapidly.

Carbon monoxide poisoning steals upon the victim in such a way that he may be overcome by the gas without warning.

Symptoms.— The symptoms are numerous, the more pronounced being headache, yawning, giddiness, ringing in the ears, weariness and a fluttering or throbbing of the heart, which is a late symptom. If the victim gets into fresh air these symptoms usually pass off, often leaving a headache. If the victim remains in the presence of carbon monoxide gas his legs collapse under him, he may stagger and sink to the ground in a semiconscious or unconscious state.

First aid.—

1. Remove the victim to fresh air as quickly as possible.
2. If breathing has stopped, is weak and intermittent, or is present only in occasional gasps, start artificial respiration at once.

If oxygen is available it should be given while artificial respiration is administered.

3. Aid circulation by rubbing the limbs, keeping the victim warm with blankets and hot water bottles.
4. Keep the victim at rest, lying down to avoid any strain on the heart.

Inhalations of oxygen for 20 minutes, when given immediately, decrease the possibility of serious after-effects. Oxygen should be given to all victims if possible.

Unconsciousness

Anyone who is unconscious is in a serious condition and should have immediate medical attention. Before the doctor arrives there are certain things which those trained in first aid should do:

A. *Bleeding?* If so, control the bleeding and dress the wound.

B. *Breathing?—"Blue unconsciousness."*—If not breathing, with a bluish or blotched face, start artificial respiration at once. Be sure there is no obstruction in the throat. Be careful of electric shock if the victim is found in contact with wires, plumbing or heating pipes or other conductors which may have become temporarily charged. Do not expose yourself to electric shock by careless handling of the victim. Be careful of carbon monoxide gas and do not become a victim yourself. Remember that persons not breathing become chilled very rapidly and must be kept warm during artificial respiration.

C. *"Red unconsciousness."*—Red face and

strong pulse. Keep victim lying down, head slightly raised, cold applications to head, give no stimulants. Prevent chilling, and transport in lying position.

D. *"White unconsciousness."*—The same as shock.

DRESSINGS AND BANDAGES

One of the most satisfactory dressings for wounds is the bandage compress. It is a piece of gauze attached to the center of a strip of bandage. The compress is to be opened without touching the inside, placed over the wound, and bound in place by the bandage tails (fig. 3).

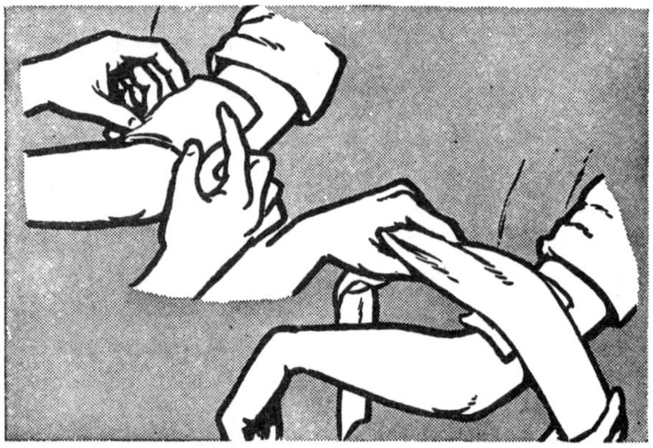

FIGURE 3

When a bandage compress is not available, use a sterile gauze pad of suitable size and thickness and bind in place with bandage or short strips of adhesive plaster. In emergency work, triangle bandages are useful for this purpose. They can be improvised from many materials. They will hold a piece of gauze in place and keep out dirt and contamination. These are intended as emergency dressings which will be replaced with more permanent dressings by the physician.

Roller bandages are excellent but are difficult to apply properly. A poorly applied roller bandage will not stay in place and will admit dirt.

THE TRIANGLE BANDAGE

The triangle bandage is very useful in first aid. It may be used to keep splints or dressings in position, as a sling to support an injured part or as a tourniquet.

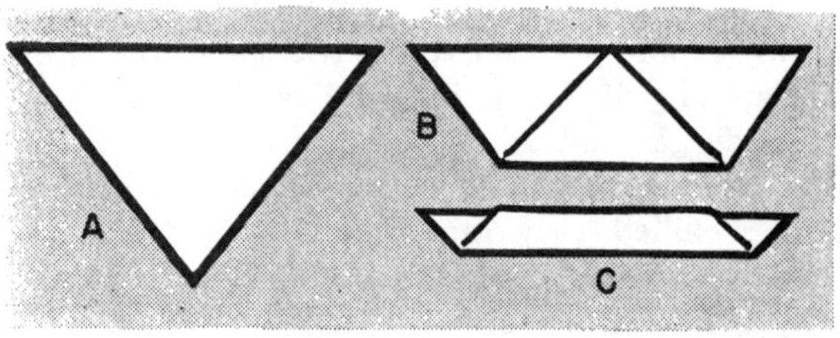

FIGURE 4

It may be used:

1. As an open triangle spread out to its full extent (fig. 4 A).

2. As a wide folded bandage (wide cravat). Carry the point (the angle opposite the longest edge) to the middle of the longest edge (B), and then fold the bandage again in the same direction (C).

3. As a narrow folded bandage (cravat). Fold the wide cravat bandage once again, long edge to long edge.

To tie a square knot.— Take one end of the bandage in each hand, pass the end in the right hand over that in the lelt and tie a single knot. Pass the end now in the left hand over that in the right and complete the knot. The ends when pulled tight will be parallel with the folds of the bandage. The rule for tying a square knot is—right over left, left over right (fig. 5).

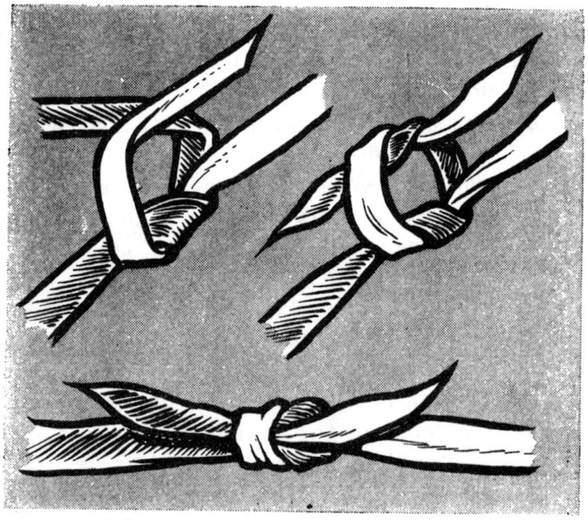

FIGURE 5

Slings

The large arm sling is used to support the forearm and hand. Spread out a triangle bandage on the front of the casualty with the point toward the injured arm. Pass the upper end around the back of the neck from the sound side so that it appears over the shoulder of the injured side. Carry the point behind the elbow of the injured arm; place the forearm across the middle of the bandage. Then carry the lower end up around the arm and tie to the upper end. Bring the point forward around the elbow and pin to the front of the sling.

Slings may be improvised (1) by pinning a coat sleeve to the front of the coat, (2) by turning up the lower edge of a coat and pinning it to the front of the coat, or (3) by passing the hand inside the coat and then buttoning it.

Bandaging Special Parts of the Body

1. *Chin and side of face* (fig. 6).—Put the center of a cravat under the chin. Pass one end over the top of the head to the temple on the

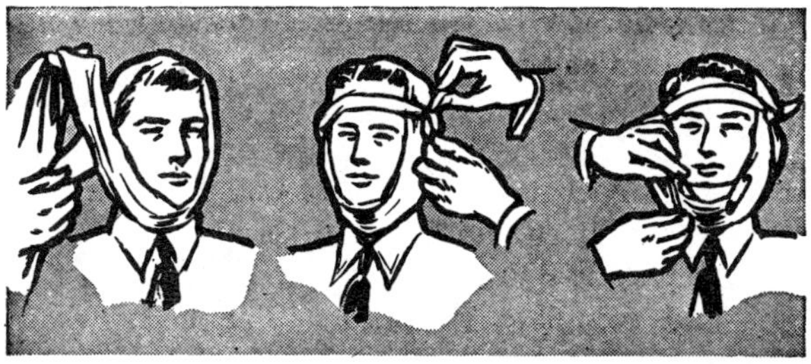

FIGURE 6

opposite side. Bring the other end to the temple, cross the bandage ends so that they go around the head in opposite directions. Tie at the side.

2. *The head* (fig. 7).—Take an unfolded triangle bandage and lay its center on top of the head so that its point is toward the back of the head and its long lower border lies along the forehead just above the eyebrows. Take a short fold in the long border and then pass the ends of the bandage around the back of the head above the ears (A). Cross the ends over the point of the bandage (B), bring the ends to the front again and tie in the middle of the forehead (C). Put your hand on the top of the head to steady the dressing and draw down the point of the bandage until the dressing is taut over the top of the head. Then turn up the point and tuck it under the bandage going around the head (D).

3. *Both eyes.*—Put the center of a wide cravat bandage over the eyes as a blindfold, carry the ends backward, cross behind the head and tie at the side. Never cover an eye affected by gas.

4. *One eye* (fig. 7E).—Lay a strip of narrow bandage about three and one-half feet long across the top of the head so that one end hangs down over the uninjured eye and the other end hangs down the back. Place the middle of a cravat over the injured eye, carry the ends obliquely around the head so as not to cover the uninjured eye and tie. Carry the loose ends of the narrow bandage strip over the top of the head and tie tightly enough to keep the cravat above the uninjured eye. If the eyeball has been injured bandage both eyes.

5. *Elbow or knee* (fig. 7F and G).—Bend the elbow or knee to a right angle and use a cravat at least 8 inches wide. Place the middle over the elbow and carry the ends around, crossing in the hollow. Carry the upper end entirely around the arm above the elbow, bringing it back to the hollow. Carry the lower end entirely around the arm below the elbow bringing it back to the hollow.

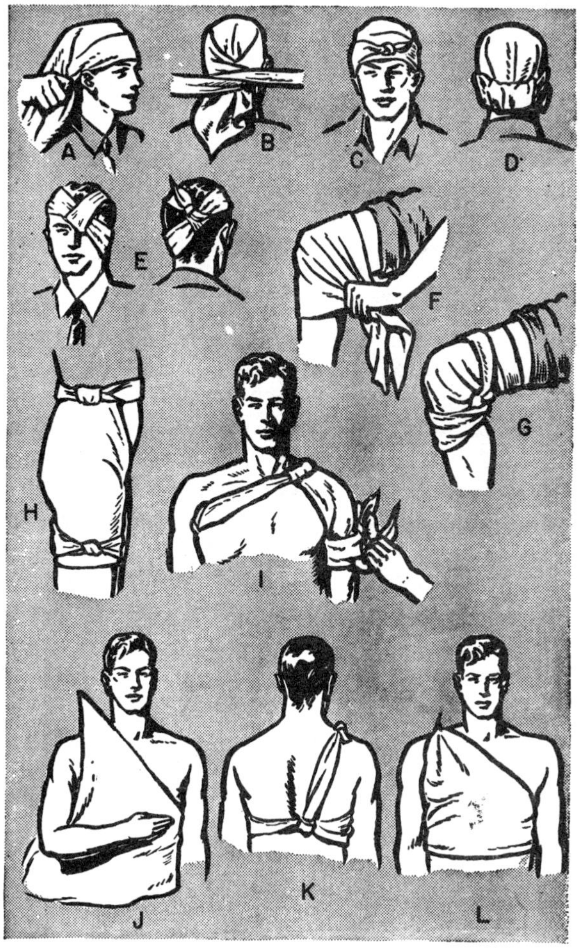

FIGURE 7

Tie snugly at the outside edge of the hollow.

The knee bandage is applied in the same manner except that the bandage is wider. In folding the bandage for the knee bring the point of an open triangle bandage to the center of the base and do not fold again.

6. *Neck.*—Put the center of a cravat bandage over the dressing, cross the ends in back, and tie over the dressing.

7. *Abdomen.*—Put the center of a wide cravat bandage over the dressing. Carry the ends around the abdomen in opposite directions and tie at the side.

8. *The hip* (fig. 7H).—Pass a cravat bandage around the waist and tie in front. Then take an unfolded triangle bandage, put the center over the hip, point upwards, with its long border folded and lying across the thigh. Pass the ends around the thigh and tie on the outer side. Draw the point upwards under the bandage around the waist, turn it down over the bandage going around the waist and tie or pin in place.

9. *Shoulder* (fig. 7I).—Lay the center of an unfolded triangle bandage on the top of the

shoulder, point toward the head, with the lower border across the middle of the upper arm. Fold the lower border, carry the ends around the arm, cross them inside and tie on the outer side. Take a cravat bandage, and carry it from the shoulder of the injured side underneath the armpit on the opposite side and tie over the shoulder on the injured side. Draw the point of the first bandage under the second bandage, fold it back on itself and tie or pin in this position. Support the arm in a sling.

10. *Chest* (fig. 7 J, K, and L).—Using an open triangle bandage, place the point over the shoulder on the injured side with the middle of the long border below the shoulder. Carry the ends around the chest and tie directly below the shoulder on the injured side. This leaves a long and a short end. Carry the long end to the bandage point and tie.

11. *The foot.*—Place the sole of the foot in the center of an unfolded bandage with the toes toward the point. Turn the point over the toes and instep. Take one of the ends in each hand close to the foot, bring them forward and cross them over the instep, covering the point. Draw the point upwards to tighten the bandage, and fold it toward the toes. Carry the bandage ends back around the ankle, cross them behind, catching the lower border of the bandage. Bring the ends forward, cross them again over the instep so as to cover the point. carry one end under the foot and tie on inner side.

12. *Lower part of the abdomen.*—Pass a cravat bandage around the waist and tie. Pass the end of a wide cravat bandage under the first at the middle of the back, fold it over and secure it with a safety pin. Bring the other end forward

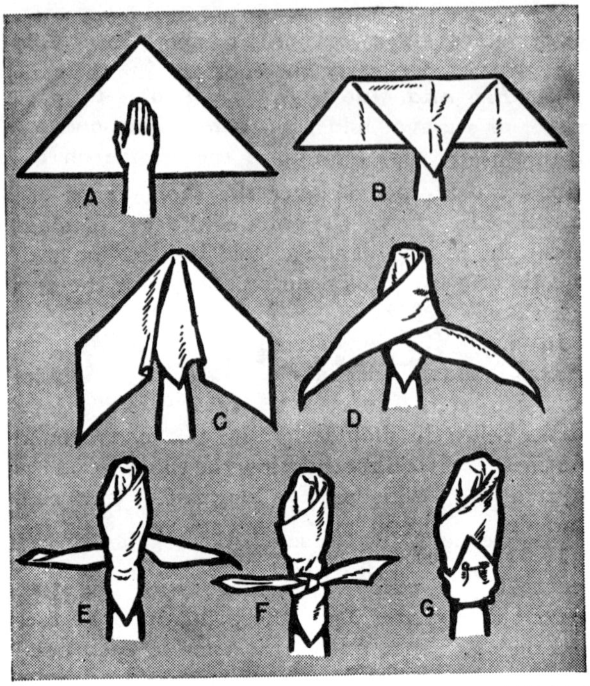

FIGURE 8

between the thighs and up to the waist bandage in the front. Pass it under the waist bandage and pin or tie.

13. *The hand* (fig. 8).—Place the hand, palm down, in the center of an unfolded triangle bandage with the fingers toward the point of the bandage (A). Bring the point over the back of the hand to the wrist (B), and pass the bandage ends around it, crossing the ends over the point (C and D). Circle the wrist and tie (E and F). Then turn the point toward the fingers and pin to the bandage (G).

First Aid Questions

The following questions are based on current first aid procedures. Some of them have appeared in actual examinations. All of them are a good indication of what kind of question to expect in future first aid questions.

DIRECTIONS for answering questions. For each question, decide which is the best answer of the choices given. Note the capital letter preceding the best answer. On machine scored examinations you will be given an answer sheet and told to blacken the proper space on that answer sheet. Near the end of this book we have provided sixteen facsimiles of such answer sheets. Tear one out, and mark your answers on it, just as you would do on an actual exam. In most machine scored examinations, competitors are instructed to "place no marks whatever on the test booklet." In other examinations, competitors are instructed to mark the answers in the booklet, but they should be careful that no other marks interfere with the legibility of the answers. It is always best not to mark the booklet unless you are sure that it is permitted. It is most important that you learn to mark the answer sheet clearly.

1. The best procedure in case of "red unconsciousness" is to keep victim lying down and
   (A) to lower the head
   (B) administer alcohol
   (C) raise the head slightly
   (D) shake the patient vigorously.

2. The most accurate of the following statements is:
   (A) when a vein is cut blood spurts forth
   (B) bleeding from small veins will not stop itself
   (C) blood going away from the heart is carried by arteries
   (D) blood from an artery flows steadily without spurting.

3. As a dressing directly over a wound, the best material to use is
   (A) a handkerchief
   (B) adhesive tape
   (C) cotton gauze
   (D) absorbent cotton.

4. If a tourniquet is kept tightened too long, which of the following may result?
   (A) Locomotor Ataxia
   (B) Delirium Tremens
   (C) Tabes
   (D) Gangrene.

5. In giving first aid treatment to wounds one should
   (A) apply antiseptic
   (B) wash them with soap and water
   (C) cover them with a dressing
   (D) encourage bleeding.

6. In heat exhaustion
   (A) cold may be applied externally to the patient
   (B) external heat may be used on the patient
   (C) the pulse of the patient is rapid and slow
   (D) place the head of the patient in an elevated position.

7. When treating an unconscious person, it must be remembered that he be given nothing to drink for it may
   (A) cause increased heart beat
   (B) cause swelling of the arteries
   (C) strangle the patient
   (D) cause death.

8. When using the mouth-to-mouth method of artificial respiration, it is important firstly to clear the mouth and throat of any visible obstructions, and secondly to:
   (A) Splash cold water on the patient's face.
   (B) Wrap the patient in a blanket
   (C) Start blowing rhythmically into the patient's mouth
   (D) Tilt the head far back

9. When applying the prone-pressure method of artificial respiration, it is best to have the pressure applied — per minute
   (A) 18-20 times (B) 4 times
   (C) 12-15 times (D) 10 times

10. A bandage should not be made too tight for it may
    (A) cut off the return flow of the veinous blood and cause a swelling
    (B) destroy the tissues around the wound
    (C) increase the blood circulation
    (D) cause immediate unconsciousness.

11. The best treatment for shock condition in the majority of first aid cases is to
    (A) give the patient an alcoholic stimulant
    (B) walk the patient
    (C) slap the patient's face
    (D) thoroughly wrap patient to prevent loss of body heat.

12. If a pressure point for the head is required, it is best to place the finger
    (A) just in front of the ear, against the skull
    (B) in the center of the forehead
    (C) at the base of skull in back of the head
    (D) against the nose.

13. Unless the wound requires other measures, it is advisable that the tips of the fingers and toes should
    (A) remain partially covered with bandages
    (B) not be covered
    (C) be completely covered
    (D) be placed in hot water.

14. When administering first aid it is most important to remember that
    (A) the patient should remain seated
    (B) the patient should walk back and forth
    (C) the patient should lie down and remain still
    (D) nothing should be done until a physician arrives.

15. There is practically no germ growth in a wound during the first
    (A) 12 hours (B) 14 hours
    (C) 15 hours (D) 6 hours.

16. It is best when rubbing a strained part to
    (A) rub from left to right
    (B) rub downward only
    (C) use the upward motion
    (D) rotate the movement.

17. In the case of burns, tannic acid jelly should be
    (A) applied to the skin
    (B) mixed with water
    (C) spread on the gauze
    (D) heated.

18. The main object when treating for poison is
    (A) dilute and wash out
    (B) to take a sample of the blood
    (C) to examine the saliva
    (D) to examine the heart-beat.

19. During an hysterical attack, it is recommended that
    (A) the patient be forced to walk
    (B) the patient be left alone
    (C) the patient be held down by feet and head
    (D) someone should knock out the patient.

20. Assume that you are called to render first aid to a person who is unconscious. Your first glance indicates that the victim's face is red. You would immediately start treatment for
    (A) heat exhaustion
    (B) sun stroke
    (C) gas asphyxiation
    (D) red unconsciousness.

21. Of the following statements concerning the treatment of wounds with severe bleeding, the LEAST accurate is
    (A) the chief duty of the first aider is to stop the bleeding at once
    (B) application of digital pressure in most severe venous bleeding may well be recommended
    (C) in all serious bleeding the first aider should think first of pressure
    (D) stimulants should be given so that the patient will not go into shock.

22. Of the following statements concerning the use of tourniquets, the LEAST accurate is
    (A) tourniquets are most frequently used in cases of severe venous bleeding
    (B) it is preferable to use a pad over the artery with a tourniquet
    (C) a tourniquet is correctly applied in only two places
    (D) a tourniquet should be loosened every fifteen or twenty minutes.

23. Assume that you are about to apply artificial respiration to a person. The LEAST useful of the following items is
    (A) a blanket
    (B) an inhalator
    (C) a hot water bottle
    (D) a radiant heater.

24. Assume that you are called on to render first aid to a man injured in an accident. You find

he is bleeding profusely in spurts, has a rash indicating a food poisoning, has a broken leg and is not breathing. The first thing for which you should treat him is
(A) profuse bleeding
(B) not breathing
(C) the broken leg
(D) food poisoning.

25. Assume that it is necessary for you to apply a tourniquet in order to stop serious bleeding. The one of the following most properly used for this purpose is
(A) thin cord (B) thick rope
(C) a necktie (D) wire.

26. Suppose that an elderly man has met with an accident and is lying on the floor awaiting the arrival of a doctor. Of the following, the best action to take in order to prevent shock is to
(A) raise him in a sitting position
(B) apply a wet cloth to his head
(C) apply artificial respiration
(D) cover him with a coat.

27. Assume that a fellow worker suddenly turns pale and his breathing becomes rapid and shallow. He is apparently suffering from heat exhaustion. Of the following, the LEAST desirable action for you to take under the circumstances is to
(A) apply cold cloths to his head
(B) place him in a reclining position
(C) give him a stimulant
(D) have him sip salt water.

28. Assume that a fellow worker is in contact with an electrically charged wire. Of the following, the best reason for not grasping the victim's clothing with your bare hands in order to pull him off the wire is that
(A) his clothing may be damp with perspiration
(B) his clothing may be 100% wool
(C) you may be standing on a dry surface
(D) you may be wearing rubber-soled shoes.

29. "Deep wounds caused by narrow, pointed instruments are particularly dangerous." Of the following, the best justification for this statement is that
(A) germs lodged in a deep wound cannot be easily reached and destroyed by an antiseptic
(B) deep wounds usually cause free bleeding
(C) narrow, pointed instruments are especially likely to sever muscles
(D) most germs cannot thrive without the presence of oxygen.

30. The reason that the iodine in a first aid kit should be kept tightly corked is that evaporation may
(A) cause the solution to lose its germicidal powers
(B) change the iodine into a non-antiseptic chemical
(C) increase the concentration of the solution
(D) thicken the solution so that it will flow easily.

31. Of the following, the most accurate statement concerning pressure points in the control of arterial bleeding is that
(A) the heart should be between the pressure point and the wound
(B) the wound should be between the pressure point and the heart
(C) pressure should be applied to a point as distant from the heart as possible
(D) a pressure point is usually a spot where the artery crosses a bone.

32. Of the following, the best reason for using gauze instead of absorbant cotton directly over a wound is that absorbent cotton
(A) clots the blood
(B) is not sufficiently sterile
(C) is porous and allows circulation of air
(D) sticks to the wound and is difficult to remove.

33. "Most serious cases of profuse bleeding involve veins rather than arteries. Of the following, the best justification for this statement is that
(A) there are a larger number of arteries than veins
(B) veins are not as well protected as arteries
(C) blood from arteries comes in spurts
(D) arteries carry blood away from the heart.

34. Of the following, the one which is NOT a symptom of carbon monoxide poisoning is
(A) headache
(B) nosebleed
(C) yawning
(D) throbbing of heart.

35. An important point that should be kept in mind about roller bandages is that
(A) they provide excellent protection
(B) they are inferior to the triangle bandage
(C) they cannot be used for a majority of wounds
(D) they are difficult to apply properly.

36. If the victim complains of a pain in the back and is unable to move his hands, he possibly suffers from
(A) apoplexy
(B) a broken neck
(C) a fractured pelvis
(D) a broken back.

37. When employing a tourniquet, a thing which must never be done is to
(A) loosen the tourniquet
(B) apply a dressing over the tourniquet
(C) mark the victim indicating presence of tourniquet
(D) make certain that the tourniquet stops the bleeding.

38. A man is found unconscious beside some fallen masonry. Blood stained material is draining from his ear. The first aider should
(A) apply a compress and bandage over the affected ear
(B) clean the ear and plug with cotton
(C) simply apply a sterile dressing over the ear
(D) apply treatment at pressure point to stop discharge.

39. An exploding boiler has severely scalded a man's chest. He is in great pain. Onlookers are offering advice. The first thing that should be done is to
(A) heed the soundest advice from the onlookers
(B) cut away the clothing and apply a compress spread with tannic acid jelly
(C) cut away the clothing and apply a cooling salve
(D) pull off the clothing as quickly as possible and apply ointment.

40. One thing that quickly identifies a fragment wound is
(A) profuse bleeding
(B) a large opening in the flesh
(C) an irregular pulse
(D) blackened edges of the wound.

41. In cases involving broken necks, it is important to keep the victims from moving their heads and to
(A) cover them with blankets
(B) give them something hot and sweet to drink
(C) apply cold cloths to their foreheads
(D) stimulate the neck muscles by massage.

42. Prostration should be treated as if it were
(A) heat stroke
(B) nausea
(C) shock
(D) fainting.

43. Successful treatment of a chemical burn can best be accomplished by
(A) diluting and washing off the chemical with large quantities of water
(B) dabbing the burn with sterile cotton soaked in alcohol
(C) applying a salve
(D) covering the burns with dry gauze.

44. When stimulants are advisable, they should be given to a patient
(A) as the first step in administering first aid
(B) when the bleeding has stopped
(C) only when it is cold
(D) before the bleeding has stopped.

45. The chief reason to control all bleeding immediately is
(A) to check the loss of blood
(B) to ease the patient psychologically by concealing blood
(C) to avoid the development of shock and infection
(D) to make the treatment of other injuries easier.

46. Victims with internal injuries should never be
(A) kept warm
(B) transported
(C) elevated
(D) given anything to drink.

47. A man has been removed from fallen debris. His chest was severely crushed. He is bleeding slightly from the mouth, and appeals for water and a cigarette. The first aider should
(A) treat for shock and keep the man warm
(B) give the man what he asks for before proceeding with treatment
(C) refuse the cigarette, but give him water
(D) refuse both cigarette and water, and place him on a stretcher, lying down.

48. Assume that a victim approaches you in a dazed condition, but does not complain of injury. There are no obvious injuries to contradict him. You should
(A) examine him for bodily injuries
(B) thoroughly examine his head first
(C) check his respiration
(D) tell him to rest until the dazed condition passes.

49. If a casualty's wound bleeds in a steady flow, you would assume the injury has occurred to
(A) an artery (B) small vessels
(C) the veins (D) a joint.

50. The rule for tying a square knot is
(A) left over right, right under left
(B) right under left, left under right
(C) left under right, right over left
(D) right over left, left over right.

51. To bandage an injury to the hand, you would use
(A) roller bandage (B) splint
(C) triangle bandage (D) sling.

52. To immobilize a fractured limb, you would use
(A) fixed traction splint
(B) improvised sling
(C) splint
(D) compress.

53. Hot, dry skin accompanied by dizziness and nausea are sure signs of
(A) shock (B) prostration
(C) strangulation (D) sun stroke.

54. To minimize the after-effects of carbon monoxide poisoning, the patient should be given
(A) large amount of fresh air
(B) inhalations of oxygen
(C) a strong stimulant
(D) barbiturates.

55. If a victim of frostbite is unable to exercise the affected part, you should
(A) thaw it slowly in water
(B) massage it
(C) apply heat with blankets
(D) rub with oil.

56. When body salt is rapidly depleted, the result may be
(A) heat stroke (B) heat exhaustion
(C) heat cramps (D) spasms.

57. If a person suffers from a stroke (apoplexy), you should
(A) place him on the back with head and shoulders slightly elevated
(B) massage him vigorously
(C) place him on the back with head lower than rest of body
(D) apply artificial respiration.

58. A responsible first aid worker will always remember that
(A) his training permits him to employ the treatment he sees fit
(B) his duty is to administer full treatment under adverse circumstances
(C) he is not a doctor
(D) he should not reach conclusions too hastily.

59. In applying first aid to injuries of the face, you should always make sure that
(A) you do not mar the victim's natural features
(B) the tongue has not fallen to the back of the throat
(C) you do not apply too many dressings
(D) the victim is not aware of the extent of his injuries.

60. To arrest bleeding from the shoulder or armpit, you should, in addition to applying pressure at side of neck behind collar bone, tilt the head
(A) away from the injured side
(B) sideways
(C) back as far as possible
(D) toward the injured side.

61. The best *immediate* first-aid if a chemical solution splashes into the eyes is to
(A) protect the eyes from light by bandaging
(B) rub the eyes dry with a towel
(C) cause tears to flow by staring at a bright light
(D) flush the eyes with large quantities of clean water. (0901)

62. An inhalator is used to:
(A) prepare one for an oxygen tent
(B) supplant artificial respiration
(C) force air into the lungs
(D) supplement artificial respiration. (593)

63. What are considered the four important things to do in first aid in the order of their importance?
(A) artificial respiration, treatment for shock, stoppage of severe bleeding, proper transportation
(B) artificial respiration, stoppage of severe bleeding, treatment for shock, proper transportation
(C) stoppage of severe bleeding, artificial respiration, treatment for shock, proper transportation
(D) stoppage of severe bleeding, treatment for shock, artificial respiration, proper transportation. (583)

64. "The eyes appear vacant and lack luster; the pupils are dilated; breathing is shallow and irregular; the skin is pale, cold and moist; and the pulse is weak." This best describes symptoms of:
(A) sunstroke
(C) coronary thrombosis
(B) high blood pressure
(D) shock (1022)

65. The most commonly used group of bandages in first aid are:
(A) the triangular, roller, and pleated 4 tail
(B) the square, horizonatal, and triangular
(C) pleated 4 tail, bulk, roller
(D) roller, round. (592)

66. When administering first aid for the accidental swallowing of poison, water is given chiefly to
(A) increase energy
(B) quiet the nerves
(C) weaken the poison
(D) prevent choking
(E) prevent vomiting.

67. Heat and exhaustion and sunstroke are alike in that in both cases the person affected
(A) has hot dry skin and a red face
(B) should lie with head high
(C) should be given stimulants
(D) has a very high temperature
(E) has been exposed to heat. (7161)

68. A man's clothes begin to burn rather strongly. The best thing for this man to do, if possible, is to
(A) wrap himself in a rug of wool
(B) run to a doctor
(C) apply oil to his body
(D) shout in order to obtain assistance
(E) wrap himself in a rug of cotton. (2001)

69. The first operation in starting an arm sling is usually at the
(A) shoulder of the injured side
(B) shoulder of the uninjured side
(C) chest
(D) elbow of the injured arm
(E) neck (586)

70. A compound fracture is one in which
(A) broken bones protrude through the skin
(B) bones are broken and shattered
(C) a large bone and its adjoining smaller bones are broken
(D) two or more bones are broken. (1611)

71. Which one of the following usually would be the *worst* type of dressing to use when administering first aid for an open second degree burn
(A) sterile absorbent cotton
(B) a clean cloth napkin
(C) a clean handkerchief
(D) sterile gauze
(E) a strip torn from a clean shirt. (1028)

72. In administering first aid to a patient who is unconscious, it is ordinarily most important to first:
(A) loosen the patient's clothing and rub his limbs vigorously
(B) determine, if possible, the cause of the patient's unconsciousness from a check of the patient and his surroundings
(C) administer artificial respiration
(D) administer an antidote as a precaution against possible poisoning. (1022)

73. In first aid, splints would be used for
(A) an infection
(B) a bruise
(C) an open cut
(D) a broken bone. (5761)

Key Answers: First Aid

1. C	20. D	39. B	58. C
2. C	21. D	40. D	59. B
3. C	22. A	41. A	60. D
4. D	23. B	42. C	61. D
5. C	24. A	43. A	62. D
6. B	25. C	44. B	63. C
7. C	26. D	45. C	64. D
8. D	27. A	46. D	65. A
9. C	28. A	47. A	66. C
10. A	29. A	48. B	67. E
11. D	30. C	49. C	68. A
12. A	31. D	50. D	69. B
13. B	32. D	51. C	70. A
14. C	33. B	52. A	71. A
15. D	34. B	53. D	72. B
16. C	35. D	54. B	73. D
17. C	36. D	55. A	
18. A	37. B	56. C	
19. B	38. C	57. A	

NUMERICAL RELATIONS

"Hark how the numbers softly clear, gently steal upon the ear . . . adding to golden numbers, golden numbers."

Solutions To Basic Problems

Ten "basic" types of problems are explained and solved in this section. They are followed by previous exam questions which you should be able to solve if you are adequately prepared for the mathematical part of your exam. Each of the ten "basic" problem types are solved in step-by-step fashion. Most of the problems you will face on an actual exam are either like one of these ten types, or a variation of one, since the principles they apply encompass a vast number and variety of problems. Study these example problems which have been solved for you, and then go to the previous exam problems. Your score on these latter problems should be at least 75%.

Profit and Loss

1. Hammers are bought for \$18.00 a dozen. In order to gain 40%, what must the selling price per hammer be?

(A) \$2.10 (B) \$2.00
(C) \$2.50 (D) \$3.00

SOLUTION: To find the selling price we must multiply the cost by the rate of profit or loss.

In this case the cost is \$18.00 divided by 12; \$18.00 being the cost of an entire dozen. Since there is a profit of 40% we must multiply the cost by 1.40 or 140%. (If we sold something at 100% of its cost, we should be getting what we paid for it.)

$$\frac{18}{12} \times 1.40 = \begin{array}{r} 18 \\ \times\ 1.40 \\ \hline 720 \\ 18 \\ \hline 25.20 \end{array}$$

Answer $12\,\overline{)\,25.20}$ = 2.10

To find the rate of profit or loss, we first find the actual profit or loss and then find what percent of the COST this is.

2. Hammers are bought for \$30.00 a dozen and sold at \$3.50 each. The rate of profit on the transaction is:

(A) 30% (B) 40%
(C) 50% (D) 45%

SOLUTION: Multiplying \$3.50 by 12 to find the cost of a dozen hammers:

$$\$3.50 \times 12 = \$42.00$$

Subtracting the cost from the selling price to find the actual profit:

$$\begin{array}{r} \$42.00 \\ -\ 30.00 \\ \hline \$12.00 \end{array}$$

Finding what percent of the cost the profit is involves converting a fraction into a percent.

We multiply the fraction by 100 and perform the indicated divisions:

$$\frac{\$12}{\$30} \times 100 = \qquad \textbf{Answer} \quad 30\overline{)1200} = 40\%$$

Addition of Fractions

3. If we add 8-1/5, 45-5/8, 2-17/20, 14-1/2, and 1-21/40 the answer will be
   (A) 70-8/10 (B) 72-7/10
   (C) 72-1/5 (D) 70-7/10.

SOLUTION: In adding mixed numbers like these, we perform three additions: The addition of the whole numbers, the addition of the fractions, and combination of the added whole numbers and fractions. Adding the whole numbers presents no difficulty. Our sum is 70.

To add the fractions we must first find the least common denominator. In this case it is 40.

Then for each separate fraction we divide the denominator into the common denominator and multiply the resulting quotient by the numerator.

We add all these products and divide by the common denominator. Here are the actual calculations:

	40
8-1/5	8
45-5/8	25
2-17/20	34
14-1/2	20
1-21/40	21

$$\frac{108}{40} = 2\frac{28}{40} = 2\frac{7}{10}$$

$$70 + 2\frac{7}{10} = 72\frac{7}{10} \quad \textbf{Answer}$$

Interest

4. \$1,850 is invested for 50 days at a rate of 5%. The interest return is
   (A) \$12.00 (B) \$10.00
   (C) \$12.67 (D) \$13.00.

SOLUTION: While there are many short cuts used by banks and commercial houses in computing interest, the best plan for the candidate is to understand thoroughly all the steps involved in this computation and to use them all intelligently.

If we multiply the principal by the rate of interest, and the length of time the money draws interest, we have the amount of interest due.

If the money were to bear interest for a year we would only have to multiply \$1,850 by 5% (5/100) in this example. However, the money only bears interest for 50 days or 50/365 of a year. The rest is done by simple cancellation.

$$\frac{\$1850 \times 5 \times 50}{100 \times 365} = \frac{925}{73} = \$12.67 \quad \textbf{Answer}$$

Expressed as a formula, interest may be computed thus: $P \times R \times T = I$. If we are given interest, principal and time, and asked to find the Rate, the operation may be expressed thus:

$$R = \frac{I}{P \times T}$$

And if we are given R, T, and I, and asked to find the Principal, this is the formula:

$$P = \frac{I}{R \times T}$$

5. What amount of money yields $40.00 per month if invested at an annual rate of 5%
(A) $9,000 (B) $9,500
(C) $9,600 (D) $9,400.

SOLUTION: To find the principal we must divide interest by rate by time.

If we multiply $40.00 per month by twelve we find the interest yield for a year. $40 × 12 = $480.00. The Time factor in this problem is now one year.

For the rest we have only to follow out our formula:

$$P = \frac{I}{R \times T} = P = \frac{\$480}{\frac{5}{100} \times 1}$$

DIVISION OF FRACTIONS: At this point an interesting difficulty presents itself: The division of fractions. To divide $80 by 5/100 we have simply to invert the fraction and multiply thus:

$$\$480 \div \frac{5}{100} = \$\overset{96}{\not{4}\not{8}\not{0}} \times \frac{100}{\underset{1}{\not{5}}} = \$9{,}600 \quad \textbf{Answer}$$

6. A woman invested $4,000 in a speculative venture for 9 months. A second woman invested $6,000 in the same business for 6 months. The net gain was $720.00. What was the second woman's return on her investment if all the profits were divided between the two women?
(A) $360 (B) $700
(C) $400 (D) $350.

SOLUTION: So far as regards dividends, the investment of $6,000 for 6 months is the same as the investment of $36,000 for 1 month. The same statement can be made regarding $4,000 for 9 months.

First Woman — $4,000 for 9 months = $36,000 for 1 month.

Second Woman— $6,000 for 6 months = $36,000 for 1 month.

Both $72,000 for 1 month.

It is a coincidence that the shares of the two women in this example are the same. However, the procedure here is exactly the same as though they had different shares.

We find what part the second woman's share bears to the total. We then take this proportion of the total income and our result is the second woman's share.

$$\frac{\overset{1}{\not{3}\not{6},\not{0}\not{0}\not{0}}}{\underset{2}{\not{7}\not{2},\not{0}\not{0}\not{0}}} \times \overset{360}{\not{7}\not{2}\not{0}} = \$360 \quad \textbf{Answer}$$

7. The rate of interest on a principal of $10,000 that will yield $80.00 in 65 days is
(A) 4% (B) 5.5%
(C) 4.49% (D) 6%.

SOLUTION: The formula here is

$$R = \frac{I}{P \times T}$$

Substituting, we have:

$$R = \frac{\$80}{10{,}000 \times \frac{65}{365}} = \frac{\$80}{\frac{650{,}000}{365}} =$$

$$\$80 \times \frac{365}{650{,}000} = \frac{29{,}200}{650{,}000}$$

CONVERTING A FRACTION INTO A PERCENT: This is a simple operation if the proper steps be known and taken. We must convert the fraction $\frac{29{,}200}{650{,}000}$ into a percent so that we may properly express the rate of interest.

To change a fraction into a percent we must multiply the fraction by 100 and then carry through the indicated division.

$$\frac{29{,}200}{650{,}000} \times 100 = \frac{2{,}920{,}000}{650{,}000} =$$

$$65\not{0},\not{0}\not{0}\not{0}\,\overline{)\,2{,}92\not{0},\not{0}\not{0}\not{0}}\quad 4.49\% \quad \textbf{Answer}$$

Assessment

8. If a piece of property is assessed at $45,700 and the tax rate on real property is $2.40 per $1,000, the amount of tax that must be paid on this property is

(A) $110 (B) $112
(C) $109.68 (D) $109.

SOLUTION: Since the tax rate is $2.40 per $1,000, we must determine how many thousands of dollars are involved. To do this, we divide $45,700 by $1,000. And the result is 45.7.

When we multiply 45.7 by $2.40, we learn the amount of the tax—

$109.68 **Answer**

9. $60,000 worth of land is assessed at 120% of its value. If the tax rate is $2.56 per 1,000 the amount of tax to be paid is

(A) $190 (B) $195
(C) $184.32 (D) $180.

SOLUTION: To find how much the land has been assessed:

$$60{,}000 \times \frac{12\not{0}}{10\not{0}} = \frac{720{,}00\not{0}}{1\not{0}} = \$72{,}000$$

If tax is $2.56 per $1,000, multiply:

```
  2.56
 × 72
  512
 1792
$184.32
```

Answer

Cubic Volume

10. A bin measures 14 feet by 9 feet by 7½ feet. Allowing 4/5 bushel of grain per cubic foot, how many bushels will the bin hold?

SOLUTION: Length × Width × Height = Cubic Area.

$$14 \times 9 \times 7\tfrac{1}{2} = \overset{7}{\not{14}} \times 9 \times \frac{15}{\not{2}} = 945 \text{ cubic ft.}$$

Since each cubic foot of space holds 4/5 bushel of grain:

$$\overset{189}{\not{945}} \times \frac{4}{\not{5}} = 756 \text{ Bushels.}$$ **Answer**

Literal Problems

11. If L explosions occur during a given month and result in Q dollars of loss, the average loss per explosion in dollars is:

(A) L × Q (B) Q/L
(C) L/A (D) 12K/2P
(E) none.

SOLUTION: This is a simple problem in determining an average. The presence of letters rather than numbers makes it slightly more difficult by imposing upon us the burden of using fundamental principles rather than habitual modes of action.

The average loss per explosion is the total loss divided by the number of explosions, or the average loss per explosion equals

$$\frac{\text{Total amount of loss}}{\text{Number of explosions}}$$

Since the total loss in a given month is Q and the number of explosions is L we may say that the average loss per explosion is $\frac{Q}{L}$ **Answer**

12. If there is a total of J garbage trucks in operation in New York City, covering a total street mileage of N miles at an average speed of F miles per hour, we can find the average street mileage per truck from the above data, without considering

(A) the number of cars
(B) the total street mileage
(C) the average speed
(D) any of these values
(E) any further data besides the above.

SOLUTION: The average street mileage per truck is the total street mileage divided by the total number of trucks, that is, the average street mileage per truck $= \frac{\text{Total street mileage}}{\text{Total No. of trucks}}$ (if we had 20 trucks covering a total street mileage of 300 miles then the average mileage covered by each truck is 15 miles or

$$\frac{300}{20} = 15 \text{ miles.)}$$

From this it is clear that the average speed of the trucks does not come into the consideration of the average mileage per truck and therefor answer(C)is correct.

13. During 1964, T families took out insurance policies, representing an increase of M families over the number taking them in 1962. In 1963, however, the number taking out insurance was P less than in 1962. If there were R insurance agents in each of these 3 years, the average number of policies written per insurance agent in 1963 was:

(A) $\frac{T - M}{P \quad R}$ (B) $\frac{T - M - P}{R}$
(C) $\frac{M + T - R}{R}$ (D) $\frac{T + M + P}{R}$

SOLUTION: We must first determine how many people took out insurance in 1963 and get this quantity in terms of T, M, and P.

in 1964—T families took out insurance.

in 1962—T − M families took out insurance (since 1964 is an increase of M over 1962.)

in 1963—(no. in 1962) − P (since it was P less than 1962) = T − M − P − Total number of Policies in 1937.

Now the average number of policies per insurance agent:

$$\frac{\text{Total number of policies in 1963}}{\text{Total number of insurance agents in 1963}} =$$

Answer $\frac{T - M - P}{R}$

14. Clerk A sorts B letters per hour, clerk C sorts D letters per hour. The D letters which clerk C sorts exceed those which clerk A sorts by 10 letters per hour. Measured in number sorted per 8-hour day, clerk C exceeds A by:

(A) $D - B \times 10$ (B) $(D - B) \times 8$
(C) $D + C - A + B$ (D) $C + D - A + B$

SOLUTION: The D letters sorted per hour by clerk C exceeds (is greater than) the B letters sorted per hour by clerk A, by an amount of 10 letters per hour, or D is 10 more than B. In symbols: $D = B + 10$.

In 8 hours, clerk C will have sorted 8 D letters while clerk A will have sorted 8 B letters and since the difference in one hour is 10 letters, in 8 hours, the difference will be 8×10. $8D = 8B + 80$ or bringing 8 B to the other side: $8D - 8B = 80$ or factoring out the 8 on the left.

We have $8(D - B) = 80$ which is the amount of letters by which clerk C's output exceeds clerk A's output and hence answer (B) above is correct.

15. The annual salary of a machinist is R dollars more than that of his assistant. His assistant earns V dollars annually. The amount in monthly salary, by which the machinist exceeds his assistant is given by:

(A) $\frac{V - R}{13}$ (B) $\frac{RV}{12}$
(C) $R - V$ (D) $12V - R$
(E) $\frac{R}{12}$

SOLUTION: The annual salary of the machinist is V + R dollars. The annual salary of his assistant is V dollars. The monthly salary of the machinist is $\frac{V}{12} + \frac{R}{12}$ dollars. (Since in a year the machinist receives 12 times as much as he receives in a month, we divide the yearly salary by 12 to find the amount earned in one month.) Similarly, the monthly salary of his assistants is $\frac{V}{12}$ dollars. Therefore the machinist's monthly salary exceeds his assistant's salary, monthly, by $\frac{R}{12}$ dollars. **Answer (E) is correct.**

16. A family of 5 has two employed members earning L dollars a month. The family receives a total semi-monthly relief allowance of M dollars. If the rent allowance is N dollars, and the amount spent for food is twice that for rent, the amount spent monthly for all items other than food and rent is:

(A) L + 2 M − 3N (B) N + L + M

(C) L + M − 2N

SOLUTION: The amount spent monthly for all items other than food and rent is the total income for one month minus the total expenditure for food and rent.

Total income = L + 2M (since M is a semi-monthly allowance, the monthly allowance is 2M or M multiplied by 2.)

Total exp. for food and rent = N (for rent) + 2N (food)—since the amount spent for other items = L + 2M − N − 2N = L + 2M − 3N. **Answer**

17. If psychological studies of college students show K per cent to be emotionally unstable, the number of college students not emotionally unstable per one hundred college students is: (A) 100 minus K (B) 100 times (K minus) (C) K minus 1

SOLUTION: Since K percent = $\frac{K}{100}$ in 100 students, K% of 100 are emotionally unstable then $\frac{K}{100} \times 100$ = K students are unstable. Therefore the remaining students are emotionally stable and they number 100 − K.

Rate, Time, and Distance Problems

In all these problems the formula to be followed is very simple:
Rate (speed) X Time = Distance.

If you are given the RATE and DISTANCE and are asked to find time then you simply make the obvious modification in the formula:

$$\text{Time} = \frac{\text{Distance}}{\text{Rate}}$$

To find rate given distance and time:

$$\frac{\text{Distance}}{\text{Time}} = \text{Rate}$$

There are many complications that can be introduced but if these fundamental ideas can be kept clearly in view few difficulties will be encountered.

18. Two hikers start walking from the city line at different times. The second hiker whose speed is 4 miles per hour starts 2 hours after the first hiker whose speed is 3 miles per hour. Determine the amount of time and distance that will be consumed before the second hiker catches up with the first.

SOLUTION: Since the first man has a 2 hour headstart and is walking at the rate of 3 miles per hour he is 6 miles from the city line when the second hiker starts.

Rate × Time = Distance.

Subtracting 3 miles per hour from 4 miles per hour gives us 1 mile per hour or the difference in the rates of speed of the two men. In other words, the second hiker gains one mile on the first hiker in every hour.

Since there is a 6 mile difference to cut down and it is cut down one mile every hour, it is clear that the second hiker will need 6 hours to overtake his companion.

In this time he will have traveled $4 \times 6 = 24$ or 24 miles. The first hiker will have been walking 8 hours since he had a 2 hour head-start $8 \times 3 = 24$.

19. The same two hikers start walking toward each other along a road connecting two cities which are 60 miles apart. Their speeds are the same as in the preceding problem, 3 and 4 miles per hour. How much time will elapse before they meet?

SOLUTION: In each hour of travel toward each other the men will cut down a distance equal to the sum of their speeds. $3 + 4 = 7$ miles per hour. To meet they must cut down 60 miles, and at 7 miles per hour this would be

$$\frac{D}{R} = T \quad \frac{60}{7} = 8\frac{4}{7} \text{hours.}$$

20. The problem might also have asked: "How much distance must the slower man cover before the two hikers meet?" In such case we should have gone through the same steps plus one additional step:

The time consumed before meeting was $8\frac{4}{7}$ hours. To find the distance covered by the slower hiker we merely multiply his rate by the time elapsed.

$$R \times T = D \quad 3 \times 8\frac{4}{7} = 25\frac{5}{7}$$ **Answer**

Time and Work Problems

21. If A does a job in 6 days, and B does the same job in 3 days, how long will it take the two of them, working together, to do the job?

SOLUTION: Almost any problem of this type can be solved quite simply by fractions, without resorting to higher mathematics.

A. If A does the whole job in 6 days, he will do 1/6 of the job in one day.
If B does the whole job in 3 days, he will do 1/3 of the job in one day.

B. $1/3 + 1/6 = 1/2$

C. 1/2 of the job will be finished in one day if the two men work together.

D. The whole job will be finished in two days.

EXPLANATION OF SOLUTION:

A. If you are given the time that a job takes you have merely to find the reciprocal of that time in order to find how much of the work would be done in one day. Finding the reciprocal simply means inverting the figure.

If you do a job in 2 1/2 days, you would do 2/5 of the job in one day.

$$2\ 1/2 = 5/2$$

Finding the reciprocal or inverting:

$$5/2 = 2/5$$

Another way of looking at the same operation:

All of the work is done in 5/2 days. In other words it takes 5 half days to finish the job. In one half day 1/5 of the job would be completed, and consequently in one day (2/2) 2/5 of the job would be completed.

CAUTION: If the total time for the job is given in HOURS you will, by getting the reciprocal, find what fraction of the work is done in one HOUR. The procedure for the rest of the problem, of course, is the same as above, except that the answer is in hours.

B. The total time must be reduced to a fraction of the total job because it would not do to simply add the time consumed by each man. 3 days and 6 days added together yield nine days, which is merely

TIME and tells us nothing of the AMOUNT OF WORK. But 1/3 and 1/6 do represent amounts of work.

C. Adding these two fractions together we discover the part of the job that would be completed in one day.

D. If we are told that a certain fraction represents the amount of work done in one day and if we wish to find how long the entire job would take, we find the reciprocal of the fraction.

1/2 in 1 day $\frac{2}{2}$ (or all) in $\frac{2}{1}$ days.

Two principles should be kept in mind.

1. To find the part, invert the time.
2. To find the time, invert the part.

22. A and B working together do a job in 4½ days. B, working alone, is able to do the job in 10 days. How long would it take A, working alone, to do the job?

SOLUTION: All of the job in 9/2 days. $\frac{2}{9}$ of the job in 1 day.
If B takes 10 days to do the job alone he will do 1/10 of the job in one day.

To find the work done by A in one day we subtract B's work from the amount of work done by the two men together in one day.

$$2/9 - 1/10 = \frac{20-9}{90} = \frac{11}{90}$$

11/90 represents the portion of the total job done by A in one day.

Inverting, we found how long it would take him to do the entire job.

$$\frac{90}{11} = 8\frac{2}{11} \text{ Days.}$$

23. If A can do a job in 6 days which B can do in 5-1/2 days, and C can do in 2-1/5 days, how long would the job take if A, B, and C were working together?

SOLUTION:

A Does the job in 6 days: 1/6 of the job in 1 day.
B Does the job in 5-1/2 days: 2/11 of the job in 1 day.
C Does the job in 2-1/5 days: 5/11 of the job in 1 day.

Adding the work done by A, B, and C in one day to find the work done by all three in one day.

$$\frac{1}{6} + \frac{2}{11} + \frac{5}{11} = \frac{11 + 12 + 30}{66} = \frac{53}{66}$$

Finding the reciprocal of $\frac{53}{66}$ in order to find how long the total job would take:

$$\frac{66}{53} = 1\frac{13}{53} \text{ Days.} \quad \textbf{Answer}$$

24. One pipe fills a pool in 20 minutes, a second can fill the pool in 30 minutes, and a third can fill it in 10 minutes. How long would it take the three together to fill the pool?

SOLUTION: First pipe—fills in 20 minutes—fills 1/20 of pool in 1 minute.
Second pipe—fills in 30 minutes—fills 1/30 of pool in 1 minute.
Third pipe—fills in 10 minutes—fills 1/10 of pool in 1 minute.

Adding three fractions together to determine what part of the pool will be filled in one minute when the three pipes are working together.

$$1/20 + 1/30 + 1/10 = \frac{3 + 2 + 6}{60} = \frac{11}{60}$$

If 11/60 of the pool is filled in one minute the reciprocal of the fraction will tell us how many minutes will be required to fill the whole pool.

$$\frac{60}{11} = 5\frac{5}{11} \text{ Minutes.} \quad \textbf{Answer.}$$

Problems in Proportions

25. If 5 men can build 6 miles of railroad track in 40 days, how many miles of track can be built by 3 men in 15 days?

SOLUTION: One of the best methods of solving such problems is by directly making the necessary cancellations, divisions, and multiplications.

In this example, we wish to find how many miles of track will be built if both the number of workers and the working time are reduced. It is easily seen that the amount of track constructed will be less than under the old conditions. But how much less?

Since we now have 3 men where before there were 5, we may assume that so far as manpower is concerned, production will be 3/5 as high as when 5 men were working. Consequently:

$$6 \times \frac{3}{5} = \frac{18}{5} = 3\frac{3}{5} \text{ Miles of track.}$$

Thus we know that if 3 men worked 40 days they would build 3-3/5 miles of track.

But another factor serves to lessen production. And that is the decrease in time. Only 15 days are expended, or 15/40 of the time that was expended before. Consequently:

$$3\frac{3}{5} + \frac{15}{40} = \frac{18}{5} \times \frac{15}{40} = \frac{270}{200} = 1\frac{7}{20} \text{ Miles of track.}$$

The two arithmetical operations just shown can, of course, be combined into one. Thus:

$$6 \times \frac{3}{5} \times \frac{15}{40} = 1\frac{7}{20} \text{ Miles of track.}$$

26. If 5 men build 6 miles of railroad track in 40 days, how many miles of track can be built by 8 men working 90 days?

SOLUTION: Here we have a problem which is similar to the previous one, with this exception: more men are working a longer period of time and consequently the answer will yield not a reduced but an increased number of miles of track.

If we multiply a number by a fraction whose value is less than one, we are reducing the value of that number. If, however, we multiply the number by a fraction whose value is more than one, we are increasing the value of that number. In solving this problem, then, we would not multiply $6 \times \frac{40}{90} \times \frac{5}{8}$. That would produce a number less than 6 and we know that our answer should be more than 6 since we have more men working a longer time than were required to produce 6 miles of track. The proper way of expressing the facts given in the example is:

$$6 \times \frac{90}{40} \times \frac{8}{5} = \frac{4320}{200} = 21\frac{12}{20} \text{ Miles of track.}$$

Answer

Some examples indicate an increase in one factor and a decrease in another.

27. If 10 men earn \$500 in 12 days, how much will 6 men earn in 15 days?

SOLUTION: The number of men involved decreases and consequently the fraction will be less than one. The smaller number will therefore be the numerator.

$$\$500 \times \frac{6}{10}$$

The number of days worked increases and so the fraction will be more than one. The larger number will therefore be the numerator.

$$\$500 \times \frac{6}{10} \times \frac{15}{12} = \frac{45{,}000}{120} = \$375$$

Answer

Mixture Problems

28. A wine merchant has 32 gallons of wine worth \$1.50 a gallon. If he wishes to reduce the price to \$1.20 a gallon, how many gallons of water must he add?

(A) 10 (B) 9
(C) 8 (D) 7.

SOLUTION: First let us find the cost of the 32 gallons of undiluted wine at the old price.

$$32 \times \$1.50 = \$48.00.$$

\$48, then, is the value of the wine that is ultimately to be mixed with water. By the conditions of the problem, \$48 will be the price realized from the sale of the wine at the new price of \$1.20.

To find how many gallons of wine we shall have at the new price let us divide \$48 by \$1.20, the new price. The answer, of course, is 40. We see then that we must have 40 gallons of the \$1.20 wine.

This is 8 gallons more than the undiluted wine. And that difference of 8 gallons is made up by water.

29. A bakery shop sold 3 kinds of cake. The prices of these three kinds were 25¢, 30¢, and 35¢ per pound. The income from these sales was \$36. If the number of pounds of each kind of cake sold was the same, how many pounds were sold?

SOLUTION: To buy all three kinds of cake would cost 25¢ + 30¢ + 35¢ = 90¢.

If we divide \$36, the total income, by 90¢, the total price of the three kinds of cake, we will know how many times each kind of cake was sold in order to realize the \$36. $\frac{\$36.00}{\$\ .90} = 40.$

Since there were just as many of each kind of cake sold, the total number of pounds sold = 40 × 3 = 120. **Answer**

30. The number of dimes in a cash register was equal to the number of quarters. There were five times as many nickels as quarters. All these coins together totalled \$120. How many of each were there?

SOLUTION: Let us again make groups, this time of coins. A group will consist of five nickels + 1 quarter + 1 dime which equals 60¢. If we divide \$120 by 60¢ we find that there are 200 such 60¢ groups contained in \$120. Since there are 5 nickels in every one of the 200 groups we multiply 200 by 5 to find the number of nickels—1,000. There are 200 dimes and 200 quarters.

FINAL REVIEW EXAMINATION

Plan on taking this test last, after you have gone through the entire book and after you have done all your testing, probing, and concentrated study on subjects in which, at first, you found yourself weak. It's unique in providing an excellent summary and review of all that you have learned (or should have learned). Your score here will give you an honest statement of where you stand. Certainly, it should be better than your other scores. If you're not satisfied, there's still time. Go back and review your weaker subjects. Then test yourself again. If you show improvement, you may congratulate yourself on having picked up a few more points on the actual exam.

The time allowed for the entire examination is 1 hour. In order to create the climate of the test to come, that's precisely what you should allow yourself . . . no more, no less. Use a watch and keep a record of your time, especially since you may find it convenient to take the test in several sittings.

PREVIOUS TEST QUESTIONS FOR PRACTICE

DIRECTIONS: Each question is followed by four suggested answers. Indicate the capital letter preceding your answer choice to the right of each question.

1. A real estate dealer buys a house and lot for \$4,400. He pays \$125 for painting, \$175 for plumbing, and \$100 for grading and walks. At what price must he sell the property to make a profit of 12½%?
(A) \$6,000 (B) \$5,400
(C) \$5,600 (D) \$5,800

2. An automobile cost \$1,200. It depreciated in value 45% the first year, 20% of the reduced value the second year, and 20 % of the second reduced value the third year. What was it worth at the end of the third year?
(A) \$425 (B) \$432.80
(C) \$180 (D) \$422.40

3. If the income of a certain city is \$6,950,000, and 1.81¢ of each dollar is expended for Parks, Libraries and Museums, the total amount spent for Parks, Libraries and Museums will be
(A) \$25,795 (B) \$135,795
(C) \$125,795 (D) \$12,579.

4. A desk has a marked price of \$100. Discounts of 20% and 25% are allowed. The dealer's profit is 30% of the selling price, and his cost of doing business is 10% of the selling price. What is the cost of the desk to the dealer?
(A) \$40 (B) \$50
(C) \$24 (D) \$36

5. What is the sum of 8-1/3, 4/5, 5-1/4, and 4-3/8?
(A) 18-91/120 (B) 17-91/120
(C) 18-17/24 (D) 17-5/24

6. If 1/3 gallon of milk is added to 4/5 gallon, how many quarts of milk will there be?
(A) 4-2/15 qts. (B) 4-1/30 qts.
(C) 4-8/15 qts. (D) 4-3/5 qts.

7. A man invests \$500 at the rate of 6%. How much interest is due him at the end of 3 years and 60 days? (Consider a year as 360 days.)

(A) \$125 (B) \$105
(C) \$85 (D) \$95

8. A mortgage on a house in the amount of \$4,000 provides for quarterly payments of \$200 plus interest on the unpaid balance at 4½%. The total second payment to be made is

(A) \$371 (B) \$285.50
(C) \$242.75 (D) \$240.00

9. A man borrowed \$1,200 at 6% on June 1, 1953; on Sept. 25, 1954, he paid the note in full with interest. What was the amount of payment made? (Consider a year as 360 days.)

(A) \$1,295.40 (B) \$1,289.55
(C) \$1,298.35 (D) \$1,295.08

10. A certain property is assessed at \$55,000, and the tax rate is \$4.85 per \$1,000. What is the amount of the tax to be paid on this property?

(A) \$256.75 (B) \$276.75
(C) \$286.75 (D) \$266.75

11. \$120,000 worth of land is assessed at 115% of its value. If the tax rate is \$2.80 per \$1,000, the amount of tax to be paid is

(A) \$384.60 (B) \$386.40
(C) \$368.80 (D) \$384.25

12. Blocks of real estate in a certain area are assessed at \$20,000 each. The tax rate is 90¢ per \$500. What amount of tax is due on each block?

(A) \$54.00 (B) \$48.00
(C) \$36.00 (D) \$28.00

13. The number of cubic feet of soil it takes to fill a flower box 3 ft. long, 8 in, wide, and 1 ft. deep is

(A) 2 (B) 4-2/3
(C) 12 (D) 24

14. If a man can get 1/3 bushel of berries per cubic foot, how many bushels can be get into a box measuring 5 ft. square by 1 ft. deep?

(A) 5 (B) 9-1/2
(C) 9-1/3 (D) 8-1/3

15. A carton is 10 ft. long, 4 ft. wide, and 6 in. deep. When packed with machine parts, the carton weighs 60 lbs. How many pounds of machine parts can be packed into a cubic foot of the carton?

(A) 10 (B) 3
(C) 6 (D) 8

16. A certain highway intersection has had A accidents over a ten-year period, resulting in B deaths. What is the yearly average death rate for the intersection?

(A) $A + B - 10$ (B) $B/10$
(C) $10 - A/B$ (D) $A/10$

17. A typist can address approximately R envelopes in a 7-hour day. A list containing S addresses is submitted with a request that all all envelopes by typed within T hours. The number of typists needed to complete this task would be

(A) $\frac{7RS}{T}$ (B) $\frac{S}{7RT}$
(C) $\frac{R}{7ST}$ (D) $\frac{S}{\frac{R}{7} \times T}$

18. Clerk X earns \$L per year. Clerk Y earns \$R less per month. Both earn yearly increments of \$T up to S years. At the end of P years, which is less than S years, the excess of Clerk X's earnings over Clerk Y's will be

(A) 12PR
(B) 12P(L minus R)
(C) 12PT(L plus R)
(D) P(T plus L minus R)

19. A car traveling a distance of 900 miles averages 50 m.p.h. the first 3 hours of travel, 45 m.p.h. for the 4th and 5th hours, and 40 m.p.h. for the remainder of the trip. How long did it take the car to go 900 miles?

(A) 16-1/2 hours (B) 18-1/2 hours
(C) 21-1/2 hours (D) 23 hours

20. An airplane on a trans-Atlantic flight took 18 hours to get from New York to its destination, a distance of 3,000 miles. To avoid a storm, however, the pilot went off his course, adding a distance of 200 miles to the flight. How fast did the plane travel?

(A) 179.6 m.p.h. (B) 163.4 m.p.h.
(C) 166.6 m.p.h. (D) 177.7 m.p.h.

21. Two cars start toward each other along a road between two cities which are 450 miles apart. The speed of the first car is 35 m.p.h. and that of the second 48 m.p.h. How much time will elapse before they meet?
(A) 5.42 hours (B) 6.01 hours
(C) 4.98 hours (D) 5.25 hours

22. A city pumping station can pump 3,600,000 gallons of water in 24 hours. The pump is operated on an average of 14 hours a day. The population of the city is 15,000. What is the average number of gallons of water pumped every day for each resident of the city?
(A) 145 gals. (B) 140 gals.
(C) 132 gals. (D) 1,200 gals.

23. Two men working together can build a cabinet in 2½ days. The first man, working alone, can build the cabinet in 6 days. How long would it take the second man to build the cabinet working alone?
(A) 5-1/7 days (B) 3-7/8 days
(C) 4-2/7 days (D) 4-3/10 days

24. One man can load a truck in 25 minutes; a second can load it in 50 minutes, and a third can load it in 10 minutes. How long would it take the three together to load the truck?
(A) 5-3/11 min. (B) 8-1/3 min.
(C) 6-1/4 min. (D) 10 min.

25. If 4 typists can type 600 letters in 3 days, how many letters can 2 typists complete in one day? (A) 100 letters (B) 120 letters
(C) 90 letters (D) 150 letters

26. If 12 factory workers produce 120 units in 20 days, how many units can 18 workers produce in 50 days?
(A) 375 (B) 350
(C) 325 (D) 450

27. If 15 construction workers earn $2,800 in 18 days, how much will 8 workers earn in 25 days?
(A) $2,900 (B) $2,074
(C) $1,843 (D) $2,650

28. Population figures for a certain area show there are 1½ times as many single men as single women in the area. Total population is 18,000. There are 1,122 married couples, with 756 children. How many single men are there in the area?
(A) 5,893 (B) 9,874
(C) 3,498 (D) 8,839

29. A dairyman has 4 gallons of milk worth 25¢ a quart. How much water must he add to make it worth 18¢ a quart?
(A) 1.2 gallons (B) 3.7 quarts
(C) 6.2 quarts (D) 3 gallons

30. A car dealer sold 3 different makes of cars. The price of the first make was $1,800, of the second $2,200, and the third $2,600. The income from these sales was $26,400. If the number of each make sold was the same, how many cars were sold?
(A) 12 (B) 10
(C) 8 (D) 6

31. If it takes 3 men 56 minutes to fill a trench 4′ × 6′ × 5′, and two of the men work twice as rapidly as the third, the number of minutes that it will take the two faster men alone to fill this trench is
(A) 70 minutes
(B) 60 minutes
(C) 50 minutes
(D) impossible to determine from the above data.

32. Your office wishes to purchase an adding machine. Company X offers you a standard model, less discounts of 10% and 5%. Company Y offers you the same model at the same list price, less discounts of 5% and 10%. Of the two plans, the total discount given by Company X, compared to that given by Company Y, is
(A) much larger (B) slightly larger
(C) equal (D) slightly less.

33. The dimensions of an office are 25 feet by 15 feet. It is to be fitted with desks 4 feet by 3 feet. The distance between the front of one desk and the rear of another should be 3 feet while the distance between the sides of 2 desks should be 4 feet. Assuming that no desk is placed closer than 1 ft. from any wall, the optimum number that can be placed in the office is
(A) 6 (B) 8
(C) 10 (D) 12

34. Two pieces of meat which together weighed 40 lbs. were sold for the same sum. What did the 12¢ piece weigh if they were worth 18¢ and 12¢ a pound?

(A) 24 (B) 20
(C) 30 (D) 40.

35. How many houses worth $12,000 each can a real estate agent buy for 1,000 bungalows worth $900 each?

(A) 75 (B) 74
(C) 73 (D) 72.

36. Suppose that the loss of water pressure in a hose due to friction is uniformly L pounds per square inch for every foot of hose. Of the following, the best estimate of the total loss in terms of pressure per square inch in a hose H feet long is

(A) H plus L pounds
(B) H times L pounds
(C) H divided by L pounds
(D) L divided by H pounds
(E) none of the foregoing.

37. Suppose that the amount of money that the Fire Department has saved the citizens of the City of New York in 1940 is estimated at P dollars. If this sum is to be increased at least 100 per cent in 1941, then the saving in 1941 must be at least

(A) equivalent to the ratio between P and 100
(B) commensurate with a sum derived by arithmetic manipulation involving P, 100, and a third value not given in the problem
(C) 100 times P dollars
(D) twice P dollars
(E) a sum of money not accurately described in any of the foregoing options.

38. The velocity of a fire engine which is traveling to a fire is computed by

(A) multiplying distance by time
(B) dividing distance by time
(C) squaring the force with which the earth attracts the engine
(D) means of the moment of inertia
(E) use of the Pythagorean Theorem.

39. Suppose that R persons were rescued from burning buildings by firemen in 1940. Suppose also that P persons perished in burning buildings in 1940. If R is less than S but greater than T and P is less than both M and N, it may safely be concluded that

(A) the sum of R and T is greater than S
(B) the sum of M and N is greater than P
(C) R is between M and N times as great as P
(D) R exceeds P to an indeterminate degree lying somewhere between S and N
(E) none of the foregoing options is correct.

40. In an experiment, a sprinkler system discharging W gallons of water per hour extinguished a fire covering a floor of A square yards in T minutes. The amount of water actually used to put out the fire was

(A) W times T divided by 60
(B) 60 times W divided by T
(C) 60 times W times T
(D) T divided by the fraction whose numerator is W and denominator 60
(E) none of the foregoing.

Correct Answers

(You'll learn more by writing your own answers before comparing them with these.)

1. B	11. B	21. A	31. A
2. D	12. C	22. B	32. C
3. C	13. A	23. C	33. B
4. D	14. D	24. C	34. A
5. A	15. B	25. A	35. A
6. C	16. B	26. D	36. B
7. D	17. D	27. B	37. D
8. A	18. A	28. D	38. B
9. D	19. C	29. C	39. B
10. D	20. D	30. A	40. A

SCORE 1	SCORE 2
.... %	.... %
NO. CORRECT	NO. CORRECT
NO. OF QUESTIONS	NO. OF QUESTIONS

PART FIVE

A Model Exam and Some Final Advice

COURT OFFICER

A VERISIMILAR EXAM

Testing your assimilation of the contents of this book. Hopefully, we are also proving your new-found ability to score high on the exam to come. Each of the included subjects is, in our judgment, likely to appear on your exam. You should be able to do equally well on all of them.

This examination enables you to display and exercise the important test-taking abilities leading to high scores . . . judgment, coolness, and flexibility. It's an actual civil service examination given for the very job you're seeking. But it was given a while ago, so names, dates, places, and events are old. Use your judgment and try to visualize the current facts they might substitute in the test questions they ask you. Don't try to use a time machine to transport yourself to the forgotten past. But do score yourself honestly and do concentrate your study on those weak subjects which you are rightly expected to know.

The time allowed for the entire examination is 3½ hours. In order to create the climate of the test to come, that's precisely what you should allow yourself . . . no more, no less. Use a watch and keep a record of your time, especially since you may find it convenient to take the test in several sittings.

Correct key answers to all these test questions will be found at the end of the test.

"Verisimilar" is a perfectly good English word meaning probable; likely; having the appearance of truth. In constructing this verisimilar exam we tried to visualize the questions you are *likely* to face on your actual exam. We tried to concern ourselves with the subjects on which they are *probably* going to test you.

And, as a result, you have before you an exam which simulates the actual test closely enough to provide you with important training.

Proceed through the entire exam without pausing after each sub-test. Remember that you are taking this exam under actual battle conditions, and therefore you do not stop until told to by the proctor. Certainly you should not lose time by trying to score each sub-test before finishing the entire exam. You'll be able to score yourself fairly when time is up for the entire exam.

Do you recall our chapter, *HOW TO BE A MASTER TEST-TAKER?* It's all quite applicable to getting a high score on this Verisimilar Exam, particularly the section entitled, *Multiple Choice Methods.* Likewise the chapter, *TEST-TAKING MADE SIMPLE.* Why not "walk through" these chapters now! They'll add points both to your Verisimilar Exam . . . and to your actual exam.

Practical Questions (Weight 50)

DIRECTIONS: Examine each of the following 100 statements numbered 1 to 100 and decide for each whether it is true or false. If you think a statement is True, encircle the T; if you think the statement is false, encircle the F. As examples, the first two statements are marked correctly.

CAUTION: Unless the context of the statement indicates otherwise, all statements refer to laws, courts and court procedure of New York State and must be answered with this in mind.

Examples: A. (T) F The person who presides over a court is called a judge.
B. T (F) New York City is the capital of New York State.

1. T F The County Clerk of each county acts as Clerk of the Supreme Court.

2. T F A summons can be served by a person twenty years of age.

3. T F Jury notices must be delivered to each prospective juror personally.

4. T F The only age restriction on a juror of a court of record, who is otherwise fully qualified, is that he be over twenty-one years of age.

5. T F An attorney regularly employed in the practice of law is entitled to exemption from jury service.

6. T F A court attendant is privileged from arrest during the actual sitting of a court at which he is in attendance.

7. T F The Appellate Division is part of the Supreme Court.

8. T F A voluntary general appearance of the defendant in an action is equivalent to personal service of the summons upon him.

9. T F In the Appellate Division no decision may be handed down unless there are five judges present.

10. T F Kings County is in the First Judicial District.

11. T F The Supreme Court is the only court of general original jurisdiction.

12. T F In a civil action in a court of record each party may peremptorily challenge not more than three of the persons drawn as jurors for the trial.

13. T F In a court of record the plaintiff must be present when the jurors deliver their verdict.

14. T F In the Supreme Court two trial terms may be held at the same time in the same county.

15. T F A New Jersey attorney who comes into New York City to conduct litigation for a client is legally immune from service of a New York court summons while there.

16. T F When a judgment is docketed it becomes a lien on the judgment debtor's real property situated within the county where judgment is entered.

17. T F A "Supplementary Proceeding" is a proceeding to levy on the earnings or income of the judgment debtor.

18. T F Ejectment is an action at law to recover the possession of personal property where a person having the right to possession is excluded from it by another.

19. T F If the volume and page number of a case is known, but not the name, a correct place to find out the name of the case is "Shepard's Citations."

20. T F "42 N.Y. 546" refers to the reports of the New York Court of Appeals.

21. T F "265 N.E. 75" refers to page 265, volume 75 of the Northeastern Reporter.

22. T F The decisions of the Appellate Division are reported in the Miscellaneous Reports.

23. T F If a person seeks to avoid service of a summons by refusing to accept the paper, service may be validly made by placing the summons at his feet and calling his attention to the fact that service is intended.

24. T F All City and Municipal Courts are courts of record.

25. T F A defendant served with a summons in the County or Supreme Court must appear or answer within 20 days from the date of service, exclusive of the day of service.

26. T F The Legislature may create local courts and confer upon them all the jurisdiction now held by the Supreme Court.

27. T F Where a court does not have jurisdiction over the subject matter, jurisdiction may be conferred by consent of the parties to the action.

28. T F The County Courts in Bronx, Kings, Queens, and Richmond Counties have no civil jurisdiction.

29. T F A summons of a county court may be served in any county within the State.

30. T F The terms "Judicial District" and "Judicial Department" always mean the same thing.

31. T F There is no jury sitting at a special term of the Supreme Court.

32. T F The Supreme Court is limited in its civil jurisdiction to cases involving more than $500.

33. T F An action for personal injury resulting from negligence can be brought any time within 6 years of the date of the cause of action.

34. T F Counterclaims and defenses are subject to the Statute of Limitations.

35. T F The summons is the mandate by which the court gains jurisdiction over the parties.

36. T F Name of the plaintiff's attorney need not be shown in a summons.

37. T F It is not proper to use the initial of the first name of the defendant in a summons if the first name is known.

38. T F If a summons is served on the wrong party and he accepts service he must assume the position of the defendant.

39. T F Where the court directs that an additional party be brought into an action as a defendant, a court order is used instead of a summons.

40. T F A plaintiff may sue in person rather than through an attorney.

41. T F The legal term used to describe judgments of $25 or less is "nominal damages."

42. T F A summons on a domestic corporation may be served on a "managing agent."

43. T F The personal service of a summons in an envelope is a valid service where the defendant immediately opened the envelope in the presence of the process server and found the summons.

44. T F Proof of service of a summons must be made by the person who actually serves the summons.

45. T F A summons may not be legally served between midnight and 4 A.M.

46. T F The parties in a civil action may consent to a trial by a jury of less than 12 persons.

47. T F Under the present law a woman cannot serve on a jury in the New York Courts.

48. T F The function of the jury in a civil case is to decide the disputed questions of fact.

49. T F There are no covenants implied in a conveyance of real property.

50. T F A deed to real property must be recorded in order to pass title.

51. T F The person who has charge of the estate of a deceased person is called a testator.

52. T F A child under 12 years of age is presumed to be incapable of committing a crime.

53. T F The legal title to property cannot, under any circumstances, pass under a deed before the deed is delivered.

54. T F Service of a summons on Sunday is void.

55. T F The defendant's plea to an indictment must be oral.

56. T F A corporation cannot be charged with the commission of a crime.

57. T F If a person receives a suspended sentence he is acquitted of the charge for which he was tried.

58. T F Only personal property is subject to attachment.

59. T F The granting of a new trial places the parties in the same positions as if no trial had been had.

60. T F If there is a quorum present a person may be indicted by a majority vote of the grand jurors.

61. T F A defendant in a criminal case who has recovered a judgment against a prospective juror in a recent negligence action may exclude him from the jury for that reason.

62. T F A court attendant may, without a warrant, arrest a person when a felony has in fact been committed and he has reasonable cause for believing that the person to be arrested committed it.

63. T F If a defendant in a criminal case refuses to answer an indictment, a plea of guilty must be entered.

64. T F If a defendant is indicted for a misdemeanor, trial may be had in his absence, if he appears by counsel.

65. T F The consent of both the counsel for the people and the counsel for the defendant is necessary in order to allow a jury, upon retiring for deliberation, to take with them papers which have been received as evidence.

66. T F The members of a jury may not take notes on the testimony for use in their deliberations.

67. T F The legal qualifications for a grand juror and for a trial juror are the same.

68. T F A jury must deliberate until they reach a unanimous verdict.

69. T F A court may not receive the verdict of a jury on Sunday.

70. T F A grand juror who, except when lawfully required by a court or officer, discloses in what manner he or any other grand juror voted upon a matter before them, is guilty of a misdemeanor.

71. T F A regularly employed school teacher must serve as a juror when called to act as such.

72. T F A person who is not worth $100 besides his clothing, necessary furniture, and the subject matter of the action, may apply to the court for leave to sue or defend as a poor person.

73. T F The defendant's pleading in a civil action is called a "reply."

74. T F A person who conceals himself in the jury room in order to listen to the deliberations of the jurors is guilty of contempt of court.

75. T F If a person is imprisoned for contempt of court, where the misconduct consists of failure to perform an act or duty, he may be imprisoned until he has performed the act, if it is yet in his power to perform it.

76. T F The Court of Claims is a court which hears claims for debts against the estates of deceased persons.

77. T F The only way to correct an error resulting from a judgment of a court lacking jurisdiction over the subject matter and parties is by appeal.

78. T F X and Y are residents of New York State. X damages real property of Y which is located in Massachusetts. Because New York State courts have no jurisdiction over the property, Y has no remedy in the New York State courts.

79. T F The Appellate Division has power to take original jurisdiction in all matters in which the Supreme Court has such power.

80. T F A Supreme Court justice cannot hold court in a county outside the district in which he was elected.

81. T F A plaintiff cannot recover costs in an action brought in the Supreme Court of a county in New York City which could have been brought in the City Court of New York City and in which the defendant shall have been served within the City of New York unless he shall recover more than $2,000.

82. T F The Statute of Limitations has the effect of discharging the obligation after the period within which action could have been brought has expired.

83. T F The lien of a mortgage is not impaired by the expiration of the time limit within which an action may be brought on the bond.

84. T F The defense of "laches" may be set up as a defense in an equity action even though the action is not barred by the Statute of Limitations.

85. T F A assigns his right to receive money under a contract to B. The contract remains unpaid and it is decided to bring action. The action must be brought in the name of A.

86. T F The person for whose benefit a contract is made may be the real party at interest.

87. T F In cases where the plaintiff is in doubt as to which of two persons is the proper defendant, he may join both so that the question of liability and extent of liability can be determined.

88. T F If the plaintiff is unable to ascertain the name of the defendant no action can be brought.

89. T F If a fire insurance policy insures the interest of the mortgagor and provides that the loss, if any, shall be payable to the mortgagee as his interest may appear, a joint action of mortgagor and mortgagee may be maintained.

90. T F An attorney cannot act as a guardian ad litem.

91. T F Legality is presumed in any situation until refuted by evidence.

92. T F A person is presumed to have intended the natural results of his acts.

93. T F All partners are presumed to have knowledge of entries in their books made by clerks in the regular course of business.

94. T F The Appellate Division cannot grant any provisional remedy which has been applied for and refused by the Supreme Court.

95. T F A highway, designated in an old deed as a boundary to a parcel of property, is presumed to be located in the same position until the contrary is shown.

96. T F If a defendant offers no evidence, but elects to stand on the plaintiff's proof, this fact cannot be used against the defendant if he fails to make a case.

97. T F In an automobile collision case, evidence of a whisky bottle found near the accident may be accepted in evidence as proof that the defendant was drunk.

98. T F Attachment is a proceeding for the seizure of property after judgment.

99. T F An order for a temporary injunction may be granted without notice.

100. T F The application for a warrant of attachment must be founded on an affidavit or verified pleading.

American History and Civics (Weight 25)

DIRECTIONS: Examine each of the following 100 statements and decide for each whether it is True or False, and encircle the proper letter as in the preceding questions.

101. T F The seizure of the Philippine Islands by Japan would violate the Monroe Doctrine.

102. T F The inhabitants of Porto Rico are citizens of the United States.

103. T F Washington in his Farewell Address warned his countrymen against the baneful effects of party spirit.

104. T F The Constitution gives Congress the power to establish uniform laws for bankruptcies throughout the United States.

105. T F In accordance with the Constitution, an Admiral in the United States Navy may not accept a present from the King of England without the consent of Congress.

106. T F The District of Columbia is entitled to two presidential electors.

107. T F Jefferson in his inauguaral address warned the people against "entangling alliances."

108. T F The Constitution of the United States declares that all men are created free and equal.

109. T F Congress has the power to declare the punishment for treason against the United States.

110. T F A State has the power to pass a law abolishing trial by jury.

111. T F Diseased aliens are barred from entering the United States.

112. T F New York State has an old age pension act.

113. T F State troopers are Federal soldiers stationed in the States.

114. T F Naturalization is the process by which aliens become citizens.

115. T F The Vice-President of the United States does not have to be a native-born citizen.

116. T F The duty of the Public Service Commission is to work for the benefit of public utility corporations.

117. T F The Constitution of the United States forbids the President of the United States to hold office for three successive terms.

118. T F Freedom of speech gives one the right to say anything he pleases.

119. T F A majority of the judges of the United States Supreme Court is sufficient to pronounce a law unconstitutional.

120. T F All national revenue bills must be introduced in the House of Representatives.

121. T F In New York State a bill to become law must be approved by the Governor within 10 days after final adjournment of the Legislature.

122. T F When a city in New York State includes a town, town government automatically ceases to function.

123. T F Supervision of immigration falls under the jurisdiction of the Federal Department of the Interior.

124. T F The Constitution of each State in the Union provides for a bicameral form of government.

125. T F The first Constitution for the State of New York was adopted in 1777.

126. T F The Constitution of the United States makes no provision for the use of the initiative and the referendum.

127. T F Since 1900 the Federal Government has abandoned Federal aid for road building.

128. T F The members of the New York State Legislature are elected by the system of proportional representation.

129. T F The House of Representatives has never been called upon to choose a President of the United States.

130. T F Our present Federal income tax is an example of progressive taxation.

131. T F Judges of the New York State Supreme Court may be removed by a two-thirds vote of the State Senate.

132. T F Conservation of our national resources is necessary because of the needs and welfare of future generations.

133. T F The President's cabinet members are members of Congress.

134. T F The Reconstruction Finance Corporation has authority to lend money to banks in the United States.

135. T F Japanese born in the United States are not eligible to citizenship.

136. T F The education of the children of New York City is supervised by the State.

137. T F The supreme law of the land is the Supreme Court.

138. T F The United States Supreme Court is composed of one Chief Justice and nine associate justices.

139. T F The county does not derive its power from the State.

140. T F The enforcement of the laws of the United States rests with the President.

141. T F The President negotiates treaties with the consent of the House of Representatives.

142. T F If a woman, native born in the United States, marries an alien, she loses her United States citizenship.

143. T F Congress does not levy a tax on the salary of State employees.

144. T F The term for which a patent may be issued under the present law is 17 years.

145. T F Diplomatic agents are free from criminal prosecution by the country to which they are accredited.

146. T F The Constitution of the United States forbids levying of an export tax.

147. T F The tariff is a direct tax levied on the consumer of the goods taxed.

148. T F An alien must reside in this country 7 years before being eligible for his final papers making him a citizen of this country.

149. T F The Government under the Constitution of the United States went into operation before Rhode Island had ratified the Constitution.

150. T F In case of war which results in the acquisition of territory, the President may govern this territory under his authority as Commander-in-Chief of the Army and Navy.

151. T F Some State Constitutions allow plural voting.

152. T F The method of settling a dispute peaceably with the aid of a third party is called arbitration.

153. T F The voter's attitude toward a political party should be "My party, right or wrong."

154. T F Congress can override a Presidential veto by a majority vote.

155. T F The Emancipation Proclamation of 1863 freed all slaves in the South.

156. T F Probation is a provision for a short sentence in a reformatory.

157. T F A franchise is a privilege granted by one company to another company to operate a bus line.

158. T F An injunction is an order by a labor union requiring its members to avoid damage to property during a strike.

159. T F Alaska was acquired by the United States through annexation from Prussia.

160. T F "The separation of powers" refers to the division of powers between the Federal and State governments.

161. T F The Hoover administration through the process of mediation made a final settlement of the Tacna-Arica dispute.

162. T F An act passed by Congress in 1935 has the effect of complete annulment of the Supreme Court's "Gold Clause" decision.

163. T F "Jus sanguinas" determines citizenship on the basis of place of birth.

164. T F The action of Congress in demonetizing silver was called, by its opponents, "the crime of 1873."

165. T F The right of Congress to restrict immigration to the United States is based on the commerce clause.

166. T F Judges in every State of the Union are bound to support the Constitution and all laws that are made under the authority of the United States.

167. T F Henry Clay assumed his duties as United States Senator from Kentucky before he was thirty years old.

168. T F An income tax is a tax on all wages, salaries and interest on investments.

169. T F A budget is absolutely necessary in government in order to save money.

170. T F Democracy is based on the principle of the equality of all men in all respects.

171. T F The 48 States that make up the United States bear the same relation to the United States that a county in New York State does to the State or a township to a county.

172. T F A declaration of war is an essential preliminary to actual warfare.

173. T F The National Government has the power to provide for the punishment of counterfeiting the securities and current coin of the United States.

174. T F Delaware was the first State to ratify the Constitution.

175. T F The Federal Constitution was an entirely original creation of ideas and principles of the members of the Constitutional Convention.

176. T F The nineteenth amendment to the Constitution conferred the right to vote on all women.

177. T F The House of Representatives chooses the President of the United States in case no candidate is elected by a majority of the electoral votes.

178. T F A sound and healthy public opinion depends upon freedom of speech and a free press.

179. T F The village is the smallest unit of local government in New York State.

180. T F A candidate must receive a majority of the popular votes to be elected President of the United States.

181. T F The President of the United States cannot veto particular items in the appropriation bills.

182. T F By an act of Congress, Indians born in the United States may become citizens of the United States.

183. T F A copyright may be granted to a foreign author provided his government grants similar protection to American authors.

184. T F Abraham Lincoln said "By uniting we stand, by dividing we fall."

185. T F The National Government receives the greatest part of its revenue from the general property tax.

186. T F The township was the leading type of local government in the early Virginia colony.

187. T F An excise tax is a tax levied on commodities manufactured in a country.

188. T F The Twentieth Amendment empowers Congress to pass a law providing for some person to act as President in case the President and Vice-President fail to be elected or to qualify.

189. T F The chief function of the probate court is to deal with trusts and frauds.

190. T F The grand jury may not make investigations on its own initiative.

191. T F In order to vote in a closed Republican primary it is necessary to be enrolled Republican.

192. T F Congress may be adjourned only with the consent of the President.

193. T F In a disputed election to a seat in the Lower House of Congress the House of Representatives decides who is duly elected.

194. T F The first ten amendments to the United States Constitution apply only to the Federal Government.

195. T F A community is a group of people occupying a definite area and bound together by common interests and common customs or laws.

196. T F The Panama Canal is used for both military and commercial purposes.

197. T F When there is a deficit in the United States Postal Department it is made up by taxation.

198. T F The provisions of the Agriculture Adjustment Act have recently been extended to include restrictions on the production of potatoes in the United States.

199. T F The provisions of the Constitution of the United States are not applicable to Alaska.

200. T F A proposed amendment becomes a part of the United States Constitution when it is ratified by the Legislatures of two-thirds of the States.

<u>Arithmetic</u> (Weight 10)

DIRECTIONS: Solve each of the following 10 problems which are numbered 201 to 210. No credit is given unless your answer is absolutely correct.

201. From 26.456 subtract 2.6465.

202. Add the following: 40¢, $2.75, $186.21, $24,865, $.74, $8.42, $2,475.28, $11,998.24.

203. Perform the indicated operations and express your answer in its simplest form: 5/8 divided by 20/3 times 7/19 divided by 63/38 times 16/21 divided by 1/14.

204. Perform the indicated operations: .020301 times 3.15 divided by .00000063.

205. Add the following fractions: 1 1/2, 2 1/6, 9 1/3, 2 1/4, 6 1/5.

206. Perform the indicated operations and express your answer in inches: 12 feet, minus 7 inches, plus 2 feet 1 inch, minus 7 feet, minus 1 yard, plus 2 yards 1 foot 3 inches.

207. Find the interest on $25,800 for 144 days at 6% per annum. Base your calculations on a 360-day year.

208. A court clerk estimates that the untried cases on the docket will occupy the court for 150 trial days. If new cases are accumulating at the rate of 1.6 trial days per day (Saturday and Sunday excluded) and the court sits 5 days a week, how many days' business will remain to be heard at the end of 60 trial days?

209. The visitors' section of a courtroom seats 105 people. The court is in session 6 hours of the day. On one particular day 486 people visited the court and were given seats. What is the average length of time spent by each visitor in the court? Assume that as soon as a person leaves his seat it is immediately filled and that at no time during the day is one of the 105 seats vacant. Express your answer in hours and minutes.

210. If paper costs $1.46 per ream and 5% discount is allowed for cash, how many reams can be purchased for $69.35 cash? Do not discard fractional part of a cent in your calculations.

<u>English</u> (Weight 15)

DIRECTIONS: Study each of the following sentences. Some of them contain errors in grammar. Consider a sentence correct if it does not contain a grammatical error, even though there may be other, perhaps better, methods of expressing the same thought. If you think a sentence is correct, encircle the C; if you think it is incorrect, encircle the I. Examples C and D are marked correctly.

Examples: C. (C) I The lamp burns brightly.
D. C (I) I have knew him many years.

211. C I He has finished typing the minutes of the trial.

212. C I The trial begun yesterday.

213. C I I have never seen a more kinder judge.

214. C I If they could put theirselves in the position of the jury, they would appreciate the difficult situation.

215. C I There is no objection to his attending the trial.

216. C I The attendant should call on the clerk more frequent.

217. C I The judge talks like he was angry.

218. C I Unless you help, this calendar will not be completed in time.

219. C I This kind of paper is expensive.

220. C I The letter was written by Mr. Smith, who is secretary to the judge.

221. C I The next one whose to testify is the brother of the defendant.

222. C I The court sat one hundred people.

223. C I It looks very serious.

224. C I The judge had other reasons besides these.

225. C I The number of books is limited.

226. C I I am not sure whether or not the judge will agree to the change in the calendar.

227. C I Not one of the witnesses has taken the oath.

228. C I I don't know as the judge will arrive today.

229. C I I wish I were a judge.

230. C I Where did you say Riverhead was?

231. C I Judge Green, of the First Judicial District, has a keener mind than any judge in the country.

232. C I Ten dollars are a heavy fine for the offense.

233. C I He desired to have taken up the study of law.

234. C I The judge, as well as the jury, is waiting to begin the trial.

235. C I Please collect together all the facts you have gathered at the trial.

236. C I He is one of the most interesting lawyers I have ever knew.

237. C I The judge which arrived yesterday is not familiar with the city.

238. C I Neither effort or money was spared in the undertaking.

239. C I I am confident that you can perform the duties properly.

240. C I There is no question but what you should remain here.

Correct Answers For The Foregoing Questions

(Please make every effort to answer the questions on your own before looking at these answers. You'll make faster progress by following this rule.)

1. T
2. T
3. F
4. F
5. T
6. T
7. T
8. T
9. F
10. F
11. T
12. F
13. F
14. T
15. F
16. T
17. F
18. F
19. F
20. T
21. F
22. F
23. T
24. F
25. T
26. F
27. F
28. T
29. T
30. F
31. T
32. F
33. F
34. T
35. T
36. F
37. T
38. F
39. F
40. T
41. F
42. T
43. T
44. F
45. F
46. T
47. F
48. T
49. T
50. F
51. F
52. T
53. T
54. T
55. T
56. F
57. F
58. F
59. T
60. F
61. T
62. T
63. F
64. T
65. T
66. F
67. F
68. F
69. F
70. T
71. T
72. T
73. F
74. T
75. T
76. F
77. F
78. F
79. T
80. F
81. F
82. F
83. F
84. T
85. F
86. T
87. T
88. F
89. T
90. F
91. T
92. T
93. T
94. F
95. T
96. T
97. F
98. F
99. T
100. T
101. F
102. F
103. T
104. T
105. T
106. F
107. T
108. F
109. T
110. F
111. T
112. T
113. F
114. T
115. F
116. F
117. F
118. F
119. T
120. T
121. F
122. T
123. F
124. F
125. T
126. T
127. F
128. F
129. F
130. T
131. F
132. T
133. F
134. T
135. F
136. T
137. F
138. F
139. F
140. T
141. F
142. F
143. F
144. T
145. T
146. T
147. F
148. F
149. T
150. T
151. F
152. T
153. F
154. F
155. F
156. F
157. F
158. F
159. F
160. F
161. F
162. F
163. F
164. T
165. F
166. T
167. T
168. T
169. T
170. T
171. T
172. F
173. T
174. T
175. F
176. F
177. T
178. T
179. T
180. F
181. T
182. T
183. T
184. F
185. F
186. T
187. F
188. T
189. F
190. F
191. T
192. F
193. T
194. F
195. T
196. T
197. F
198. T
199. F
200. F
201. 23.8095
202. $39,537.04
203. 2/9
204. 101.505
205. 21-9/20
206. 129 inches
207. $619.20
208. 186 trial days
209. 1 hr. 17-7/9 mins.
210. 50 reams
211. C
212. I
213. I
214. I
215. C
216. I
217. I
218. C
219. C
220. C
221. I
222. I
223. C
224. C
225. C
226. C
227. C
228. I
229. C
230. I
231. I
232. I
233. I
234. C
235. I
236. I
237. I
238. I
239. C
240. I

SCORE 1	SCORE 2	SCORE 3	SCORE 4	SCORE 5
.... %	.... %	.... %	.... %	.... %
NO. CORRECT	NO. CORRECT	NO. CORRECT	NO. CORRECT	NO. CORRECT
NO. OF QUESTIONS ON THIS TEST	NO. OF QUESTIONS ON THIS TEST	NO. OF QUESTIONS ON THIS TEST	NO. OF QUESTIONS ON THIS TEST	NO. OF QUESTIONS ON THIS TEST

COURT OFFICER

TEST—TAKING MADE SIMPLE

Having gotten this far, you're almost an expert test-taker because you have now mastered the subject matter of the test. Proper preparation is the real secret. The pointers on the next few pages will take you the rest of the way by giving you the strategy employed on tests by those who are most successful in this not-so-mysterious art.

BEFORE THE TEST

T-DAY MINUS SEVEN

You're going to pass this examination because you have received the best possible preparation for it. But, unlike many others, you're going to give the best possible account of yourself by acquiring the rare skill of effectively using your knowledge to answer the examination questions.

First off, get rid of any negative attitudes toward the test. You have a negative attitude when you view the test as a device to "trip you up" rather than an opportunity to show how effectively you have learned.

APPROACH THE TEST WITH SELF-CONFIDENCE. Plugging through this book was no mean job, and now that you've done it you're probably better prepared than 90% of the others. Self-confidence is one of the biggest strategic assets you can bring to the testing room.

Nobody likes tests, but some poor souls permit themselves to get upset or angry when they see what they think is an unfair test. The expert doesn't. He keeps calm and moves right ahead, knowing that everyone is taking the same test. Anger, resentment, fear . . . they all slow you down. "Grin and bear it!"

Besides, every test you take, including this one, is a valuable experience which improves your skill. Since you will undoubtedly be taking other tests in the years to come, it may help you to regard this one as training to perfect your skill.

Keep calm; there's no point in panic. If you've done your work there's no need for it; and if you haven't, a cool head is your very first requirement.

Why be the frightened kind of student who enters the examination chamber in a mental coma? A test taken under mental stress does not provide a fair measure of your ability. At the very least, this book has removed for you some of the fear and mystery that surrounds examinations. A certain amount of concern is normal and good, but excessive worry saps your strength and keenness. In other words, be prepared EMOTIONALLY.

Pre-Test Review

If you know any others who are taking this test, you'll probably find it helpful to review the book and your notes with them. The group should be small, certainly not more than four. Team study at this stage should seek to review the material in a different way than you learned it originally; should strive for an exchange of ideas between you and the other members of the group; should be selective in sticking to important ideas; should stress the vague and the unfamiliar rather than that which you all know well; should be businesslike and devoid of any nonsense; should end as soon as you get tired.

One of the *worst* strategies in test taking is to do *all* your preparation the night before the exam. As a reader of this book, you have scheduled and spaced your study properly so as not to suffer from the fatigue and emotional disturbance that comes from cramming the night before.

Cramming is a very good way to *guarantee poor test results.*

However, you would be wise to prepare yourself factually by *reviewing your notes* in the 48 hours preceding the exam. You shouldn't have to spend more than two or three hours in this way. Stick to salient points. The others will fall into place quickly.

Don't confuse cramming with a final, calm review which helps you focus on the significant areas of this book and further strengthens your confidence in your ability to handle the test questions. In other words, prepare yourself FACTUALLY.

Keep Fit

Mind and body work together. Poor physical condition will lower your mental efficiency. In preparing for an examination, observe the commonsense rules of health. Get sufficient sleep and rest, eat proper foods, plan recreation and exercise. In relation to health and examinations, two cautions are in order. Don't miss your meals prior to an examination in order to get extra time for study. Likewise, don't miss your regular sleep by sitting up late to "cram" for the examination. Cramming is an attempt to learn in a very short period of time what should have been learned through regular and consistent study. Not only are these two habits detrimental to health, but seldom do they pay off in terms of effective learning. It is likely that you will be *more confused* than better prepared on the day of the examination if you have broken into your daily routine by missing your meals or sleep.

On the night before the examination go to bed at your regular time and try to get a good night's sleep. Don't go to the movies. Don't date. In other words, prepare yourself PHYSICALLY.

T-HOUR MINUS ONE

After a very light, leisurely meal, get to the examination room ahead of time, perhaps ten minutes early . . . but not so early that you have time to get into an argument with others about what's going to be asked on the exam, etc. The reason for coming early is to help you get accustomed to the room. It will help you to a better start.

Bring all necessary equipment . . .

. . . pen, two sharpened pencils, watch, paper, eraser, ruler, and any other things you're instructed to bring.

Get settled . . .

. . . by finding your seat and staying in it. If no special seats have been assigned, take one in the front to facilitate the seating of others coming in after you.

The test will be given by a test supervisor who reads the directions and otherwise tells you what to do. The people who walk about passing out the test papers and assisting with the examination are test proctors. If you're not able to see or hear properly notify the supervisor or a proctor. If you have any other difficulties during the examination, like a defective test booklet, scoring pencil, answer sheet; or if it's too hot or cold or dark or drafty, let them know. You're entitled to favorable test conditions, and if you don't have them you won't be able to do your best. Don't be a crank, but don't be shy either. An important function of the proctor is to see to it that you have favorable test conditions.

Relax . . .

. . . and don't bring on unnecessary tenseness by worrying about the difficulty of the examination. If necessary wait a minute before beginning to write. If you're still tense, take a couple of deep breaths, look over your test equipment, or do something which will take your mind away from the examination for a moment.

If your collar or shoes are tight, loosen them.

Put away unnecessary materials so that you have a good, clear space on your desk to write freely.

You Must Have *TO GIVE YOUR* **Best Test** *PERFORMANCE*

(1) A GOOD TEST ENVIRONMENT

(2) A COMPLETE UNDERSTANDING OF DIRECTIONS

(3) A DESIRE TO DO YOUR BEST

WHEN THEY SAY "GO" — TAKE YOUR TIME!

Listen very carefully to the test supervisor. If you fail to hear something important that he says, you may not be able to read it in the written directions and may suffer accordingly.

If you don't understand the directions you have heard or read, raise your hand and inform the proctor. Read carefully the directions for *each* part of the test before beginning to work on that part. If you skip over such directions too hastily, you may miss a main idea and thus lose credit for an entire section.

Get an Overview of the Examination

After reading the directions carefully, look over the entire examination to get an over-view of the nature and scope of the test. The purpose of this over-view is to give you some idea of the nature, scope, and difficulty of the examination.

It has another advantage. An item might be so phrased that it sets in motion a chain of thought that might be helpful in answering other items on the examination.

Still another benefit to be derived from reading all the items before you answer any is that the few minutes involved in reading the items gives you an opportunity to relax before beginning the examination. This will make for better concentration. As you read over these items the first time, check those whose answers immediately come to you. These will be the ones you will answer first. Read each item carefully before answering. It is a good practice to read each item at least twice to be sure that you understand it.

Plan Ahead

In other words, you should know precisely where you are going before you start. You should know:

1. whether you have to answer all the questions or whether you can choose those that are easiest for you;
2. whether all the questions are easy; (there may be a pattern of difficult, easy, etc.)
3. The length of the test; the number of questions;
4. The kind of scoring method used;
5. Which questions, if any, carry extra weight;
6. What types of questions are on the test;
7. What directions apply to each part of the test;
8. Whether you must answer the questions consecutively.

Budget Your Time Strategically!

Quickly figure out how much of the allotted time you can give to each section and still finish ahead of time. Don't forget to figure on the time you're investing in the overview. Then alter your schedule so that you can spend more time on those parts that count most. Then, if you can, plan to spend less time on the easier questions, so that you can devote the time saved to the harder questions. Figuring roughly, you should finish half the questions when half the allotted time has gone by. If there are 100 questions and you have three hours, you should have finished 50 questions after one and one half hours. So bring along a watch whether the instructions call for one or not. Jot down your "exam budget" and stick to it INTELLIGENTLY.

EXAMINATION STRATEGY

Probably the most important single strategy you can learn is to do the easy questions first. The very hard questions should be read and temporarily postponed. Identify them with a dot and return to them later.

This strategy has several advantages for you:

1. You're sure to get credit for all the questions you're sure of. If time runs out, you'll have all the sure shots, losing out only on those which you might have missed anyway.
2. By reading and laying away the tough ones you give your subconscious a chance to work on them. You may be pleasantly surprised to find the answers to the puzzlers popping up for you as you deal with related questions.
3. You won't risk getting caught by the time limit just as you reach a question you know really well.

A Tested Tactic

It's inadvisable on some examinations to answer each question in the order presented. The reason for this is that some examiners design tests so as to extract as much mental energy from you as possible. They put the most difficult questions at the beginning, the easier questions last. Or they may vary difficult with easy questions in a fairly regular pattern right through the test. Your survey of the test should reveal the pattern and your strategy for dealing with it.

If difficult questions appear at the beginning, answer them until you feel yourself slowing down or getting tired. Then switch to an easier part of the examination. You will return to the difficult portion after you have rebuilt your confidence by answering a batch of easy questions. Knowing that you have a certain number of points "under your belt" will help you when you return to the more difficult questions. You'll answer them with a much clearer mind; and you'll be refreshed by the change of pace.

Time

Use your time wisely. It's an important element in your test and you must use every minute effectively, working as rapidly as you can without sacrificing accuracy. Your exam survey and budget will guide you in dispensing your time. Wherever you can, pick up seconds on the easy ones. Devote your savings to the hard ones. If possible, pick up time on the lower value questions and devote it to those which give you the most points.

Relax Occasionally and Avoid Fatigue

If the exam is long (two or more hours) give yourself short rest periods as you feel you need them. If you're not permitted to leave the room, relax in your seat, look up from your paper, rest your eyes, stretch your legs, shift your body. Break physical and mental tension. Take several deep breaths and get back to the job, refreshed. If you don't do this you run the risk of getting nervous and tightening up. Your thinking may be hampered and you may make a few unnecessary mistakes.

Do not become worried or discouraged if the examination seems difficult to you. The questions in the various fields are purposely made difficult and searching so that the examination will discriminate effectively even among superior students. No one is expected to get a perfect or near-perfect score.

Remember that if the examination seems difficult to you, it may be even more difficult for your neighbor.

Think!

This is not a joke because you're not an IBM machine. Nobody is able to write all the time and also to read and think through each question. You must plan each answer. Don't give hurried answers in an atmosphere of panic. Even though you see a lot of questions, remember that they are objective and not very time-consuming. Don't rush headlong through questions that must be thought through.

Edit, Check, Proofread . . .

. . . after completing all the questions. Invariably, you will find some foolish errors which you needn't have made, and which you can easily correct. Don't just sit back or leave the room ahead of time. Read over your answers and make sure you wrote exactly what you meant to write. And that you wrote the answers in the right place. You might even find that you have omitted some answers inadvertently. You have budgeted time for this job of proofreading. PROOFREAD and pick up points.

One caution, though. Don't count on making major changes. And don't go in for wholesale changing of answers. To arrive at your answers in the first place you have read carefully and thought correctly. Second-guessing at this stage is more likely to result in wrong answers. So don't make changes unless you are quite certain you were wrong in the first place.

FOLLOW DIRECTIONS CAREFULLY

In answering questions on the objective or short-form examination, it is most important to follow all instructions carefully. Unless you have marked the answers properly, you will not receive credit for them. In addition, even in the same examination, the instructions will not be consistent. In one section you may be urged to guess if you are not certain; in another you may be cautioned against guessing. Some questions will call for the best choice among four or five alternatives; others may ask you to select the one incorrect or the least probable answer.

On some tests you will be provided with worked out fore-exercises, complete with correct answers. However, avoid the temptation to skip the directions and begin working just from reading the model questions and answers. Even though you may be familiar with that particular type of question, the directions may be different from those which you had followed previously. If the type of question should be new to you, work through the model until you understand it perfectly. This may save you time, and earn you a higher rating on the examination.

If the directions for the examination are written, read them carefully, at least twice. If the directions are given orally, listen attentively and then follow them precisely. For example, if you are directed to use plus (+) and minus (−) to mark true—false items, then don't use "T" and "F". If you are instructed to "blacken" a space on machine-scored tests, do not use a check (✓) or an "X". Make all symbols legible, and be sure that they have been placed in the proper answer space. It is easy, for example, to place the answer for item 5 in the space reserved for item 6. If this is done, then all of your following answers may be wrong. It is also very important that you understand the method they will use in scoring the examination. Sometimes they tell you in the directions. The method of scoring may affect the amount of time you spend on an item, especially if some items count more than others. Likewise, the directions may indicate whether or not you should guess in case you are not sure of the answer. Some methods of scoring penalize you for guessing.

Cue Words. Pay special attention to qualifying words or phrases in the directions. Such words as *one, best reason, surest, means most nearly the same as, preferable, least correct,* etc., all indicate that *one* response is called for, and that you must select the response which best fits the qualifications in the question.

Time. Sometimes a time limit is set for each section of the examination. If that is the case, follow the time instructions carefully. Your *exam budget* and your watch can help you here. Even if you haven't finished a section when the time limit is up, pass on to the next section. The examination has been planned according to the time schedule.

If the examination paper bears the instruction "Do not turn over page until signal is given," or "Do not start until signal is given," follow the instruction. Otherwise, you may be disqualified.

Pay Close Attention. Be sure you understand what you're doing at all times. Especially in dealing with true-false or multiple-choice questions it's vital that you understand the meaning of every question. It is normal to be working under stress when taking an examination, and it is easy to skip a word or jump to a false conclusion, which may cost you points on the examination. In many multiple-choice and matching questions, the examiners deliberately insert plausible-appearing false answers in order to catch the candidate who is not alert.

Answer clearly. If the examiner who marks your paper cannot understand what you mean, you will not receive credit for your correct answer. On a True-False examination you will not receive any credit for a question which is marked both true and false. If you are asked to underline, be certain that your lines are under and not through the words and that they do not extend beyond them. When using the separate answer sheet it is important *when you decide to change an answer,* you erase the first answer completely. If you leave any graphite from the pencil on the wrong space it will cause the scoring machine to cancel the right answer for that question.

Watch Your "Weights." If the examination is "weighted" it means that some parts of the examination are considered more important than others and rated more highly. For instance, you may find that the instructions will indicate "Part I, Weight 50; Part II, Weight 25, Part III, Weight 25." In such a case, you would devote half of your time to the first part, and divide the second half of your time among Parts II and III.

A Funny Thing . . .

. . . happened to you on your way to the bottom of the totem pole. You *thought* the right answer but you marked the *wrong* one.

1. You *mixed answer symbols*! You decided (rightly) that Baltimore (Choice D) was correct. Then you marked *B* (for Baltimore) instead of *D*.
2. You *misread* a simple instruction! Asked to give the *latest* word in a scrambled sentence, you correctly arranged the sentence, and then marked the letter corresponding to the *earliest* word in that miserable sentence.
3. You *inverted digits!* Instead of the correct number, 96, you wrote (or read) 69.

Funny? Tragic! Stay away from accidents.

Record your answers on the answer sheet one by one as you answer the questions. Care should be taken that these answers are recorded next to the appropriate numbers on your answer sheet. It is poor practice to write your answers first on the test booklet and then to transfer them all at one time to the answer sheet. This procedure causes many errors. And then, how would you feel if you ran out of time before you had a chance to transfer all the answers.

When and How To Guess

Read the directions carefully to determine the scoring method that will be used. In some tests, the directions will indicate that guessing is advisable if you do not know the answer to a question. In such tests, only the right answers are counted in determining your score. If such is the case, don't omit any items. If you do not know the answer, or if you are not sure of your answer, then *guess.*

On the other hand, if the directions state that a scoring formula *will* be used in determining your score or that you are *not to guess,* then *omit* the question if you do not know the answer, or if you are not sure of the answer. When the scoring formula is used, a percentage of the *wrong* answers will be subtracted from the number of *right* answers as a correction for haphazard guessing. It is improbable, therefore, that mere guessing will improve your score significantly. *It may even lower your score.* Another disadvantage in guessing under such circumstances is that it consumes valuable time that you might profitably use in answering the questions you know.

If, however, you are uncertain of the correct answer but have *some* knowledge of the question and are able to eliminate one or more of the answer choices as wrong, your chance of getting the right answer is improved, and it will be to your advantage to *answer* such a question rather than *omit* it.

BEAT THE ANSWER SHEET

Even though you've had plenty of practice with the answer sheet used on machine-scored examinations, we must give you a few more, last-minute pointers.

The present popularity of tests requires the use of electrical test scoring machines. With these machines, scoring which would require the labor of several men for hours can be handled by one man in a fraction of the time.

The scoring machine is an amazingly intricate and helpful device, but the machine is not human. The machine cannot, for example, tell the difference between an intended answer and a stray pencil mark, and will count both indiscriminately. The machine cannot count a pencil mark, if the pencil mark is not brought in contact with the electrodes. For these reasons, specially printed answer sheets with response spaces properly located and properly filled in must be employed. Since not all pencil leads contain the necessary ingredients, a special pencil must be used and a heavy solid mark must be made to indicate answers.

(a) Each pencil mark must be heavy and black. Light marks should be retraced with the special pencil.

(b) Each mark must be in the space between the pair of dotted lines and entirely fill this space.

(c) All stray pencil marks on the paper, clearly not intended as answers, must be completely erased.

(d) Each question must have only one answer indicated. If multiple answers occur, all extraneous marks should be thoroughly erased. Otherwise, the machine will give you *no* credit for your correct answer.

Be sure to use the special electrographic pencil!

HERE'S HOW TO MARK YOUR ANSWERS ON MACHINE-SCORED ANSWER SHEETS:

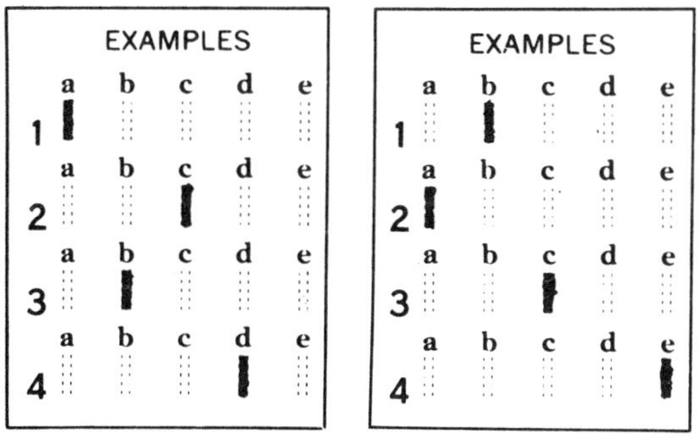

Make only ONE mark for each answer. Additional and stray marks may be counted as mistakes. In making corrections, erase errors COMPLETELY. Make glossy black marks.

Your answer sheet is the only one that reaches the office where papers are scored. For this reason it is important that the blanks at the top be filled in completely and correctly. The proctors will check this, but just in case they slip up, make certain yourself that your paper is complete.

Many exams caution competitors against making any marks on the test booklet itself. Obey that caution even though it goes against your grain to work neatly. If you work neatly and obediently with the test booklet you'll probably do the same with the answer sheet. And that pays off in high scores.

ARCO BOOKS

CIVIL SERVICE AND GENERAL TEST PREPARATION

Able Seaman, Deckhand, Scowman	01376-1	5.00
Accountant—Auditor	00001-5	6.00
Addiction Specialist, Senior, Supervising, Principal, Turner	03351-7	8.00
Administrative Assistant	00148-8	8.00
Air Traffic Controller, Turner	02088-1	8.00
American Foreign Service Officer	04219-2	8.00
Apprentice, Mechanical Trades	00571-8	5.00
Assistant Accountant—Junior Accountant—Account Clerk	00056-2	6.00
Assistant Station Supervisor, Turner	03736-9	6.00
Associate and Administrative Accountant	03863-2	8.00
Attorney, Assistant—Trainee	01084-3	8.00
Auto Machinist	00513-0	6.00
Auto Mechanic, Autoserviceman	00514-9	6.00
Bank Examiner—Trainee and Assistant	01642-6	5.00
Battalion and Deputy Chief, F.D.	00515-7	6.00
Beginning Office Worker	00173-9	6.00
Beverage Control Investigator	00150-X	4.00
Bookkeeper—Account Clerk, Turner	00035-X	6.00
Bridge and Tunnel Officer—Special Officer	00780-X	5.00
Building Custodian	00013-9	8.00
Bus Maintainer—Bus Mechanic	00111-9	5.00
Bus Operator	01553-5	5.00
Buyer, Assistant Buyer, Purchase Inspector	01366-4	6.00
Captain, Fire Department	00121-6	10.00
Captain, Police Department	00184-4	8.00
Carpenter	00135-6	6.00
Case Worker, Turner	01528-4	8.00
Cashier, Housing Teller	00703-6	6.00
Cement Mason—Mason's Helper, Turner	03745-8	6.00
Chemist—Assistant Chemist	00116-X	5.00
City Planner	01364-8	6.00
Civil Engineer, Senior, Associate, & Administrative, Turner	00146-1	8.00
Civil Service Arithmetic and Vocabulary	00003-1	4.00
Civil Service Course, Gitlin	00702-8	5.00
Teacher's Manual for Civil Service Course, Gitlin	03838-1	2.00
Civil Service Handbook	00040-6	2.00
Claim Examiner—Law Investigator	00149-6	5.00
Clerk New York City	00045-7	4.00
Clerk—Steno Transcriber	00838-5	6.00
College Office Assistant	00181-X	5.00
Complete Guide to U.S. Civil Service Jobs	00537-8	2.00
Construction Foreman—Supervisor—Inspector	01085-1	5.00
Consumer Affairs Inspector	01356-7	6.00
Correction Captain—Deputy Warden	01358-3	8.00
Correction Officer	00186-0	6.00
Court Officer	00519-X	6.00
Criminal Law Quizzer Salottolo	02399-6	8.00
Criminal Science Handbook, Salottolo	02407-0	5.00
Detective Investigator, Turner	03738-5	6.00
Dietitian	00083-X	6.00
Draftsman, Civil and Mechanical Engineering (All Grades)	01225-0	6.00
Electrical Engineer	00137-2	5.00
Electrical Inspector	03350-9	8.00
Electrician	00084-8	8.00
Electronic Equipment Maintainer Turner	01836-4	8.00
Elevator Operator	00051-1	3.00
Employment Interviewer	00008-2	6.00
Employment Security Clerk	00700-1	6.00
Engineering Technician (All Grades), Turner	01226-9	6.00
Exterminator Foreman—Foreman of Housing Exterminators	03740-7	6.00
File Clerk	00962-4	5.00
Fire Administration and Technology	00604-8	10.00
Firefighting Hydraulics, Bonadio	00572-6	7.50
Fireman, F.D.	00010-4	6.00
Food Service Supervisor—School Lunch Manager	01378-8	6.00
Foreman	00191-7	5.00
Foreman of Auto Mechanics	01360-5	6.00
Gardener, Assistant Gardener	01340-0	6.00
General Entrance Series, Arco Editorial Board	01961-1	4.00
General Test Practice for 92 U.S. Jobs	00011-2	5.00
Guard—Patrolman	00122-4	5.00
Heavy Equipment Operator (Portable Engineer)	01372-9	5.00
Homestudy Course for Civil Service Jobs, Turner	01587-X	6.00
Hospital Attendant	00012-0	4.00
Hospital Care Investigator Trainee (Social Case Worker I)	01674-4	5.00
Hospital Clerk	01718-X	3.00
Hospital Security Officer	03866-7	6.00
Housing Assistant	00054-6	5.00
Housing Caretaker	00504-1	4.00
Housing Inspector	00055-4	5.00
Housing Manager—Assistant Housing Manager	00813-X	5.00
Housing Patrolman	00192-5	5.00
How to Pass Employment Tests, Liebers	00715-X	5.00
Internal Revenue Agent	00093-7	5.00
Investigator—Inspector	01670-1	5.00
Junior Administrator Development Examination (JADE)	01643-4	5.00
Junior and Assistant Civil Engineer	01228-5	5.00
Junior Federal Assistant	01729-5	6.00
Laboratory Aide, Arco Editorial Board	01121-1	5.00
Laborer—Federal, State and City Jobs	00566-1	4.00
Landscape Architect	01368-0	5.00
Laundry Worker	01834-8	4.00
Law and Court Stenographer	00783-4	6.00
Law Enforcement Positions	00500-9	6.00
Librarian	00060-0	8.00
Lieutenant, F.D.	00123-2	8.00
Lieutenant, P.D.	00190-9	8.00
Machinist—Machinist's Helper	01123-8	6.00
Mail Handler—U.S. Postal Service	00126-7	5.00
Maintainer's Helper, Group A and C—Transit Electrical Helper	00175-5	6.00
Maintenance Man	04349-0	6.00
Management and Administration Quizzer	LR 01727-9	8.50
Management Analyst, Assistant-Associate	03864-0	8.00
Mathematics, Simplified and Self-Taught	00567-X	4.00
Mechanical Apprentice (Maintainer's Helper B)	00176-3	5.00
Mechanical Aptitude and Spatial Relations Tests	00539-4	6.00
Mechanical Engineer—Junior, Assistant & Senior Grades	03314-2	8.00
Messenger	00017-1	3.00
Mortuary Caretaker	01354-0	6.00
Motor Vehicle License Examiner	00018-X	5.00
Motor Vehicle Operator	00576-9	4.00
Motorman (Subways)	00061-9	6.00

MILITARY EXAMINATION SERIES

Practice for Army Classification and Placement (ASVAB)	03845-4	6.00
Practice for the Armed Forces Tests	00063-5	6.00
Practice for the Navy's Basic Test Battery	01300-1	5.00
Practice for Air Force Placement Tests	04270-2	6.00
Practice for Officer Candidate Tests	01304-4	6.00
U.S. Service Academies	01544-6	6.00

GED PREPARATION

Comprehensive Math Review for the High School Equivalency Diploma Test, McDonough	03420-3	4.00
High School Equivalency Diploma Tests, Turner	00110-0	5.00
Preliminary Arithmetic for the High School Equivalency Diploma Test	02165-9	4.00
Preliminary Practice for the High School Equivalency Diploma Test	01441-3	4.00
Preparation for the Spanish High School Equivalency Diploma (Preparacion Para El Exam De Equivalencia De La Escuela Superior—En Espanol)	02618-9	6.00
Step-By-Step Guide to Correct English, Pulaski	03402-5	3.95

General Education Development Series

Correctness and Effectiveness of Expression (English HSEDT), Castellano, Guercio & Seitz	03688-5	4.00
General Mathematical Ability (Mathematics HSEDT), Castellano, Guercio & Seitz	03689-3	4.00
Reading Interpretation in Social Sciences, Natural Sciences, and Literature (Reading HSEDT), Castellano, Guercio & Seitz	03690-7	4.00
Teacher's Manual for the GED Series,	03692-3	2.50

COLLEGE BOARD ACHIEVEMENT TESTS

American History and Social Studies Achievement Test, Altman	01722-8	1.45
Chemistry Achievement Test, Spector & Weiss	LR 01261-7	4.50
College Board Achievement Test: Biology, Solomon	04094-7	3.95
College Board Achievement Test: Chemistry, Solomon	04101-3	3.95
English Composition Achievement Test	01247-1	.95
French Achievement Teest, Biezunski & Boisrond	01668-X	1.45
German Achievement Test, Greiner	01698-1	1.45
Latin Achievement Test	01743-0	1.45
Mathematics: Level I Achievement Test, Bramson	03847-0	3.00
Mathematics: Level II Achievement Test, Bramson	01456-3	.95
Physics Achievement Test, Bruenn	01265-X	1.95
Spanish Achievement Test, Jassey	01741-4	1.45

ARCO COLLEGE CREDIT TEST-TUTORS

American History: CLEP and AP Subject Examination, Woloch	03804-7	4.95

PROFESSIONAL CAREER EXAM SERIES

Action Guide for Executive Job Seekers and Employers, Uris	01787-2	3.95
Automobile Mechanic Certification Tests, Sharp	03809-8	6.00
Bar Exams	01124-6	5.00
The C.P.A. Exam: Accounting by the "Parallel Point" Method, Lipscomb	02020-2	15.00
Certificate in Data Processing Examination, Morrison	04032-7	12.00
Certified General Automobile Mechanic, Turner	02900-5	6.00
Computer Programmer, Luftig	01232-3	6.00
Computers and Automation, Brown	01745-7	5.00
Dental Admission Test, Arco Editorial Board	04293-1	6.00
Graduate Management Admission Test	03926-4	6.00
Graduate Record Examination Aptitude	00824-5	5.00
Health Insurance Agent (Hospital, Accident, Health, Life)	02153-5	5.00
How a Computer System Works, Brown & Workman	03424-6	5.95
How to Become a Successful Model, Krem	03625-7	5.00
How to Get Into Medical and Dental School, Shugar, Shugar & Bauman	02523-9	4.00
How to Make Money in Music, Harris & Farrar	04089-0	5.95
The Installation and Servicing of Domestic Oil Burners, Mitchell & Mitchell	00437-1	10.00
Insurance Agent and Broker	02149-7	6.00
Law School Admission Test, Turner	00840-7	5.00
Life Insurance Agent	02343-0	6.00
Medical College Admission Test, Turner	04289-3	6.00
Miller Analogies Test—1400 Analogy Questions	01114-9	4.00
The 1977-78 Airline Guide to Stewardess and Steward Careers, Morton	04350-4	5.95
Notary Public	00180-1	6.00
Nursing School Entrance Examinations, Turner	01202-1	6.00
Oil Burner Installer	00096-1	6.00
The Official 1976-77 Guide to Airline Careers, Morton	03955-8	5.95
Playground and Recreation Director's Handbook	01096-7	6.00
Principles of Data Processing	04268-0	7.50
Quizzer for Students of Education, Walton	01447-4	4.00
Real Estate License Examination, Gladstone	03755-5	6.00
Refrigeration License Manual, Harfenist	02726-6	10.00
Resumes for Job Hunters, Shykind	03961-2	4.00
Resumes That Get Jobs, revised edition, Resume Service	03909-4	3.00
Security Representatives' Examinations, Stefano	01934-4	5.00
Simplify Legal Writing, Biskind	03801-2	5.00
Spanish for Nurses and Allied Health Science Students, Hernandez-Miyares & Alba	04127-7	10.00
Stationary Engineer and Fireman	00070-8	6.00
The Test of English as a Foreign Language (TOEFL), Moreno, Babin & Scallon	02944-7	6.00
Veterinary College Admissions	04147-1	6.00
Your Resume—Key to a Better Job, Corwen	03733-4	4.00

ADVANCED GRE SERIES

Biology: Advanced Test for the G.R.E., Miller	04310-5	4.95
Business: Advanced Test for the G.R.E., Berman, Malea & Yearwood	01599-3	4.95
Chemistry: Advanced Test for the G.R.E., Weiss	01069-X	4.95
Economics: Advanced Test for the G.R.E., Zabrenski & Heydari-Darafshian	01557-8	4.95
Education: Advanced Test for the G.R.E., Beckoff	01223-4	4.95
Engineering: Advanced Test for the G.R.E., Ingham & Nesbitt	01604-3	4.95
French: Advanced Test for the G.R.E., Dethierry	01070-3	3.95
Geography: Advanced Test for the G.R.E., White	01710-4	3.95
Geology: Advanced Test for the G.R.E., Dolgoff	01071-1	3.95
History: Advanced Test for the G.R.E., Smith	01072-X	4.95
Literature: Advanced Test for the G.R.E.	01073-8	3.95
Mathematics: Advanced Test for the G.R.E., Bramson	04264-8	4.95
Music: Advanced Test for the G.R.E., Murphy	01471-7	3.95
Philosophy: Advanced Test for the G.R.E., Steiner	01472-5	3.95
Physical Education: Advanced Test for the G.R.E., Rubinger	01609-4	3.95
Physics: Advanced Test for the G.R.E., Bruenn	01074-6	4.95
Political Science: Advanced Test for the G.R.E., Meador & Stewart	01459-8	3.95
Psychology: Advanced Test for the G.R.E., Millman & Nisbett	01145-9	4.95
Sociology: Advanced Test for the G.R.E., Reddan	01444-X	4.95
Spanish: Advanced Test for the G.R.E., Jassey	01075-4	3.95
Speech: Advanced Test for the G.R.E., Graham	01526-8	3.95

S3556